How To Use This Book

Teach Yourself Database Programming with Delphi in 21 Days
As the name of this book implies, it is expected that you'll complete a chapter a day. However, you should work at your own rate. If you think you can complete two (or more) chapters a day, then go for it! Also, if you think that you should spend more than one day on a certain chapter, spend as many hours as you need.

Each day ends with a Q&A section containing answers to common questions related to the day's material. There is also a Quiz that tests your knowledge of the concepts presented that day. One or more exercises are included as well so that you can put your new skills to use.

Who Should Read This Book?

Do you need any previous programming experience to benefit from this book? The answer is no. Naturally, if you have programming experience (with any programming language), you'll find the code-writing portions of this book easier to do. However, no previous Delphi programming experience is assumed.

There are two phases of developing a Delphi program: the visual programming phase and the code-writing phase. Visual programming is similar to the way you operate the Paintbrush program that comes with Windows. For example, you "pick up" an object with the mouse, and you place it in a window.

The visual programming of Delphi is only half the job, though! Once you place objects in your programs' windows, you write Pascal code. For instance, you place a button in your application's window, and the user clicks this button during the execution of your program. When the user clicks the button, code is executed. What code? The Pascal code you write with Delphi. You don't need any Pascal experience to write this code—you learn all the Pascal information you need as you implement the programs in this book.

Conventions Used in This Book

Special features are used throughout the book to highlight certain kinds of information.

 Notes: These provide essential background information so that you not only learn to do things with Delphi, but have a good understanding of what you're doing and why.

 Tips: It would be nice to remember everything you've previously learned, but that's just about impossible. If there is important Delphi material that you have to know, these tips will remind you.

 Cautions: Here's where the authors share their insight and experience as professional programmers to help you avoid pitfalls. Learn from their experiences.

Teach Yourself DATABASE PROGRAMMING with DELPHI®

in 21 Days

Teach Yourself

DATABASE PROGRAMMING
with DELPHI ®
in 21 Days

Nathan Gurewich
Ori Gurewich

SAMS
PUBLISHING

201 West 103rd Street
Indianapolis, Indiana 46290

Publisher	*Richard K. Swadley*
Acquisitions Manager	*Greg Wiegand*
Development Manager	*Dean Miller*
Managing Editor	*Cindy Morrow*
Marketing Manager	*Gregg Bushyeager*

Acquisitions Editor
Chris Denny

Development Editor
Angelique Brittingham

Production Editor
Kristi Hart

Copy Editor
Johnna VanHoose

Technical Editor
Danny Thorpe,
Borland International

Editorial Coordinator
Bill Whitmer

Technical Edit Coordinator
Lynette Quinn

Formatter
Frank Sinclair

Editorial Assistant
Sharon Cox

Cover Designer
Tim Amrhein

Book Designer
Alyssa Yesh

Production Team Supervisor
Brad Chinn

Production
Mary Ann Abramson, Carol Bowers, Mona Brown, Michael Brumitt, Charlotte Clapp, Mike Dietsch, Steph Mineart, Louisa Klucznik, Kevin Laseau, Mark Walchle, Angelina Ward

Indexer
Cheryl Dietsch

Overview

Contents

Acknowledgments

We would like to thank Chris Denny, the acquisitions editor for this book, Angelique Brittingham, the development editor, Kristi Hart, the production editor, and all the other people at Sams Publishing who contributed to this book.

Thanks also to Borland International who supplied us with technical information and various betas and upgrades of the software product. In particular, thanks to Ms. Nan Borreson from Borland International.

About the Authors

Nathan Gurewich and Ori Gurewich are the authors of several best-selling books in the areas of Visual Basic for Windows, C/C++ programming, multimedia programming, database design and programming, and other topics.

Nathan Gurewich

Nathan Gurewich holds a master's degree in electrical engineering from Columbia University, New York, and a bachelor's degree in electrical engineering from Hofstra University, Long Island, New York. Since the introduction of the PC, Nathan has been involved in the design and implementation of commercial software packages for the PC. He is an expert in the field of PC programming and in providing consulting services in the areas of local area networks, wide area networks, database management and design, and software marketing. Nathan can be contacted via CompuServe (CompuServe ID 75277,2254).

Ori Gurewich

Ori Gurewich holds a bachelor's degree in electrical engineering from Stony Brook University, Stony Brook, New York. His background includes working as a senior software engineer and as a software consultant engineer for companies, and developing professional multimedia and Windows applications. He is an expert in the field of PC programming and network communications, and he has developed various multimedia algorithms for the PC. Ori can be contacted via CompuServe (CompuServe ID 72072,312).

Introduction

This book teaches you how to use the Delphi software package by Borland International. Delphi contains many programs, the most important of which are

- The Delphi program
- The Database Desktop program
- The ReportSmith program

In this book, the term *Delphi* refers to the Delphi program.

The Delphi Program

Let's start with the Delphi program. Delphi is a visual programming language. This means that you design your programs by visual means. As you know, Windows programs contain graphic objects (buttons, scrollbars, editboxes, and so on). You use Delphi to create Windows programs, and so you have to create windows with buttons, scrollbars, and other objects in your programs' windows. You place these objects by using the mouse. The visual programming aspect is very similar to the way you operate the Paintbrush program that comes with Windows, for example. You "pick up" an object with the mouse, and you place it in a window. As you can imagine, the visual programming aspect of your program, therefore, amounts to a lot of clicking and dragging with your mouse.

Is the visual programming aspect easy? Yes. Delphi is designed so that the visual programming of your programs is easy.

The visual programming of Delphi is only half the job, though! Once you place objects in your programs' windows, you'll write programming code.

For example, during the visual programming phase of development, you place a button in the window of your application. Later, when your user executes your program and clicks the button, a certain code is executed. Which code? The code that you write with Delphi.

The code you write with Delphi is written with the Pascal programming language, but don't worry. Even if you've never used Pascal before, you learn all the Pascal information you need as you implement the programs in this book.

Do you need any previous programming experience? Naturally, if you have any programming experience (with any programming language), you'll find the code-writing portion easier. However, no previous Delphi programming experience is assumed (and no Pascal, either).

The Types of Programs You Can Write with Delphi

With Delphi, you can write any Windows program you can think of! Delphi is equipped with all the tools and programming power you need to write state-of-the-art, powerful Windows applications. You can use Delphi for writing games, database applications, communications, 3D virtual reality programs, and so on. Although you can write complex programs with Delphi, the engineers of Borland International designed Delphi so it's especially easy to design database applications.

Database Applications

What is a database application? A database application is an application dealing with data that is stored in tables. The collection of tables is called a *database.*

This book assumes no previous experience of database design. During the course of this book, you learn all the database information you need as you implement the programs in this book.

What makes Delphi so special that it is easy to write database applications? Database applications have existed for a long time. Before the invention of the PC, database applications were implemented on mainframe computers. Since the introduction of the PC, many database applications have been written for the PC. Examples of database applications are applications dealing with invoices, payroll, inventory, and so on. It is not an overstatement to say that a big portion of PC use is executing database applications. You might even say that the one of the main reasons PCs are so popular is because PCs and PC software enable programmers to write database programs.

Over the years, a huge amount of experience was accumulated regarding writing database applications. Sure, database applications are different from each other, but there are some fundamental things that you must do when designing database applications—no matter what the exact nature of your database application. Delphi's programming language is designed to have all the important things you need during the design of your database programs. For example, you'll no doubt need to write programs that perform a search for certain data. As you might have expected, the Delphi program is designed so you can implement a search mechanism with great ease. The bottom line is that, based on the vast experience accumulated over the years, the engineers who designed Delphi designed the product with all the database "goodies" already incorporated into the Delphi programming language.

If you write a database application using a programming language that was not designed specifically for designing database applications, you spend a lot of time doing things that are already incorporated into a programming language that was specifically designed for writing

database applications. By using Delphi for writing database applications, you save yourself a lot of programming time.

Although you can write any Windows program with Delphi, this book concentrates on using Delphi for designing database applications.

The Database Desktop Program

One important program in the Delphi package that you'll use a lot during the course of this book is the Database Desktop program.

Because the programs you write "operate" on databases, you need some databases with which you can experiment. The Database Desktop program enables you to generate the databases quickly and easily. No previous experience with the Database Desktop program is assumed.

The ReportSmith Program

Another important component of the Delphi package is a program called ReportSmith.

There are many database-related tasks you must implement during the course of your database projects. You must display data on the screen, display windows that take user's input, search for particular data among many pieces of data, sort the data in a variety of ways, filter out a certain amount of data, and perform many other database-related tasks. You can implement all these tasks by writing Delphi programs as described in this book.

There's one additional task that you must perform: the very important task of printing reports. A report is a printed hard copy of data. It can be a list of employees, an inventory list, a list of invoices, and anything else that is a printout of your data arranged in a particular format.

ReportSmith is a program that enables to you print reports with great ease. ReportSmith is equipped with almost everything you need to generate powerful reports. It also enables you to design reports visually. That is, you mainly use the mouse device to click and drag objects for implementing the reports. In this respect, ReportSmith is different than writing programs with the Delphi program because generating reports with ReportSmith requires almost no programming.

The Accompanying CD-ROM

The inside back cover of this book contains a CD-ROM that includes the following:

- Delphi programs' source code (so you can compare your work with the provided source code).
- EXE files of the book's programs (so you can execute the book's programs and gain a better understanding of what the programs are supposed to do).
- All the databases and tables required for the implementation of, and that are used by, the book's programs. With this information, you can compare your Database Desktop work with the tables that are provided on the CD.
- During the course of this book, you need runtime modules (VBX files) that are required for the implementation of state-of-the-art-technology Delphi programs that perform database, multimedia, and encyclopedia-type applications. The CD includes the required software so you can execute and implement the book's programs.
- Other files that are needed for the execution and implementation of the book's programs, such as WAV sound files, MIDI sound files, movie AVI files.

To install the CD, follow the instructions included in the ReadMe.TXT file that resides in the CD's root directory.

Teach Yourself Delphi Database Programming in 21 Days

As the name of this book implies, there are 21 chapters in this book, and it is expected that you'll complete a chapter a day. However, you should work at your own rate. If you think you can complete two (or more) chapters a day, then go for it! Also, if you think that you should spend more than one day on a certain chapter, spend as many hours as you need.

So relax, and prepare yourself for a very pleasant journey.

1

Before you can build a sophisticated, state-of-the-art Windows application with Delphi, you have to know what building materials Delphi offers. In your first week, you learn about the programming building blocks of Delphi.

You immediately dive into the water on Day 1, "Creating Your First Delphi Application," where you'll build a program called Hello.EXE. This is a simple program that displays the message Hello. Although simple, this program illustrates a variety of important Delphi topics.

On Day 2, "Databases," you learn how to use the Database Desktop program that comes with Delphi. Database Desktop is a program that enables you to create databases. During the course of this book, you design and implement many programs, and you'll need databases to practice with. The Database Desktop program is an ideal program for this purpose because it enables you to create the databases you need quickly.

On Day 3, "Creating Your First Delphi Database Program," you write your first Delphi database-based application. You build a simple database program that uses the database you built on Day 2 using the Database Desktop program.

On Day 4, "Reading and Writing Field Values," you further enhance the Delphi database program you built on Day 3 by adding code to the program. Today, you learn important Delphi programming topics.

On Day 5, "Calculated Fields," you learn about the important topic of calculated fields by implementing a program that uses this feature.

On Day 6, "Linking Tables," you learn about secondary indexes and how to use Delphi for creating a linkage between tables.

On Day 7, "Searching For and Validating Data," you learn about the important topics of searching for and validating data in the tables.

Creating Your
First Delphi
Program

Welcome to the Fascinating World of Delphi

Delphi is a powerful programming language. As you'll see during the course of this book, it enables you to create *any* conceivable Windows application. What is so special about Delphi? It's very easy to use. Moreover, as you'll discover, Delphi is fun and pleasant to work with. In fact, you'll be able to design and create sophisticated state-of-the-art applications in a fraction of the time it would take you to create the same applications with other programming languages.

Delphi and Databases

Delphi is closely related to databases. To understand this statement, consider the fact that many programming languages do not include any special mechanism to handle databases. Delphi, on the other hand, provides many features that enable you to interface with databases with great ease. In this respect, you could consider Delphi a programming environment designed for creating Windows applications that use databases.

Many programmers use Delphi for creating applications that have nothing to do with databases. Why? Because it is a very easy programming language to learn and to use. Nevertheless, keep in mind that the main feature of Delphi is that it can be used to write database-related applications, and that is what this book teaches you about: the database aspects of Delphi. You'll learn what a database is as well as how to create one with Delphi. You might already be familiar with terms such as *tables, linked tables, one-to-one, one-to-many, one-to-many-to-many,* and so on. If not, they are all database terms and are explained and used in this book.

Creating Your First Delphi Project

Before you can start doing database work with Delphi, you must understand several basics about Delphi. In this chapter, you'll create a simple program with Delphi. The objective for creating this program is for you to become comfortable with Delphi's terminology, the various software tools that come with Delphi, and to learn how to use Delphi's basic tools.

Note: If you browse through subsequent chapters of this book, you'll realize that the material presented in this chapter is presented differently than in other chapters. This chapter takes you through a detailed, step-by-step tutorial, whereas subsequent chapters assume that you already know how to perform basic Delphi operations.

Let's go to work! Your first step is to start the Delphi program. Take a look at Figure 1.1. It shows you the Delphi program group, which contains all the programs that come with Delphi. As you can see, there are several programs in the Delphi program group, but the only one you need to worry about now is the Delphi program.

Figure 1.1.
The Delphi program group.
The Delphi program icon is
shown magnified.

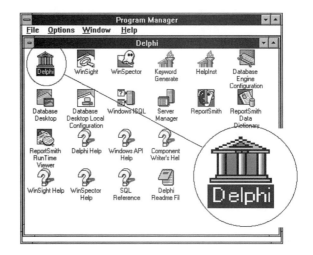

☐ Start the Delphi program by double-clicking the Delphi icon shown in Figure 1.1.

Windows responds by executing the Delphi program, and various windows are displayed.
These windows are Delphi's tools—the software tools that enable you to write Delphi
programs. You'll learn to appreciate these tools during the course of this book.

Now that you've started Delphi, it's time to create your first project. Here is how you create it:

☐ Select New Project from Delphi's File menu.

Whenever you're instructed to create a new project, just select New Project from the File menu.

Before proceeding, save the new project. Even though you didn't do anything to the new project yet, it's a good idea to save it at this early stage.

Note: The following steps presume that your hard disk has a directory called C:\DProg\Ch01. Save the work that you perform in this chapter in this directory.

If your hard disk doesn't have the C:\DProg\Ch01 directory, switch to Windows File Manager, create the directory C:\DProg, and then create the subdirectory C:\DProg\Ch01.

To save your project, do the following:

☐ Select Save Project As from the File menu.

Delphi responds by displaying the Save As dialog box.

Note that Delphi suggests saving a file by the name: Unit1.Pas. However, you don't want to save the file as Unit1.Pas. You also don't want to save the file in the directory that Delphi suggests. So don't click the OK button. Instead, save the file as follows:

☐ Save the file as CHello.Pas in the C:\DProg\Ch01 directory. That is, set the Save dialog box as shown in Figure 1.2, and then click the OK button.

Delphi responds by displaying another Save dialog box. This time, Delphi suggests saving a file as Project1.Dpr.

Figure 1.2.
*Saving the Pas file as
CHello.Pas in the
C:\DProg\Ch01 directory.*

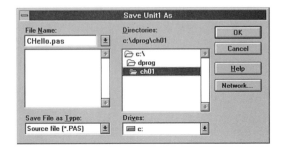

You don't want to save the file as Project1.Dpr, so don't click the OK button. Instead, save the file as follows:

☐ Save the file as Hello.Dpr in the C:\DProg\Ch01 directory. That is, set the Save dialog box as shown in Figure 1.3, and then click the OK button.

Figure 1.3.
*Saving the Hello.Dpr project
in the C:\DProg\Ch01
directory.*

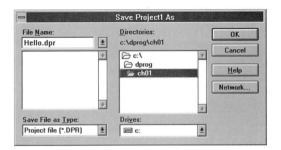

Let's review what you've done so far. First, you saved a file by the name CHello.Pas. As you'll soon see, the CHello.Pas file contains the code of the program.

You then saved a file by the name Hello.Dpr. This is the *project file*.

☐ Use Windows File Manager to examine the C:\DProg\Ch01 directory. As shown in Figure 1.4, the directory contains the following files:

CHello.dfm
CHello.pas
Hello.dpr
Hello.opt
Hello.res

Figure 1.4.
After saving the project, Delphi generates several files.

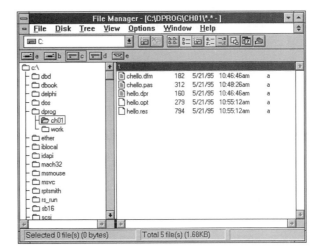

The reason you preceded the name of the Pas file with the character *C* (CHello.Pas) is because the CHello.PAS file contains code. Because you named the Pas file as CHello.Pas, Delphi automatically generated the file: CHello.DFM. Preceding the file name with the character *C* is not a Delphi requirement, but it makes things easy for you in terms of understanding the various files that Delphi generates.

Because you saved the Dpr file (the project file) as Hello.Dpr, Delphi automatically generated several Hello files with various extensions. In subsequent steps today, you'll generate the EXE program. Because you named the Dpr file as Hello.Dpr, the name of the EXE file that Delphi will generate is Hello.EXE.

> **Note:** As you develop Delphi applications, you'll use other Windows applications. As you probably know, sometimes an application does not function well and causes Windows to collapse. In this case, you have to start Windows again, and if you didn't save your Delphi work, you have to start the project all over again.
>
> To be safe, save your project from time to time.
>
> To save your project, select Save Project from the File menu.

The *Form1* Form

One of the windows you see on Delphi's desktop has the caption (the title in the window's title bar): Form1, as shown in Figure 1.5.

Figure 1.5.

The Form1 window.

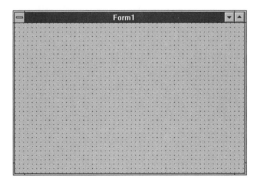

> **Note:** Your Delphi desktop should contain the Form1 window. If, for some reason, it is not present on your desktop, follow these steps to display it:
>
> ☐ Select Forms from the View menu.
>
>   *Delphi responds by displaying the View Form dialog box, as shown in Figure 1.6.*
>
> The list of forms in the dialog box shown in Figure 1.6 contains one form, the Form1 form.
>
> ☐ Select the Form1 item, and then click the OK button.
>
>   *Delphi responds by displaying Form1 window.*

Figure 1.6.
The View Form dialog box that Delphi displays after selecting Forms from the View menu.

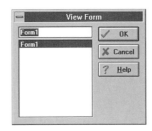

What is this Form1 window? This is the window of the program you're now writing! In other words, you're writing a program called Hello.EXE. When you execute the Hello.EXE program, a window will pop up. Which window? The Form1 window.

Changing the Properties of *Form1*

It's your job as the programmer of Hello.EXE to change the appearance of Form1 so it looks as you want it to look. What is wrong with the current appearance of Form1? One thing is that the form's caption is Form1. You want the caption to be something more friendly, such as The Hello Program. (In this book the term *form's caption* means the title of the form.)

In the following steps, you change the caption of the Form1 window from Form1 to **The Hello Program**. Note that the terms *form* and *window* are interchangeable because a window is the same thing as a form.

Another window on Delphi's desktop is the Object Inspector window shown in Figure 1.7. If, for some reason, you don't see the Object Inspector window, select Object Inspector from the View menu to display the Object Inspector window.

Figure 1.7.
The Object Inspector window.

Note: You read earlier that if you do not see the Form1 window on the desktop, then you can display the Form1 window by selecting Forms from the View menu.

You also read that if you do not see the Object Inspector window on the desktop, then you can display the Object Inspector window by selecting Object Inspector from the View menu.

Guess what? As you do your Delphi work, whenever you don't see a certain window that you need, just select the window from the View menu.

As its name implies, the Object Inspector is a tool that enables you to inspect objects. Delphi works with objects. For example, the Form1 form is an example of an object. Later in this chapter you learn about the pushbutton object. There are many other objects, such as scroll bars, edit boxes, option buttons, check boxes, and so on. The Object Inspector window enables you to view the properties of the object. For example, in Figure 1.7, the Caption property of Form1 is Form1. This is why the caption in Figure 1.5 is Form1. Your objective now is to change the caption to The Hello Program.

☐ Click in the cell to the right of the Caption item in the Object Inspector window, use the keyboard to delete the word Form1, and type the text **The Hello Program**.

Take a look at your Form1 (see Figure 1.8). The caption of the form is now The Hello Program.

Figure 1.8.
The caption of the Form1
form is now The Hello
Program.

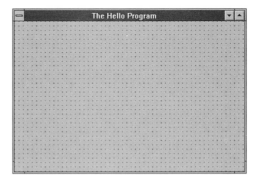

Congratulations, you know how to change the form's properties. You can set the properties of the form to any desired value by changing the properties in the Object Inspector window.

Let's change another property.

☐ In the Object Inspector window, search for the Color property (the properties are arranged alphabetically), and click in the cell that appears to the right of the Color property.

☐ Click the down-arrow icon in the cell.

Delphi responds by dropping down a list of colors.

☐ Use the scroll bar listing the colors to select the clBlue item, as shown in Figure 1.9.

Delphi responds by changing Form1's color to blue!

Figure 1.9.
Setting the Color *property of* Form1 *to* clBlue.

Setting the *Name* Property of the Form

What you've done so far with the Hello program is known as *visual design*. As you can see, the visual design amounts to a lot of selecting and clicking with the mouse. In fact, about 50 percent of your programming time will be spent on visual design. The other 50 percent of the time you'll spend writing code (and as you'll soon see, writing code with Delphi is also easy).

When you write the code, you'll refer to the Form1 form somehow. How you refer to Form1 depends on the Name property of the form. For example, if you set the Name property to Form1, your code refers to the form as Form1. If you set the Name property of the form to Form2, your code refers to the form as Form2, and so on.

☐ Look at the Name property of Form1 in the Object Inspector window.

As you can see, Delphi set the Name property of the form to Form1.

There is nothing wrong with setting the Name property to Form1. However, it's better to give objects more descriptive names. For example, in this book all the form names start with the characters *frm* to make your code easier to read and understand. Every time you see the text *frmXXXX*, you'll know that it is the name of a form. This naming scheme is not a Delphi requirement, but it will help you during the development of your projects.

☐ Set the Name property to **frmHello**.

That's it! From now on, you won't refer to the form as Form1 because it is formally known as frmHello.

☐ Select Forms from the View menu.

Delphi responds by displaying the View Form dialog box, as shown in Figure 1.10.

As you can see, Delphi now recognizes the frmHello form.

Figure 1.10.
The View Form dialog box after setting the Name *property of the form to* frmHello.

☐ Click the Cancel button in the View Form dialog box to close the dialog box. The only reason you were instructed to display the View Form dialog box was to show you that from now on Delphi knows about the form by its name, frmHello.

During the course of this book you'll have a chance to experiment with other form properties, but for now, save the work you've done so far.

☐ Select Save Project from the File menu.

Note: During your Delphi work, select Save Project from the File menu from time to time. This saves all the files that were changed since the last time you selected Save Project from the File menu.

Placing a Button in the *frmHello* Form

As you know, Windows applications have buttons in the application windows. Now place a button in the frmHello form.

Figure 1.11 shows the Delphi top window. This window includes various tabs (Standard, Additional, Data Access, and so on); the Standard tab is selected. Because the Standard tab is selected, Delphi displays the icons corresponding to the Standard tab.

☐ Click the Additional tab.

As shown in Figure 1.12, the icons corresponding to the Additional tab are displayed. Compare the icons that are displayed above the tabs in Figures 1.11 and 1.12, and note that the icons are different in each figure. In Figure 1.11, you see the Standard page, and in Figure 1.12, you see the Additional page.

Figure 1.11.
The icons on the Standard page.

Figure 1.12.
The icons on the Additional page.

Place a button in the frmHello form. The button's icon is displayed on the Standard page, so go ahead and select the Standard tab.

☐ Select the Standard tab.

☐ Double-click the Button icon. The Button icon is located three icons to the right of the A icon (see Figure 1.11). The button icon looks like a button, and it has the word OK on it as shown in Figure 1.13.

Delphi responds by placing a button in the frmHello *form, as shown in Figure 1.14.*

Figure 1.13.
The Button icon on the Standard page.

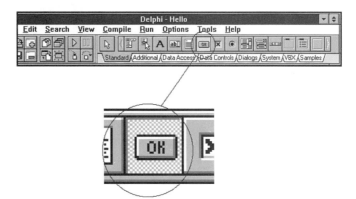

Figure 1.14.
The frmHello *form after placing a button in it.*

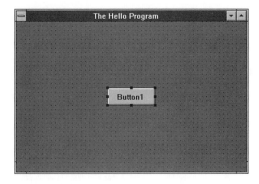

The button you placed serves as the Exit button. The user clicks the Exit button to terminate the Hello.EXE program.

The Exit button really shouldn't be in the center of the form, as shown in Figure 1.14. Typically, you place the Exit button in one of the corners of the form.

☐ Use the mouse to drag the button to a different place, as shown in Figure 1.15.

Figure 1.15.
Placing the button that will serve as the Exit button in the lower-left corner of the frmHello *form.*

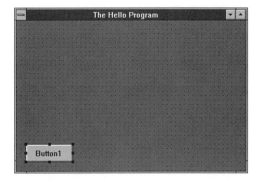

Because the button you placed serves as the Exit button, change the Caption property of the button as follows:

☐ Make sure that the button is selected. The button is selected when it is enclosed with a black rectangle that has four little solid black squares on each side of the enclosing rectangle. If the button is not selected, click it to select it.

☐ Change the Caption property of the button (in the Object Inspector window) to **E&xit**.

The Object Inspector with the new Caption property of the button set to E&xit is shown in Figure 1.16.

Figure 1.16.

The Object Inspector with the new Caption *property of the button set to* E&xit.

Note: When you change object properties, be careful to change the property of the correct object! Many objects have the Caption property. In the preceding steps, you changed the Caption property of the button, but how do you make sure that the Object Inspector displays the properties of the button and not the properties of the frmHello form?

Look at the top of the Object Inspector in Figure 1.16, It says: Button1: TButton. This means that the Object Inspector now displays the properties of the button that you placed in the frmHello form.

You can click the down-arrow icons of the combobox located on the top of the Object Inspector window. As shown in Figure 1.17, the list of objects contains two objects: the frmHello form and the Button1 object. By selecting the proper object from the list, the Object Inspector displays the properties of the object you selected from the list.

Figure 1.17.

Selecting an object.

After you set the button's Caption property to E&xit, the frmHello form looks as shown in Figure 1.18.

Figure 1.18.

The frmHello *form after setting the button's* Caption *property to* E&xit.

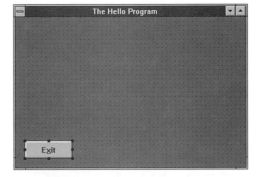

> **Note:** Note that the *x* of the Exit in Figure 1.18 is underlined. This is because you set the button's Caption property to E&xit. When you precede a character in the Caption property with an ampersand (&) (this is typed by pressing Shift+7), the character is underlined.
>
> Why do you want to underline the *x* in Exit? During the execution of the Hello.EXE program, when the user clicks the Exit button, the Hello.EXE program should terminate. However, because you have the *x* underlined, the user can use the keyboard to push the Exit button. Pressing the Alt+x key combination has the same effect as clicking the Exit button. The *x* in Exit is sometimes referred to as a *hot key* or *accelerator key*.

Currently, the Name property is Button1. Because this button serves as the Exit button, it is a better idea to name it as cmdExit. Just as you start the names of forms with *frm*, you start the names of buttons with the characters *cmd*. Again, this is not a Delphi requirement, but it makes your programs easier to read and understand. (In Windows literature, a pushbutton is also called a *command button*. This is the reason for prefixing the name of the pushbuttons with *cmd*.)

☐ Make sure that the Object Inspector window displays the button's properties, and set the Name property to cmdExit.

☐ Save your work (select Save Project from the File menu).

It's time to execute the program.

☐ Select Run from the Run menu, or press F9.

Delphi responds by creating the file Hello.EXE in the C:\DProg\Ch01 directory and executing the Hello.EXE program.

The Hello.EXE program appears, as shown in Figure 1.19.

Figure 1.19.
Executing the Hello.EXE program.

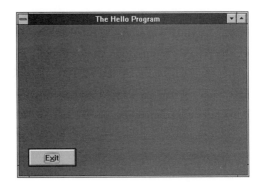

☐ Click the Exit button.

Although the Hello.EXE program should terminate because you clicked the Exit button, you can see that nothing happens. Clicking the Exit button didn't cause the Hello.EXE program to terminate because you haven't attached code to the Exit button.

Terminate the Hello.EXE program as follows:

☐ Click the minus-sign (–) icon that appears on the upper-left corner of the Hello.EXE window, and select Close from the system menu that pops up.

Windows responds by terminating the Hello.EXE program.

Attaching Code to the Exit Button

Attach code to the Exit button so that when the user clicks the Exit program, the Hello.EXE program is terminated.

At the bottom of the Object Inspector window are two tabs: Properties and Events. When you set the properties of an object, you must click the Properties tab. In Figure 1.16, the Properties tab is selected.

You're now ready to attach code to the Exit button's OnClick event. As its name implies, the button's OnClick event occurs when the user clicks the button—the code you attach to this event is executed automatically when the user clicks the Exit button.

To attach code to the Exit button's OnClick event, use the following steps:

☐ Make sure the cmdExit button is selected, and then click the Events tab in the Object Inspector window.

☐ One of the events is the OnClick event. Double-click the cell that appears to the right of the OnClick item.

Delphi responds by displaying a window where you write the code for the Exit button's OnClick event, as shown in Figure 1.20.

Figure 1.20.

The window in which you type the code for the Exit button's OnClick event.

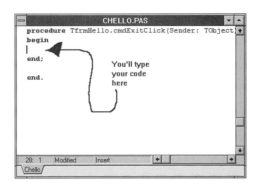

There are several things that you should note about Figure 1.20.

The window's title is CHello.PAS. Recall that when creating the new project, you saved the PAS file as CHello.Pas in the C:\DProg\Ch01 directory. Now you write code into this file.

The text in the window shown in Figure 1.20 is as follows:

```
procedure TfrmHello.cmdExitClick(Sender: TObject);
begin

end;

end.
```

Delphi already wrote some code for you. Don't worry about this code because Delphi knows what it is doing. Your job is simply to insert code that terminates the Hello.EXE program when the user clicks the Exit button.

Look at the first line that Delphi wrote for you; it contains the following text:

```
TfrmHello.cmdExitClick
```

This is the procedure that is executed when the user clicks the cmdExit button you placed in the frmHello form. Again, at this point don't worry that the word TfrmHello appears instead of frmHello.

Also, there is other text in the window, such as the word *end* (it appears twice), and the word *begin*. You should insert your code after the line containing the word *begin*.

☐ Type the following code in the `cmdExitClick` procedure.

```
{Terminate the Hello.EXE program}
Application.Terminate;
```

After typing the above code, the `cmdExitClick` procedure should look as follows. Notice that we've bolded the lines that Delphi wrote for you; this is a convention we use throughout the book.

```
procedure TfrmHello.cmdExitClick(Sender: TObject);
begin

{Terminate the Hello.EXE program}
Application.Terminate;

end;

end.
```

When typing the preceding code, don't forget to type the semicolon (;) at the end of the line:

```
Application.Terminate;
```

Before we go over the code you typed, execute the Hello.EXE program:

☐ Select Save Project from the File menu.

> **Note:** In the following steps, you execute the Hello.EXE program.
>
> Whenever you are instructed to execute a program, do one of the following:
>
> ☐ Press F9. This executes the program.
>
> or,
>
> ☐ Select Run from the Run menu. This is the same as pressing F9.
>
> or,
>
> ☐ Click the Run icon. This also is the same as selecting Run from the Run menu. The Run icon is shown in Figure 1.21.

☐ Execute the Hello.EXE program.

☐ Click the Exit button.

As you can see, the code you attached to the `OnClick` event of the Exit button works! The Hello.EXE program terminates.

Figure 1.21.
The Run icon.

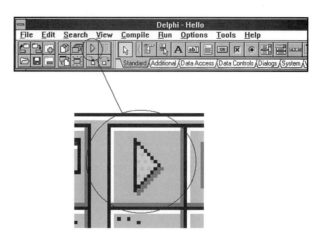

☐ Execute the Hello.EXE program again.

☐ Press Alt+x on your keyboard.

As you can see, the Hello.EXE program terminates. Because the Caption of the Exit button has its x underlined, pressing Alt+x has the same effect as clicking the Exit button.

The Exit Button Code

After you attached code to the cmdExitClick procedure, the procedure looks as follows:

```
procedure TfrmHello.cmdExitClick(Sender: TObject);
begin

{Terminate the Hello.EXE program}
Application.Terminate;

end;

end.
```

Delphi's programming language is Pascal. And as you'll see during the course of this book, Pascal is actually an easy programming language. You'll be able to write code with Pascal even if you've never used it before.

The first line you typed is

```
{Terminate the Hello.EXE program}
```

In Pascal, you can insert comments in your procedures. A comment must be enclosed with the curly brackets ({}). During program execution, comments are ignored. You can write whatever you wish in the curly brackets. The comments are for you, the programmer, so that you can document the code.

A comment can be spread over more than one line. Thus, the following comments are all valid.

```
{Terminate the Hello.EXE program}
```

```
{Terminate the
Hello.EXE program}
```

```
{Terminate the
Hello.EXE
program}
```

The next line of code that you typed in the cmdExitClick procedure is

```
Application.Terminate;
```

As you might have guessed, this statement terminates the application. Whenever the user clicks the Exit button, the cmdExitClick procedure is executed automatically and the Hello.EXE program is terminated.

When you typed the Application.Terminate; statement, you typed a semicolon at the end of it. In Pascal, statements *must* be separated with the semicolon.

The *Application.Terminate* Statement

Terminating the Hello.EXE program was easy; you simply executed the Application.Terminate statement. In a similar manner, you write other statements that perform other operations, but the main question is: how do you know what to type to accomplish a certain operation? For example, you want to terminate the Hello.EXE program whenever the user clicks the Exit button. You know that you have to attach code to the Exit button's OnClick event, but what do you type in the procedure? As you saw, you have to type **Application.Terminate**. But where do you get this information? The answer is that you should consult Delphi's Help feature. Without consulting any books or manuals, you should be able to find out what to type in the procedure.

As an exercise, suppose you don't know that the Application.Terminate statement terminates the program. Let's find this information out from Delphi's Help mechanism.

☐ Select Contents from the Help menu.

   Delphi responds by displaying the Help window.

☐ Click the Search button in the Help window.

   Delphi responds by displaying the Search window.

You're looking for information about the termination of the program, and so the keyword that may lead you to what you're looking for is *terminate.*

☐ In the edit box of the Search dialog box, slowly type the word **terminate**. As shown in Figure 1.22, when you are done typing the first three letters, the search list already highlights the word Terminate.

Figure 1.22.
The Search mechanism found the Terminate topic.

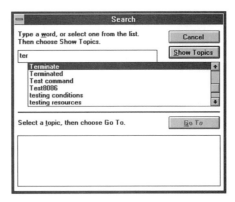

There's a good chance that the highlighted word `Terminate` has something to do with the termination of the program.

☐ Click the Show Topic button to show all topics related to the Terminate topic.

As shown in Figure 1.23, the Search mechanism found one item: the Terminate Method item.

Figure 1.23.
The Terminate Method topic is listed.

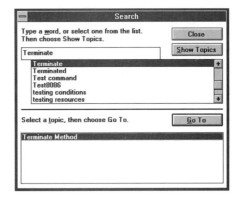

Typically, when you perform the search as discussed in the preceding steps, several items are found and listed in the bottom list. You then have to select item after item in the bottom list until you find what you need. In this case, only one item was found, the Terminate Method item. To see the contents of the Terminate Method item, do this:

☐ Make sure the Terminate Method item is highlighted in the bottom list, and click the Go To button.

   Delphi responds by displaying the Help window for the Terminate Method item, as shown in Figure 1.24.

Figure 1.24.
The Terminate Method help window.

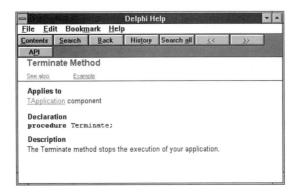

You can read the contents of the Terminate Method to determine whether this is the information that you need. In this case, you are lucky; this is indeed the information you need! It specifically says so in the description:

`The Terminate method stops the execution of your application.`

At this point, you know that the Terminate method is what you need. But how should you use the Terminate method?

☐ Click the sample green text that appears in the Terminate Method Help window.

> *Delphi responds by displaying an example that shows how to use the Terminate method, as shown in Figure 1.25.*

Figure 1.25.
An example showing how to use the Terminate method.

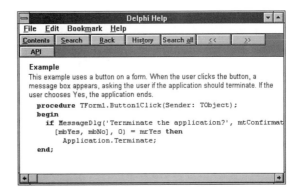

By reading the example, you can see that you terminate the program by executing the following statement:

`Application.Terminate;`

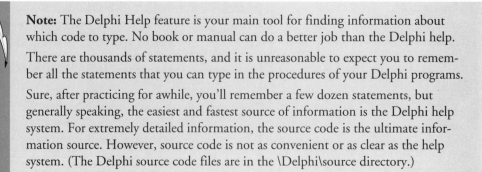

> **Note:** The Delphi Help feature is your main tool for finding information about which code to type. No book or manual can do a better job than the Delphi help.
>
> There are thousands of statements, and it is unreasonable to expect you to remember all the statements that you can type in the procedures of your Delphi programs.
>
> Sure, after practicing for awhile, you'll remember a few dozen statements, but generally speaking, the easiest and fastest source of information is the Delphi help system. For extremely detailed information, the source code is the ultimate information source. However, source code is not as convenient or as clear as the help system. (The Delphi source code files are in the \Delphi\source directory.)

To close the Help window, click the minus icon of the Help window, and select Close from the system menu.

Adding an Edit Box and Two More Buttons to the *frmHello* Form

In this section, you continue implementing the Hello.EXE program. In particular, you'll add an edit box and another two buttons to the frmHello form.

After placing the edit box and the two buttons in the frmHello form and setting their properties, the frmHello form looks as shown in Figure 1.26.

Figure 1.26.
The frmHello form with the edit box and two additional buttons.

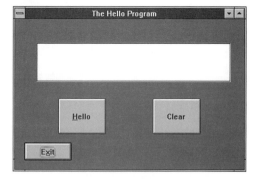

☐ When the user clicks the Hello button, the edit box displays the word Hello, as shown in Figure 1.27.

☐ When the user clicks the Clear button, the text in the edit box is cleared.

Figure 1.27.
*After clicking the Hello
button, the edit box displays
the word* Hello.

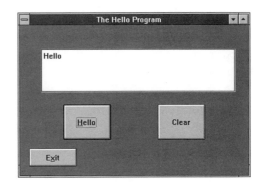

Now that you know what the Hello.EXE program should do, implement it.

☐ Place two more buttons in the frmHello form.

☐ Move the buttons to their new locations, as shown in Figure 1.26, and then drag the
selection handles to enlarge the buttons, also as shown in Figure 1.26. The handles are
small, solid black squares enclosing the button when it is selected.

☐ Set the Caption property for the left button to &Hello.

☐ Set the Name property for the left button to cmdHello.

☐ Set the Caption property for the right button to &Clear.

☐ Set the Name property for the right button to cmdClear.

☐ Place an edit box in the form, and then move it and change its size so it looks as shown
in Figure 1.26. The Standard pages Edit box icon (which is displayed after you select the
Standard tab) is shown in Figure 1.28.

Figure 1.28.
*The Edit box icon in the
Standard page.*

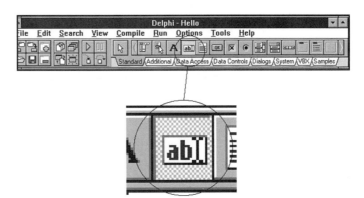

☐ Set the Name property of the edit box to txtHello.

Attaching Code to the Hello Button

Attach code to the Hello button. Recall that when the user clicks the Hello button, the edit box should display the word Hello.

☐ Make sure that the Hello button is selected. Select the Events page of the Object Inspector window, and then double-click the cell to the right of the OnClick event.

Delphi responds by displaying the code for the cmdHelloClick *procedure as follows:*

```
procedure TfrmHello.cmdHelloClick(Sender: TObject);
begin

end;

end.
```

You'll now type code between the begin line and the end line. The code that you'll add should display the word Hello in the txtHello edit box when the user clicks the Hello button.

☐ Type code in the cmdHelloClick procedure. After typing the code, the cmdHelloClick procedure looks as follows:

```
procedure TfrmHello.cmdHelloClick(Sender: TObject);
begin

txtHello.Text:='Hello';

end;

end.
```

The code you added sets the Text property of the txtHello edit box to Hello.

☐ Select Save Project from the File menu.

☐ Execute the Hello.EXE program.

The window shown in Figure 1.29 appears.

Yes, there is something wrong with the Hello program: txtHello appears in the edit box. For now, ignore it; you'll correct it later in this chapter.

☐ Click the Hello button.

As shown in Figure 1.27, the word Hello appears in the edit box.

Of course, at this point, clicking the Clear button will not do any good because you haven't attached any code to the button.

☐ Click the Exit button to terminate the Hello program.

Figure 1.29.
*The window that appears
when you execute the Hello
program.*

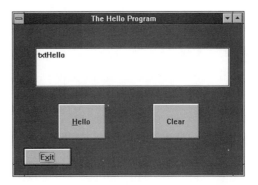

Attaching Code to the Clear Button's *OnClick* Event

Attach code to the Clear button by following these steps:

☐ Select the cmdClear button in the frmHello form, click the Events tab of the Object
Inspector window, double-click the cell to the right of the OnClick event item, and type
the following code in the cmdClearClick procedure:

```
txtHello.Text :='';
```

The cmdClearClick procedure should now look as follows:

```
procedure TfrmHello.cmdClearClick(Sender: TObject);
begin

txtHello.Text :='';

end;

end.
```

Set the Text property to nothing (null). This means that the txtHello edit box displays no text
in it.

☐ Select Save Project from the File menu.

☐ Execute the Hello program.

☐ Click the Hello button.

   Hello responds by displaying the word Hello *in the* txtHello *edit box.*

☐ Click the Clear button.

   Hello responds by clearing the text from the txtHello *edit box.*

☐ Experiment with the Hello program, and then click its Exit button to terminate it.

Setting the Edit Box's Other Properties

You've finished writing the Hello program. Now you can spend time making all types of cosmetic changes to it. In fact, you can make the Hello program as pretty as you want it by setting various properties. This section enables you to do just that.

To begin with, when the program starts, there should not be any text in the txtHello edit box. This can be easily solved as follows:

☐ In the Object Inspector window, set the txtHello edit box's Text property to null. Because the default value set for the Text property is txtHello, you should erase this text. The result is shown in Figure 1.30.

Figure 1.30.

Setting the Text *property of the* txtHello *edit box to empty.*

☐ Execute the Hello program, and verify that when executing the program, the txtHello edit box does not contain text.

☐ Experiment with the Hello program, and then terminate it by clicking its Exit button.

Do you like the way the word Hello is displayed in the txtHello edit box? Would you prefer that the text be displayed with a different font?

☐ Set the Font property of the txtHello edit box to a different font. Select the txtHello edit box, click the cell to the right of the Font property in the Object Inspector window, and select a new font and a new font size.

☐ Execute the Hello program, and verify that the text in the txtHello edit box appears with the same font and size that you set for the Font property.

□ Experiment with the Hello program, and then terminate it by clicking its Exit button.

As your last cosmetic enhancement for the Hello program, do the following:

□ Execute the Hello program.

□ Click in the txtHello edit box.

□ Type something in the txtHello edit box.

There is nothing wrong with being able to type in the edit box. In fact, this is the reason for placing edit boxes in the form—so the user can type something in them. However, in the Hello program, the txtHello edit box is only for displaying text, and so it would be nice if you could prevent the user from entering text into the txtHello edit box.

Here is how you do that:

□ In the Object Inspector window, set the ReadOnly property of the txtHello edit box to True.

□ Execute the Hello program, and note that you no longer can type in the txtHello edit box.

□ Experiment with the Hello program, and then terminate it by clicking its Exit button.

Shorthand Notation

In this chapter, you learned how to implement the frmHello form. As you become more familiar with implementing forms, you'll find the long, detailed step-by-step instructions of implementing forms annoying rather then helpful. Thus, in subsequent chapters, you'll be instructed to implement forms by following Properties tables. For example, the frmHello form has the Properties table shown in Table 1.1, which is self-explanatory. What you have to do is simply follow the table line by line. In Table 1.1, the first object is the frmHello form, and so you must set the form's Name property to frmHello, as shown in the Property and Setting columns. You then continue with the rest of the lines of the table until you set all the form properties.

Then, as dictated by Table 1.1, you place a button in the form, set its Name property to cmdExit, set its Caption property to E&xit, and so on.

After practicing for a while, you'll see that the Properties table is the easiest way to implement the book's forms.

Table 1.1. The Properties table of the `frmHello` form.

Object	Property	Setting
Form	Name	frmHello
	Caption	The Hello Program
	Color	clBlue
Button	Name	cmdExit
	Caption	E&xit
Button	Name	cmdHello
	Caption	&Hello
Button	Name	cmdClear
	Caption	&Clear
Edit Box	Name	txtHello
	ReadOnly	True

Summary

In this chapter, you learned Delphi terms, such as *properties, events, objects, methods*, and others. The Hello.EXE program you implemented demonstrates how you place objects in the form and then attach code to the object events.

Q&A

Q I know Visual Basic. It looks to me that Delphi is a lot like Visual Basic. Right?

A Yes. Implementing Delphi programs is very similar to implementing Visual Basic programs. However, in Delphi you write Pascal code, and in Visual Basic you write Basic code. Also, Delphi was designed so that you can implement database-related applications with great ease. Many database-related features are incorporated into Delphi's core objects and tools. This book does not assume that you know Visual Basic.

Q The title of this book is *Teach Yourself Delphi Database Programming in 21 Days*. Should I complete the book in 21 days?

A The book is organized so that you can complete a chapter a day. Nevertheless, we recommend that you work at a speed that makes you comfortable. If you feel comfortable, complete two (or more) chapters a day. Also, if you feel that you want to spend more than one day on a certain chapter, then do it.

Q I don't know Pascal. Is this book for me?

A Yes. Pascal is not a prerequisite for this book. All the Pascal topics you need during the implementation of your Delphi projects are discussed in this book.

Q From my previous experience with visual programming languages, I know that an object, such as the pushbutton for example, is sometimes referred to as a *control* and sometimes as a *component*. What is it, a control or a component?

A In Delphi, a *control* is any object you can see on the screen when your program is running. *Component* is a more general term that includes visible controls as well as objects that are not visible when your program runs. So, just as you can say a car is a kind of machine, you can say a control is a kind of component. In conversation, people often interchange these terms. There's no harm in that; just keep in mind that a control is a special (visible) kind of component. Delphi has many other kinds of components, such as the database components you'll examine in the next chapter.

Quiz

1. The first thing to do when starting a new project in Delphi is _____.
2. The button's OnClick event occurs when?
    a. There is no such event.
    b. Never.
    c. Always.
    d. When the user clicks the button.

Exercise

Add a button to the frmHello form. The button will serve as the Beep button. When the user clicks the Beep button, the PC should beep. Implement this button. **Hint:** To cause the PC to beep, use the following statement:

```
MessageBeep(1);
```

Answers to Quiz

1. Select New Project from the File menu.
    ☐ Select Save Project As from the File menu.

☐ Save the Pas (code) file (preferably with the character *C* as the first character of the filename).

☐ Save the Dpr (project) file.

2. d.

Answer to Exercise

Here is the answer:

☐ Place a button in the frmHello form.

☐ Set the Name property of the button to cmdBeep.

☐ Set the Caption property of the button to &Beep.

☐ Type the following code in the cmdBeepClick procedure:

```
procedure TfrmHello.cmdBeepClick(Sender: TObject);
begin

{Beep}
MessageBeep(1);

end;

end.
```

The code you typed uses the MessageBeep() function to cause the PC speaker to beep:

```
MessageBeep(1);
```

Windows comes with many functions that are used for normal Windows operations. For example, if you do something illegal in Windows, it causes the PC speaker to beep. To cause the PC speaker to beep, Windows executes the MessageBeep() function, which is an integral part of Windows. Many programming languages take advantage of the built-in functions that Windows uses. In Delphi, you can use these built-in Windows functions. In this exercise, you used the MessageBeep() function. (When using the MessageBeep() function, you have to type the parentheses, and insert *1* in the parentheses, as in MessageBeep(1).)

The functions used by Windows and that also are available for use from within other programming languages are called *API functions*. The MessageBeep() function is an example of an API function.

The Delphi Help menu provides you with a list of API functions. To learn how to use an API function, select Windows API from the Help window. You'll have a chance to practice with additional API functions during the course of this book.

2

Databases

As mentioned in Chapter 1, "Creating Your First Delphi Application," Delphi has many database features. It enables you to write programs that deal with databases. In subsequent chapters, you'll learn how to write these types of programs, but you must first create a database to be used by your programs. This chapter teaches you how to build databases.

The Database Desktop

One of the programs that comes with the Delphi package is the Database Desktop program (see Figure 2.1). The Database Desktop program enables you to create databases and perform other related database operations. These databases are used by the programs that you will create in subsequent chapters.

Figure 2.1.
The Database Desktop program icon.

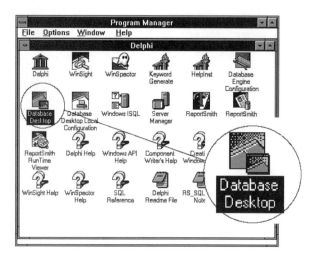

☐ Double-click the Database Desktop icon in the Delphi program group (see Figure 2.1).

Windows responds by executing the Database Desktop program, and the window shown in Figure 2.2 appears.

Figure 2.2.
The Database Desktop program window.

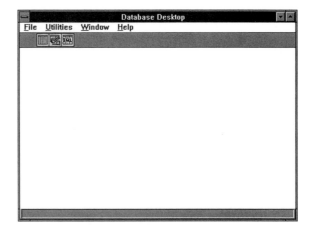

Setting the Working Directory

During the execution of your Delphi programs that use databases, your programs look for the directory in which the database files reside. This directory is called the *working directory.*

Now tell Delphi the name of the directory where the database files reside.

Note: The following steps assume that your hard drive contains the directory C:\DProg\Work.

If you don't have this directory on your hard drive, create it now.

☐ Select Working Directory from the Database Desktop program's File menu.

The Database Desktop program responds by displaying the Set Working Directory dialog box, as shown in Figure 2.3. Your objective now is to set the working directory to C:\DProg\Work.

Figure 2.3.
The Set Working Directory dialog box.

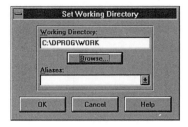

☐ Click the Browse button in the Set Working Directory dialog box.

> *Database Desktop responds by displaying the Directory Browser dialog box, as shown in Figure 2.4.*

☐ Set the name of the directory to C:\DProg\Work, as shown in Figure 2.4, and then click the OK button.

Figure 2.4.
The Directory Browser dialog box.

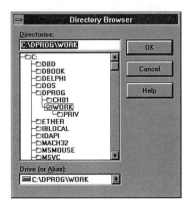

Database Desktop closes the Directory Browser dialog box and displays the Set Working Directories dialog box.

☐ Click the OK button in the Set Directories dialog box to close the dialog box.

Now your working directory is C:\DProg\Work.

Setting an Alias for the Working Directory

It's a good idea to assign an alias name for the working directory. Why? During your work, you have to type the name of the working directory many times. Setting an alias enables you to simply

type the alias name instead of the long, working-directory pathname. Also, at some point, you might decide to change your working directory to another directory. In that case, all that you have to do is change the assignment for the alias name.

Here is how you assign an alias name for the working directory.

☐ Select Aliases from the Database Desktop File menu.

> *Database Desktop responds by displaying the Alias Manager dialog box as shown in Figure 2.5.*

Figure 2.5.
The Alias Manager dialog box.

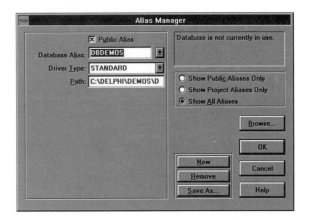

You use the Alias Manager dialog box to set the alias for the C:\DProg\Work working directory.

☐ In the Path edit box, type `C:\DProg\Work`.

☐ Click the New button because you are creating a new alias.

Database Desktop now lets you enter a new alias name in the Database Alias edit box.

☐ In the Database Alias, edit box type `MYWORK`.

Your Alias Manager dialog box should now appear as shown in Figure 2.6.

☐ Click the OK button in the Alias Manager dialog box.

> *Database Desktop responds by displaying the dialog box shown in Figure 2.7.*

☐ Click the Yes button in the dialog box shown in Figure 2.7. The setting for the new alias is saved into the configuration file that is used for determining aliases.

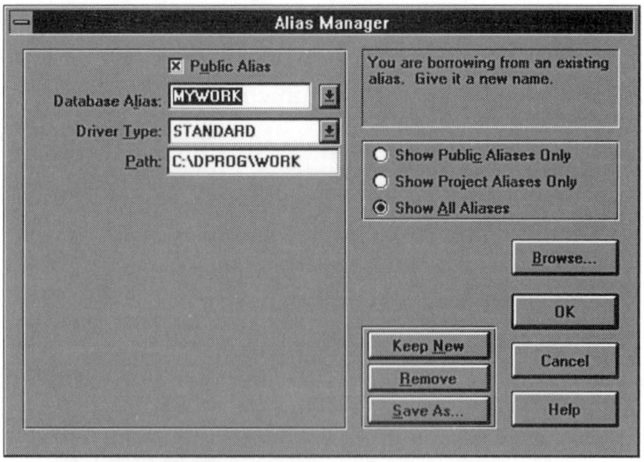

Figure 2.6.
Setting the C:\DProg\Work directory alias to MYWORK.

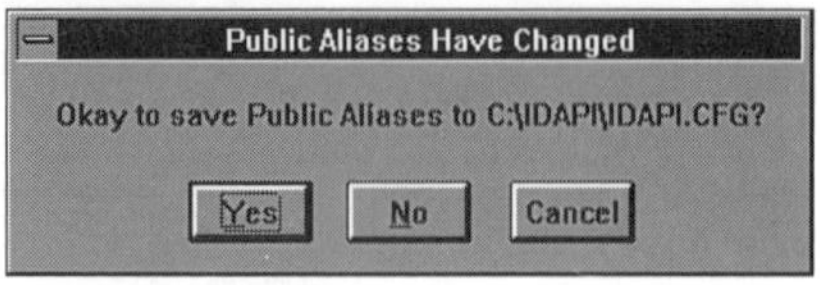

Figure 2.7.
Saving a new configuration file.

Creating Tables with the Database Desktop

Now create a table with the Database Desktop program. A *table* is a collection of data arranged in columns and rows, such as the table shown in Table 2.1.

Table 2.1. A table of customers.

CustNum	LastName	FirstName
1001	Kennedy	Tom
1002	Anderson	Jean
1003	George	Tim
1004	Sam	Jean

The table columns are called *fields*. Table 2.1 has three fields: `CustNum`, `LastName`, and `FirstName`.

There are four entries in Table 2.1. In database terminology, each entry (row) is called a *record*. Table 2.1 has three fields and four records.

Here is how you construct Table 2.1 using Database Desktop.

☐ Select New from the Database Desktop File menu.

Database Desktop responds by displaying another submenu.

☐ Select Table from the new submenu because you now want to create a new table.

Database Desktop responds by displaying the dialog box shown in Figure 2.8.

Figure 2.8.

*Setting the table type as
Paradox 5.0 for Windows.*

If you click the down arrow in the Table Type combobox, you'll see that you can choose from several types of tables. Basically, it doesn't matter which table type you select because, except for some minor differences, Delphi can work with all the listed tables. In order to duplicate the tutorials presented in this book (which use the Paradox 5.0 for Windows table type), always select the Paradox 5.0 for Windows table type.

☐ Click the OK button in the Table Type dialog box.

*Database Desktop responds by displaying the dialog box shown in Figure 2.9. Use the
dialog box shown in Figure 2.9 to construct the table shown in Table 2.1.*

Figure 2.9.

*The Create Paradox 5.0 for
Windows Table dialog box.*

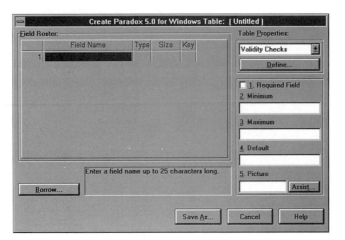

Note: The dialog box shown in Figure 2.9 appears provided that you set the Table Type as Paradox 5.0 for Windows.

You do not have to own the Paradox 5.0 for Windows package to work with these tables in Delphi.

☐ Click in the row below the Field Name, and type **CustNum**. This represents the name of the first field as dictated by Table 2.1.

☐ Use the mouse or the Tab key to move to the row under the Type column, and right-click the mouse.

Database Desktop responds by displaying a menu with various types of data.

☐ Select the Number item because you want the customer number field to be a number.

When the field is a number, you don't specify the field size, and so you can now move to the Key column.

☐ Double-click the cell under the Key column.

Database Desktop responds by placing an asterisk in the Key column. This means that the CustNum field is a key field. You learn more about the key field later in this chapter.

☐ Set the LastName and FirstName fields as shown in Figure 2.10. The type of both these fields is Alpha. The size of the LastName field is 30 characters, and the size of the FirstName field is 25 characters. Neither of these two fields is a key field.

Figure 2.10.

Setting the LastName and FirstName fields.

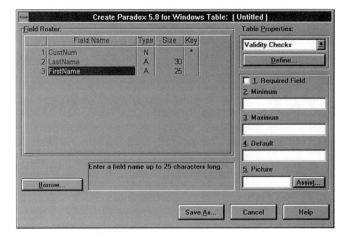

☐ Click the Save As button located at the bottom of the window to save the table you just created.

Database Desktop responds by displaying the Save Table As dialog box, shown in Figure 2.11.

Figure 2.11.
The Save Table As dialog box.

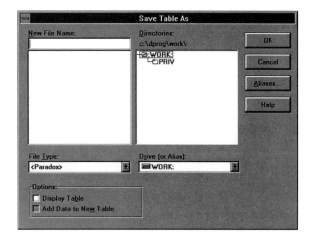

☐ In the New File Name edit box, type **Customer**, and then click the OK button.

You've now completed the Customer table. If you examine the C:\DProg\Work directory, you'll find that Database Desktop saved several files into this directory.

Note: As you can see from Figure 2.10, there are additional features that you can assign to the table.

For example, you can set a validity check, meaning that while the user inputs data into the customer table, a validity check is performed. For instance, if you have a field that holds the person's age, your validity check can consist of a check that doesn't allow the user to type a negative number.

For simplicity's sake, you weren't instructed to set any validity checks at this point.

Entering Data in the Customer Table

In the previous section you created the Customer table. You designed and implemented the Customer table structure. Now you enter data into the Customer table.

> **Note:** Naturally, you can enter data in the Customer table by writing a Delphi program which does that. You learn how to create such programs in subsequent chapters. In this chapter, you learn how to enter the data into tables by using the Database Desktop program.

☐ Select Open from the Database Desktop File menu, and then select Table from the popup menu.

Database Desktop responds by displaying the Open Table dialog box (see Figure 2.12).

Figure 2.12.
The Open Table dialog box.

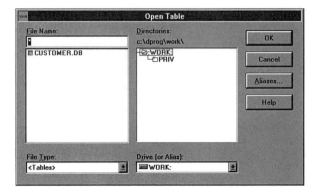

☐ Select the Customer.DB table from the C:\DProg\Work directory, and then click the OK button.

Database Desktop responds by displaying the Customer.DB table, as shown in Figure 2.13.

Figure 2.13.
The empty Customer.DB table.

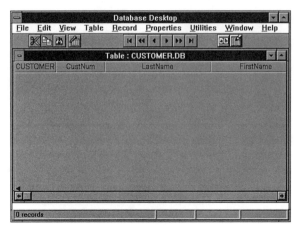

Naturally, Customer.DB is currently empty because you haven't entered any data into it.

Add four records to the Customer.DB table as follows:

☐ Select Edit Data from the View menu.

> *Database Desktop responds by placing the Customer.DB table in an edit mode (so that you now can enter data into the table).*

☐ Enter the data shown in Table 2.1 into the Customer table. To enter data into a field, click in the field, and then type the data. Use the keyboard arrow keys to move from one field to another and from one record to another. When you finish entering the data, the Customer table should appear as shown in Figure 2.14.

Figure 2.14.
The Customer.DB table with four records in it.

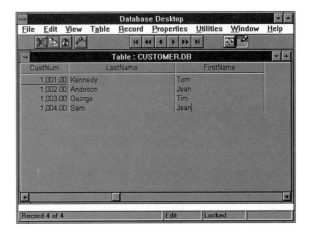

Note: There is no need to save the Customer.DB table data because Database Desktop automatically saves the data when you complete entering or modifying data in any of the records. So, the only thing you have to do for Database Desktop to save the data is to move from the current record to another record.

There are many things you can do to the appearance of the Customer.DB table. For one thing, the Customer Number appears as currency. Instead of having Customer Number equal to 1001, the Customer Number appears as 1,001.00.

You also can make the font of the data look different as well as make many other cosmetic changes. Changing the font now is equivalent to doing it with Paradox 5.0 for Windows, but this is not the objective of this book. The objective of this book is to use Delphi for doing such operations. In subsequent chapters, you learn how to write a Delphi program that uses the

Customer.DB table. When writing Delphi programs, you have practically unlimited ways of presenting the data, taking user input and updating the tables, validating the data, and whatever else you can think of.

The only reason we constructed the Customer.DB table with the Database Desktop program was to construct a very simple table so that you can have a database to work with in subsequent chapters.

Ordering the Table Records

Remember that during the construction of the Customer table, you set the CustNum field as a key field? This means that the Customer table is ordered by the CustNum field.

Every Paradox table must have at least one key field, and the first key field of a table is called the *primary key field.*

To see ordering in action, do the following:

☐ Change the value of the Kennedy customer number 1001 to 2001.

Remember, to make the change in data effective, you must move to another record.

☐ Use the keyboard arrow keys to move to another record.

Database Desktop automatically orders the records according to the key field. This means that the record with CustNum equal to 2001 now appears as the last record (see Figure 2.15).

Figure 2.15.
The records are ordered by the key field.

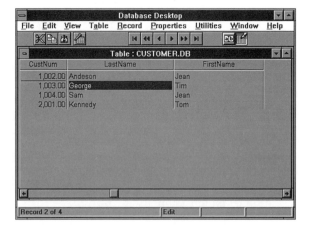

☐ Change the value of customer number 2001 back to 1001 to return the table data to its original state.

Key Field Records Must Be Unique

One thing that you must keep in mind about the key field is that this field *must* be unique. This means that if one of the records has its CustNum field equal to 1001, for example, then no other record in this table can have its CustNum field equal to 1001. You can verify this as follows:

☐ Use the arrow keys to move to the last empty row to add a new record.

☐ Set the fields of the new records as follows:

```
CustNum    1001
LastName   aaa
FirstName  bbb
```

☐ Try to move to another record.

Database Desktop does not allow you to move to another record. Why? Because the Customer table already has a record with CustNum equal to 1001.

☐ Select Delete from the Record menu to delete the new record that you attempted to add.

Be careful, however, with having a blank value for the key field, as demonstrated by the following steps:

☐ Use the arrow keys to move to the last empty row to add a new record.

☐ Set the fields of the new records as follows:

```
CustNum    Leave it blank
LastName   aaa
FirstName  bbb
```

☐ Try to move to another record.

Database Desktop agrees to take the last record that you entered. As a matter of fact, as shown in Figure 2.16, because CustNum is empty, Database Desktop sorts the table as if an empty value for CustNum is the smallest CustNum.

Now do the following:

☐ Use the arrow keys to move to the last empty row to add a new record.

☐ Set the fields of the new records as follows:

```
CustNum    Leave it blank
LastName   ccc
FirstName  ddd
```

☐ Try to move to another record.

Figure 2.16.
Having a record with no value for CustNum.

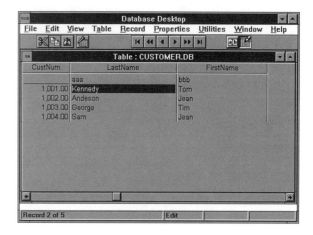

Database Desktop will not take the new record because you already have one record with blank value for the CustNum record.

☐ Delete the record that you tried to add by selecting Delete from the Record menu.

☐ Delete the record with the empty CustNum field by moving to that record and then selecting Delete from the Record menu.

Moving from Record to Record

As you saw in the previous sections, you can move from record to record by using the arrow keys of your keyboard. However, you also can use the control shown in Figure 2.17 for moving from record to record.

Figure 2.17.
Moving in the table by using the Navigator *control.*

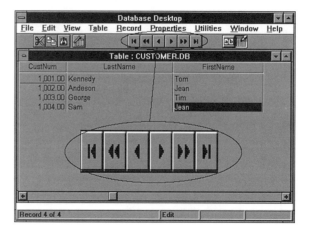

The leftmost button of the control shown in Figure 2.17 places the current record position on the first record. The second button from the left scrolls the list of records backward (toward the first record) by one page. If your table does not have at least one windowful of records, you cannot see this button in action.

The third button from the left places the current record position one record backward, and the third button from the right places the current position one record forward. The second button from the right places the current record one page forward. Again, if your table does not have enough records in it to fill a window, you will not be able to see this button in action. The rightmost button places the current position of the record at the last record of the table.

Databases, Tables, and All That Jazz

As you design and implement Delphi programs that deal with database and tables throughout this book, you'll have a chance to experiment with databases and tables. For now, though, let's go over some basic rules and topics related to the concept of databases.

Designing Table Structures

Suppose you're designing a table called Customers that contains a list of customers. One possible rendition of this table could contain the following fields:

```
Customer Last Name
Customer First Name
Customer Street Address
Customer Town
Customer State
Customer Zipcode
Customer Phone Number
```

Now suppose you want to maintain a table that contains the list of items the customers purchased. A bad solution would be to add the following fields to the Customers table:

```
Part Number 1
Quantity 1
Unit Price 1

Part Number 2
Quantity 2
Unit Price 2
```

```
Part Number 3
Quantity 3
Unit Price 3
```

The Customers table would then look as follows:

```
Customer Last Name
Customer First Name
Customer Street Address
Customer Town
Customer State
Customer Zipcode
Customer Phone Number
Part Number 1
Quantity 1
Unit Price 1
Part Number 2
Quantity 2
Unit Price 2
Part Number 3
Quantity 3
Unit Price 3
```

Each record would contain information about the customer as well as fields that contain information about the purchases. If you added the preceding fields, you would be able to update each record with a maximum of three purchases per customer. But what if the customers expect to make more than three purchases? As you can see, it isn't practical to keep adding fields to the Customer table every time a customer makes an additional purchase.

The optimal solution is to create a new table called Items. The Items table can include the following fields:

```
Part Number
Quantity
Unit Price
```

Whenever a purchase is made, you can record the information inside the Items table. For example, the following are some records in the Items table:

Part Number	Quantity	Unit Price
3001	42	$32.99
3011	1	$100.00
3502	3	$76.00

Can you tell what's wrong with the Items table? It doesn't provide you with any information about which customer purchased item number 3001, which customer purchased item 3011, and so on.

You might say that the answer to the preceding problem is simply to add two additional fields to the Items table: `Customer Last Name` and `Customer First Name`. Now the records of the Items table would look as follows:

Last Name	First Name	Part Number	Quantity	Unit Price
Smith	Jim	3001	42	$32.99
Richardson	Rich	3011	1	$100.00
Davidson	David	3502	3	$76.00

At first glance, it looks as if adding the `Last Name` and `First Name` fields to the Items table is a good solution. After all, the Items table now tells you that `Smith Jim` purchased 42 units of part number `3001` at `$32.99` apiece, `Richardson Rich` purchased part number `3011` at a unit price of `$100.00`, and so on. One problem with this solution is that there could be two customers with the same last name and first name. For example, you may have two `Smith Jim` customers in the Customers table.

You might start applying all types of "creative" solutions to the problem of having customers with the same last name and same first name. For example, one bad solution would be to attach numbers to the last names so that when you enter the last name of the first `Smith`, you would enter `Smith1`. If a second `Smith` is entered into the Customers table, this `Smith` would be entered as `Smith2`, and so on. You should feel intuitively that this solution is not a good one.

The beauty of database design is that this industry has been around for a long time, and a huge amount of experience has been accumulated. Because of this, all you have to do is simply learn what other database designers found to be the best way to design databases and tables.

In particular, looking at the example of the Customers and Items tables, the solution is as follows:

☐ Add a `Customer Number` field to the Customers table so that the Customers table has the following fields:

```
Customer Number
Customer Last Name
Customer First Name
Customer Street Address
Customer Town
Customer State
Customer Zipcode
Customer Phone Number
```

Whenever a customer is added to the Customers table, he or she is assigned a unique customer number. The term *unique* means that no two customers can have the same customer number. For example, when entering the first customer into the Customers table, the customer is assigned customer number 1001. The second customer is assigned customer number 1002, and so on. Once 1002 is used, no other customer can be assigned with 1002.

Here are some of the records in the Customers table:

Customer Number	Last Name	First Name	Street	...
1001	Richardson	Rich	...	...
1002	Davidson	David	...	...
1003	Smith	Jim	...	...

Now let's take a look at the Items table. Instead of putting the Last Name and First Name fields in the Items table, add the Customer Number field to the Items table.

After adding the Customer Number field to the Items table, some of its records of the Items table may look as follows:

Customer Number	Part Number	Quantity	Unit Price
1003	3001	42	$32.99
1001	3011	1	$100.00
1002	3502	3	$76.00

It's not clear from looking at the Items table now who purchased part number 3001. You can see that customer number 1003 purchased 42 units of part number 3001 at a unit price of $32.99, but who is customer number 1003? To figure out who customer number 1003 is, you have to consult the Customers table, where you can see that customer 1003 is Smith Jim.

To humans, the process of cross-referencing two tables is not convenient. In fact, on your way to find who customer number 1003 is, you can make a mistake by looking at the wrong row in the Customers table. But PCs do not make mistakes. And the correlation between customer 1003 and Smith Jim can be performed very fast and without any mistakes by your Delphi programs.

Note that the Items table has to be linked to the Customers table. The linkage is performed by using the Customer Number field. The collection of two tables (Customers and Items) is called a *database*. In this sample database, there are only two tables, but you can have more than two tables in a database.

What did you gain by only including the Customer Number field in the Customers table? Several things! Let's review the advantages of designing the Customers and Items tables so that they can be linked by the Customer Number field.

☐ *Saving hard-disk space.* The name `Smith Jim` appears only once on your hard disk; it appears inside the file that contains the Customers table. If the `Last Name` and `First Name` fields were included in the Items table, the name `Smith Jim` would appear many times on the hard disk. For example, if `Smith Jim` purchased three items, `Smith Jim` would have three records in the Items table, and the name `Smith Jim` would appear four times on the hard disk (one time in the Customer table and three times in the Items table).

When `Last Name` and `First Name` are not used in the Items table, the name `Smith Jim` appears only once on your hard disk. As you can see, this represents a tremendous amount of hard-disk space.

☐ *Fast performances.* Typically, databases are shared by several users. Several people may be involved in the process of entering data into the tables of the database, reading the data, and so on. In this situation, the database resides on the hard disk of one PC. Other PCs read data from and write data to the database by using a LAN (Local Area Network) where several PCs are connected via cables in an office or a building. If a program on one of the PCs that use the database has to load some records from the database, a minimum amount of information is transferred over the LAN. In the `Smith Jim` example, only the `1003` is transferred over the LAN (instead of transferring `Smith Jim`). If during a work week, a certain PC loaded a record of `Smith Jim` 10,000 times, the customer number `1003` was transferred 10,000 times over the LAN (instead of transferring the nine characters `Smith Jim` 10,000 times). Transferring less data means that the particular operation can be performed faster.

The preceding example assumes that the users of the PCs are connected via a LAN. In some cases, however, the users of the PC are connected via a WAN (Wide Area Network), where telephone lines and other long-distance equipment are used for transferring data from one location to another. This way of communication must use a database designed in a similar way to the Customers and Items tables. Why? Because typically, when you are using the telephone lines for data communication, the data is transferred at a low rate of speed. This is due to the limitation of the telephone equipment (which was designed for transferring voice, not data). The more data you're transferring over the telephone lines, the longer it takes to transmit it.

☐ *Easy data entry and easy maintenance.* Another important advantage of setting the Customers and Items tables as discussed is that it's easy to enter data into the tables. For example, suppose the user enters a new record into the Items table. If the user has to type the name `Smith Jim`, chances are that some typo will occur. Using the `Customer Number` field in the Items tables enables the user to type (or select with the mouse) the number `1003`. In other words, your Delphi programs will display the Customers table and an empty record of the Items table. The user will select the `1003` record from the Customer table, and by clicking a button, the `Customer Number` field of the Items table will be filled. There are fewer chances for errors now because the user sees the Customers table and sees that `Customer Number 1003` is `Smith Jim`.

51

Can you imagine what happens if one day `Smith Jim` calls and says that there is an error in the Customers table and that his correct name is `Smithson`? If the `Last Name` and `First Name` fields are part of the Items table, the person in charge of the Items table will have to locate all the records in the Items table that have `Last Name` equal to `Smith` and change these records to `Smithson`. By not including `Last Name` and `First Name` in the Items table, the person in charge of maintaining the database will have to change `Smith` to `Smithson` in only one place—the Customers table.

To summarize, when designing tables, you should avoid having redundant fields. Each table must contain only fields that are absolutely necessary. If certain data can be extracted from another table, don't include a field for this data. For example, don't include the `Last Name` field in the Items table because this field can be extracted from the Customers table.

> **Note:** The Customers table has a unique field called `Customer Number`, and the Items table can have many records with the same `Customer Number` field.
>
> So, for each record in the Customer table, there can be several records in the Items table. This linkage between the Customers and Items tables is called *one-to-many*.

Additional Linking

In the preceding section, you saw that the Items table has the following fields:

```
Customer Number
Part Number
Quantity
Unit Price
```

But what is the description of the part number? And how many units of this part number exist in stock?

You can see that the description of the part number and the number of items in stock should not be included in the Items table. Instead, the database should have an additional table called Parts. The Parts table could have the following fields:

```
Part Number
Part Description
Stock Quantity
```

The Part Number field should be a unique field. For example, only one record in the Parts table should have its Part Number field equal to 3001.

Now suppose that the Delphi program you're writing has to generate a report about one of the items from the Items table. In particular, suppose that a full detailed description is to be generated from the following record of the Items table:

Customer Number	Part Number	Quantity	Unit Price
1003	3001	42	$32.99

At first glance, it looks as if there is almost no information in the preceding record. However, the Delphi program you'll write has all the information that it needs! It can now display an attractive window with a lot of information in it. Based on the Customer Number field, your Delphi program will access the Customers table and display many details about this customer number—for example, the Last Name, First Name, Address, and everything else that exists in the Customers table. Also, your Delphi program will access the Parts table, and based on the Part Number, the description of the part number and the number of items in stock can be extracted from the Parts table.

During the course of this book, you'll learn many other database-design topics. These topics will be discussed on a need-to-know basis using practical examples.

Summary

In this chapter, you learned how to use the Database Desktop program that comes with Delphi. As you saw, the Database Desktop enables you to create a table as well as to enter records into the table. The Database Desktop program also enables you to manipulate the tables in various ways and perform various operations, such as displaying the data of the tables in different fonts and other cosmetic aspects.

We introduced you to the Database Desktop program because it is part of Delphi, and you can use it to perform simple tasks. As you develop Delphi programs, from time to time you'll need to use a table for experimenting and testing your Delphi programs. In such cases, using the Database Desktop program is the easiest and quickest way to construct tables. However, the objective of this book is to teach you how to program using Delphi. You can use Delphi to build a program like the Database Desktop (or a program that is better than the Database Desktop program).

Q&A

Q   **After playing with Database Desktop for awhile, I can see that I can do a lot with it. Why do I need Delphi?**

A   As stated in the chapter summary, Delphi is the tool that enables you to design an application like the Database Desktop. Basically, Database Desktop is for people like you who need to construct databases and tables quickly. However, would you give the Database Desktop program to a person who takes orders over the phone? The answer is no. The person who takes orders from customers over the phone needs a much friendlier program. This person needs to concentrate on sales, not on operating the Database Desktop program. By using Delphi, you can design programs that enable the person who uses it to enter and extract information in the friendliest and easiest way.

Q   **I've heard about database terms such as *one-to-many, one-to-many-to-many, linked tables,* and others. When will I learn about these topics?**

A   You'll learn about these important database topics in later chapters on a need-to-know-basis. That is, rather than loading too much database material on you at this early stage of your study, you first design a Delphi program that uses the simple Customer table you created in this chapter.

Then you'll learn additional database material and immediately proceed to apply your knowledge by designing a corresponding Delphi program.

Quiz

1. What is a key field?
    a. The field by which the table is ordered.
    b. The field that contains keys, knobs, and doors.
    c. A Paradox table does not need a key field.
2. The value of key field must be unique.
    a. True.
    b. False.
3. A unique value for a field means that _____.
4. The U.S. government uses a unique field in its database. Give an example.

Exercise

Practice with the Customer table by adding records, deleting records, and so on. Also add and delete fields from the table. However, no matter what you are doing, at the end of your practice, make sure that the table remains as shown in Figure 2.14, because in subsequent chapters it is assumed that the Customer table is as shown in Figure 2.14. (See the hint in the answer to this exercise.)

Answers to Quiz

1. a.
2. a.
3. No other record in the table can have the same value in the unique field.
4. Each person in the USA has a Social Security number. No two people can have the same social security number. This means that if you construct a table with all the social security numbers, the social security number can serve as a key field because this field is unique.

Answer to Exercise

If you are new to database and table design, you could do so much damage to the Customer.DB table that you won't be able to repair it. If you get into this situation, do the following:

☐ Terminate the Database Desktop application.

☐ Delete all the files that reside in the working directory (C:\DProg\Work).

☐ Start constructing the Customer table as discussed in this chapter, and enter data into it so that it will appear as shown in Figure 2.14. Subsequent chapters assume that the Customer table works and that it has the data shown in Figure 2.14.

This exercise also instructs you to add and delete fields from the table. This means that you have to restructure the table. You can restructure the table by clicking the Restructure icon (see Figure 2.18). When you click the Restructure icon, Database Desktop displays the window that enables you to add and delete fields from the table.

Figure 2.18.
The Restructure icon.

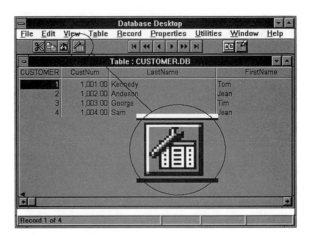

Creating Your First Delphi Database Program

In Chapter 2, "Databases," you designed the Customer.DB table and entered data into it. In this chapter, you design and implement a Delphi program that uses the Customer.DB table.

Data Controls

Figure 3.1 shows Delphi's standard controls. You'll notice that you've already used some of the controls that appear on the Standard page from your work in Chapter 1, "Creating Your First Delphi Application." You placed pushbuttons and the txtHello edit box from the Standard page into the frmHello form.

Figure 3.1.

The Standard page contains standard components.

Now look at Figure 3.2, which shows the Data Access page. The Data Access page contains icons that enable you to perform data-access operations.

Figure 3.2.

The Data Access page contains database components.

In essence, you use the data-access controls the same way you use the standard controls. However, the pushbutton control, for example, is a very simple control. You set its Name property, its Caption property, and maybe some other cosmetic aspects, such as its size and location in the form. The data-access controls of Delphi, on the other hand, are more powerful, and hence more complex, than the standard controls. The data-access controls (and the data controls on the Data Controls page) enable your program to interface with database tables with great ease. Setting the properties of these controls is not so easy! In other words, you must set several properties before the data controls can do a useful job for you.

Luckily, the job of setting the properties of the data controls can be automated by using a special Delphi feature, which we introduce you to in this chapter.

Now you're ready to create a new Delphi project. The form of this project will contain several data controls. As you'll see, you'll let Delphi automatically set the properties of the data controls.

Placing Data Controls in a Form

Here's how you let Delphi place data controls in your project's form:

☐ If your Database Desktop program is running, close it.

☐ Start Delphi.

In the following steps, you'll save files to the C:\DProg\Ch03 directory. Make sure that your hard drive has this directory. If it doesn't, use Windows File Manager to create the directory.

☐ Select New Project from the File menu.

☐ Select Save Project As from the File menu, and save the Pas file as CMyCust.Pas in the C:\DProg\Ch03 directory. Save the Dpr file (the project file) as MyCust.Dpr in the C:\DProg\Ch03 directory.

As you can see, you're going to design a program called MyCust.EXE. As implied by its name, this program uses the Customer.DB table that you created in Chapter 2, which means you have to use certain data controls (because the data controls enable you to access the Customer.DB table).

The following steps illustrate how you let Delphi automatically place the data controls in your form as well as automatically set the properties of these controls.

☐ Select Database Form Expert from the Help menu.

Delphi responds by displaying the window shown in Figure 3.3.

Figure 3.3.
The Database Form Expert window.

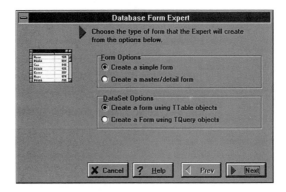

☐ Set the options of the Database Form Expert window as shown in Figure 3.3. These options tell the Database Expert that you are creating a simple form.

A *simple form* can use data from a single table, such as the Customer.DB table. (In subsequent chapters, you use data controls to extract data from several tables.)

Also, as shown in Figure 3.3, you have to select the option button, Create a form Using TTable Objects. Why? Because the MyCust program uses the Table component (which in Delphi lingo is called the *TTable* component).

☐ Click the Next button.

Delphi responds by displaying the window shown in Figure 3.4.

Figure 3.4.

The Database Form Expert asks you to specify the table that you want to use.

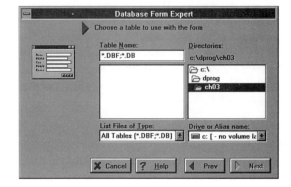

As you can see from this figure, the Database Form Expert asks you to specify the name of the table you want to use. If you had not used the Database Form Expert feature, you would have to set a data-control property with the name of the table. Using the Database Form Expert feature takes you step by step to your objective.

☐ Set the Table Name edit box to the C:\DProg\Work\Customer.DB file, as shown in Figure 3.5.

Figure 3.5.

Setting the name of the table to Customer.DB.

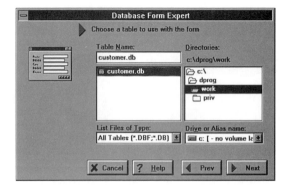

☐ Click the Next button.

Delphi responds by displaying the window shown in Figure 3.6.

Figure 3.6.
The Database Form Expert window asks you to specify the field names.

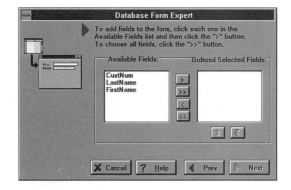

The window shown in Figure 3.6 asks you to specify the field names that are to appear in the form of the MyCust.EXE program. A table might have dozens of fields, but in many cases, you don't need to display all the table fields in your application's form. Now you're asked to specify which fields should be included in the MyCust.EXE program form. Remember, you *could* set the fields to be included in your application by first placing certain data controls in the form and then setting the controls' properties in the Object Inspector window, but you're doing it the easy way for now.

More importantly, specifying the fields with the Database Form Expert prevents you from making errors. Altogether, you're saving yourself time.

☐ Click the button that has a picture of two right-pointing arrows. You could select an individual field from the left list of fields and then click the button that has a picture of one arrow pointing to the right to move the field to the list on the right. In this case, however, you want to copy *all* the fields in the left list to the right list, and the double-arrow button does just that.

After copying all the fields from the left list to the right list, the window of Database Form Expert should look like the one shown in Figure 3.7.

Figure 3.7.
All the fields from the Customer.DB table are used in the MyCust program's form.

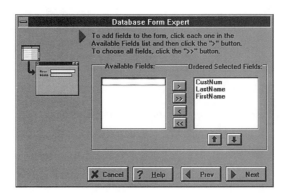

☐ Click the Next button.

Delphi responds by displaying the window shown in Figure 3.8.

Figure 3.8.
Selecting the layout arrangement.

Your application's form (MyCust.EXE program's form) can display the Customer.DB table fields in a variety of ways. The window shown in Figure 3.8 enables you to select the proper layout.

☐ Select the Grid option button.

The Database Form Expert window should now appear as shown in Figure 3.9.

Figure 3.9.
The Customer.DB table data is displayed in a grid.

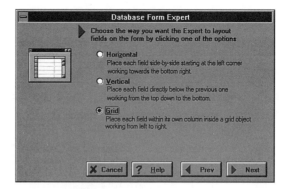

☐ Click the Next button.

Delphi responds by displaying the window shown in Figure 3.10.

Figure 3.10.
Everything is ready for generating the form according to your specifications.

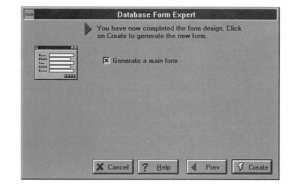

The window shown in Figure 3.10 is waiting for you to click the Create button. Everything is now ready to create the form according to the specifications you made in the previous steps. All you need to do now is click the Create button.

☐ Click the Create button.

> *Delphi responds by creating the Form2 form as shown in Figure 3.11.*

Figure 3.11.
The Form2 form was created by Database Form Expert.

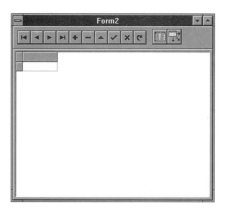

☐ Make sure that the Form2 form is selected, select Save File As from the File menu, and save the file as CData.Pas in the C:\DProg\Ch03 directory.

Understanding the Form Generated by Database Form Expert

Before going any further, it's very important that you understand what Database Form Expert did for you.

Basically, Database Form Expert generated the Form2 form and placed various controls in it.

Figure 3.12 shows the Grid control in the Form2 form. Note that we clicked the Grid control to select the control. It is enclosed with a black rectangle, just as the pushbutton is enclosed with the black rectangle when it is selected. As you can see in Figure 3.12, the Grid control is the size of the entire Form2 area.

Figure 3.12.
The Grid *control in the*
Form2 *form.*

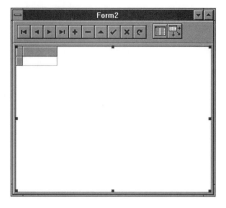

Figure 3.13 shows the Object Inspector window with the properties of the Grid control shown.

Figure 3.13.
The Object Inspector
window displaying the Grid
control properties in the
Form2 *form.*

As you can see, Database Form Expert sets various Grid control properties. For example, the control's Name property was set to DBGrid1.

If you wanted to (if you don't like the easy way), you could do the same thing without using the Database Form Expert. You could, instead, double-click the DBGrid control on the Data Controls page, and then set its properties in the Object Inspector window. The DBGrid control icon on the Data Controls page is shown in Figure 3.14.

Figure 3.14.

The DBGrid *control on the Data Controls page.*

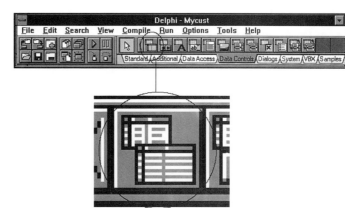

The DBGrid control is not the only control that was placed in the Form2 form. In Figure 3.15, the Navigator control that Database Form Expert placed in Form2 is shown as the selected control.

Figure 3.15.

The DBNavigator *control that Database Form Expert placed in* Form2.

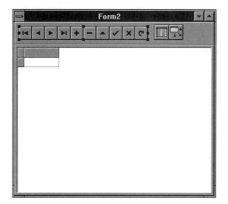

Of course, Database Form Expert also set various properties of the Navigator control. In Figure 3.16, you can see that the Object Inspector displays the properties of the Navigator control and that the Name property of the Navigator control is set to DBNavigator.

Figure 3.16.

The Object Inspector window displays the Navigator *control properties placed in the* Form2 *form.*

You could have placed the Navigator control on the form by yourself (without using Database Form Expert). The Navigator control icon is shown on the Data Controls page in Figure 3.17.

Figure 3.17.

The Navigator *control icon on the Data Controls page.*

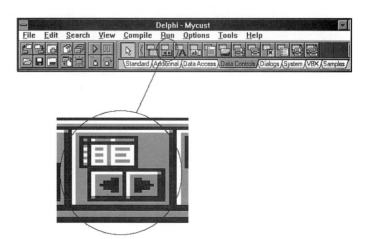

Figure 3.18 shows a component that Database Form Expert placed on the Form2 form: the Table component, which is shown selected in the figure.

Figure 3.18.

The Table *component is shown selected in the* Form2 *form.*

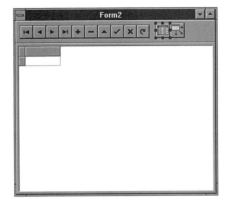

The Object Inspector window in Figure 3.19 shows the Table component properties. As you can see, Database Form Expert set the Name property of the component to Table1. Figure 3.20 shows the Table component icon on the Data Access page.

Figure 3.19.

The Object Inspector window displays the Table *component properties placed in the* Form2 *form.*

Figure 3.20.

The Table *component icon on the Data Access page.*

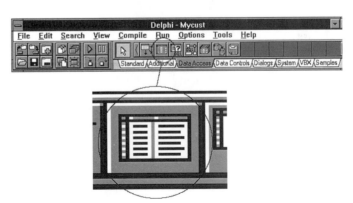

Database Form Expert also placed the component shown selected in Figure 3.21: the DataSource component. In Figure 3.22, you can see that Database Form Expert set the component's Name property to DataSource1.

Figure 3.21.

The DataSource component is shown selected in the Form2 *form.*

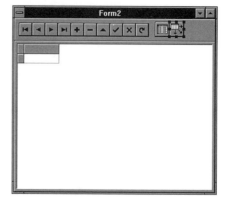

Figure 3.22.

The Object Inspector window displays the DataSource *component properties placed in the* Form2 *form.*

The DataSource component icon on the Data Access page is shown in Figure 3.23.

For cosmetic reasons, Database Form Expert placed another control in Form2: the Panel control, which is shown selected in Figure 3.24. It contains the Navigator control as well as the Table and DataSource components.

The Object Inspector window shown in Figure 3.25 displays the Panel control properties.

Figure 3.23.

The DataSource *component icon on the Data Access page.*

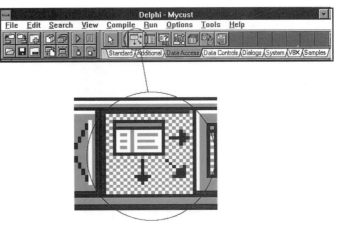

Figure 3.24.

Database Form Expert placed a Panel *control in the* Form2 *form.*

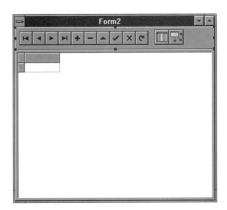

Figure 3.25.

The Object Inspector window displays the Panel *control properties placed in the* Form2 *form.*

The Panel control icon is shown on the Standard page in Figure 3.26.

Figure 3.26.

The Panel control icon on the Standard page.

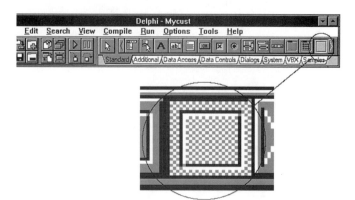

Executing the MyCust Program

Although you haven't yet written a single line of code, the MyCust program already performs a few functions. To see it in action, do the following:

☐ Execute the MyCust program.

The MyCust program window appears, as shown in Figure 3.27.

Figure 3.27.

The MyCust program windows.

When you execute the MyCust program from Delphi, Delphi compiles the program and generates an EXE file, namely, the MyCust.EXE file in the C:\DProg\Ch03 directory.

☐ Close the Delphi project, and then execute the MyCust.EXE program by using the File Manager (or the Run item from the Program Manager's File menu). (Remember, the MyCust.EXE program resides in the C:\DProg\Ch03 directory.)

When the MyCust program executes, it displays the Customer.DB table data. You can use your keyboard arrow keys to move from record to record and from field to field. Alternatively, you can use the Navigator control buttons.

The *Navigator* Control

As was shown in Figure 3.27, Database Form Expert placed the Navigator control in your form. The Navigator control has 10 buttons: some are enabled, and some are disabled or *dimmed*. According to the particular status of the records on your screen, the Navigator control buttons are enabled or disabled.

To see the Navigator control in action, do the following:

☐ Use your keyboard arrow keys to make the second record the current record.

The first button on the left places the current record position at the beginning of the table. Try it:

☐ Click the first button on the left.

As a result, the current record position is now the first record in the table.

The second button from the left moves the current record position one record backward, and the third button from the left moves the current record position one record forward. The fourth button from the left moves the current record position to the last record.

The button with the plus-sign (+) icon is the Insert button. You can place the current record position on a particular record, and then click the Insert button. This creates a new empty row one row above the current row. You can now enter new data into the empty row, but you must be careful not to enter a value for the CustNum field that already exists in the table. Why? Because the CustNum field is a key field, and hence it must be unique. If you execute the MyCust.EXE program by using the File Manager program (that is, you execute the MyCust program as you would any other Windows application), and then you attempt to enter a non-unique value for CustNum, MyCust.EXE refuses to accept the value (you are prompted with a Key Violation message box). To delete the record that has a non-unique value for CustNum (or any other record that you want to delete), place the current record on the row you want to delete, and then click the button with the minus-sign (–) icon on it.

Note that once you insert a new record with a unique value for CustNum, you can move to another record, and the records are automatically ordered according to CustNum. Assume, for example, that you insert a record with CustNum equal to 2000 before the record with CustNum 1003. After moving to another record, the record with CustNum equal to 2000 is displayed in its proper ordered position.

The button with the up-arrow icon is the Edit button. In the MyCust program, the table is always in Edit mode (you always can edit the record data). In other programs you'll write, the table will be in non-Edit mode, and the user will have to click the Edit button to be able to edit the data.

The button with the X icon is the Cancel button. This icon is used to cancel the current record being edited. For example, the user starts to modify a particular record. If, before moving to another record, the user clicks the Cancel button, the values of the record are returned to their original values.

The first button on the right is the Refresh button, which causes the form to display the current data contained in the Customer.DB table. As this statement implies, the data displayed on your screen isn't necessarily the table's current data. For instance, suppose you're working on a network, and you are sharing the Customer.DB table (which resides on a PC other than yours) with other users. When you execute the MyCust program, data is extracted from Customer.DB and delivered to your PC screen over the network. If someone else on the network modifies the Customer.DB table while you're still viewing data on your screen, the updated data in the table will not be displayed on your screen until you click the Refresh button.

Likewise, if you modify the data on your screen, you can update the Customer.DB table by clicking the Post button (third button from the right), which updates the Customer.DB immediately.

Note that the Post and Refresh buttons cause immediate data updating no matter where the Customer.DB table resides. Customer.DB could reside on your PC or on another PC on the network.

☐ Experiment with the various Navigator control buttons.

☐ Click the minus-sign icon that appears in the upper-left corner of the application's window, and select Close from the system menu that pops up.

About the MyCust Project Forms

A project can have one or more forms. For example, the Hello program you implemented in Chapter 1 has a single form, the frmHello form.

The MyCust project has two forms right now:

- When you created the MyCust project, Delphi automatically created Form1.
- When you used the Database Form Expert, Delphi created the Form2 form.

You can find out how many forms your project has as follows:

☐ Select Project Manager from the View menu.

Delphi responds by displaying the window shown in Figure 3.28.

Figure 3.28.
The MyCust project has two forms.

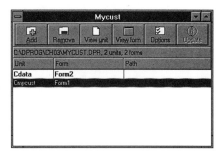

Alternatively, you can select Forms from the View menu to display a list of the forms.

When you used the Database Form Expert, you instructed it to generate a new form and to set the new form as the main form (refer back to Figure 3.10). When a program starts, it loads one of its forms, and so the Hello program in Chapter 1 loads the frmHello form because it's the only form that the project has.

The MyCust project contains two forms, and so you may wonder which form is loaded and displayed when the MyCust program executes. As you saw in Figure 3.23, Form2 is loaded and displayed because it is the main form.

You can find out which form is the main form by doing this:

☐ Click the Options button in the Project Manager window. The Project Manager window is displayed, as shown in Figure 3.28, because you selected Project Manager from the View window.

Once you click the Options button, Delphi responds by displaying the Project Options window, as shown in Figure 3.29.

Note that the Main form combobox contains the entry, Form2. The entry in this box specifies the form that should be displayed when the MyCust program executes—in this case, Form2.

If you want to set a different form as the main form, you can click the down arrow of the Main form combobox to display the forms available for the current project (see Figure 3.30), and select the form you want from the list. For now, make sure that Form2 is the main form.

Figure 3.29.
The Project Options window.

Figure 3.30.
Selecting the main form.

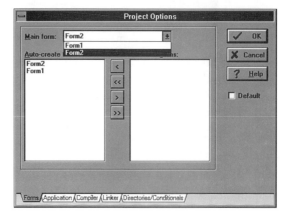

What Else Is There To Do?

So far, you've implemented a program without typing a single line of code! In the next chapter, you work further on the MyCust program. You now have a form (Form2) that has data controls in it. These controls enable you to access the Customer.DB table. You can customize the MyCust program in any conceivable way: you can attach pushbuttons and scroll bars, and design the MyCust program to do whatever you want it to do. The most difficult portion of the implementation, however, is placing the data controls in the form and setting the control properties, but guess what? Using the Database Form Expert, it will take you less than a minute to place the data controls and set their properties!

Summary

In this chapter, you learned about the importance of the Database Form Expert. This feature places the data controls in your form and sets their properties. Once you accomplish this, you can continue implementing the program in the same manner that you implemented the Hello program in Chapter 1. You have a chance to do this in subsequent chapters.

Q&A

Q I see that to display table data, such as that in the Customer.DB table, several controls are used. Why?

A As you learn in subsequent chapters, each control has its own purpose. For example, the Grid control is simply a way to display table data. The Panel control is just a cosmetic thing, the Navigator control enables the user to navigate through the data, and the Table and DataSource controls are the actual interface between the table and your program.

Quiz

1. You can use the Database Form Expert by selecting it from where?
   a. From the Help menu.
   b. From within the Database Desktop program.
2. Every control that Database Form Expert placed in the form can be manually placed by you.
   a. True.
   b. False.
3. What is/are the advantage(s) of using Database Form Expert?

Exercise

It's extremely important to practice using Delphi tools, so here's a chance for you to practice. Create a new program called MyTry.EXE. In order not to destroy the work that you've done in this chapter, save it into a new directory called C:\Try. The MyTry program should be identical to the MyCust program.

> **Caution:** Whatever you do, don't destroy the work you accomplished in this chapter. Subsequent chapters assume that the Customer.DB table is in good working condition in the C:\DProg\Work directory, and that the MyCust project resides in the C:\DProg\Ch03 directory.
>
> If you accidentally alter your existing work, don't panic. Instead, just follow the steps outlined in this chapter to create the MyCust program (and, if needed, the Customer.DB table) all over again.

Use the Database Form Expert feature to create a new form in your project and to place data controls in your form. Your MyTry program should use the Customer.DB table. (Alternatively, you could use Database Desktop to create a new table (for example, MyTable.DB) and let Database Form Expert create the connection between your MyTable.DB table and your MyTry program.)

Answers to Quiz

1. a.
2. a.
3. Database Form Expert also sets the properties of the data controls so that you don't have to do it manually.

Answer to Exercise

Your table, forms, and data should be the same as those of the MyCust program. Test your program by executing it. Using the tools described in this chapter, verify that everything is correct.

Reading and Writing Field Values

In the previous chapter, you implemented the MyCust.EXE program. However, you did not write a single code in it. You let Database Form Expert do all the work for you. As such, the MyCust program is quite limited; it doesn't have many features.

In this chapter, you start adding your own code to the MyCust program.

Data Component Properties

Before starting to add your own code to the MyCust program, take a look at some of the properties that Database Form Expert set for the data components that it placed in the Form2 form of the MyCust project. As you see, you can modify the MyCust program by setting different values for the component properties that Database Form Expert placed.

The *Active* Property of the *Table* Component

One of the controls that Database Form Expert placed in the Form2 form is the Table component. Database Form Expert set the Name property of this component to Table1.

One of the Table component properties is the Active property. To see the Active property in action, follow these steps:

☐ Select the Table1 component in the Form2 form by clicking on the component.

☐ Use the Object Inspector to inspect the Active property of Table1.

As you can see, the Active property is set to False.

☐ Set the Active property of Table1 to True.

  Delphi responds by displaying the values of the records during design time.

☐ Set the Active property of Table1 back to False.

The *DataBaseName* Property of the *Table* Component

The MyCust program uses a single table, Customer.DB. As you'll see in subsequent chapters, Delphi enables you to write applications that use several tables. (You learn how to link the tables for extracting various information from the collection of the tables). The group of tables is called a *database*. A database is composed of several tables. The DataBaseName property of the Table1 component specifies the database.

☐ Use the Object Inspector to examine the value of the DataBaseName property of Table1.

As you can see, Database Form Expert sets the values of this property to C:\DProg\Work.

Recall that you saved the Customer.DB table to the C:\DProg\Work directory, which is the working directory. If there were additional tables to be used in the MyCust program, the other tables would have to reside in the C:\DProg\Work directory because this is where the database resides.

The *TableName* Property of the *Table* Component

☐ Use the Object Inspector to examine the value of the TableName property of Table1.

As you can see, Database Form Expert set the value of this property to Customer.DB. Because the DataBaseName property was set to C:\DProg\Work, the Table component knows that Customer.DB resides in C:\DProg\Work.

The *ReadOnly* Property of the *Table* Component

An important property of the Table component is the ReadOnly property.

☐ Use the Object Inspector to examine the value of the ReadOnly property of **Table1**.

Database Form Expert set the value of this property to False. This means that during the execution of the MyCust program, the user can write new data to the Customer.DB table. In fact, in the previous chapter you were instructed to experiment with the MyCust program by modifying the values of the Customer.DB table.

However, you seldom will give your user the freedom to directly change data in the tables as the MyCust program does! As a Delphi programmer, one of your prime concerns is to not allow the user to alter the tables. Thus, you write, for example, code that checks whether user-typed data is valid, and only if the data is valid does your code update the database tables with the new data.

☐ Make sure that the Active property of the Table1 component is set to False, and then set the ReadOnly property of Table1 to True. You can change the ReadOnly property only if the Active property is set to False.

☐ Run the MyCust program.

As you can see, you can now read the values of the Customer.DB table, but you cannot modify the table. Note that some of the Navigator buttons are always dimmed because the Customer.DB table is now in read-only mode.

☐ Terminate the MyCust program.

The *DataSource* Component

The Database Form Expert placed the DataSource component in the Form2 form.

☐ Use the Object Inspector window to examine the DataSource component's Name property.

The Name property is now set to DataSource1.

Also note that the Database Form Expert set the DateSet property of DataSource1 to Table1. This means that the data is supplied to the MyCust program from Table1 (which is set to Customer.DB). As you can see, the DataSource component serves as a link between the database and your application.

The *DBGrid* Control

Database Form Expert placed the DBGrid control in the Form2 form.

☐ Use the Object Inspector to examine the DBGrid control properties.

As you can see, Database Form Expert set the Name property of the control to DBGrid1.

Which data is displayed in the DBGrid control? This is set by the DBGrid control's DataSource property. You can examine the DBGrid1 control's DataSource property to verify that its DataSource property is set to DataSource1. You already know that the DataSet property of DataSource1 is set to Table1. So, putting it all together, the DBGrid1 control displays the Customer.DB data.

The *Navigator* Control

Database Form Expert also placed the Navigator control in the Form2 form.

☐ Use the Object Inspector window to examine this control's properties.

As you can see, this control's Name property is DBNavigator.

Because the DataSource property of DBNavigator is DataSource1, the DBNavigator knows in which table it should navigate.

If you examine the DBNavigator control's VisibleButtons property, you see that this property is composed of a long expression (see Figure 4.1).

Figure 4.1.

The Navigator *control's*
VisibleButtons *property.*

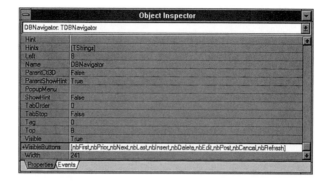

☐ Double-click the plus sign (+) that appears to the left of the VisibleButtons cell.

Delphi responds by expending the VisibleButtons *item as shown in Figure 4.2.*

You now can set the properties of the nbFirst item, for example. When this property is set to True, the First button of the Navigator control (the first button from the left) is visible. Setting the nbFirst property to False causes the First button to be invisible.

Figure 4.2.

The various items of the
VisibleButtons *property.*

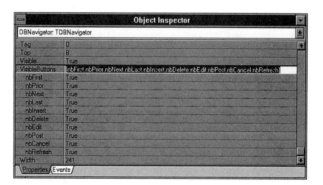

☐ Set the nbFirst property to False.

☐ Run the MyCust program.

As you can see in Figure 4.3, the Navigator control now has only nine buttons (the First button is invisible).

Figure 4.3.

The Navigator *control has only nine buttons.*

☐ Terminate the MyCust program.

☐ Set the Navigator control's nbFirst property back to True.

In a similar manner, you can set the properties under the VisibleButtons item so that other buttons will be visible or invisible.

> **Note:** Whenever you see a plus sign (+) to the left of a property in the Object Inspector window, double-click it to expand it.
>
> To un-expand the property, double-click it again. (In its expandable state, the property has a minus sign to its left.)

> **Note:** You saw in this chapter that you can set the Table component's ReadOnly property to True, which disables the user from entering data.
>
> When the table is read only, you may argue that it is acceptable to set the nbEdit property to False (to make the Navigator control's Edit button invisible) because this button is always dimmed.
>
> However, it also may be argued that it's a good idea to make all the buttons visible (even if they are always dimmed). Why? Because a dimmed button provides information to the user. For example, when the user sees the Navigator control's Edit button dimmed, the user has a visual indication that the table cannot be edited. Also, by always displaying the 10 buttons, the user becomes used to the 10-button arrangement. That is, the second button from the left is always the Prior button, and so on.

The *FormCreate* Event

The Database Form Expert created the Form2 form and placed components in it for you. Database Form Expert also wrote some code for you. To see this code, follow these steps:

☐ Make Form2 the selected window, and then click the down-arrow icon that appears on the top of the Object Inspector window.

   Object Inspector responds by dropping down a list of all the objects in Form2.

☐ Select the Form2 object from the list.

   Object Inspector responds by displaying the properties of Form2.

☐ Click the Events tab to display the Form2 form's events.

As shown in Figure 4.4, the OnCreate Event has the FormCreate item to its right.

Figure 4.4.
The Event page of Form2 in the Object Inspector window.

☐ Double-click the FormCreate cell that appears to the right of the OnCreate event cell.

   Delphi responds by displaying the window with the code of the FormCreate procedure as follows:

```
procedure TForm2.FormCreate(Sender: TObject);
begin

   Table1.Open;

end;
```

As you can see, Database Form Expert wrote the statement

```
Table1.Open;
```

The FormCreate procedure is automatically executed when the form is created, and so when you start the MyCust program, Form2 is first created and then displayed. The FormCreate procedure gives you a chance to write code that you want to execute prior to displaying the form.

Database Form Expert also wrote code that opens `Table1`. This is why when the `Form2` form is displayed, the data is shown in the `Grid` control (because the `Table1` component is open already).

Database Form Expert named the components with mechnical names, such as `Table1` for the `Table` component.

It's your job to change the component's `Name` properties set by Database Form Expert to more friendly names that enable you to better understand your project.

The following steps illustrate how you set a new value for the `Table1` component's `Name` property.

The `Table1` component that Database Form Expert placed does not really give you any indication about the role of this component in the MyCust program. A better name for this component is `CustomerTable` because this `Table` component is connected to the Customer.DB table.

☐ Make sure that the `Table1` component is selected, and then in the Object Inspector window change the `Name` property from `Table1` to `CustomerTable`.

If you execute the MyCust program now, you get an error! Why? Because in the `FormCreate` procedure in `Form2`, you have code written by Database Form Expert referring to the `Table` component as `Table1`.

Thus, you must manually change every occurrence of `Table1` in the project to `CustomerTable`. You can use the Find and Find Next menu items on the Search menu to find `Table1` and replace it with `CustomerTable`.

☐ Search for the occurrence of `Table1` using the Find item from the Search menu.

Delphi finds `Table1` in the `FormCreate` procedure of `Form2`.

☐ Replace the text `Table1` with the text `CustomerTable`. After replacing the text, the `FormCreate` procedure should appear as follows:

```
procedure TForm2.FormCreate(Sender: TObject);
begin

   CustomerTable.Open;

end;
```

☐ Search for additional occurrences of `Table1` using Find Next from the Search menu.

Delphi does not find any more occurrences of `Table1`.

☐ Run the MyCust program to verify that everything is working, and then terminate the program.

You can use Delphi's powerful Replace dialog also to search for and replace text all in one step. If a search-and-replace operation doesn't go quite the way you intended, you can always undo the operation (by selecting Undo from the Edit menu) and try again.

Using the Fields Editor

When you used the Database Form Expert to generate Form2 with various components in it, you specified that you want all the fields by clicking the button with the right-pointing double arrow. By specifying *all* the fields, you specified that the MyCust program can use every field. But do you really want to display all the fields? If, during the Database Form Expert session, you specified that you want all the fields, your form will be able to use every field. In this section, you learn how to select only some of the fields so that only the selected fields are displayed. To do this, you need to use the Fields Editor tool.

Here is how you use the Fields Editor.

☐ Set the Active property of the CustomerTable's Table component (formally known as Table1) to True.

☐ Double-click the CustomerTable control.

> *Delphi responds by displaying the Fields Editor dialog box, as shown in Figure 4.5, which does not include any fields.*

Figure 4.5.
The Fields Editor dialog box.

☐ Click the Add button in the Fields Editor dialog box.

> *Delphi responds by listing all the fields of the Customer.DB table, as shown in Figure 4.6.*

Figure 4.6.
Listing all the fields from the Customer.DB table.

Select the `CustNum` and `LastName` fields:

☐ Click the `CustNum` field.

☐ Press the Ctrl button, and while holding the Ctrl button down, click the `LastName` item.

The `CustNum` and `LastName` fields are now highlighted.

☐ Click the OK button.

The Fields Editor window now contains the `CustNum` and `LastName` fields, as shown in Figure 4.7.

Figure 4.7.
The list contains only two fields from the Customer.DB table.

☐ Click the minus-sign (–) icon located on the upper-left corner of the Fields Editor window, and select Close from the system menu that pops up.

Look at `Form2`; it contains only the `CustNum` and `LastName` fields.

☐ Run the MyCust program.

The MyCust window appears as shown in Figure 4.8.

Figure 4.8.
Only the `CustNum` *and* `LastName` *fields appear in the grid.*

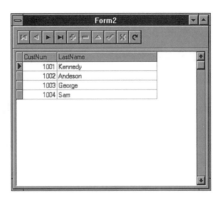

☐ Terminate the MyCust program.

Figure 4.9.
The LastName field is listed first in the Fields Editor window.

Figure 4.10.
The arrangement of the columns in the grid corresponds to the order of the fields in Figure 4.9.

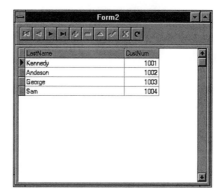

About the *CustNum* and *LastName* Fields in the Form

In the previous steps, you included the CustNum and LastName fields with the Fields Editor window. Once you included these fields, Delphi actually placed two additional components in Form2! You can't see these components because they are invisible, but you can examine and set the properties of them just like any other component.

First, verify that Delphi indeed placed these components in Form2.

☐ Click the down-arrow icon on the combobox at the top of the Object Inspector window.

As shown in Figure 4.11, the list of objects in Form2 includes the CustomerTableCustNum object and the CustomerTableLastName object.

Figure 4.11.

The form now contains the
CustomerTableCustNum
object and the
CustomerTableLastName
object.

Let's examine the properties of the CustomerTableCustNum object. This is the object corresponding to the CustNum field of the CustomerTable table.

☐ Use the Object Inspector to examine the properties of CustomerTableCustNum.

As shown in Figure 4.12, this control's Name property is CustomerTableCustNum. Delphi composed this component's name by combining the Table control's Name property (CustomerTable) and the field's name (CustNum).

Figure 4.12.

Examining the
CustomerTableCustNum
object properties.

> **Note:** Look at the combobox at the top of the Object Inspector window in Figure 4.12. The `CustomerTableCustNum` object is a control of type `TFloatField`.
>
> If you display the `CustomerTableLastName` field properties, you'll see that this component is of type `TStringField`.
>
> Because `CustNum` is a numeric field that can hold float numbers, Delphi placed the `TFloatField` component for the `CustNum` field; and because `LastName` is a string field, Delphi placed the `TStringField` control for `LastName`.
>
> As you can see, Delphi places the `TxxxField` component where *xxx* stands for the data type that the field supports.

Note that the `Alignment` property of the `CustomerTableCustNum` component is set to `taRightJustify`. You can set a different value for this property to display the `CustNum` column in different alignment.

Delphi is a visual programming environment. That is, most of your programming you do visually by using the mouse and doing a lot of clicking. Also, a large part of your development time is spent on the cosmetic aspects of the program you're developing. As you saw, the `CustomerTableCustNum` component's `Alignment` property enables you to display the column in different alignments.

Another cosmetic property is the `CustomerTableCustNum` component's `DisplayLabel` property. In Figure 4.8, note the `CustNum` column heading. Is that a useful heading? For you, the programmer, it is because you know that `CustNum` is the name of the field corresponding to this column. For your end user, this looks like a misspelling of Customer Number.

☐ Set the `CustomerTableCustNum` component's `DisplayLabel` property to `Customer Number`.

☐ Run the MyCust program.

As shown in Figure 4.13, now the column corresponding to the `CustNum` field has the heading you set with the `DisplayLabel` property.

☐ Terminate the MyCust program and then use the Object Inspector window to examine the `CustomerTableCustNum` component's `FieldName` property, which is set to `CustNum`. This, of course, makes a lot of sense because this component represents the `CustNum` field of the Customer.DB table.

Note that the `CustomerTableCustNum` component's `ReadOnly` property is set to `False`. This means that the user can read and write to this field. However, you can set this property to `True` so the user won't be able to modify the value of this field.

Figure 4.13.
The heading of the CustNum
column is now Customer
Number.

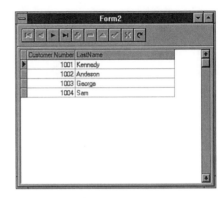

Another useful property is the Visible property. To see this property in action, do the following:

☐ Set the CustomerTableCustNum object Visible property to False, and then run the MyCust program.

As you can see, the Customer Number column is now invisible. (See Figure 4.14.)

Figure 4.14.
Making the Customer
Number *column invisible.*

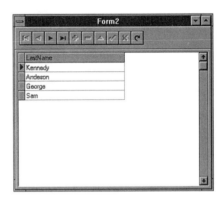

☐ Terminate the MyCust program.

☐ Set the Visible property back to True.

As you can see from the preceding steps, you have a lot of control over the fields you included in the grid by simply setting their properties. So far, you've set the properties by using the Object Inspector, but you can, of course, set the component properties from within your code as outlined in the following sections.

Changing Field Properties from Within Your Code

Currently, the Grid control covers the entire client area (the entire useable area of Form2).

☐ Examine the Grid control's Align property, and notice that the Align property is set to alClient. This is why the Grid control covers the entire client area.

☐ Drag the edges of Form2, and note that the Grid control automatically changes its size to fit the entire client area of Form2. Drag the edge of the Grid control, and note that no matter how you size the Grid control, it always returns to a size that fills the entire client area.

Add standard controls to Form2 now. You need area in Form2 in which to place the standard controls.

☐ Set the Grid control's Align property to alNone.

Now that the Grid control's Align property is set to alNone, you can change the size of the Grid control.

☐ Set the Grid control size, as shown in Figure 4.15.

Figure 4.15.
Making the Grid *control smaller.*

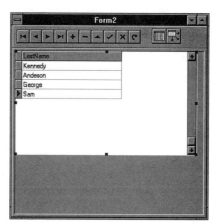

☐ Click the Standard page, click the Checkbox icon, and then click in a free area of Form2.

Delphi responds by placing a checkbox in Form2.

☐ Again click the Checkbox icon on the Standard page, and then click again in a free area of Form2.

Delphi responds by placing a second check box in Form2.

☐ Click the pushbutton icon in the Standard page, and then click in a free area of Form2.

Delphi responds by placing a pushbutton in Form2.

☐ Arrange the two checkboxes and the pushbutton you placed in Form2, as shown in Figure 4.16.

Figure 4.16.

Placing two check boxes and one pushbutton in Form2.

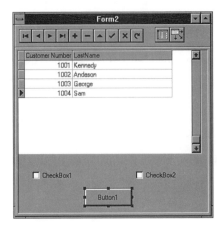

Designing the Exit Button

So far, whenever you were instructed to run and then terminate the MyCust program, you had to click the minus (–) icon in the upper-left corner of the MyCust window, and select Close from the system menu that pops up.

To make things easier, implement the Exit button so that you can just click this button whenever you want to terminate the MyCust program.

☐ Set the pushbutton's Caption property to E&xit.

☐ Set the pushbutton's Name property to cmdExit.

Don't forget to select Save Project from the File menu from time to time.

Attach code to the cmdExit button's OnClick event as follows:

☐ Double-click the OnClick cell in Object Inspector while displaying the Events page of the cmdExit button.

Delphi responds by displaying the cmdExitClick *procedure code.*

☐ Type code in the cmdExitClick procedure. After typing the code, the cmdExitClick procedure should appear as follows:

```
procedure TForm2.cmdExitClick(Sender: TObject);
begin
```

```
Application.Terminate;
```

end;

☐ Execute the MyCust program, and verify that clicking the Exit button terminates the program.

Designing the Checkboxes

☐ Set the checkbox properties as shown in Table 4.1. After doing so, Form2 should appear as shown in Figure 4.17.

Table 4.1. The checkbox properties.

Object	Property	Setting
Checkbox	Name	chkVisible
	Caption	&Visible
	Checked	True
Checkbox	Name	chkCenter
	Caption	&Center
	Checked	False

Figure 14.17.
The Form2 form with the Exit button and two checkboxes.

☐ Execute the MyCust program.

Of course, at this point you have not attached any code to the checkboxes, so checking and unchecking the checkboxes doesn't do anything. However, note that clicking the checkbox places or removes the checkmarks from the checkboxes.

☐ Terminate the MyCust program.

As implied by the name of the chkVisible checkbox, you now attach code to this checkbox that makes the CustomerTableCustNum field visible or invisible.

Note that during design time you set the Invisible checkbox's Checked property to True. This means that when starting the program, a checkmark appears in this checkbox.

☐ Attach the following code to the OnClick event of the chkVisible checkbox.

```
procedure TForm2.chkVisibleClick(Sender: TObject);
begin

If (chkVisible.Checked = True) Then
   CustomerTableCustNum.Visible := True
else
   CustomerTableCustNum.Visible := False;

end;
```

The chkVisibleClick procedure is executed automatically whenever the user clicks the Visible checkbox. The code you typed uses an If statement to examine the Checked property of the chkVisible property.

```
If (chkVisible.Checked = True) Then
   CustomerTableCustNum.Visible := True
else
   CustomerTableCustNum.Visible := False;
```

If the Checked property is equal to True, there is a checkmark in the Visible checkbox. Because the If condition is satisfied, the code between the If and the Else statements is executed:

```
CustomerTableCustNum.Visible := True
```

The code after the If sets the CustomerTableCustNum's Visible property to True, which makes the Customer Number column visible.

When the Checked property of the Visible checkbox is not True (there is no checkmark in the Visible checkbox), the code after the Else statement is executed.

```
CustomerTableCustNum.Visible := False;
```

The preceding code makes the Customer Number column invisible.

Note that the statement starts with If and ends with False, and a semicolon (;) is placed at the end of the statement. In other words, you typed a single statement that spans four lines.

☐ Select Save project from the File menu.

☐ Execute the MyCust program.

☐ Click the Visible checkbox, and note that when there is a checkmark in the Visible checkbox, the Customer Number column appears. When there is no checkmark in the Visible checkbox, the Customer Number column is invisible.

☐ Experiment with the MyCust program, and then click its Exit button to terminate the program.

In a similar manner, you now attach code to the Center checkbox. The code you attach displays the data in the LastName column as either centered or left-aligned.

☐ Attach the following code to the chkCenter checkbox OnClick event:

```
procedure TForm2.chkCenterClick(Sender: TObject);
begin

If (chkCenter.Checked = True) Then
   CustomerTableLastName.Alignment := taCenter
else
   CustomerTableLastName.Alignment := taLeftJustify;

end;
```

The chkCenterClick procedure is executed whenever the user clicks the Center checkbox. The code you typed is very similar to the code you typed in the chkVisibleClick procedure. However, when there is a checkmark in the Center checkbox, the LastName column is centered:

```
CustomerTableLastName.Alignment := taCenter
```

When there is no checkmark in the Center checkbox, the column is left-justified:

```
CustomerTableLastName.Alignment := taLeftJustify;
```

How do you know what values should be assigned to the Alignment property? You can examine the CustomerTableLastName component's Alignment property in the Object Inspector window, and examine the various values that can be set for this property.

☐ Select Save Project from the File menu,

☐ Execute the MyCust program.

☐ Experiment with the checkboxes. Note that when the Center checkbox is checked, the data in the LastName column appears centered.

☐ Experiment with the MyCust program, and then click its Exit button to terminate it.

Reading Field Values

As you develop your Delphi programs, you'll need to read the field values, and assign them to variables. Now enhance the MyCust program by adding to it some standard controls and attaching code to the controls. This enhancement serves as an illustration of how you read the field values.

☐ Place a Label control and a pushbutton in Form2 according to the specifications of Table 2.2. When implementing Table 2.2, you have to drag the edges of Form2 to enlarge it. When you finish, Form2 should appear as shown in Figure 4.18.

Table 2.2. The properties of the `lblValue` and `cmdCustomerNumber` buttons.

Object	Property	Setting
Pushbutton	Name	cmdCutomerNumber
	Caption	C&ustomer Number
Label	Name	lblValue
	Caption	Customer Number:

Figure 4.18.

Placing the Customer Number button and a label in Form2.

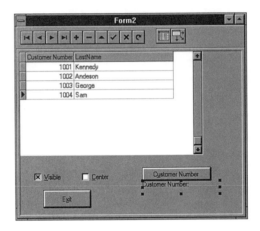

☐ Attach the following code to the `OnClick` event of the `cmdCustomerNumber` pushbutton:

```
procedure TForm2.cmdCustomerNumberClick(Sender: TObject);
begin

lblValue.Caption :=
    'Customer Number: ' +
    CustomerTableCustNum.AsString;

end;
```

The code you attached to the `cmdCustomerNumberClick` procedure is executed whenever the user clicks the Customer Number pushbutton. This code assigns a value to the `Caption` property of the `lblValue` label as follows:

```
lblValue.Caption :=
    'Customer Number: ' +
    CustomerTableCustNum.AsString;
```

You could have typed the entire statement on a single line, but spreading the statement over three lines makes it easier to read.

The `Label` control's `Caption` property is a string. You must assign strings to this property.

You assigned two strings to the lblValue label's Caption property. The first string is

```
'Customer Number: '
```

Then you used the plus (+) character to add a second string to the end of the first string. The second string is

```
CustomerTableCustNum.AsString;
```

The second string is the value of the CustomerTableCustNum (the CustNum field value) expressed as a string. Recall that when you designed the Customer.DB table, you set the CustNum field as a numerical field. This is why a conversion from a number to a string is required (by using the AsString).

☐ Select Save Project from the File menu.

☐ Execute the MyCust program.

☐ Click any of the records. This sets the current record position to the record on which you clicked.

☐ Click the Customer Number button.

MyCust responds by updating the lblValue *label's* Caption *property with the current record's* CustNum *value (see Figure 4.19).*

Figure 4.19.
Clicking the Customer Number button updates the Caption *property of the* lblValue *label.*

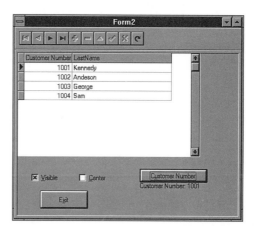

☐ Experiment with the MyCust program, and then click its Exit button to terminate it.

Note that the CustomerTableCustNum component has the Value property. This property is available only during runtime, hence you do not see this property in the Object Inspector window. Because the CustNum field is a numeric field, you cannot use the following statement:

```
{Error!!!}
lblValue.Caption := CustomerTableCustNum.Value;
```

Why? Because the `Label` control's `Caption` property expects a string. On the other hand, the following statement is acceptable:

```
lblValue.Caption := CustomerTableLastName.Value;
```

This statement is allowed because the `LastName` field is a string, and the `Label` control's `Caption` property expects a string.

The following statement is also acceptable:

```
lblValue.Caption := CustomerTableCustNum.AsString;
```

This statement is acceptable because the `AsString` converts the numeric value of the `CustNum` field to a string.

> **Note:** You learned that to convert the numeric value of a field object to a string, you use the `AsString`, as in the following statement:
>
> ```
> lblValue.Caption :=
>     'Customer Number: ' +
>     CustomerTableCustNum.AsString;
> ```
>
> In a similar manner, you can use the following properties to convert a field:
>
> | Property | Use |
> | --- | --- |
> | AsBoolean | Used when you assign a field value to a control that can be either True or False. |
> | AsDateTime | Used when you assign a field value to a control that can hold Date and Time. |
> | AsFloat | Used when you assign a field value to a control that can hold float numbers. |
> | AsInteger | Used when you assign a field value to a control that can hold integer numbers. |
> | AsString | Used when you assign a field value to a control that can hold a string. |

Assigning Field Values to Variables

You've already seen how you can assign a field value to a control. Now, you learn how to assign a field value to a variable.

☐ Look at the CData.Pas file (this is the file in which you type code). To display the code window, select Project Manager from the View menu to display the Project Manager window. Then, select the CData row, and click the View Unit button.

Delphi responds by displaying the CData.Pas window (where code is written).

☐ Scroll the CData.Pas window to the top of the window.

As you can see, the code starts as follows:

```
unit Cdata;

interface

uses
  SysUtils, WinTypes, WinProcs, Messages, Classes, Graphics, Controls,
  StdCtrls, Forms, DBCtrls, DB, DBGrids, DBTables, Grids, ExtCtrls;

type
  TForm2 = class(TForm)
    DBGrid1: TDBGrid;
    DBNavigator: TDBNavigator;
    ....
    ....
    ....
  private
    { private declarations }
  public
    { public declarations }
  end;

var
  Form2: TForm2;

implementation
...
```

Note the var section. There is only one item after the var section. The var section declares variables used in the form.

```
var
  Form2: TForm2;
```

Now add a variable called MyVariableString to the var section.

☐ Add code to the var section. After adding the code, the var section should appear as follows:

```
var
  Form2: TForm2;
  MyVariableString: String;
```

In the preceding statement, you declared a variable called MyVariableString. You must decide at declaration time what type of data the variable will hold. You do that as follows:

```
MyVariableString: String;
```

Terminate the variable name with a colon (:), and then enter the type of variable followed by a semicolon (;). In the preceding declarations, the variable was declared as a string. Delphi does not require that you mention the variable type in the variable name. It's acceptable to declare the following variable:

```
MyVariable: String;
```

However, including the variable type in its name makes your programming job easier because this can determine the variable type simply by inspecting its name. For example, the following variable declarations declare variables with names that tell their types:

```
HisVariableInt: Integer;
HerVariableDouble: Double;
```

☐ Change the code in the `cmdCustomerNumberClick` procedure. After changing the code, the procedure should appear as follows:

```
procedure TForm2.cmdCustomerNumberClick(Sender: TObject);
begin

{
lblValue.Caption :=
   'Customer Number: ' +
   CustomerTableCustNum.AsString;
}

MyVariableString := CustomerTableCustNum.AsString;
lblValue.Caption :=
   'Customer Number: ' +
   MyVariableString;

end;
```

The code you typed encloses the first statement with curly brackets, which means that the statement is commented out.

```
{
lblValue.Caption :=
   'Customer Number: ' +
   CustomerTableCustNum.AsString;
}
```

Why did you comment out the preceding statement? Because, for the sake of illustrating a point, you added code that updates the `MyVariableString` variable with the `CustNum` field's contents and then assigns the contents of the `MyVariableString` variable set to the `Label` control's `Caption` property. Thus, the first statement that does this by assigning the contents of the field directly to the `Label` control's `Caption` property is no longer needed.

Here is how you assign the `CustomerTableCustNum` object contents to the `MyVariableString` variable:

```
MyVariableString := CustomerTableCustNum.AsString;
```

Note that an `AsString` is required because the `CustNum` field is a number, whereas the `MyVariableString` variable is a string.

You then set the `Label` control `Caption` property as follows:

```
lblValue.Caption :=
   'Customer Number: ' +
   MyVariableString;
```

☐ Select Save Project from the File menu.

☐ Execute the MyCust program, and verify that clicking the Customer Number button causes the `Label` control to display the current record's `CustNum` field value.

☐ Experiment with the MyCust program, and then click its Exit button to terminate the program.

> **Note:** You saw that to assign a value to the `MyVariableString` variable you use the following statement:
>
> ```
> MyVariableString := CustomerTableCustNum.AsString;
> ```
>
> The `AsString` is needed because `MyVariableString` is a string, whereas the `CustNum` field is a number.
>
> No conversion is needed if you assign the `LastName` field (a string field) to the `MyVariableString` variable. You do this as follows:
>
> ```
> MyVariableString := CustomerLastName.Value;
> ```
>
> Because there is no performance penalty for using `AsString` when the field type is already `string`, it's good programming style to use the `AsXXX` field properties all the time, instead of the `Value` property. This practice makes your source code easier to read, and it insulates your code from changes in the database structure.
>
> For example, if an `integer` field is changed to a `float` in the database table, `AsInteger` source code references to that field will continue to work, but any source code that uses the `Value` property of that field will have to be changed.

4

Setting Field Values

In the preceding steps, you learned how to read the field value (to assign the field value to a control, such as the `Label` control or to a variable such as the `MyVariableString` variable).

In this section, you learn how to assign a value to a field from within your code.

☐ Enlarge Form2 because you are now going to place another pushbutton and an Edit box in the form.

☐ Place a pushbutton and an Edit box in Form2 as specified in Table 4.3. When you finish, Form2 should appear as shown in Figure 4.20.

Table 4.3. The `cmdUpdateLastName` button and `txtUpdateLastName` editbox properties.

Object	Property	Name
Pushbutton	Name	cmdUpdateLastName
	Caption	U&pdate Last Name
Editbox	Name	txtUpdateLastName
	Text	*Leave it empty*

Figure 4.20.
The form with the Update Last Name pushbutton and the txtUpdateLastName editbox.

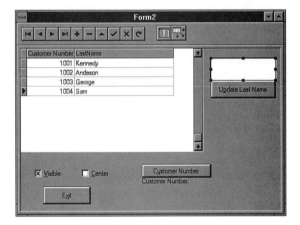

☐ Set the CustomerTable component's Active property to False.

☐ Set the CustomerTable component's ReadOnly property to False.

Note: In the following steps, you write code that modifies the LastName field. This means that the CustomerTable component's ReadOnly property must be set to False.

However, you cannot set certain properties of the table while the Table component's Active property is True.

This is why you were instructed first to set the CustomerTable Active property to False, and only then set the CustomerTable ReadOnly property to False.

☐ Attach the following code to the OnClick event of the cmdUpdateLastName button:

```
procedure TForm2.cmdUpdateLastNameClick(Sender: TObject);
begin

CustomerTable.Edit;

CustomerTableLastName.AsString := txtUpdateLastName.Text;
CustomerTable.Post;

end;
```

The code you typed places the CustomerTable in edit mode.

```
CustomerTable.Edit;
```

You can place the CustomerTable table in edit mode even if the CustomerTable is already in an edit mode.

The value in the txtUpdateLastName editbox is assigned to the LastName field as follows.

```
CustomerTableLastName.AsString := txtUpdateLastName.Text;
```

Finally, the actual database is updated by issuing the Post command:

```
CustomerTable.Post;
```

☐ Select Save Project from the File menu.

☐ Execute the MyCust program.

☐ Click in the txtUpdateLastName editbox, and enter a name in it.

☐ Click the Update Last Name button.

> *MyCust responds by updating the LastName field of the current record with the contents of the txtUpdateLastName edit box.*

☐ Experiment with the MyCust program, and then click its Exit button to terminate the program.

Global and Local Variables

Previously, you added the MyVariableString variable to the var section of the program (at the beginning of the CData.Pas file) as follows:

```
var
  Form2: TForm2;
  MyVariableString: String;
```

Because you did so, from now on you can use the MyVariableString variable in any Form2 procedure. When the variable is declared in a var section in the interface section of a unit (at the top of the file), the variable is accessible from any other form procedure as well as from any other unit in the program that uses this unit. The variable in this case is called a *global* or *public* variable.

Alternatively, you can declare a *local* variable (also called a *private* variable) in a procedure. In this case, the variable is accessible only in the procedure where the variable is declared. To see this in action, do the following:

☐ Comment out the MyVariableString variable declaration in the var section at the beginning of the CData.Pas file. So now the var section looks as follows:

```
var
  Form2: TForm2;
  {MyVariableString: String;}
```

If you compile the MyCust program now, you get an error because you use the MyVariableString variable in the cmdCustomerNumberClick procedure, but this variable is no longer declared.

Declare the MyVariableString variable in the cmdCustomerNumberClick procedure. Only the cmdCustomerNumberClick procedure can access this variable.

☐ Between the first line of the procedure and the word begin, add the var declaration as follows:

```
procedure TForm2.cmdCustomerNumberClick(Sender: TObject);

var
 MyVariableString: String;

begin


{
lblValue.Caption :=
    'Customer Number: ' +
    CustomerTableCustNum.AsString;
}


MyVariableString := CustomerTableCustNum.AsString;
lblValue.Caption :=
    'Customer Number: ' +
    MyVariableString;


end;
```

In the preceding code, you added the variable declaration as follows:

```
var
 MyVariableString: String;
```

Because MyVariableString is declared in the cmdCustomerNumberClick procedure, this procedure's code can use the MyVariableString variable. However, you cannot use this variable from other procedures.

☐ Save Project from the File menu, and then execute the MyCust program to verify that everything is working.

Summary

In this chapter, you learned how to use the Fields Editor for selecting the fields and placing the TxxxField components in the form. For example, with the Fields Editor, you selected the CustNum field, and so Delphi placed the invisible CustomerTableCustNum object (an invisible object of type TFloatField) in the form. This component is of type TFloatField because the CustNum field is a numeric field. Likewise, Delphi placed the CustomerTableLastName component, a component of type TStringField, in the form. This field is of type TStringField because LastName is a field of type string.

You learned that you can then set the properties of the field components by using the Object Inspector window or from within your code. You also learned how to set the values of the fields from within your code.

Finally, you learned how to declare a variable in the var section of the code and about global (public) and local (private) variables.

Q&A

Q It looks like there is a lot going on! To use a table field, I have to use the Fields Editor, and then Delphi places invisible components in the form. Why not let me use the field in an easier manner?

A Delphi is a highly modular programming language. It is called an OOP (Object-Oriented Programming) language. At first glance, it looks as if there is a lot of work for just using a field from within your form, but the benefit is that you deal with objects.

Working with objects has several advantages. One advantage that you can appreciate right now is that you deal with the field objects in the same manner that you deal with other objects (pushbuttons, checkboxes, and so on). In essence, after practicing for a while, you'll get accustomed to the way the objects are programmed—for example, attaching code to the object events and setting the object properties by using Object Inspector. This makes your life as a programmer easier because you have fewer things to remember. Once you understand the concept of properties and events, you'll be able to program any object. During the course of this book, you learn to appreciate the OOP nature of Delphi and to realize the other advantages that an object-oriented programming language offers.

Quiz

1. The Fields Editor is used for _____.

2. To access a field from within your program you treat the field as

    a. A string.

    b. A float number.

    c. An object.

3. A global (public) variable is declared in _____.

4. A local (private) variable is declared in _____.

5. You can access a global variable from _____.

6. You can access a local variable from _____.

Exercises

1. The MyCust program has a `cmdCustomerNumber` button. Clicking this button causes the `lblValue` to display the selected record's customer number. Modify the program by adding the Last Name button. Clicking the Last Name button should display the value of the `LastName` field.

2. Some of the sample code shown in this chapter is more verbose than required, in the interest of tutorial clarity. Study the `TForm2.chkCenterClick` method shown in this chapter. See if you can find a way to perform the same operation in fewer lines of code. (**Hint**: Look at the values being assigned.)

Answers to Quiz

1. The Fields Editor is used for selecting fields from the table.

2. c.

3. A global (public) variable is declared inside the `var` section at the beginning of the Pas code file.

4. A local (private) variable is declared in a procedure.

5. You can access a global variable from any procedure of the form.

6. You can access a local variable from the procedure in which the variable was declared.

Answers to Exercises

1. Here's what to do:

   ☐ Add a pushbutton to the form.

   ☐ Set the pushbutton's Name property to cmdLastName.

   ☐ Set the pushbutton's Caption property to &Last Name.

   ☐ Attach code to the cmdLastName button's OnClick event. After adding the code, the cmdLastNameClick procedure should appear as follows:

   ```
   procedure TForm2.cmdLastNameClick(Sender: TObject);
   begin

   lblValue.Caption :=
       'Last Name: ' +
       CustomerTableLastName.Value;

   end;
   ```

   In the preceding code, you assigned the sum of two strings to the lblValue control's Caption property. Note that the second string is the CustomerTableLastName component's Value property. Because the LastName field is a string field, you can add its Value property without using AsString.

2. The TForm2.chkVisibleClick method tests the value of a Boolean property to determine how to set the value of another Boolean property. If chkVisible is True, set CustomerTableCustNum.Visible to True. If chkVisible is False, set CustomerTableCustNum.Visible to False. Because the value of the test condition always matches the value you want to assign to CustomerTableCustNum.Visible, you can simplify the code by eliminating the If statement, like this:

   ```
   procedure TForm2.chkVisibleClick(Sender: TObject);
   begin

     CustomerTableCustNum.Visible := chkVisible.Checked;

   end;
   ```

Calculated Fields

In this chapter, you learn about calculated fields. You work with several tables, and the program you implement will display data from these tables.

Constructing and Designing Databases

When you design a database (a collection of tables), keep in mind that each table should contain the minimum number of fields required. Here is an illustration of the concept of designing a database.

Suppose you're designing a database to keep track of sales for a certain company. Your job as a Delphi programmer is to write a program to print invoices. As you know, an invoice can consist of several items.

Here is one way to implement such a database.

One table is the Customer.DB table that consists of the following fields:

```
CustNum
LastName
FirstName
```

For simplicity's sake, don't add other fields to the Customer.DB table, such as the customer's address, phone number, and so on.

The next table is the Parts.DB table. This table consists of the following fields:

```
PartNum
Description
QtyInStock
SellingPrice
```

As you can see, the Parts.DB table includes the QtyInStock field, which shows how many units of this PartNum are in stock.

A third table, called Invoice.DB, consists of the following fields:

```
InvoiceNum
CustNum
```

The last table you need is the Items.DB table, which consists of the following fields:

```
InvoiceNum
PartNum
QtySold
```

Each record in the Items.DB table describes an invoice item. Suppose that Mr. Kennedy (CustNum 1001) purchased the following items:

```
P/N:10003 QtySold: 3
P/N:11004 QtySold: 1
```

He received an invoice (invoice number 23222) with these two items listed.

On another date, Mr. Kennedy made another purchase of the following items:

```
P/N:10003 QtySold: 6
P/N:11004 QtySold: 2
P/N:12001 QtySold: 3
```

For this purchase, Mr. Kennedy received an invoice (invoice number 32000) with three items on it.

The two purchases Mr. Kennedy made produce five records in the Items.DB table:

```
P/N:10003 QtySold: 3 Invoice Number: 23222 CustNum: 1001
P/N:11004 QtySold: 1 Invoice Number: 23222 CustNum: 1001
P/N:10003 QtySold: 6 Invoice Number: 32000 CustNum: 1001
P/N:11004 QtySold: 2 Invoice Number: 32000 CustNum: 1001
P/N:12001 QtySold: 3 Invoice Number: 32000 CustNum: 1001
```

Mr. Kennedy pays at the end of each month, and so at the end of the month, the Delphi program has to send invoices to him. In our case, the Delphi program has to send two invoices to Mr. Kennedy. You could argue that the program should send one invoice with five items on it, but for the sake of illustrating the point, let's say that the program should print two invoices.

Here's how your program should generate the two invoices.

☐ The program should look at the records in the Items.DB table and print all records corresponding to invoice number 23222. As you know, the Items.DB table does not have enough information to print an invoice. From the records of the Items.DB table, the program does not know who the customer is, but each record of the Items.DB table includes the InvoiceNum field. The Invoice.DB table contains records with invoice numbers, and these records include the CustNum fields.

Putting it all together, then, the program can extract the information about the name of the customer by looking at the Items.DB table's InvoiceNum field. This leads the program to the Invoice.DB table, which tells the program the CustNum that corresponds to the invoice. The program then accesses the Customer.DB table, which has information about the CustNum.

The description of the various part numbers the customer purchased also should be mentioned on the printed invoice. Each record in the Items.DB table contains the PartNum, but the description is not included in the Items.DB table record! Well, your program accesses the Parts.DB table and extracts the description of the part number based on the PartNum field.

The invoice should list the selling price, but not every Items.DB table record includes the unit price. Again, your program accesses the Parts.DB table, and based on the Items.DB table's PartNum field, the unit price can be extracted from the Parts.DB table.

Each table contains a minimum number of fields. When it comes to working with the tables (such as printing invoices), the program you write with Delphi accesses the various tables to extract the proper information.

The Customer.DB, Parts.DB, Invoices.DB, and Items.DB tables are the database. From this database, you can write a Delphi program that prints invoices.

Of course, you have to add additional fields to the various tables. For example, the Invoices.DB table should include the `PaidInFull` field (a Boolean field that can have a `True` or `False` value). Naturally, your Delphi program should check the `PaidInFull` field, and if the invoice was paid, it should not be printed or sent.

Calculated Fields

In the previous section, you learned that each table should contain only the necessary information. Information that can be extracted from another table is not necessary. Storing only necessary information in each table enables the tables to be small because, for example, the customer's name and address are stored in only one table (the Customer.DB table). For example, if you search the hard disk containing the database for the word `Kennedy`, you find it in only one file, the Customer.DB file. By designing your tables this way, you save hard-disk space. But more importantly, the person maintaining the database does not have to enter information more than once.

For example, suppose that Mr. Kennedy changed his address. The person maintaining the database must update the new information in only one record: Mr. Kennedy's record in the Customer.DB table. If the Items.DB table included Mr. Kennedy's address, and Mr. Kennedy purchased 100 items, the person entering information to the database would have to enter Mr. Kennedy's new address in 100 records in the Items.DB table. If Mr. Kennedy were a good customer who purchased 1,000 items in the last 10 years, the Items.DB table would have 1,000 records with Mr. Kennedy's purchases. Naturally, you don't want the person maintaining the database to enter Mr. Kennedy's address 1,000 times.

This leads us now to calculated fields. You saw in database design that you store a minimum amount of information. There is no need to store redundant information. Now suppose that Mr. Kennedy purchased three items of one part number, and each item cost $100.00. The total price Mr. Kennedy must pay is 3×$100.00, or $300.00. Would you include the `TotalPrice` field in the Items.DB table? No, because the result of the multiplication (3×100) can be performed when you print the invoices. In this case, you can consider the `TotalPrice` field as a calculated field in the program that prints the invoices.

Now you're ready to construct various tables using the Database Desktop program discussed on Day 2, "Databases," and write a program called TotPrice.EXE that uses the calculated fields feature of Delphi.

Using Database Desktop to Construct Your Tables

Use the Database Desktop program to construct various tables you need for this chapter. If you forgot how to use Database Desktop, refer back to Day 3, "Creating Your First Delphi Database Program." Save all the tables to the C:\DProg\Work directory.

Note: Because the size of the field is not applicable when you construct a numeric field, the tables containing the information you need to implement the tables have n/a (not applicable) as the field size. See the Size column in Table 5.1, for example.

☐ Use Database Desktop to construct the Items.DB table per the Table 5.1 specifications.

Table 5.1. The Items.DB table structure.

Field	Type	Size	Key
ItemNum	Autoincrement	n/a	Yes
CustNum	Numeric	n/a	Yes
PartNum	Numeric	n/a	Yes
QtySold	Numeric	n/a	No

The Items.DB table's ItemNum field is of type Autoincrement. Whenever you add a record to the Items.DB table, the ItemNum field is automatically filled with a number that serves as a serial number. When you enter the data for the first record, ItemNum is automatically set to 1. When you enter data for the second record, ItemNum is automatically set to 2, and so on.

Why do you need the ItemNum field? Because the Items.DB table needs a unique key field. The first keyed field of a table is called a *primary key*, and the values of this field must be unique in the table.

You cannot make the CustNum field the first key field because a customer can have more than one record in the Items.DB. Remember, the primary key field must be unique.

PartNum cannot be the primary key field either because several records in the Items.DB table can have the same PartNum. Of course, the QtySold field can have several records with the same value. The solution is to create the ItemNum field as the primary key field. In essence, the ItemNum field serves as a dummy field. You use it because you must have the primary field of the Items.DB table, and you cannot use any of the other Items.DB table fields.

5

Note that Table 5.1 instructs you to include the CustNum field in the Items.DB table. Typically, you do not include this field in the Items.DB table. Rather, the Items.DB table includes the field InvoiceNum. The CustNum information is extracted from the Invoice.DB table records. However, for the sake of simplicity, the TotPrice.EXE program you'll write uses only three tables: Customer.DB, Items.DB, and Parts.DB. The Invoices.DB table is not used, and hence you are not instructed to implement the Invoices.DB table.

☐ Implement the Parts.DB table according to the information provided in Table 5.2.

Table 5.2. The Parts.DB table structure.

Field	Type	Size	Key
PartNum	Numeric	n/a	Yes
Description	Alpha	40	No
QtyInStock	Numeric	n/a	No
SellingPrice	Numeric	n/a	No

☐ Make sure that the Customer.DB table has the structure shown in Table 5.3.

Table 5.3. The Customer.DB table structure.

Field	Type	Size	Key
CustNum	Numeric	n/a	Yes
LastName	Alpha	30	No
FirstName	Alpha	25	No

Implementing the TotPrice.EXE Program

Implement the TotPrice.EXE program as follows:

☐ Start Delphi.

☐ Select Database Form Expert from the Help menu.

> *Delphi responds by displaying the Database Form Expert window.*

☐ Set the options button as shown in Figure 5.1 by selecting the Create a simple form and Create a form using TTable objects options.

Figure 5.1.
*The Database Form Expert's
initial window.*

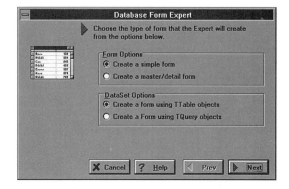

☐ Click the Next button.

> *Delphi responds by displaying the next window in which you are asked to select a table.*

☐ Select the Items.DB table from the C:\DProg\Work directory (see Figure 5.2), and then
click the Next button.

> *Delphi responds by displaying the window in which you are asked to specify the fields.*

Figure 5.2.
*Selecting the Items.DB
table.*

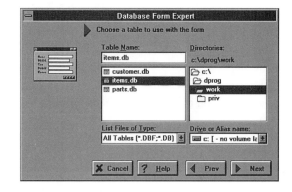

☐ Click the button displaying a right-pointing double arrow.

> *Delphi responds by moving all the fields from the left list to the right list (see Figure 5.3).*

☐ Click the Next button.

> *Delphi responds by displaying the window that lets you select the layout for displaying the
data.*

☐ Select the Grid option (see Figure 5.4), and then click the Next button.

Figure 5.3.
Selecting the fields.

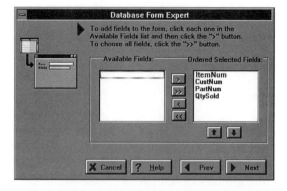

Figure 5.4.
Selecting the Grid option.

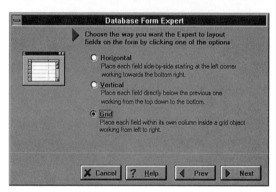

☐ Make sure that the Generate a main form checkbox has a checkmark in it (see Figure 5.5), and then click the Create button.

Delphi responds by creating Form2 as shown in Figure 5.6.

Figure 5.5.
Generating the form as the main form.

Figure 5.6.
The form generated by Database Form Expert.

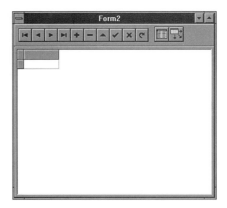

Now you need to save the project files you've just created. Make sure that your hard disk includes the directory C:\DProg\Ch05. If you don't have this directory, create it with File Manager.

☐ Make sure that Form2 is selected, select Save File As from the File menu, and save Form2 as CItems.Pas in the C:\DProg\Ch05 directory.

Currently, the project includes two forms: Form1 and Form2. Database Form Expert placed various controls in Form2. Form1 is not used in the project, and so you can delete it. Here's how to delete Form1 from the project.

☐ Make sure Form1 is selected, and then select Remove file from the File menu.

Delphi responds by displaying the dialog box shown in Figure 5.7.

5

Figure 5.7.
The Remove From Project dialog box.

In this figure, the project contains two forms: Form1 and Form2.

☐ Make sure Form1 is selected, and then click the OK button.

Delphi responds by displaying the dialog box shown in Figure 5.8. Delphi noticed that you want to remove Form1 and did not yet save Form1.

Figure 5.8.
The Confirm dialog box.

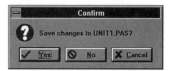

☐ Click the No button because Form1 is not used in the project, and so there's no need to save it.

☐ Select Save Project As from the File menu, and save the project file as TotPrice.Dpr in the C:\DProg\Ch05 directory.

Let's review what you've accomplished so far.

• When you start Delphi, a new project is created with Form1.
• You used Database Form Expert to create Form2.
• You saved Form2 as CItems.Pas in the C:\DProg\Ch05 directory.
• There is no need for Form1, and so you removed it without saving it.
• Finally, you saved the project file as TotPrice.Dpr in the C:\DProg\Ch05 directory.

Just to verify that everything is working, do the following:

☐ Execute the TotPrice program.

The TotPrice program displays the Items.DB table. Currently, there are no records in the Items.DB table.

☐ Use the TotPrice program to enter the data shown in Figure 5.9. When entering the record data, do not fill the ItemNum field because as you move from the current record to another record, it is filled automatically.

Figure 5.9.
The Items.DB table data.

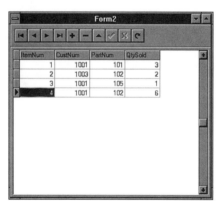

☐ Click the minus-sign (–) icon that appears in the window's upper-left corner, and then select Close from the system menu that pops up.

The TotPrice program terminates itself.

Entering Data into the Parts.DB and Customer.DB Tables

To experiment with the TotPrice program, you need some data in the Parts.DB and Customer.DB tables. Use the Database Desktop program to enter data into the tables.

☐ Use Database Desktop to enter the data shown in Figures 5.10 and 5.11.

☐ Terminate the Database Desktop program.

Figure 5.10.
The Parts.DB table.

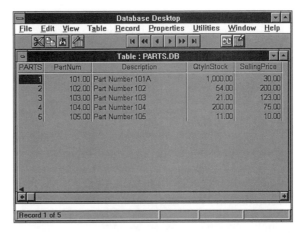

Figure 5.11.
The Customer.DB table.

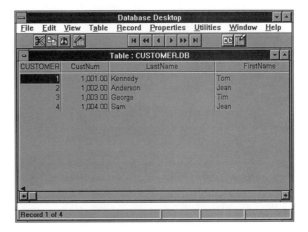

Using the Fields Editor to Add Field Objects

To place invisible field components in Form2, use the Fields Editor.

Before using the Fields Editor, however, change the name of the Table1 object that Database Form Expert placed in Form2.

☐ Change the Name property of Table1 to **ItemsTable**.

Because you changed the Name property of Table1 to ItemsTable, you have to change Table1 to ItemsTable in the CItems.Pas file.

☐ Use the Find item on the Search menu to find Table1.

Delphi finds Table1 in the FormCreate procedure.

☐ In the FormCreate procedure, change the word Table1 to **ItemsTable**. After changing the text, the FormCreate procedure should appear as follows:

```
procedure TForm2.FormCreate(Sender: TObject);
begin

    ItemsTable.Open;

end;
```

☐ Use the Find Next item from the Search menu to verify that there are no more occurrences of the word Table1 in the project.

☐ Execute the TotPrice program to verify that everything is working.

☐ Terminate the TotPrice program.

☐ Double-click the ItemsTable control.

Delphi responds by displaying the Fields Editor window (see Figure 5.12).

Figure 5.12.
The Fields Editor window.

☐ Click the Add button.

The Fields Editor window now displays all the Items.DB table fields, as shown in Figure 5.13.

Figure 5.13.
Selecting all the fields in the Items.DB table.

☐ Make sure that all the fields are selected, and then click the OK button.

☐ Close the Fields Editor window.

☐ Verify that Delphi placed four invisible field controls in Form2. Click the down-arrow icon of the combobox in the Object Inspector window, and verify that you see the following items in the list (see Figure 5.14):

```
ItemsTableCustNum
ItemsTableItemNum
ItemsTablePartNum
ItemsTableQtySold
```

Figure 5.14.
The four field objects that Delphi placed in Form2.

Currently, the user can edit ItemNum. However, as you know, this field should be filled automatically because it is of type Autoincrement. It's a good idea to make this field a read-only field.

☐ Set the `ItemsTableItemNum`'s `ReadOnly` field property to `True`.

☐ Select Save Project from the File menu.

☐ Execute the TotPrice program.

☐ Experiment with the TotPrice program, and note that you cannot enter data into the `ItemNum` field.

☐ Terminate the TotPrice program.

Implementing an Exit Button

Implement an Exit button as follows:

☐ Set the `Grid` control's `Align` property to `alNone`.

☐ Size the `Grid` control so there'll be room in `Form2` to place a button.

After sizing the `Grid` control, `Form2` should appear as shown in Figure 5.15.

Figure 5.15.
Sizing the Grid *control.*

☐ Place a pushbutton in `Form2`, and set its properties as follows:

```
Caption   E&xit
Name      cmdExit
```

After placing the Exit button, `Form2` should appear as shown in Figure 5.16.

Figure 5.16.
Placing the Exit button in
Form2.

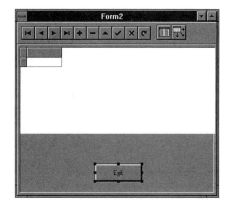

☐ Attach the following code to the cmdExitClick procedure:

```
procedure TForm2.cmdExitClick(Sender: TObject);
begin

Application.Terminate;

end;
```

☐ Select Save Project from the File menu.

☐ Execute the TotPrice program, and verify that the Exit button works as expected.

Placing Calculated Fields

Everything is now prepared for placement of a calculated field, the ItemDescription field, in Form2. Remember that the Items.DB table does not have the ItemDescription field. Which table has a Description field? The Parts.DB table does. You're going to place the ItemDescription in the Grid control. This field displays the Parts.DB table's Description field data.

☐ Double-click the ItemsTable control in Form2.

Delphi responds by displaying the Fields Editor window. (Yes, the Fields Editor window is used for defining the calculated fields.)

☐ Click the Define button because you're going to define a calculated field.

Delphi responds by displaying the Define Field window, as shown in Figure 5.17.

Calculated Fields

Figure 5.17.
The Define Field window.

☐ In the Field name field, enter **ItemDescription**. This is the name of the calculated field.

Note that as you enter the name of the calculated field, Delphi fills the Component name field with text.

☐ Set the Field type to StringField.

☐ Make sure that the Calculated checkbox is checked.

When you complete the preceding steps, the Define Field window should appear as shown in Figure 5.18.

Figure 5.18.
Defining the calculated field.

☐ Click the Define Field window's OK button.

☐ Examine the list of objects in the Object Inspector.

As you can see, the ItemsTableItemDescription object is among the objects on Form2 (see Figure 5.19).

Figure 5.19.
ItemsTableItemDescription
is among the objects in
Form2.

You can now treat the `ItemsTableItemDescription` object like any other `Form2` object. You can attach code to its events and set its properties from the Object Inspector or from within your code.

☐ Select Save Project from the File menu.

☐ Execute the TotPrice program.

The window of TotPrice appears as shown in Figure 5.20. Note that the `ItemDescription` column appears in the figure.

Figure 5.20.
The TotPrice window with
the ItemDescription
column in it.

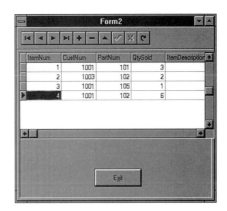

Your disappointment at this point should be that the `ItemDescription` column does not display data in it. We want the first row's `ItemDescription` to display the part number description mentioned in the `PartNum` field of the first row, and so on.

Delphi doesn't have any idea that this is what you want to do because it doesn't know the connection between the `ItemDescription` column and the `PartNum` field.

How should you tell Delphi the connection between ItemDescription and PartNum? There are basically two ways of accomplishing this:

- You can link the Items.DB table with the Parts.DB table, and during the linking, you tell Delphi that the linking between the Items.DB table and the Parts.DB table is based on the PartNum field. Delphi looks at the current record of Items.DB, takes note of the PartNum field value, accesses the Parts.DB table, and extracts the Description field value from the Parts.DB table. The extracted value is then placed in the ItemDescription column.

- You can write code that performs the linking.

For this exercise, use the second way of linking. Write code that fills the ItemDescription field with values from the Parts.DB table. In a later chapter, you learn how to tell Delphi to perform the linking.

☐ Terminate the TotPrice program.

Adding the Parts.DB Table to the TotPrice Project

The ItemDescription calculated field should be filled with the Description field's contents from the Parts.DB table.

You must include the Parts.DB table in Form2. This means that you have to do the same job that Database Form Expert did with the Items.DB table.

☐ Place a Table component in Form2.

Form2 should now appear as shown in Figure 5.21.

Figure 5.21.

Placing a Table *component in* Form2.

You must connect Form2 with the Parts.DB table, which means that you must place a DataSource component in Form2.

☐ Place a DataSource control in Form2. You may have to enlarge Form2 to make room for the component.

Form2 should now appear as shown in Figure 5.22.

Figure 5.22.
Placing a DataSource component in Form2.

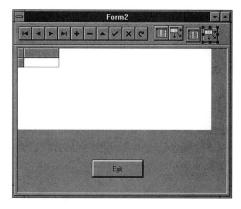

Next, you need to place a Grid control in Form2. This Grid control displays the data of Parts.DB. Typically, just because the program uses Parts.DB does not mean that you have to display its data. Here is how to place a Grid control for Parts.DB—just to illustrate that it can be done.

☐ Place a Grid control in Form2. First make the Items.DB Grid control a little smaller, and then place in Form2 a DBGrid Grid control from the Data Controls page. If necessary, enlarge Form2. After adding the Grid control, Form2 should appear as shown in Figure 5.23.

Figure 5.23.
Placing a Grid control in Form2.

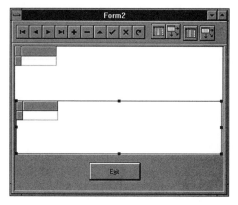

You also could place a `Navigator` control for the `Grid` control that you placed, but for now we are keeping things simple.

☐ Select Save Project from the File menu.

☐ Execute the TotPrice program.

The window of TotPrice appears as shown in Figure 5.24.

Figure 5.24.

The TotPrice program with two Grid controls in its window.

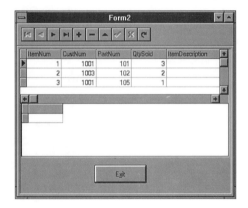

Of course, the second `Grid` control does not display any data because you didn't set the properties of the second `Table` control, `DataSource` control, and `Grid` control, that you placed in `Form2`. Now set the properties of these controls so that the second `Grid` control displays the Parts.DB data.

☐ Terminate the TotPrice program.

☐ Set the properties of the second `Table` control as follows:

```
Name          PartsTable
DatabaseName  MYWORK
TableName     PARTS.DB
```

By specifying that the `DatabaseName` is MYWORK, you are telling Delphi where the table resides. MYWORK is the working directory. Alternatively, you can set `DatabaseName` to C:\DProg\Work.

☐ Set the properties of the second `DataSource` component as follows:

```
Name     DataSource2
DateSet  PartsTable
```

☐ Set the properties of the second Grid control as follows:

    Name   DBGrid2
    DataSource   DataSource2

To verify that everything is working properly, do the following:

☐ Set the PartsTable control's Active property to True.

Delphi responds by displaying data in DBGrid2, as shown in Figure 5.25.

Figure 5.25.
The second Grid control displays the data of PartsTable (Parts.DB).

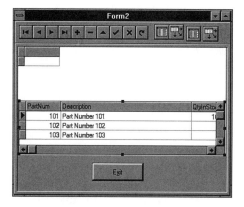

Note: As you saw in the preceding step, setting the Table component's Active property to True enables you to verify that the Table and DataSource components and the Grid control are set correctly.

5

Add field objects to Form2 from the PartsTable Table control.

☐ Double-click the PartsTable control.

Delphi responds by displaying the Fields Editor window for the PartsTable control, as shown in Figure 5.26.

☐ Click the Add button in the Fields Editor window.

Delphi responds by displaying the fields of the Parts.DB table, as shown in Figure 5.27.

Figure 5.26.
*The Fields Editor window
for the* PartsTable *table.*

Figure 5.27.
*The fields of the Parts.DB
table in the Fields Editor
window.*

☐ Make sure that all the Parts.DB table fields are selected, and then click the OK button.

☐ Close the Fields Editor window.

☐ Click the down-arrow icon in the combobox at the top of the Object Inspector
window, and verify that Delphi placed field components for the PartsTable fields (see
Figure 5.28).

Figure 5.28.
*Each of the fields in
Parts.DB has a correspond-
ing control in* Form2.

☐ Select Save Project from the File menu.

☐ Execute the TotPrice program, and verify that everything is working properly. As shown in Figure 5.29, the ItemDescription column of the upper grid is still empty because you didn't yet make the connection between the Parts.DB table and the ItemDescription column.

Figure 5.29.

The TotPrice program displaying the Items.DB and Parts.DB tables. The calculated field ItemDescription *is not yet filled with data.*

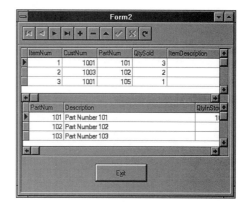

☐ Click the Exit button to terminate the TotPrice program.

Filling the *ItemDescription* Field with Values from the Parts.DB Table

In this section, you write code that fills the ItemDescription column with data.

One of the events of the ItemsTable Table control is the CalcFields event.

☐ Double-click the cell to the right of the OnCalcFields cell in the ItemsTable Table control's Events page.

Delphi responds by displaying the ItemsTableCalcFields *procedure code as follows:*

```
procedure TForm2.ItemsTableCalcFields(DataSet: TDataset);
begin

end;
```

With the framework in place, you can type code into this procedure. The ItemsTableCalcFields procedure is executed automatically whenever Delphi senses a need to calculate the value of a calculated field.

For example, as you display the data, Delphi needs to place data in the current record. One of the fields is the ItemDescription calculated field. Delphi automatically executes the ItemsTableCalcFields procedure when you move the cursor to a new record while the TotPrice program is running.

131

☐ Type the following code in the `ItemsTableCalcFields` procedure:

> **Caution:** Make sure that you are attaching the code to the `OnCalcFields` event of the `ItemsTable` control because the calculated field belongs to this `Table` component.

```
procedure TForm2.ItemsTableCalcFields(DataSet: TDataset);

var
FindResultBoolean: Boolean;

begin

end;
```

You declared a local variable called `FindResultBoolean` as a *Boolean* variable (a variable that can be `True` or `False`).

☐ Enter additional code in the `ItemsTableCalcFields` procedure.

After entering the code, the `ItemsTableCalcFields` procedure should appear as follows:

```
procedure TForm2.ItemsTableCalcFields(DataSet: TDataset);

var
FindResultBoolean: Boolean;

begin

FindResultBoolean :=
    PartsTable.FindKey([ItemsTablePartNum]);

if FindResultBoolean then
   begin
   ItemsTableItemDescription.Value :=
        PartsTableDescription.Value;

   end;

end;
```

The code you typed uses the `FindKey` method to find the record in the `PartsTable` whose `PartNum` field is equal to the value of the current record's `PartNum` in Items.DB.

```
FindResultBoolean :=
     PartsTable.FindKey([ItemsTablePartNum]);
```

For example, suppose that the first record in the Items.DB table is the current record, and suppose that the first record's `PartNum` field value is `101`. The `FindKey` method searches for a record in the Parts.DB table whose `PartNum` field is equal to `103`. If such a record exists, Delphi moves the record pointer of Parts.DB to the found record.

The result of the search is assigned to the `FindResultBoolean` variable that you declared.

If a record in the Parts.DB table is found, `FindResultBoolean` is equal to `True`. If there is no such record in Parts.DB, `FindResultBoolean` is set to `False`.

An `if` statement is then executed to examine the value of `FindResultBoolean`.

```
if FindResultBoolean then
   begin
   ItemsTableItemDescription.Value :=
        PartsTableDescription.Value;
   end;
```

If `FindResultBoolean` is equal to `False`, the statements after the `if` statements are not executed. If it is equal to `True`, the statements after the `if` statement are executed.

```
begin
   ItemsTableItemDescription.Value :=
        PartsTableDescription.Value;
end;
```

You can insert several statements after the `if...then` statement. The statements start with the keyword `begin` and end with the keyword `end` followed by a semicolon (;).

In your case, you have a single statement between the keywords `begin` and `end`.

The statement sets the `ItemDescription` column value to the Parts.DB table's `Description` field value.

```
ItemsTableItemDescription.Value :=
        PartsTableDescription.Value;
```

☐ Select Save Project from the File menu.

☐ Execute the TotPrice program.

The window of TotPrice appears as shown in Figure 5.30. Note that the `ItemDescription` column is updated with the Parts.DB table's `Description` field values.

5

Figure 5.30.

The ItemDescription
*column is updated with
the Parts.DB table's*
Description *field values.*

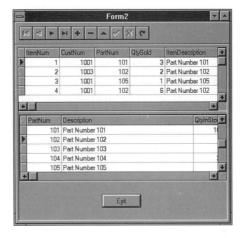

Note: Delphi is a powerful package. However, as with any other powerful package, you (as a new user) occasionally will take Delphi out of sequence, and Delphi will not perform as expected!

If you get into a situation where Delphi keeps prompting you with dialog boxes that indicate errors, do the following:

☐ Quit Delphi.

☐ Make sure that you entered the code correctly.

☐ Set the Active property of the table components to False. Some table properties cannot be changed while the table is open (Active = True).

Currently, the TotPrice program has a little flaw in it. To see the flaw in action, do the following:

☐ Click on one of the Parts.DB table records, and change its value. For example, change the Description of PartNum 101 to **101 is a good P/N.**

☐ Move to another record in the Parts.DB table.

As you can see, the data in the ItemDescription column did *not* change. Currently, the ItemDescription column does not reflect the Description field data.

☐ Click the Navigator control's Refresh button (the rightmost button).

TotPrice responds by updating the ItemDescription *column with data corresponding to the* Description *field of the Parts.DB table. You take care of this problem in the next section by writing code that updates the* ItemDescription *automatically without the need to click the Refresh button.*

☐ Experiment with the TotPrice program, and then click its Exit button to terminate it.

Refreshing the Items.DB Table

As you've seen, you must click the Refresh button for the `ItemDescription` column to be updated. In this section, you write code that clicks the Refresh button automatically.

Attach code to the `PartsTable` control's `AfterPost` event by following these steps.

☐ Double-click the cell to the right of the `AfterPost` cell on the `PartsTable` Events page.

Delphi responds by displaying the `PartsTableAfterPost` *procedure as follows:*

```
procedure TForm2.PartsTableAfterPost(DataSet: TDataset);
begin

end;
```

☐ Add the following code to the `PartsTableAfterPost` procedure.

```
procedure TForm2.PartsTableAfterPost(DataSet: TDataset);
begin

ItemsTable.Refresh;

end;
```

The code you typed refreshes the `ItemsTable` table.

☐ Select Save Project from the File menu.

☐ Execute the TotPrice program.

☐ Modify the `Description` field of one of the Parts.DB table records, and then move to another record.

Once you move to another record, the `Post` method for the Parts.DB table is executed automatically. Then, Delphi automatically generates the `AfterPost` event, and the `PartsTableAfterPost` procedure is executed.

The code you typed in the `PartsTableAfterPost` procedure has the same effect as clicking the `Navigator` control's Refresh button. As a result, the Items.DB table is refreshed.

Note that the `ItemDescription` column is considered a field in Items.DB. When you created Items.DB with Database Desktop. you did not create the `ItemDescription` field. However, in this chapter, you did create the calculated field `ItemDescription`. From a programming point of view, you can think of the Items.DB table as having the `ItemDescription` field.

Calculating the Total Price

The program is called TotPrice because it calculates the total price in each Items.DB record. You now add a calculated field called `TotalPrice`, and calculate the value of this field based on the `QtySold` field of the Items.DB record and the `SellingPrice` field in the Parts.DB table.

☐ Double-click the ItemsTable control.

Delphi responds by displaying the Fields Editor window.

☐ Click the Define button in the Field Editor window.

Delphi responds by displaying a window that lets you define a calculated field.

☐ Set the Field name edit box to TotalPrice. This will be another calculated column in the DBGrid1 Grid control.

☐ Set the FieldType to **FloatField**. The calculated column holds float numbers.

☐ Make sure that the Calculated checkbox is checked.

The Define Field window should now appear as shown in Figure 5.31.

Figure 5.31.
Defining the Total Price calculated field.

☐ Click the OK button in the Define Field window.

Delphi responds by adding the TotalPrice calculated field to the DGrid2 grid, and you can verify that the ItemsTableTotalPrice object was added to Form2.

☐ Close the Field Editor window.

☐ Make the Active property of the ItemsTable Table control True so that you can see the DBGrid1 control displaying the TotalPrice column. As shown in Figure 5.32, you have to scroll the DBGrid1 control to the left so you can see the TotalPrice column.

Figure 5.32.
The `TotalPrice` *column.*

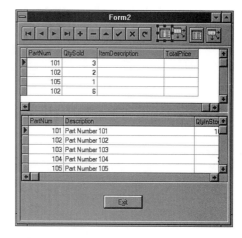

Add code that updates the `TotalPrice` column as follows:

☐ In the `ItemsTableCalcFields` procedure, add code that updates the `TotalPrice` column. After adding the code, the `ItemsTableCalcFields` procedure should appear as follows:

```
procedure TForm2.ItemsTableCalcFields(DataSet: TDataset);

var
FindResultBoolean: Boolean;

begin

FindResultBoolean := PartsTable.FindKey([ItemsTablePartNum]);

if FindResultBoolean then
   begin
   ItemsTableItemDescription.Value :=
        PartsTableDescription.Value;

ItemsTableTotalPrice.Value :=
  PartsTableSellingPrice.Value * ItemsTableQtySold.Value;

   end;

end;
```

The code you added calculates the `ItemsTableTotalPrice` as follows:

```
ItemsTableTotalPrice.Value :=
  PartsTableSellingPrice.Value * ItemsTableQtySold.Value;
```

☐ Select Save Project from the File menu.

☐ Execute the TotPrice program.

You might have to scroll the grids to see the rightmost columns of the grids.

As shown in Figure 5.33, the `TotalPrice` column is updated.

Figure 5.33.

The `TotalPrice` column is updated.

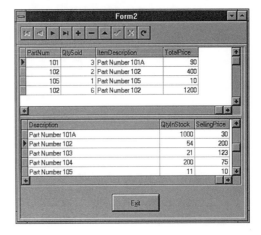

☐ Experiment with the TotPrice program, and then click its Exit button to terminate it.

Summary

In this chapter, you learned how to incorporate calculated fields into your Delphi programs. As you saw, Delphi is designed so that once you define the calculated field, you then can treat the calculated field like an object, which means that you can set its properties as you would any other object.

Q&A

Q After adding the `ItemDescription` calculated field, Delphi added the `ItemDescription` column to the grid displaying the Items.DB table, and `ItemsTableItemDescription` was added as an invisible object to `Form2`. Is this complication necessary?

A Delphi is a highly modular, object-oriented programming language. By making the calculated field an object, you now can treat this object as you would any other object (for example, a regular object field or pushbutton). This means that you now can set the calculated field object's properties in design time by using the Object Inspector as well as set the calculated field's properties from within your code.

Quiz

1. Explain the reason for including the ItemNum field in the Items.DB table.
2. The CalcFields event occurs when _____.
3. The FindKey() method is used for which of the following?
   a. Finding a key.
   b. Finding a table record whose key field is equal to the FindKey() method's parameter.

Exercises

1. Modify the TotPrice program so the TotPrice column displays values with a 10 percent discount.
2. Add another column to the upper grid of the TotPrice program. This column should display the names of the customers.

Answers to Quiz

1. The Items.DB table must have its first field keyed just like any other Delphi table. In tables, the first keyed field must be a unique field. As it turns out, all the Items.DB table fields are non-unique fields. For example, one customer can have many records in Items.DB, and so the ItemNum field was introduced as a dummy field that serves as the first keyed field.

2. The CalcFields event occurs when a certain operation occurs requiring the display of calculated fields. For example, upon displaying Form2 for the first time, the TotalPrice column is displayed, and its values must be calculated. Therefore, the CalcFields event occurs.
3. b.

Answers to Exercises

1. The formula for the new total price is

   ```
   Total Price = SellingPrice * QtySold * 0.9

   ItemsTableTotalPrice.Value :=
   PartsTableSellingPrice.Value*ItemsTableQtySold.Value*0.9;
   ```

The code in the ItemsTableCalcFields procedure should be modified as follows:

```
procedure TForm2.ItemsTableCalcFields(DataSet: TDataset);

var
FindResultBoolean: Boolean;

begin

FindResultBoolean := PartsTable.FindKey([ItemsTablePartNum]);

if FindResultBoolean then
   begin
   ItemsTableItemDescription.Value :=
        PartsTableDescription.Value;

ItemsTableTotalPrice.Value :=
PartsTableSellingPrice.Value*ItemsTableQtySold.Value*0.9;

   end;

end;
```

2. In the following steps, you must increase the size of Form2 and make DBGrid1 and DBGrid2 smaller.

☐ Place a Table component in Form2.

☐ Set the Name property of the Table component to **CustomerTable**.

☐ Set the TableName property of CustomerTable to **Customer.DB**.

☐ Set the DatabaseName property of the CustomerTable Table control that you placed in Form2 to MYWORK.

☐ Place a DataSource component in Form2.

☐ Set the Name property of the DataSource component that you placed in Form2 to **DataSource3**.

☐ Set the DataSet property of DataSource to **Customer.DB**.

☐ Place a DBGrid control in Form2.

☐ Set the Name property of the new Grid control to **DBGrid3**.

☐ Set the DataSource property of DBGrid3 to **DataSource3**.

☐ Set the Active property of DBGrid3 to True, and verify that during design time you can view the Customer.DB table data.

☐ Double-click the CustomerTable Table control.

Delphi responds by displaying the Fields Editor window.

☐ Click the Add button.

Delphi responds by listing the Customer.DB table fields.

☐ Double-click the CustomerTable Table control.

☐ Make sure all the fields are selected, and then click the OK button.

☐ Verify that in the Object Inspector window you see the objects corresponding to the Customer.DB table fields.

☐ Double-click the ItemsTable Table control.

  Delphi responds by displaying the Fields Editor window of the Items.DB table.

☐ Click the Define button.

  Delphi responds by displaying the Define Field window.

☐ Set the Field name to **CustomerName**.

☐ Set the field type to **StringField**.

☐ Make sure that the Calculated checkbox is checked, and then close the Define Field window.

☐ Make sure that the Object Inspector combobox includes the ItemsTableCustomerName object.

  Now add code that fills the DBGrid1 control's CustomerName column.

☐ In the ItemsTableCalcFields procedure, add code. After adding the code, the ItemsTableCalcFields procedure should appear as follows:

```
procedure TForm2.ItemsTableCalcFields(DataSet: TDataset);

var
FindResultBoolean: Boolean;
begin

FindResultBoolean := PartsTable.FindKey([ItemsTablePartNum]);

if FindResultBoolean then
   begin
   ItemsTableItemDescription.Value :=
        PartsTableDescription.Value;

ItemsTableTotalPrice.Value :=
  PartsTableSellingPrice.Value * ItemsTableQtySold.Value;

   end;
```

5

```
FindResultBoolean := CustomerTable.FindKey([ItemsTableCustNum]);

if FindResultBoolean then
   begin

      ItemsTableCustomerName.Value :=
         CustomerTableLastName.Value + ' ' +
            CustomerTableFirstName.Value;

   end;

end;
```

The code you added to the procedure uses the FindKey() method to find the Customer.DB record that has a CustNum field value equal to the value of CustNum in the Items.DB table's current record:

```
FindResultBoolean := CustomerTable.FindKey([ItemsTableCustNum]);
```

An if statement is then used to update the value of the CustomerName column, provided that the record was found in the Customer.DB table.

```
if FindResultBoolean then
   begin

      ItemsTableCustomerName.Value :=
         CustomerTableLastName.Value + ' ' +
            CustomerTableFirstName.Value;

   end;
```

Note that the CustomerTable column is updated by adding three strings: the LastName field of Customer.DB, a space, and then the FirstName field of Customer.DB.

6

Linking Tables

In Chapter 5, "Calculated Fields," you implemented the TotPrice.EXE program. You wrote code to link the Parts.DB and Items.DB tables and to extract data from the Parts.DB table and place it in the Items.DB table. In this chapter, instead of writing code to link tables, you use the Database Form Expert's table-linking capabilities.

The One2Many Program

You'll now experiment with the one-to-many relationship. What is a one-to-many relationship? The program you write in this chapter, One2Many.EXE, illustrates the concept of a one-to-many table relationship. During the course of executing and implementing the One2Many program, you'll gain a full understanding of this important database topic. Before you start writing the code, however, let's first specify what it should do:

☐ When you start the One2Many program, the window shown in Figure 6.1 appears.

Figure 6.1.

The One2Many.EXE program window.

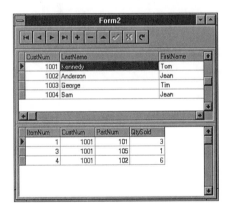

The top grid shown in the figure displays the Customer.DB table data, and the bottom grid displays data from the Items.DB table.

☐ As you move from record to record in the Customer.DB table, the bottom grid displays the records corresponding to the CustNum currently selected in the Table.DB table.

For example, CustNum 1001 has three records in Items.DB. The lower grid in Figure 6.1 displays three items, which correspond to CustNum 1001.

In Figure 6.2, the bottom grid displays the item corresponding to CustNum 1003, which has one record in Items.DB.

Figure 6.2.
The data displayed in the bottom grid corresponds to the Items.DB records of the CustNum *in Customer.DB.*

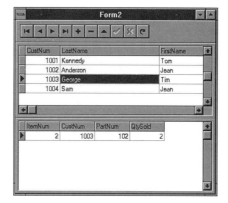

 Note: The One2Many program illustrates the concept of a one-to-many relationship. One record in Customer.DB can have many corresponding records in Items.DB, hence the term *one-to-many*.

Primary and Secondary Indexes

As stated in previous chapters, the first field of a Paradox table must be keyed. When you construct the table using Database Desktop, you must double-click the Key column of the first field in the table, and this places an asterisk (*) character in the field's Key column. The table is ordered by this field. The first keyed field is called a *primary indexed* field, and the values of this field must be unique. For example, in the Customer.DB table, CustNum is the first keyed field (the primary index), and so you can't have two records in Customer.DB with the same CustNum.

You also can create a *secondary indexed* field. As it turns out, to implement the One2Many program, you need to create a secondary indexed field for Items.DB.

6

☐ Terminate the Delphi program.

☐ Start the Database Desktop program.

☐ Select Restructure from the Utilities menu, and then select Items.DB from the C:\DProg\Work directory.

Database Desktop responds by displaying the Items.DB structure shown in Figure 6.3.

Figure 6.3.
The Items.DB structure.

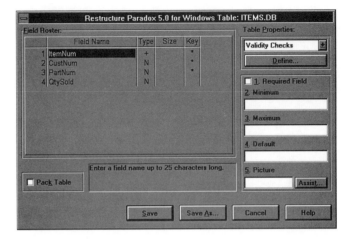

As you can see from this figure, the first field of Items.DB is a keyed field that is the primary index field.

Make the CustNum field (the second field of Items.DB) the secondary indexed field.

☐ Click the down-arrow icon in the combobox located below the Table Properties label (see Figure 6.4).

Database Desktop responds by dropping the list shown in Figure 6.4.

Figure 6.4.
Listing Table Properties.

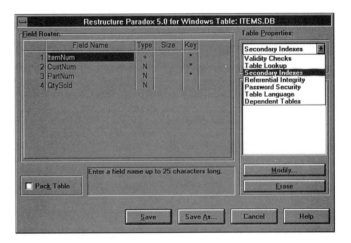

☐ Select the Secondary Indexes item from the list.

Database Desktop responds by making the Define button available.

☐ Click the Define button.

Database Desktop responds by displaying the window shown in Figure 6.5.

Figure 6.5.
The Define Secondary Index window.

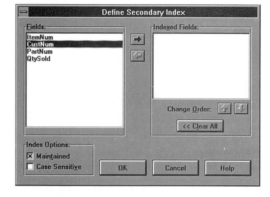

☐ Select the CustNum field because this is the field you want to make a secondary index field, and then click the button that has the right-pointing arrow on it.

Database Desktop responds by copying the CustNum field to the righthand list, as shown in Figure 6.6.

Figure 6.6.
Making CustNum the secondary indexed field.

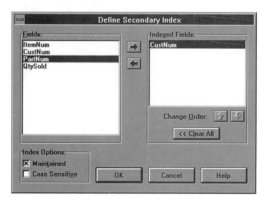

☐ Click the OK button in the Define Secondary Field window.

Database Desktop responds by displaying the Save Index As dialog box.

☐ In the Save Index As dialog box type **ByCustNum**.

Your Save Index As Dialog box should now appear as shown in Figure 6.7.

Figure 6.7.

*The Save Index As
dialog box.*

☐ Click the OK button in the Save Index As dialog box.

The Items.DB structure window should now look like Figure 6.8. Note that when the Secondary Indexes item is selected in the Table Properties combobox, the ByCustNum item appears in the list below the combobox (see Figure 6.8). When the combobox has the Secondary Indexes in it, the ByCustNum appears in the list as a secondary index.

Figure 6.8.

*The Items.DB structure
window.*

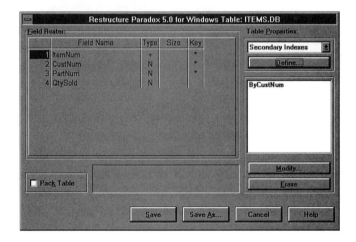

☐ Click the Save button.

☐ Terminate the Database Desktop program.

Now that you have the Items.DB table with a secondary index, you can start implementing the One2Many program.

Implementing the One2Many Program

To implement the One2Many.EXE program, follow these steps.

☐ Start Delphi.

☐ Select New Project from the File menu.

☐ Select Database Form Expert from the Help menu.

Delphi responds by displaying the first window of the Database Form Expert.

☐ Set the options buttons in the first window of Database Form Expert, as shown in Figure 6.9, by selecting them: Create a master/detail form, and Create a form using TTable objects. Note that in previous chapters you selected the Create a simple form option, but now you are creating a one-to-many linking, and so you have to select the Create a master/detail form option.

Figure 6.9.
The first window of Database Form Expert.

☐ Click the Next button.

Database Form Expert responds by displaying a window allowing you to select the master table.

☐ Select the Customer.DB table from the C:\DProg\Work directory, as shown in Figure 6.10. In the One2Many program, each record of Customer.DB can produce many records in Items.DB. The Customer.DB table is the *one* in the one-to-many, and the Items.DB table is the *many*. In this linking, Customer.DB is called the *master* table, and the Items.DB table is called the *detail* table.

Figure 6.10.
Selecting the master table.

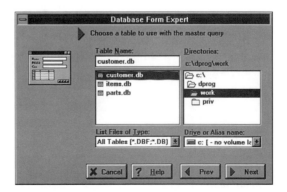

☐ Click the Next button.

Database Desktop Expert responds by displaying a window that enables you to select the fields to be included.

☐ Click the button picturing a right-pointing double arrow.

Database Form Expert responds by moving the field from the left list to the right list, as shown in Figure 6.11.

Figure 6.11.
Selecting all the Customer.DB fields.

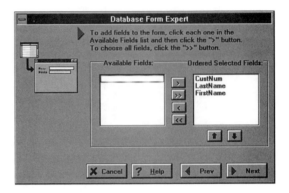

☐ Click the Next button.

Database Form Expert responds by displaying a window that enables you to choose how the Customer.DB data is displayed.

☐ Select the Grid option button, as shown in Figure 6.12.

Figure 6.12.
Selecting the Grid option for displaying the master table (Customer.DB).

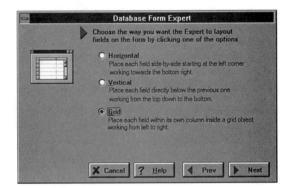

☐ Click the Next button.

Database Form Expert responds by displaying a dialog box that enables you to select the detail table.

☐ Select the Items.DB table from the C:\DProg\Work directory, as shown in Figure 6.13.

Figure 6.13.
Selecting the Items.DB table as the detail table.

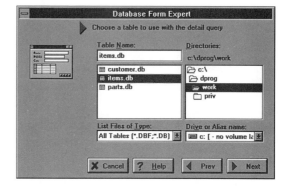

☐ Click the Next button.

Database Form Expert responds by displaying a window that enables you to select fields from the Items.DB table.

☐ Click the button picturing a right-pointing double arrow.

Database Form Expert responds by moving the fields from the left list to the right list, as shown in Figure 6.14.

Figure 6.14.
Selecting the fields in the Items.DB table.

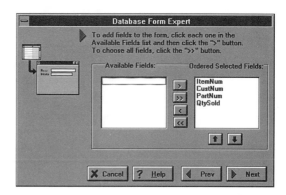

☐ Click the Next button.

Database Form Expert responds by displaying a window that enables you to select the way the Items.DB data are displayed.

☐ Select the Grid option button, as shown in Figure 6.15.

Figure 6.15.
Selecting the Grid as how to display the Items.DB data.

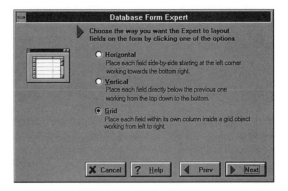

☐ Click the Next button.

> *Database Form Expert responds by displaying the window you use to define the linking between Customer.DB and Items.DB, as shown in Figure 6.16.*

Figure 6.16.
The window that enables you to define the linking relationship between Customer.DB and Items.DB.

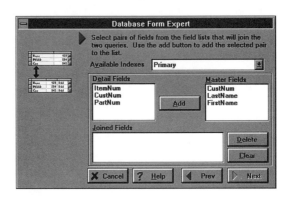

☐ Set the Available Indexes combobox to ByCustNum. This is the secondary index of Items.DB that you created at the beginning of this chapter.

☐ Select the CustNum item in the left list and the CustNum item in the right list.

Your Database Form Expert should now appear as shown in Figure 6.17.

☐ Click the Add button.

> *Database Form Expert responds by filling the Joined Fields list, as shown in Figure 6.18.*

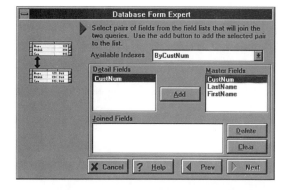

Figure 6.17.
Preparing the linking relationship between Customer.DB and Items.DB.

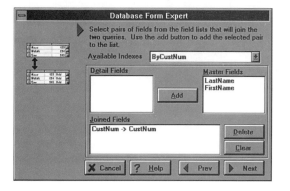

Figure 6.18.
The Joined Fields list of Database Form Expert is now ready.

Note: Database Form Expert dims the Next button if it determines that the relationship doesn't make sense.

☐ Click the Next button.

Database Form Expert responds by displaying the window shown in Figure 6.19.

☐ Make sure that the Generate a main form checkbox is checked, and then click the Create button.

Database Form Expert responds by creating Form2, *as shown in Figure 6.20.*

Figure 6.19.

Ready to generate the form with the Customer.DB table as the master table, and Items.DB as the detail table.

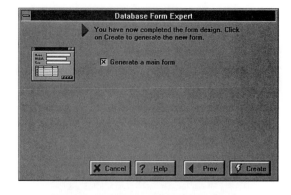

Figure 6.20.

Form2 as generated by Database Form Expert.

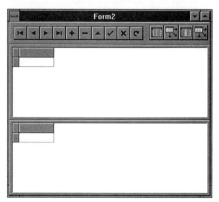

Saving the Project Files

Now that you've created the project files, you need to save them.

☐ Select the Form2 form, select Save File As from the File menu, and save the form as C2Tables.Pas in the C:\DProg\Ch06 directory.

☐ Select Remove File from the File menu, then select Form1 from the list of forms displayed, and remove the Form1 form. When Delphi asks you if you want to save Form1 before removing it, click the No button. Currently, the project is composed of two forms: Form1 and Form2. Database Form Expert placed controls in Form2. Form1 was created automatically when you first created the project. Because Form1 isn't used, there's no need to save it.

☐ Select Save Project As from the File menu, and save the project as One2Many.Dpr in the C:\DProg\Ch06 directory.

☐ Execute the One2Many program.

Note that listed on the bottom grid are items corresponding to the selected CustNum in the top grid.

☐ Experiment with the One2Many program, and then terminate it.

> **Note:** Database Form Expert did all the hard work for you. It placed the controls in `Form2` and set the necessary properties to establish the linking relationships as you defined them during the Database Form Expert session.
>
> You now can continue to customize the One2Many program according to your needs.

Changing the *Table* Component's *Name* Properties

Database Form Expert placed two `Table` components in `Form2`: `Table1`, corresponding to Customer.DB, and `Table2`, corresponding to Items.DB.

Change the `Name` properties of `Table1` and `Table2`, as follows:

☐ Select the `Table1` Table component, and change its `Name` property from `Table1` to **CustomerTable**.

☐ Select the `Table2` Table component, and change its `Name` property from `Table2` to **ItemsTable**.

☐ Select Find from the Search menu, search for the word *Table1*, and change it to **CustomerTable**.

☐ Select Search Again, and verify that the word *Table1* doesn't appear in the project.

☐ Select Find from the Search menu, search for the word *Table2*, and change it to **ItemsTable**.

☐ Select Search Again, and verify that the word *Table2* does not appear in the project.

In the preceding steps, you found that the words *Table1* and *Table2* appeared only in the `FormCreate` procedure. After changing the text, the `FormCreate` procedure should appear as follows:

```
procedure TForm2.FormCreate(Sender: TObject);
begin

  CustomerTable.Open;
  ItemsTable.Open;

end;
```

☐ Select Save Project from the File menu.

☐ Execute the One2Many program, and verify that everything is working as expected.

☐ Terminate the One2Many program.

Placing an Exit Button

Now place an Exit button in Form2.

☐ Set the Align property of the upper grid to clNone so that you can size the grid.

☐ Set the Align property of the lower grid to clNone so that you can size the grid.

> **Note:** Database Form Expert places three Panel controls in Form2 for cosmetic reasons. The controls of Form2 were placed in the Panel controls. When the Align property of a Panel control is set to clTop, the Panel control is placed at the top of the window. Thus, it is appropriate for the top Panel control (the control with the Navigator control in it) to have its Align property set to clTop.
>
> When the second Panel control (the control with the Customer.DB in it) has its Align property set to clTop, Delphi places the Panel control at the top of the window. Because the top of the window is already occupied by the first Panel control, Delphi places the second Panel control below the first Panel control, and the same goes for the third Panel control.

☐ Move the two lower Panel controls and the Grid controls they contain to make room for the Exit button.

Form2 should now appear as shown in Figure 6.21.

Figure 6.21.
Form2 with a free area where you can place the Exit button.

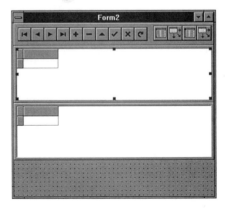

☐ Place a pushbutton control in Form2 as shown in Figure 6.22. Set the properties of the button as follows:

```
Name      cmdExit
Caption   E&xit
```

Figure 6.22.
Form2 with the Exit pushbutton.

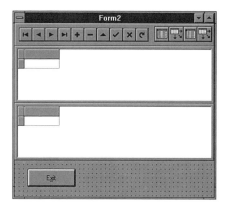

☐ Attach code to the OnClick event of the Exit button. After attaching the code, the cmdExitClick procedure should appear as follows:

```
procedure TForm2.cmdExitClick(Sender: TObject);
begin

    Application.Terminate;

end;
```

☐ Select Save project from the File menu.

☐ Execute the One2Many program.

☐ Verify that the Exit button terminates the program.

> **Note:** The point of the One2Many program is to illustrate the one-to-many concept, and so we didn't have you place additional code or add features to the program.
>
> However, it's important for you to understand that everything Database Form Expert did, you can do yourself by placing the appropriate controls and then setting their properties. Thereafter, you can continue developing the program as you always do.
>
> For example, you can double-click the Table controls to display the Fields Editor window and add field objects to Form2. You then can make any field a Read Only field, place calculated fields, and so on.

Creating Additional Secondary Indexes

You saw in the One2Many program that the Items.DB table has a secondary index called ByCustNum that is indexed on the CustNum field.

In Figure 6.1 for example, the CustNum in the Customer.DB table is customer number 1001. As a result, the lower grid displays all the records in Items.DB that have the CustNum field equal to 1001.

However, what if you want, for example, to have the Parts.DB table as the master table, and you want to display all the items in Items.DB whose PartNum fields are equal to the PartNum of the current record of Parts.DB? This is possible, but you need to create another secondary index for the Items.DB table.

You accomplish this by doing the following:

☐ Terminate Delphi.

☐ Start the Database Desktop program.

☐ Select Restructure form the Utilities menu.

Database Desktop responds by displaying a dialog box that enables you to load a table.

☐ Select the Items.DB table from the C:\DProg\Work directory.

Database Desktop responds by displaying the Items.DB structure.

☐ Select the Secondary Indexes from the Table Properties combobox.

As you can see, the Items.DB table already has one secondary index: the ByCustNum secondary index you created earlier in this chapter.

☐ Click the Define button.

Database Desktop responds by displaying the Define Secondary Index dialog box.

☐ Select the PartNum from the left list, and then click the button picturing the right-pointing arrow.

Database Desktop responds by moving the PartNum field to the right list, as shown in Figure 6.23.

Figure 6.23.
Making the secondary index on the PartNum field of the Items.DB table.

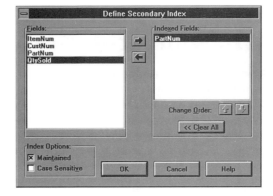

☐ Click the OK button in the Define Secondary Index window.

> *Database Desktop responds by displaying the Save Index As dialog box.*

☐ Save the index as ByPartNum.

As you can see in Figure 6.24, the Items.DB table now has two secondary indexes.

Figure 6.24.
The Items.DB table has two secondary indexes.

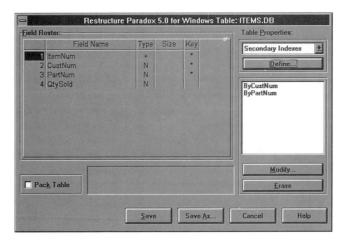

☐ Click the Save button of the Restructure window.

☐ Terminate the Database Desktop program.

Creating the Parts.DB and Items.DB One-to-Many Relationship

Now use the Database Form Expert to build the PartItem.EXE program, a program that displays the Parts.DB table data as the master table and the Items.DB data as the detail table. For each Parts.DB table record, the Items.DB table displays the records corresponding to the PartNum.

☐ Start Delphi.

☐ Select Database Form Expert from the Help menu.

Delphi responds by displaying the first window of the Database Form Expert.

☐ Select the two option buttons: Create master/detail form, and Create a form using TTable object.

☐ Click the Next button.

Delphi responds by displaying the window that enables you to select the master table.

☐ Select as the master table the Parts.DB table from the C:\DProg\Work directory.

☐ Click the Next button.

Database Form Expert responds by displaying the window that enables you to select the field from the Parts.DB table.

☐ Click the button picturing a right-pointing double arrow.

Database Form Expert responds by listing all the fields in the right list.

☐ Click the Next button.

Database Form Expert responds by displaying the window that enables you to select the layout.

☐ Select the Horizontal option button. You already saw what happens when you select the Grid option button. Let's see how the Parts.DB table data appears when you select the Horizontal option button.

☐ Click the Next button.

Database Form Expert responds by displaying a dialog box that enables you to select the detail table.

☐ Select the Items.DB table from the C:\DProg\Work directory.

☐ Click the Next button.

Database Form Expert responds by displaying a window that enables you to select the fields from the Items.DB table.

☐ Click the button picturing a right-pointing double arrow.

Database Form Expert responds by listing all the Items.DB's fields in the right list.

☐ Click the Next button.

Database Form Expert responds by displaying a window that enables you to select the layout of the data for the Items.DB table.

☐ Select the Grid option button.

☐ Click the Next button.

Database Form Expert responds by displaying the window that enables you to establish the relationship between Parts.DB and Items.DB, as shown in Figure 6.25.

☐ Select ByPartNum from the Available Indexes comboboxes, and select PartNum in the right list.

Your Database Form Expert window should now appear as shown in Figure 6.25.

Figure 6.25.
Establishing the master/detail relationship.

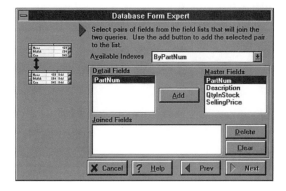

☐ Click the Add button.

Database Form Expert responds by listing the relationship in the Joined Fields list, as shown in Figure 6.26.

Figure 6.26.
The master/detail relationship.

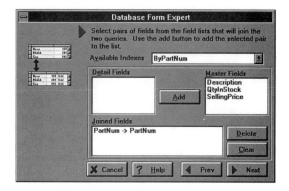

☐ Click the Next button.

Database Form Expert responds by displaying the last window for this session.

☐ Make sure the Create main form checkbox is checked, and then click the Create button.

Database Form Expert responds by creating the Form2 form, as shown in Figure 6.27.

Figure 6.27.
Form2 that was created by Database Form Expert.

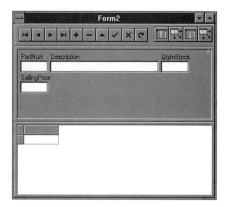

Note that the upper section of Form2 displays the Parts.DB fields horizontally, and the lower portion of Form2 is a regular grid, as you specified during the Database Form Expert session.

Saving the Project Files

Save the project files.

☐ Select Form2, select Save File As from the File menu, and then select the file as CPrtItem.Pas in the C:\DProg\Ch06 directory.

☐ Remove Form1 from the project because it isn't used.

☐ Select Save Project As from the File menu, and save the project as PartItem.Dpr in the C:\DProg\CH06 directory.

☐ Execute the PartItem program.

As shown in Figures 6.28 and 6.29, when a record in Parts.DB is selected, the Items.DB grid displays the Items.DB records that have the same PartNum.

Figure 6.28.
The PartItem program window.

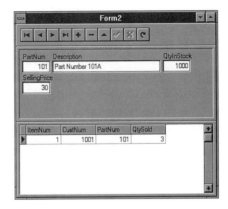

Figure 6.29.
The lower grid control displays records from the Items.DB table corresponding to the PartNum displayed on the upper portion of the window.

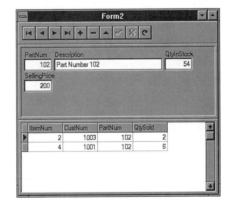

☐ Move from record to record in Table.DB by using the Navigator control, and notice the results in the Items.DB grid.

☐ Experiment with the PartItem program, and then terminate the program.

Summary

In this chapter, you learned about the important concept of one-to-many relationships. As you saw, the Database Form Expert enables you to create a one-to-many relationship by displaying various windows, and it enables you to design the relationship by clicking the mouse on various options.

You also learned about what secondary indexes are and that a table can have multiple secondary indexes.

Q&A

Q Before implementing the One2Many program, I was instructed to create a secondary index for Items.DB. Why?

A The relationship between Customer.DB and Items.DB requires an index on the detail table so that when the master table changes records, the corresponding records of the detail table can be extracted.

Quiz

1. A primary keyed field is _____.
2. A secondary indexed field is _____.
3. A field that is keyed and is not the first field in the table is a secondary field.
    a. True
    b. False

Exercises

1. Make the lower grid of the One2Many program a read-only grid.
2. Clean up the PartItem program a little bit.

Answers to Quiz

1. A primary keyed field is the first keyed field of a table.
2. A secondary indexed field is a key field that you assigned as a secondary indexed field with the Database Desktop tools.
3. False. To make a secondary field, it is not enough to make the field a key field. You must use the Database Desktop tools as outlined in this chapter to make the secondary index.

Answers to Exercises

1. The answer is as follows:

   ☐ Set the ReadOnly property of the lower grid control to True.

2. Replace the words *Table1* and *Table2* in the program code with PartsTable and ItemsTable.

   ☐ Move the Grid control to make room for an Exit button.

   ☐ Place a pushbutton in Form2, and set its properties as follows:

   ```
   Name     cmdExit
   Caption  E&xit
   ```

   ☐ Attach the following statement to the cmdExit button's OnClick event:

   ```
   Application.Terminate;
   ```

6

WEEK
1

Searching For and Validating Data

In this chapter, you learn about two fundamental topics in database programming: searching for and validating data.

As the terms imply, *searching for* data is the process of searching for a particular record. *Validating* data is the process of examining the user's input, determining whether it is acceptable, and accepting or rejecting the input accordingly.

The SearchMe Program

The SearchMe program illustrates how searching for a particular record is performed. Before writing the SearchMe program, review its specifications. Here is what the program should do.

☐ When starting the SearchMe program, the window in Figure 7.1 appears.

Figure 7.1.
The SearchMe program window.

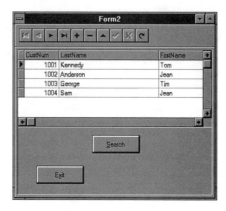

The SearchMe program window has a Search button in it.

☐ When the Search button is clicked, the input dialog box shown in Figure 7.2 appears.

Figure 7.2.
The input dialog box asks the user to enter the Customer Number.

☐ The user now can enter the customer number and then click the OK button in the input dialog box.

> *The SearchMe program responds by searching the Customer.DB table for a record with* CustNum *field equal to the value the user entered in the input dialog box.*

> *If a record with the same* CustNum *isn't found, the SearchMe program responds by displaying a dialog box (see Figure 7.3) telling the user that the record was not found.*

If the record was found, the Grid control displaying the Customer.DB table shows the found record as the current record.

Figure 7.3.
*A record was
not found.*

Implementing the SearchMe Program

Implement the SearchMe program by following these steps:

☐ Start Delphi.

☐ Use Database Form Expert to create a simple form that is displayed as a grid. You should use the Customer.DB table that resides in the C:\DProg\Work directory.

When you complete the Database Form Expert session, the Form2 form that Database Form Expert created should appear as shown in Figure 7.4.

Figure 7.4.
Form2 *generated by Database Form Expert.*

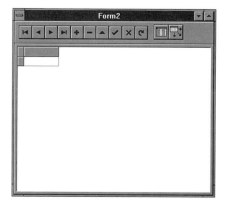

☐ Size the Grid control to make room at the bottom of Form2. Don't forget to set the Grid control's Align property to clNone so you'll be able to make the Grid control smaller.

☐ Save Form2 as CSearch.Pas in the C:\DProg\Ch07 directory.

☐ Remove Form1 from the Project.

☐ Save the project as SearchMe.Dpr in the C:\DProg\Ch07 directory.

☐ Execute the SearchMe program to verify that everything is working properly.

☐ Terminate the SearchMe program.

☐ Set the Table1 Table control's Name property to CustomerTable, and replace the word Table1 in the FormCreate procedure with the word **CustomerTable**.

The FormCreate procedure should now appear as follows:

```
procedure TForm2.FormCreate(Sender: TObject);
begin

   CustomerTable.Open;

end;
```

☐ Execute the SearchMe program to verify that everything is working properly.

☐ Terminate the SearchMe program.

☐ Place an Exit button in Form2 with the following properties:

```
   Caption    E&xit
   Name       cmdExit
```

☐ Attach the following code to the cmdExit button's OnClick event:

```
procedure TForm2.cmdExitClick(Sender: TObject);
begin

Application.Terminate;

end;
```

☐ Save the project.

☐ Execute the SearchMe program.

The SearchMe program window now appears as shown in Figure 7.5.

Figure 7.5.
The SearchMe program
with its Exit button.

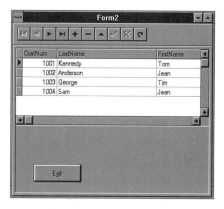

☐ Verify that the Exit button terminates the program.

Implementing a Search Button

Implement a Search button by following these steps:

☐ Place a pushbutton in Form2, and set its properties as follows:

```
Caption    &Search
Name       cmdSearch
```

☐ Attach code to the cmdSearch button's OnClick event. After attaching the code, the cmdSearchClick procedure should appear as follows:

```
procedure TForm2.cmdSearchClick(Sender: TObject);

var
CustNumToSearchString: String;
ResultBoolean: Boolean;

begin

CustNumToSearchString :=
   InputBox ('Search',
             'Type the Customer Number to be searched:',
             '');

ResultBoolean := CustomerTable.FindKey([CustNumToSearchString]);

if not ResultBoolean then
   MessageDlg('Cannot find!',
              mtInformation,
              [mbOK],
              0);

end;
```

The code you typed declares the following two local variables that are used in the procedure:

```
var
CustNumToSearchString: String;
ResultBoolean: Boolean;
```

The `InputBox` function is then executed:

```
CustNumToSearchString :=
   InputBox ('Search',
             'Type the Customer Number to be searched:',
             '');
```

An input box is displayed. The user types a string in the input box, and the string is assigned to the `CustNumToSearchString` variable.

The `InputBox` function parameters determine how the input box looks. The first parameter of the `InputBox` function specifies the input box title. The second parameter is the instruction to the user, and the third parameter is the default string that is displayed in the input box. Because you don't want a default string, you typed `''`.

When the user executes the SearchMe program after clicking the Search button, the input box shown in Figure 7.2 appears.

A search is then performed, and the result of the search is assigned to the `ResultBoolean` variable, as follows:

```
ResultBoolean := CustomerTable.FindKey([CustNumToSearchString]);
```

If the search is successful (a record is found), `ResultBoolean` is set to `True`. If no record is found, `ResultBoolean` is set to `False`. What was searched? The `CustomerTable` was searched for a record whose `CustNum` field is equal to `CustNumToSearchString`. Recall that the first field of Customer.DB is `CustNum`, and this field is keyed.

If the search is successful, the grid containing the Customer.DB table data shows the found record as the current record.

An `if` statement is then executed to examine the `ResultBooleanString` variable.

```
if not ResultBoolean then
   MessageDlg('Cannot find!',
              mtInformation,
              [mbOK],
              0);
```

If `ResultBoolean` is equal to `False`, the statement after the `if` statement is executed. This statement displays a message box. The title of the message box is: `Cannot find!` (the `MessageDlg` function's first parameter).

The message box has the Information icon, which is the second parameter of the `MessageDlg` function.

The message box also has an OK button. (The third parameter of the `MessageDlg` function.)

The last parameter of the `MessageDlg` function is `0` because there is no Help associated with the message box.

If you execute the SearchMe program now, you get an error because you used the `InputBox` function without telling the program that `InputBox` is used.

Tell the program that the `InputBox` is used, as follows:

☐ At the beginning of the CSearch.Pas window you see the following code:

```
unit Csearch;

interface

uses
  SysUtils, WinTypes, WinProcs, Messages, Classes,
  Graphics, Controls, StdCtrls, Forms, DBCtrls, DB,
  DBGrids, DBTables, Grids, ExtCtrls;

type
...
```

Under uses, you see a list of all the components that the program uses. You don't see the `Dialogs` keyword in the list, hence the program cannot use the `InputBox`.

☐ Add the `Dialogs` keyword to the list of uses. After adding `Dialogs` to the list, the beginning of the CSearch.Pas file should appear as follows:

```
unit Csearch;

interface

uses
  SysUtils, WinTypes, WinProcs, Messages, Classes,
  Graphics, Controls, StdCtrls, Forms, DBCtrls, DB,
  DBGrids, DBTables, Grids, ExtCtrls,
  Dialogs;

type
...
```

☐ Save the project.

☐ Execute the SearchMe program, and verify its proper operation.

☐ Terminate the SearchMe program.

7

Errors During Runtime

You can execute the SearchMe program either from within Delphi, or by using the File Manager and executing the SearchMe.EXE program like any other program in Windows.

When you run the program from Delphi, it first compiles the program (Delphi creates the SearchMe.EXE program) and then executes it. If you want to create SearchMe.EXE without running the program, select Compile from the Compile menu. If you select Compile All from the Compile menu, Delphi compiles all the project files—even files that were not modified since the last time you compiled the project.

When an error occurs during program execution, the user is prompted with an error message. The message displayed depends on how you executed the program. If you executed the program by using the File Manager and an error occurred during execution, the user can read the message, and, in most cases, can click the OK button in the message box and continue with program execution.

If a program is executed by using the Delphi debugger and an error occurs during execution, some of the message boxes displayed are intended for you, the developer. In this case, read the message, click its OK button, and then select Step Over from the Run menu.

☐ Execute the SearchMe program from Delphi, and search for Tom.

Delphi informs you that you can't search for Tom because the search is performed according to the CustNum field, which has to be a number.

☐ Click the error message's OK button, select Run from the Run menu, and then terminate the SearchMe program.

More about the *FindKey()* Method

The FindKey method you executed in the SearchMe program can be used to search a keyed field (a field with an asterisk on the Key column in Database Desktop).

The FindKey() method searches for the value supplied as its parameter in all the keyed fields. In the SearchMe program example, only one parameter was supplied to FindKey (the string that was typed in the input box). Because CustNum is the first key field, the program searches for a match between the CustNum field and the parameter of the FindKey().

To use FindKey() to search also for the LastName and FirstName in Customer.DB, these fields must be keyed.

☐ Close any open tables in your Delphi project. If in doubt, close the project itself.

☐ Start Database Desktop.

☐ Select Restructure from the Utilities menu, load the Customer.DB table, and double-click the Key column of the LastName and FirstName fields.

The Customer.DB structure should now look like Figure 7.6.

Figure 7.6.

The LastName and FirstName fields of Customer.DB are key fields.

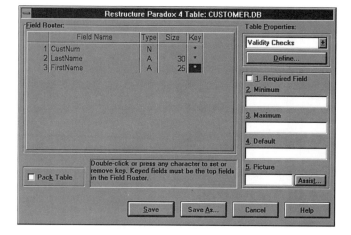

Note: When you develop Delphi programs, Database Desktop is very useful.

Before going to Database Desktop to restructure the table, you must close all open references to that table. This means you should close any TTable or TQuery components (set their Active property to False) in your Delphi projects that refer to the table you plan to restucture; or, simply close the project. A table cannot be restructured while it is in use.

☐ Select Save to save the new structure.

☐ Terminate Database Desktop.

☐ Start Delphi and load the SearchMe project from the C:\DProg\Ch07 directory.

You can use FindKey() with three parameters to search for a record in Customer.DB. The first parameter of FindKey() is the CustNum field, the second parameter is the LastName field, and the third parameter is the FirstName field.

To see this in action, do the following:

☐ Change the code in the cmdSearchClick procedure as follows:

```
procedure TForm2.cmdSearchClick(Sender: TObject);

var
```

```
    CustNumToSearchString: String;
    ResultBoolean: Boolean;

begin

    {
    CustNumToSearchString :=
        InputBox ('Search',
                  'Type the Customer Number to be searched:',
                  '');
    }

    {
    ResultBoolean := CustomerTable.FindKey([CustNumToSearchString]);
    }

    ResultBoolean :=
        CustomerTable.FindKey([ '1002','Anderson','Jean']);

    if not ResultBoolean then
        MessageDlg('Cannot find!',
                   mtInformation,
                   [mbOK],
                   0);

end;
```

The code you entered comments out the statement that displays an input box:

```
{
CustNumToSearchString :=
    InputBox ('Search',
              'Type the Customer Number to be searched:',
              '');
}
```

It also comments out the statement that searches for the record:

```
{
ResultBoolean := CustomerTable.FindKey([CustNumToSearchString]);
}
```

The following statement was added to the procedure:

```
ResultBoolean :=
    CustomerTable.FindKey([ '1002','Anderson','Jean']);
```

The FindKey() has three parameters. The first parameter corresponds to the CustNum field, the second parameter corresponds to the LastName field, and the third parameter corresponds to the FirstName field, and so the FindKey() parameters must correspond to the table's key fields.

☐ Execute the SearchMe program.

☐ Click the Search button.

If you have a record with CustNum equal to 1002, LastName equal to Anderson, and FirstName equal to Jean, the record will be found.

☐ Terminate the Search program.

The preceding steps illustrate how you can search for a record by examining more than one field.

If you replace the FindKey statement with the following statement, the search fails if there is no record matching CustNum equal to 1002, LastName equal to Anderson, and FirstName equal to JJJJean:

```
ResultBoolean :=
    CustomerTable.FindKey([ '1002','Anderson','JJJJean']);
```

That's it for experimenting with the FindKey() method for now. At the end of this chapter, you learn how to search for a particular last name.

☐ Return to the original code of the cmdSearchClick procedure. So the cmsSearchClick procedure should now appear as follows:

```
procedure TForm2.cmdSearchClick(Sender: TObject);

var
CustNumToSearchString: String;
ResultBoolean: Boolean;

begin

CustNumToSearchString :=
    InputBox ('Search',
              'Type the Customer Number to be searched:',
              '');

ResultBoolean := CustomerTable.FindKey([CustNumToSearchString]);

end;
```

Validating User Input Data

To examine whether the user enters valid data in the tables, you can use the table-based validation technique. As you probably noticed, when you create a table with Database Desktop, you can set various validity checks. For example, you can set the minimum-allowed and maximum-allowed field values.

The good thing about using Database Desktop for data validation is that you don't have to write code that validates the data. The validation you set with Database Desktop is embedded in the tables, and if the user enters invalid data, the program has in it all the code required to display errors during runtime. Typically, the user is able to understand the error messages. The bad thing about using the table-level validation feature is that you don't have control over the error messages your user receives. As a programmer, you want to have control over your program, and you want your code to display the error messages during runtime. This means you have to write code to accomplish this.

To write your own code that validates the user's data, you can attach code to the OnValidate event. When you implement the program form, you use the Fields Editor window to place field objects corresponding to the table fields. When the user modifies a field, the object field's OnValidate event occurs automatically, and the code you typed for this event is executed. This code should check the user's data and accept or reject the data accordingly.

To see the OnValidate event in action, follow these steps:

☐ Double click the CustomerTable's Table control.

Delphi responds by displaying the Fields Editor window.

☐ Click the Add button and then the OK button to place field objects in Form2 for all the Customer.DB fields.

Delphi responds by placing the following invisible field objects in Form2:

```
CustomerTableCustName
CustomerTableLastName
CustomerTableFirstName
```

Suppose you want to prohibit your user from entering a record that has LastName equal to Smith.

☐ Attach code to the BeforePost event of the CustomerTable's Table control. After entering the code, the CustomerTableBeforePost procedure should be as follows:

```
procedure TForm2.CustomerTableBeforePost(DataSet: TDataset);
begin

if CustomerTableLastName.Value = 'Smith' then
   begin
   MessageBeep(1);

   MessageDlg(
   'Inside CustomerTableBeforePost:' +
   'LastName Cannot be Smith!',
    mtInformation,
   [mbOK],
    0);

   end;

end;
```

The code you typed uses an `if` statement to determine if the value of `LastName` is equal to `Smith`.

```
if CustomerTableLastName.Value = 'Smith' then
   begin
   ...
   end;
```

If the user typed `Smith` in one of the `LastName` fields, the code after the `if` statement is executed.

The code after the `if` statement causes the user's PC to beep.

```
MessageBeep(1);
```

It also displays a message box.

```
MessageDlg(
   'Inside CustomerTableBeforePost:' +
   'LastName Cannot be Smith!',
   mtInformation,
   [mbOK],
   0);
```

We included the text `InsideCustomerTableBeforePost` in the message box so that during program execution, you'll realize that the message box that appears is the one you displayed in the `CustomerTableBeforeTable` procedure.

☐ Select Save Project from the File menu.

☐ Execute the SearchMe program.

☐ Change the `LastName` field of one of the records to **Smith**.

☐ Move to another record.

SearchMe responds by beeping and then displaying the message box shown in Figure 7.7.

Figure 7.7.
The message box that SearchMe displays after entering Smith *as the* LastName *of one of the records.*

Note that the `Smith` in the `LastName` field remains in the field after you moved to another record! In other words, the user was warned that `Smith` was unacceptable, but besides warning the user, the program did not reject the `Smith` entry.

☐ Experiment with the SearchMe program. Before terminating the program, make sure that none of the `LastName` fields is `Smith`. Terminate the program.

In the preceding code, you attached code to the `CustomerTableBeforePost` procedure. This procedure is executed just before the Post operation is performed. For example, after the user moves from the current record to another record, a Post operation is performed. Therefore, the `CustomerTableBeforePost` procedure is executed after the user moved from the current modified record to another record. As you can see, the `BeforePost` event enables you to write code that is executed before the Post operation is performed.

Raising an Exception

In the previous section, the user was warned about the fact that `Smith` was entered as `LastName`. Even so, the Post operation was performed. The bottom line is that the user was able to enter `Smith` as `LastName`.

You now write code that actually raises an exception. The program refuses to accept `Smith` as `LastName`.

☐ Comment out all the code you typed in the `CustomerTableBeforePost` procedure.

☐ Attach code to the `OnValidate` event of the `CustomerTableLastName` object. After attaching the code, the `CustomerTableLastNameValidate` procedure should appear as follows:

```
procedure TForm2.CustomerTableLastNameValidate(Sender: TField);
begin

if CustomerTableLastName.Value = 'Smith' then
   begin

MessageBeep(1);
raise Exception.Create('Cannot have LastName equal Smith');

   end;

end;
```

The `CustomerTableLastName` object's `OnValidate` event occurs when the user tries to move away from the `LastName` field, and so the code you typed checks the validity of the `LastName` field contents.

An `if` statement checks if `LastName` is equal to `Smith`.

```
if CustomerTableLastName.Value = 'Smith' then
   begin
   ....
   end;
```

The code after the `if` statement makes the user's PC beep.

```
MessageBeep(1);
```

The `raise Exception` statement then is executed.

```
raise Exception.Create('Cannot have LastName equal Smith');
```

If the LastName field contains Smith, the program refuses to move to another record or to another field on the same record, and a message box with the following message is displayed:

```
Cannot have LastName equal to Smith
```

☐ Select Save Project from the File menu.

In the following steps, you're instructed to execute the SearchMe program by using the File Manager to execute the program like a regular Windows application. Why? Because the purpose of the exercise is to demonstrate the error message your program displays. When executing the program from within Delphi, you may see two types of messages: messages from the Delphi debugger to you, the programmer, and those from your program to the user. When the Delphi debugger prompts you with an exception-notification message box, you must select Run from the Run menu to continue with the execution. The program's error message response to the exception (if any) will appear after the Delphi debugger notification. The debugger notification exsists to help you debug your application—it shows you the source code line closest to where the exception was raised. You then can examine variables to figure out why the exception was raised, or you can single-step to debug the execution of the exception handlers. If you're not interested in debugging exception conditions, the debugger's exception-notification message boxes can become tiresome. You can disable them in the Options | Environment dialog's Preferences page by unchecking the Break on Exception checkbox. Or, as in the following exercise, you can simply run the program outside the Delphi environment.

☐ Use File Manager to execute SearchMe.EXE.

☐ In one of the LastName fields, type **Smith**.

☐ Try to move to another record or another field on the same record.

SearchMe prompts you with a message telling you that the LastName field cannot be Smith.

☐ Experiment with the SearchMe.EXE program, and then terminate it.

Note: The raise Exception statement is a powerful one. Without writing elaborate code, it causes the program to refuse to move to another record. Use the raise Exception statement whenever possible, rather than writing your own code that refuses to accept a certain value for a field.

Generally speaking, whenever Delphi offers a feature that does what you require, use that feature rather than write code to accomplish the same task. This is demonstrated in the next section with the Required property.

7

The *Required* Property

In addition to requiring users to enter a particular type of data into a field, you can require them to fill the LastName field. Suppose a user either deletes the LastName contents of an existing record or enters a new record without filling the LastName field, and then the user tries to move to another record. You can set the Required property so the user is forced to fill the LastName field.

☐ Set the CustomerTableLastName object's Required property to True.

☐ Select Save project from the File menu.

☐ Use File Manager to execute the SearchMe.EXE program.

☐ Move to an existing record, and delete the contents of the LastName field.

> *SearchMe.EXE responds by displaying a message box telling you that* LastName *must be filled. The user is now forced to fill* LastName.

☐ Fill the LastName field of the current record.

☐ Add a new record by using the down-arrow key on your keyboard and moving to a new empty record past the last record.

☐ In the new record, fill the CustNum field.

☐ Move to the LastName field, and then, without filling the LastName field, try to move away from it.

> *SearchMe responds by displaying a message box telling you that you must fill the* LastName *field.*

☐ Experiment with the SearchMe.EXE program, and then terminate it.

Because Delphi provides the Required feature, use it rather than write your own code that examines whether the LastName field is filled.

About the Key Field

As you know, the first key field of a table must be unique. Because the CustNum field of the Customer.DB table is the first key field, you cannot have more than one record with the same CustNum.

However, if you now try to add a record to the Customer.DB table, you see that you can add another record with the same CustNum. Why? Because earlier in this chapter you made the LastName and FirstName fields key fields, too, so that CustNum, LastName, and FirstName are all key fields. This means you can't enter a record that has the same CustNum, LastName, and FirstName to the Customer.DB table.

To see this in action, follow these steps:

☐ Use Database Desktop to make sure that the CustNum, LastName, and FirstName fields are key fields.

☐ Use File Manager to execute the SearchMe.EXE program.

☐ Add a new record. The new record should have a CustNum that already exists in the Customer.DB table, but the LastName and FirstName fields of the new record should have values that no other records in Customer.DB have.

☐ Move to another record.

As you can see, it is all right to have such a record; Delphi doesn't complain.

☐ Modify the new record you added so that it has a CustNum, LastName, and FirstName of another record.

☐ Try to move to another record.

A key violation message is displayed.

☐ Modify the new record so that its CustNum field is unique, move to another record, and then terminate the SearchMe.EXE program.

Typically, the CustNum field should be the first field and the only key field in Customer.DB because you want this field to be unique. Each customer must have a unique customer number. Recall that we made the LastName and FirstName fields key fields because we wanted to demonstrate how the FindKey() method is used for searching several key fields.

☐ Use Database Desktop to modify the Customer.DB structure so that only CustNum is a key field. LastName and FirstName should not be key fields.

☐ Use File Manager to execute the SearchMe.EXE program.

☐ Add a new record with a CustNum that already exists in the Customer.DB table.

The user is prohibited from entering a non-unique CustNum value.

☐ Terminate the program by clicking its Exit button.

Searching by Other Fields

So far, you've seen that the Customer.DB table can be searched by CustNum. Recall that CustNum is the first keyed field of the Customer.DB table. CustNum is the primary field and must be unique. What if you want to search the Customer.DB table by LastName? In this case, you first must create a secondary index for the LastName field. You must use Database Desktop to create a secondary index for the LastName field of Customer.DB.

☐ Make sure that Customer.DB has only its first field (the CustNum field) as a key field.

☐ Use Database Desktop to create a secondary index for the LastName field of Customer.DB. If you forgot how to create a secondary field, refer to Day 6, "Linking Tables.") When creating the secondary field for LastName, save the secondary field as ByLastName.

☐ Comment out the statements in the cmdSearchClick procedure, and add code to the procedure. The code you add searches for a record with LastName equal to Anderson, as follows:

```
procedure TForm2.cmdSearchClick(Sender: TObject);

var
CustNumToSearchString: String;
ResultBoolean: Boolean;

begin

{
...
... Previous code is commented out
...
}

CustomerTable.IndexName := 'ByLastName';

ResultBoolean :=
CustomerTable.FindKey(['Anderson']);

CustomerTable.IndexName := '';

if not ResultBoolean then
    MessageDlg('Cannot find!',
                mtInformation,
                [mbOK],
                0);

end;
```

The code you typed sets the CustomerTable's IndexName property as follows:

```
CustomerTable.IndexName := 'ByLastName';
```

This statement makes the secondary index you created the active index by which the Customer.DB table is ordered. From now on, think of it as if the primary key field were not CustNum, but LastName. Of course, unlike a real primary field, LastName can be a non-unique field. The LastName of Anderson, for example, can appear several times in the Customer.DB table.

You now can search for a record as if LastName were a primary field.

```
ResultBoolean :=
CustomerTable.FindKey(['Anderson']);
```

That's it! ResultBoolean is now updated either with True (if the record with LastName equal to Anderson was found) or with False (if a record with this LastName was not found).

The next statement returns IndexName to its original setting (which is the CustNum field as the primary field). You do that by setting IndexName to null as follows:

```
CustomerTable.IndexName := '';
```

☐ Execute the program, and verify that when one of the records has LastName equal to Anderson, clicking the Search button causes the program to find the record.

As stated, because LastName is not the primary field, you can have several records with LastName equal to Anderson. When performing the search, the FindKey() method finds the first record with LastName equal to Anderson.

☐ Comment out the statement that returns IndexName to the primary field as follows:

```
{ CustomerTable.IndexName := ''; }
```

☐ Execute the program.

☐ Click the Search button.

As you can see, because IndexName is set to ByLastName, the table records are ordered by LastName. So, the fact that the FindKey() method found only the first occurrence of Anderson is not a problem because all the records with LastName as Anderson are displayed one after another.

☐ Terminate the program.

☐ Return to the original code of the cmdSearchClick procedure.

Summary

In this chapter, you implemented the SearchMe program, a program that illustrates how to use the FindKey() method for searching a record by the table's key field(s). As you saw, you can search by one or more key fields.

You also learned about the BeforePost event, the OnValidate event, and the Required property.

Q&A

Q Should I execute the Delphi programs that I write from Delphi or from the File Manager?

A You should do both. That is, during development, execute the program from Delphi because if there is any error, the message box error you get may provide a clue of what you did wrong.

Your user gets different error messages because the error messages displayed when the program is executed with File Manager are different than the error messages that Delphi displays.

As you develop Delphi programs, you'll write code preventing the user from inputting invalid data, and this code will cause runtime errors. However, in many cases, you won't be able to prevent the user from doing something that causes runtime error. In complex applications, there are so many possibilities for creating runtime errors that your user will manage to create a runtime error.

In most cases, the error messages the program displays during runtime (when the program is executed as a regular Windows application) contain valuable information for the user, and most users are able to understand what they did wrong. In other words, the runtime error messages are not embarrassing to the developer, such as `Your code is invalid`. Nevertheless, always try to write code that examines whether the user entered valid data.

Q Do I need to enclose the statements after the `if` with `begin` and `end` as in the following?

```
if MyVariable = 3 then
begin
...
end;
```

A If you have only one statement after the `if` statement, you don't need the `begin` and `end`. However, if you have more than one statement after `if`, you do need the `begin` and `end`. Don't forget to place a semicolon after the `end`.

Some programmers think it's good practice to enclose the statements after the `if` statement with `begin` and `end` even if you have only one statement after `if`. Why? Because you may want to add another statement after `if` later. With the `begin` and `end` statements already there, all you have to do is add the additional statement between them.

Quiz

1. The `FindKey()` method is used to search for:

   a. Values in keyed fields.

   b. Values in keyed and non-keyed fields.

2. When using the `InputBox` function, the `Dialogs` keyword must be listed in the `uses` section at the beginning of the Pas file.

   a. True

   b. False

Exercises

1. Modify the SearchMe program so that when a record is found, the user receives a visual indication that the record was found.
2. Currently, the SearchMe.EXE program does not let the user enter Smith as the LastName of a record. However, the user can enter the name SMITH, SmItH, or any other combination of uppercase and lowercase characters. Modify the SearchMe program so it doesn't let the user enter the name smith as the LastName regardless of the capitalization.

Answers to Quiz

1. a.
2. a.

Answers to Exercises

1. Modify the cmdSearchClick procedure so that it appears as follows:

```
procedure TForm2.cmdSearchClick(Sender: TObject);

var
CustNumToSearchString: String;
ResultBoolean: Boolean;

begin

CustNumToSearchString :=
   InputBox ('Search',
            'Type the Customer Number to be searched:',
            '');

ResultBoolean := CustomerTable.FindKey([CustNumToSearchString]);

if not ResultBoolean then
   MessageDlg('Cannot find!',
              mtInformation,
              [mbOK],
              0);

if ResultBoolean then
   MessageDlg('Record found!',
              mtInformation,
              [mbOK],
              0);

end;
```

The code you typed after the `if` statement uses another `if` statement to display a message box telling the user that the record was found.

```
if ResultBoolean then
    MessageDlg('Record found!',
              mtInformation,
              [mbOK],
              0);
```

Alternatively, instead of using two `if` statements, you can use `if...else`.

2. The user's data in the `LastName` field is detected in the `CustomerTableBeforePost` procedure. Here is the code of the `CustomerTableBeforePost` procedure.

```
procedure TForm2.CustomerTableBeforePost(DataSet: TDataset);
begin

if CustomerTableLastName.Value = 'Smith' then
    begin
    MessageBeep(1);

    MessageDlg(
    'Inside CustomerTableBefore Post:' +
    'LastName Cannot be Smith!',
     mtInformation,
    [mbOK],
     0);

    end;

end;
```

Evidently, you have to modify the `if` statement. To do so, follow these steps:

☐ Select Search Topic from the Help menu of Delphi, and search for help on the UpperCase topic. As you enter the word `UpperCase`, you see the UpperCase topic.

☐ Display the `UpperCase` function's help window.

As you can see, the `UpperCase` function converts to uppercase the string supplied as its parameter. For example, after executing the following statement, the `MyVariableString` variable is equal to `MY COMPUTER`:

```
MyVariableString := UpperCase('My Computer');
```

Note: There are thousands of statements, functions, methods, and so on, in Delphi. It's unreasonable to expect you to remember all these things. Whenever you need to find the syntax of an operation you want to perform, the best source is the Delphi Help. No book or manual can supply you with more complete and accurate information as Delphi's Help feature can.

Now that you know about the UpperCase() function, modify the
CustomerTableLastNameValidate procedure so that it appears as follows:

```
procedure TForm2.CustomerTableLastNameValidate(Sender: TField);
begin

if UpperCase(CustomerTableLastName.Value) = 'SMITH' then
begin

MessageBeep(1);
raise Exception.Create('Cannot have LastName equal Smith');

end;

end;
```

The if statement now appears as follows:

```
if UpperCase(CustomerTableLastName.Value) = 'SMITH' then
begin
...
end;
```

The uppercase value of the LastName is compared with SMITH. If the user types SmItH as
the LastName field, the if statement detects it.

☐ Save the project.

☐ Use File Manager to execute the SearchMe.EXE program, and verify that you
cannot enter sMiTh as the LastName.

☐ Terminate the SearchMe.EXE program.

On Day 8, "Implementing Data-Entry Forms," you start applying the knowledge you acquired last week (Days 1 through 7) for creating a data-entry forms. A data-entry form is a form that enables the user to enter data into a table. Today, you learn about the DBText and DBEdit controls as well as how to search for sub-strings.

On Day 9, "Lookups and Lists," you learn more about how to use some Delphi controls that enable you to implement powerful data-entry forms. You learn about controls such as DBComboBox and DBLookupList. Referential Integrity is also discussed today.

On Day 10, "Queries and Ranges," you learn how to issue SQL statements—static and dynamic SQL statements. You also learn how to select a range of records.

On Day 11, "Multiple Forms and Printing Forms," you implement a project that is composed of several forms. You also learn about important topics, such as printing your forms and bookmarking.

On Day 12, "Graphics and Memos with Delphi," you implement programs that use Memo and Graphics fields. You implement an animation program that demonstrates how to move from record to record in a table from within the code of your program.

You can give users the sophisticated, state-of-the-art software they expect by adding sound capability to your Delphi programs. In addition to displaying a textual message that instructs your user to do something, your program also can play an audio message that says the same thing. On Day 13, "VBX and Sound in Your Delphi Program," you implement a program that demonstrates how to play WAV files (sound files) through the PC speaker (which every PC has) from within a Delphi program.

On Day 14, "Writing Multimedia Database Applications with Delphi (Part 1)," you learn how to create a multimedia application with Delphi. As you'll see, the MM.EXE program you implement enables the user to play movies, WAV sound files, and MIDI sound files. This application uses many of the database features you learned on previous days. You also use some new database features in the MM program. Due to the length of the MM program, its implementation is spread over two days (Day 14 and Day 15).

Implementing
Data-Entry Forms

In previous chapters, you learned about the basic programming building blocks of Delphi. You implemented a form (Form2) that displays table data in the form of a Grid control. However, when designing database applications with Delphi, you often don't let your user enter table data by using the Grid control. Grids are a very powerful and compact way to manage complex data, but they're often too complicated and too powerful for average users of your program to use safely. Rather, you implement forms to enable users to enter table data. What is a form? A form is a window resembling a regular paper form. A form is designed so the user can enter form data easily. Delphi is equipped with a variety of controls to help you design sophisticated forms.

The Clients Program

In this section, you design a program called Clients.EXE, which is a program used to enter new clients into a table called Clients.DB. This program also is used for viewing Clients.DB table data.

As usual, you first must create the Clients.DB table by using Database Desktop.

☐ Use Database Desktop to implement the Clients.DB table according to the information presented in Table 8.1. The Clients.DB Structure window is shown in Figure 8.1.

Table 8.1. The Clients.DB structure.

Field Name	Type	Size	Key
CustNum	Autoincrement	n/a	Yes
LastName	Alpha	30	No
FirstName	Alpha	20	No
Street	Alpha	40	No
City	Alpha	30	No
State	Alpha	10	No
Area Code	Alpha	3	No
Phone	Alpha	8	No

Depending on the particular database project you're developing, you may need additional fields in the Clients.DB table. For example, you may consider adding a Fax field, a MrMs field (a field indicating the customer's gender or title), and DateEntered field (a field indicating the date the customer was first entered into the Clients.DB table), as well as other fields that may be applicable to the particular project you're developing.

Figure 8.1.
The Clients.DB structure window.

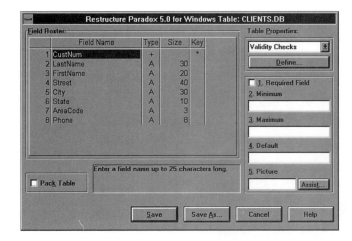

About the *CustNum* Field

The CustNum field is a numeric field that is incremented automatically whenever a new record is added to the Clients.DB table.

If you let the user insert the very first record of Clients.DB, the program automatically assigns the number 1 to the CustNum field. The second record assigned to CustNum is 2, and so on.

Typically, you want the CustNum to be a number with several digits. There are several reasons for this. For example, if a new company is established, you don't want your customer to know that he or she is customer number 1.

Also, it is useful for the Clients.DB table operator to get accustomed to the fact that the customer number is a number composed of, say, five digits.

Here's how you can force the program to start assigning customer numbers that have five digits.

☐ Using Database Desktop, display the Clients.DB table structure.

☐ Set the CustNum field Type to **Numeric**. You do this so you'll be able to edit the CustNum field. When the CustNum field is Autoincrement, you cannot edit it.

☐ Save the new Clients.DB structure.

☐ Display the Clients.DB table data (the Clients.DB table currently has no records in it).

☐ Place the Clients.DB table in Edit mode (from the View menu).

☐ Set the CustNum field in the first new record to **10000**.

☐ Move to a new empty row so that the new first record is saved. Then, without placing any data in the second record, move back to the first row.

☐ Restructure the Clients.DB table to its original structure. (Set the CustNum field to Autoincrement.)

Database Desktop prompts you with several dialog boxes because you restructured a table that has a record in it already.

☐ Save the new Clients.DB structure, and then terminate Database Desktop.

The next record added to the Clients.DB table is a record with CustNum equal to 10001, the next record will be 10002, and so on.

Do not think of CustNum as a counter that counts the number of records in the Clients.DB table.

For example, suppose that a new record was added to Clients.DB, and the program automatically assigned the number 10500 to the CustNum field. After adding many more records to the Clients.DB table (where, for example, a new record is now assigned with CustNum equal to 20000), the Clients.DB table operator decides to delete the record with CustNum 10500 from the Clients.DB table. Nevertheless, the next record that will be added to Clients.DB is one with CustNum equal to 20001. CustNum 10500 can never be used again unless you use the same trick discussed earlier. That is, you must temporarily set the CustNum field Type to **Numeric**. However, this trick is not recommended because when the table has many records in it already, such an operation can adversely affect the table.

The bottom line is that CustNum cannot serve as a counter to indicate the number of records in Clients.DB. As discussed in previous chapters, CustNum serves as a field that assigns unique values to each record in Clients.DB.

Creating the Clients Project

Now that the Clients.DB table is ready, you can start implementing the Clients.EXE program.

Note: As you see during the implementation of the Clients.EXE program, a significant part of your development time will be spent on the cosmetic aspects of the program. In fact, due to the powerful data controls that Delphi offers, you must write only a small amount of code for this project.

The cosmetic aspects of the program are very important. The advantage of using Delphi is that you can modify the appearance of the form at any time.

Typically, you must listen to complaints, suggestions, and recommendations from your program's users, and then modify the form accordingly.

Nevertheless, don't fall into the trap of spending too much time on the cosmetic aspects of your forms. Your form serves as a vital tool for displaying and receiving data from the users of the Clients.DB table. The form you design is not intended to entertain your users.

To design a form without using Database Form Expert, do the following:

☐ Start Delphi.

☐ Select New Project from the File menu.

When creating a new project, Delphi automatically places an empty form called Form1 in the new project.

☐ Select the Form1 form, select Save File As from the File menu, and save the file as CClients.Pas in the C:\DProg\Ch08 directory.

☐ Select Save Project As from the File menu and save the project file as Clients.Dpr in the C:\DProg\Ch08 directory.

Next, you place controls in the form so that it appears as shown in Figure 8.2.

Figure 8.2.
The frmClients form.

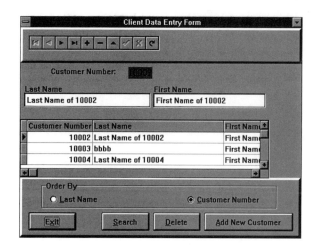

☐ Modify the Name property of Form1 to be **frmClients**.

☐ Set the Caption property of frmClients to **Client Data Entry Form**.

Delphi's Standard page includes the Panel icon, as shown in Figure 8.3.

Figure 8.3.

The Panel icon on the
Standard page.

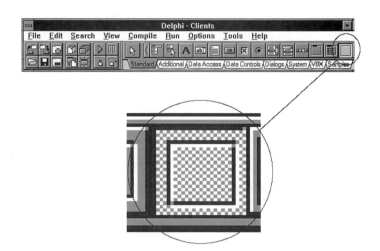

☐ Place a `Panel` control in the `frmClients` form, and set its properties as follows:

```
Name      pnlTop
Caption   Make it empty
Align     alTop
```

Setting the `Panel` control's `Align` property to `alTop` causes Delphi to place the panel at the top of the `frmClients` form.

When designing forms, you'll spend time on the cosmetic aspects of the form. Although the `frmClients` form will work well with or without the `Panel` controls, by including `Panel` controls and then placing controls on the `Panel` controls, you make your forms easier to work with.

☐ Set the `BevelWidth` property of the `pnlTop` `Panel` control to **4**.

The `BevelWidth` property determines the amount of 3D effect that the control has.

☐ Place another `Panel` control from the Standard page in the `frmClients` form, and set its properties as follows:

```
Name         pnlBottom
Caption      Make it empty
Align        alBottom
BevelWidth   4
```

When setting the `Align` properties to `alTop` or `alBottom`, the control's width is automatically adjusted to the width of the `frmClients` form. If, during the implementation of the `frmClients` form, you need to enlarge the form's size, the `Panel` controls adjust themselves automatically.

Implementing the Exit Button

Implement the Exit button as shown in Figure 8.2.

☐ Place a `Pushbutton` control on the `pnlBottom Panel` control, and set the properties of the `Pushbutton` control as follows:

```
Name        cmdExit
Caption     E&xit
```

You can spend as much time as you want on the cosmetic aspects of the form. For example, you can set the `Font` properties of the `cmdExit` button to a different font and different size.

☐ Attach code to the `OnClick` event of the `cmdExit` button.

After attaching the code, the `cmdExitClick` procedure should appear as follows:

```
procedure TfrmClients.cmdExitClick(Sender: TObject);
begin

Close;

end;
```

The code you typed closes the `frmClients` form. In previous chapters, you wrote code that terminates the program as follows:

```
Application.Terminate;
```

However, you just now wrote code that terminates the application by closing the form. The main and only project form is the `frmClients` form. Closing this form terminates the application.

All your database projects usually will be concentrated in a single project. For example, when starting the database program you're developing, your user sees a main form that has several buttons on it. One of the buttons is the Clients Data Entry Form button. Another button is the Parts Data Entry Form, another is Print Invoices, and so on.

Clicking the Clients Data Entry Form button causes the a form such as `frmClients` to appear, and so the user now can access the Clients.DB table. When the user clicks the Exit button, the application does not terminate. Rather, the `frmClients` form is closed, and the user sees the main form of the project again.

Placing *Table* and *DataSource* Components and a *DBGrid* Control in the Form

First, you place a `Table` component and a `DataSource` component in the `frmClients` form. Instead of using the Database Form Expert, place these components manually.

☐ Place a `Table` component from the Data Access page on the upper `Panel` control.

☐ Set the properties of the `Table` component as follows:

```
Name            ClientsTable
DatabaseName    MYWORK (or C:\DProg\Work)
TableName       Clients.DB
```

The `Table` component is now set to the Clients.DB table.

☐ Place a `DataSource` component from the Data Access page on the upper `Panel` control.

☐ Set the properties of the `DataSource` component as follows:

```
Name            ClientsDataSource
DatabaseName    MYWORK (or C:\DProg\Work)
TableName       Clients.DB
DataSet         ClientsTable
```

The `DataSource` component is now set to the Clients.DB table.

☐ Place a `DBGrid` control from the Data Controls page in the `frmClients` form (not on any of the `Panel` controls).

☐ Set the properties of the `DBGrid` control as follows:

```
Name          DBGridClients
DataSource    ClientsDataSource
ReadOnly      True
```

The `ReadOnly` property of `DBGridClients` is set to `True` because you don't want the user to be able to access the Clients.DB table by modifying `DBGrid` control data. The only reason you placed the `Grid` control in the form is so that the user can see the Clients.DB table records one after the other.

☐ Set the `ClientsTable` Table control `Active` property to `True` so that you are able to see the Clients.DB data during design time.

Placing a *DBText* Control in the Form

One of the icons on the Data Controls page of Delphi is the `DBText` control icon (see Figure 8.4).

The `DBText` control resembles the Standard page `Label` control. The user can't type anything in the `DBText` control. What will the contents of the `DBText` control be? You're going to set the properties of the `DBText` control so it displays the Clients.DB table `CustNum` field contents.

Figure 8.4.

The DBText *control icon on the Data Controls page.*

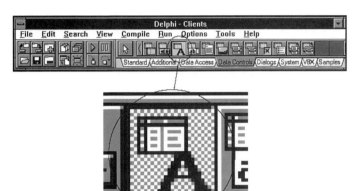

☐ Place a DBText control from the Data Controls page in the frmClients form.

☐ Set the properties of the DBText control as follows:

```
Name         DBTextCustNum
DataSource   ClientsDataSource
DataField    CustNum
Alignment    taCenter
AutoSize     True
```

When setting the DBText control's AutoSize property to True, the control size is automatically adjusted so that it perfectly encloses the text displayed by the control.

Now the DBTextCustNum control is connected to the Clients.DB table CustNum field. The user cannot type into the DBText control. This is the nature of this control. You're displaying the value of the CustNum field of the Clients.DB table's current record. It's appropriate not to allow the user edit the CustNum field because this field is of type Autoincrement. Whenever a new record is added to the Clients.DB table, the CustNum field should be filled automatically. The user has no security rights to modify the field contents.

☐ For cosmetic reasons, set the Color property of the DBTextCustNum to **clRed**, and set the Font property to a different font and font size.

☐ Place a Label control from the Standard page to the left of the DBTextCustNum control.

☐ Set the properties of the Label control that you just placed as follows:

```
Name      lblCustNum
Caption   Customer Number:
```

The *FormCreate* Procedure

Recall that whenever you used the Database Form Expert, the Form2 form was created and code was written in the FormCreate procedure.

Because you are not using Database From Expert right now, you must write the code in the FormCreate procedure yourself.

☐ Attach code to the OnCreate event of the frmClients form.

After attaching the code, the FormCreate procedure should appear as follows:

```
procedure TfrmClients.FormCreate(Sender: TObject);
begin

ClientsTable.Open;

end;
```

Upon creating the frmClients form, the Clients.DB table is opened.

Placing a *Navigator* Control on the Top Panel

To place a Navigator control on the top panel, follow these steps.

☐ Place a DBNavigator control from the Data Controls page on the top panel.

☐ Set the properties of the Navigator control as follows:

Name	DBNavigator Clients
DataSource	ClientsDataSource

Now the Navigator control is set so that clicking its button causes the proper navigation in the Clients.DB table.

Other Cosmetics Aspects

As you can see from the Object Inspector window, there is a lot more you can do to the form in terms of cosmetics.

For example, you can expand the BorderIcons property of the frmClients form and set the biMaximize property to False so that, during runtime, the user cannot maximize the program

window. You also can select the frmClients form's Icon property and set the application icon to any ICO file. This way, when the user minimizes the application window, the icon you selected is displayed.

Although you haven't finished implementing the Clients.EXE program, execute it to be sure that everything works so far.

☐ Select Save Project from the File menu.

To see the Clients program in action, you need a few records in Clients.DB.

☐ Use Database Desktop to add records to the Clients.DB table. Don't forget to set the Clients Table control Active property to False before starting Database Desktop program.

> **Note:** During the development of your Delphi program, you need to work with tables that contain data. When entering data to the tables, you can, of course, enter any fictitious data you like, but you may find it helpful to enter data, such as the following:
>
> | CustNum | LastName | FirstName |
> |---------|----------|-----------|
> | 10000 | Last Name of 10000 | First Name of 10000 |
> | 10001 | Last Name of 10001 | First Name of 10001 |
> | 10002 | Last Name of 10002 | First Name of 10002 |
> | 10003 | Last Name of 10003 | First Name of 10003 |
>
> Using data like this, you'll be able to tell that the program is working correctly as you develop it. For example, in the LastName field of record 10002 you expect to see the data Last Name of 100024, and so on.
>
> Of course, if you prefer, you can enter real names to the Clients.DB table.
>
> To save time, you can enter names such as bbb, ccc, and so on.

☐ Terminate the Database Desktop program.

☐ Execute the Clients program.

The Clients program window appears, as shown in Figure 8.5.

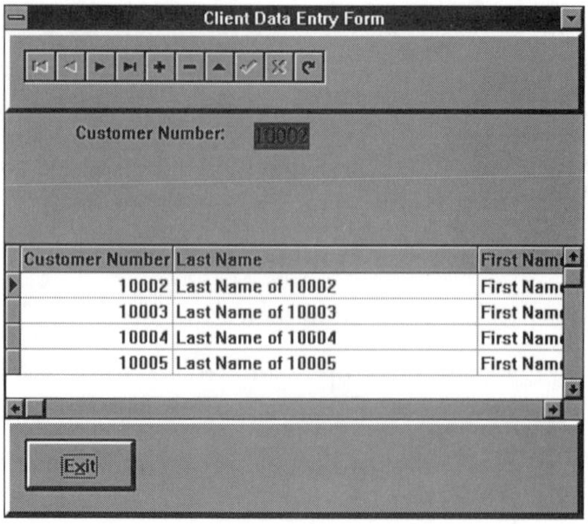

Figure 8.5.

The Clients program window with the DBText control in it.

☐ Verify that the DBTextCustNum control cannot be edited (this is the nature of this control). Also verify that you cannot edit data by using the DBGrid control (because you set the Grid control's ReadOnly property to True).

In fact, in the Clients program's current status, you cannot edit any data in the Clients.DB table.

☐ Verify that as you move from record to record, the DBTextCustNum control displays the CustNum field value.

☐ Experiment with the Clients program, and then click its Exit button to terminate it.

Placing *DBEdit* Controls in the Form

At this point in the program's development, the user cannot edit any of Clients.DB table's fields.

Place two DBEdit controls in the frmClients form. These controls let the user edit the Clients.DB table's LastName and FirstName fields.

☐ Place a DBEdit control from the Data Controls page in the frmClients form. The DBEdit control icon on the Data controls page is shown in Figure 8.6.

☐ Set the properties of the DBEdit control as follows:

```
Name         DBEditLastName
DataSource   ClientsDataSource
DataField    LastName
```

Figure 8.6.

The DBEdit icon on the Data Controls page.

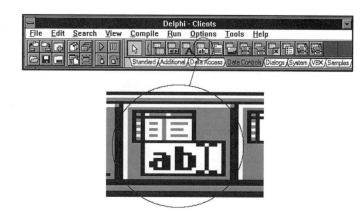

The DBEdit control is an editbox that lets you enter data in it. You set the control's DataSource property to ClientsDataSource and the DataField property to LastName. This means that whatever you type in the editbox goes directly to the LastName field in the Clients.DB table's current record. This control displays its corresponding field's data in the current record.

During runtime, the user doesn't know that the DBEditLastName control is set as the Clients.DB table's LastName field, and so you must place a Label control explaining to the user the purpose of this editbox.

☐ Place a Label control from the Standard page in the frmClients form, and place the label above the DBEditLastName control.

☐ Set the properties of the Label control as follows:

```
Name        lblLastName
Caption     Last Name
```

You now place a second DBEdit control in the frmClients form. This DBEdit control serves as the place to edit or view the Clients.DB table's FirstName field.

```
Name        DBEditFirstName
DataSource  ClientsDataSource
DataField   FirstName
```

DBEditFirstName is now set to hold the FirstName field of the Clients.DB table.

☐ Place a Label control from the Standard page above the DBEditFirstName control, and set its properties as follows:

```
Name        lblFirstName
Caption     FirstName
```

The `frmClients` form should now appear as shown in Figure 8.7.

Figure 8.7.

The `frmClients` *form with the two* `DBEdit` *controls in it (design mode).*

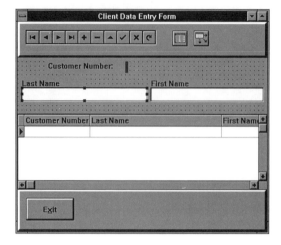

Although you haven't finished writing the Clients program, execute it now.

☐ Select Save Project from the File menu.

☐ Execute the Clients program.

The Clients program window appears, as shown in Figure 8.8.

Figure 8.8.

The Clients program with the Last Name and First Name ready to be edited.

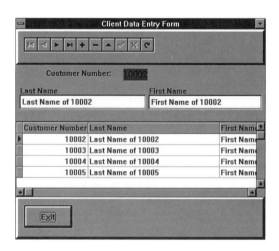

☐ Use the `Navigator` control to move from record to record.

As you move from record to record, the Customer Number DBText control displays the current record's customer number, and the DBEdit controls display the current record's Last Name and First Name.

Add a new record to the Clients.DB table as follows:

☐ Click in the DBEditLastName control, and then click the Insert button on the Navigator control. This is the button with the plus sign (+) on it.

> *The Clients program responds by displaying the window shown in Figure 8.9. As you can see in the figure, the Customer Number DBText control has no value in it, and the Last Name and First Name DBEdit controls have no data in them.*

Figure 8.9.

Adding a new record to the Clients.DB table.

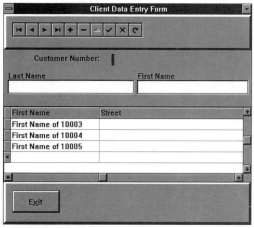

☐ Fill the Last Name Edit control with **Anderson**.

☐ Click the First Name Edit control, and type **Jean**.

☐ Move to another record. For example, click the Navigator control's Next button.

Once you move to another record or click the Post button on the Navigator control, the Clients program accepts the new record, and a customer number is assigned to the new record.

☐ Experiment with the Clients program. Add records; use the Navigator control's Delete button to delete records; and move from record to record.

☐ Terminate the Clients program by clicking its Exit button.

User Interface Considerations

Is the Clients program easy to use? This depends on the way the users are trained. As you can see, the Clients program in its present form depends heavily on the Navigator control.

You can make the Clients program easier to use by not depending on the Navigator control. We'll demonstrate how you do that by placing two buttons in the frmClients form that have the identical functionality as two buttons of the Navigator control.

Implementing the Insert Record Button in the *frmClients* Form

You'll now place the Insert button, a pushbutton serving the exact function as the plus-sign (+) button of the Navigator control.

☐ Place a pushbutton from the Standard page in the bottom Panel control.

☐ Set the properties of the button as follows:

```
Name       cmdNewCustomer
Caption    &Add New Customer
```

The frmClients form should now appear as shown in Figure 8.10.

Figure 8.10.
The frmClients *form with the Add New Customer button.*

☐ Attach code to the OnClick event of the cmdNewCustomer button. After attaching the code, the cmdAddCustomerClick procedure should appear as follows:

```
procedure TfrmClients.cmdNewCustomerClick(Sender: TObject);
begin

ClientsTable.Edit;
ClientsTable.Insert;

end;
```

The code you typed has the same effect as clicking the Insert button of the `Navigator` control.

☐ Select Save Project from the File menu.

☐ Execute the Clients program.

☐ Click the Add New Customer button.

☐ Click in the Last Name editbox, and type a last name. Click in the First Name editbox and type a first name.

☐ Move to another record.

As you can see, a new customer number was assigned to the new record.

☐ Experiment with the Clients program, and then click its Exit button to terminate it.

> **Note:** You should make your programs easy to use, but don't fall into the trap of helping the user too much. That is, sometimes, programmers fall into the trap of adding more complexity to their programs in an attempt to make the program easy to use. Don't forget: Your users are Windows users. A basic understanding of how Windows programs work is expected from your users.

Place a pushbutton in the `frmClients` form to emulate the Delete button of the `Navigator` control.

☐ Place a pushbutton in the bottom `Panel` control of the `frmClients` form.

☐ Set the properties of the pushbutton as follows:

```
Name       cmdDelete
Caption    &Delete
```

The `frmClients` form with the Delete button is shown in Figure 8.11.

Figure 8.11.

The frmClients *form with the Delete button (design mode).*

☐ Attach code to the cmdDelete button's OnClick event.

After attaching the code, the cmdDeleteClick procedure should appear as follows:

```
procedure TfrmClients.cmdDeleteClick(Sender: TObject);
begin

ClientsTable.Edit;
ClientsTable.Delete;

end;
```

The code you typed places the table in Edit mode, and then the current record is deleted.

☐ Save the project, execute the program, and experiment with the Delete button.

☐ Click the Exit button to terminate the program.

If you decide that your program should include additional pushbuttons that emulate the Navigator control, you must make your form larger so there is free space where you can place the pushbuttons.

Ordering the Table

In some applications, when the user enters a new customer to Clients.DB, the user has to do some checking before adding the new customer. For example, the user may want to check if this customer already has a customer number.

Right now, however, the Clients.DB table is ordered by the CustNum field. If the Clients.DB table has 1,000 records in it, it's unreasonable to expect the user to scroll through hundreds of records and search to see if the new customer already has a record.

This means that your form needs to provide the user with a mechanism for ordering the table by the LastName field. Using this mechanism, your user can order the table by the LastName field and scroll the records in the grid. Also, because the records are ordered by the LastName field, the user can easily tell whether the new customer already has a record in the Clients.DB table.

Use the following steps to implement a mechanism by which the user can order the Clients table by different fields.

☐ Enlarge the area of the bottom Panel control. You're going to place a RadioGroup control in the bottom Panel control. The RadioGroup control icon on the Standard page is shown in Figure 8.12.

Figure 8.12.
The RadioGroup *control icon on the Standard page.*

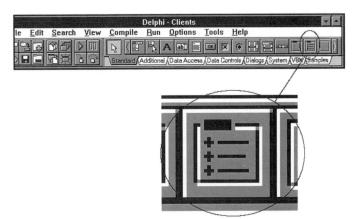

☐ Place a RadioGroup control from the Standard page in the bottom panel, and set its properties as follows:

```
Name      radOrderBy
Caption   Order By
```

Place two RadioButton controls from the Standard page in the RadioGroup control.

☐ Place two radio buttons from the Standard page in the RadioGroup control.

☐ Set the properties of the two radio buttons as follows:

```
Name      optLastName
Caption   &Last Name
Checked   False

Name      optCustNum
Caption   &Customer Number
Check     True
```

After placing the two RadioButton controls, the frmClients should look like the one shown in Figure 8.13.

Figure 8.13.

The frmClients form ordered by radio buttons.

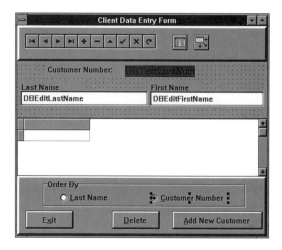

Before writing additional code, execute the Clients program to verify that everything works so far.

☐ Select Save project from the File menu.

☐ Execute the Clients program.

☐ Click the radio buttons, and note that without writing any code, the radio buttons' check status changes. If you click the Customer Number radio button, the Last Name radio button becomes unchecked, and the Customer Number radio button becomes checked. If you then click the Last Name radio button, the Customer Number radio button becomes unchecked, and the Last Name radio button becomes checked.

☐ Terminate the Clients program by clicking its Exit button.

As you saw in the preceding steps, there is no need to write code that toggles the radio buttons' state.

A Secondary Index for the *LastName* Field

The Clients.DB table is ordered by the CustNum field because the CustNum field is the first field in the Clients.DB structure, and this field is a key field. To be able to order the Clients.DB table by the LastName field, you must first create a secondary index for the LastName field.

☐ Use Database Desktop to create a secondary index for the LastName field of the Clients.DB table. If you forgot how to create a secondary index, refer to Chapter 6, "Linking Tables." When saving the secondary index, save it as **ByLastName**.

Attaching Code to the *OnClick* Events of the Radio Buttons

To attach code to the OnClick events of the radio buttons, follow these steps.

☐ Attach code to the OnClick event of the optLastName radio button. After attaching the code, the optLastNameClick procedure should appear as follows:

```
procedure TfrmClients.optLastNameClick(Sender: TObject);
begin

ClientsTable.IndexName := 'ByLastName';
ClientsTable.Refresh;

end;
```

The code you typed sets the IndexName property to ByLastName, and then the Refresh method is executed so the user can see that the table is indeed ordered according to the LastName field.

☐ Attach code to the OnClick event of the optCustNum radio button. After attaching the code, the optCustNumClick procedure should appear as follows:

```
procedure TfrmClients.optCustNumClick(Sender: TObject);
begin

ClientsTable.IndexName := '';
ClientsTable.Refresh;

end;
```

The code you typed sets the IndexName property to the primary field (CustNum), and then the Refresh method is executed so the user can see that the table is indeed ordered according to the CustNum field. When setting the IndexName as null, the table is ordered according to the primary field.

☐ Select Save Project from the File menu.

☐ Execute the Clients program.

☐ Experiment with the Last Name button and the Customer Number button. Note that when the Customer Numberbutton is selected, the table is ordered by the CustNum field, and when the Last Name button is selected, the table is ordered by the LastName field.

☐ Terminate the Clients program by clicking its Exit button.

Attaching a Search Button

You should never forget that your program may be used with a table that has hundreds of thousands of records in it. Suppose that your Clients.DB table has 100,000 records in it. Do you expect the user to scroll through them to find a particular last name? Of course not. This is why you should implement a Search button that enables the user to search for a record.

☐ Place a pushbutton in the bottom Panel control.

☐ Set the properties of the pushbutton as follows:

```
Name      cmdSearch
Caption   &Search
```

☐ Attach code to the OnClick event of the cmdSearch button.

After attaching the code, the cmdSearchClick procedure should appear as follows:

```
procedure TfrmClients.cmdSearchClick(Sender: TObject);
var
ClientLastNameString: String;

begin

ClientsTable.IndexName := 'ByLastName';

ClientLastNameString :=
   InputBox ('Search',
            'Type the Customer Last Name to be searched:',
            '');

ClientsTable.FindNearest([ClientLastNameString]);

if optCustNum.Checked = True then
   begin
   ClientsTable.IndexName := '';
   ClientsTable.Refresh;
   end;

end;
```

The code you typed declares a local variable.

```
var
ClientLastNameString: String;
```

The code then sets the ClientsTable IndexName property as follows:

```
ClientsTable.IndexName := 'ByLastName';
```

This means that the Clients.DB table is now ordered by the LastName field, and you can perform a search by the LastName field.

An InputBox is displayed to the user.

```
ClientLastNameString :=
   InputBox ('Search',
             'Type the Customer Last Name to be searched:',
             '');
```

The InputBox asks the user to type the last name to be located. Recall that you must include `Dialogs` in the uses section at the beginning of the Pas file.

The search is performed using `FindNearest()`.

```
ClientsTable.FindNearest([ClientLastNameString]);
```

`FindNearest()` lets you search for a portion of a string, and capitalization is not important. If the Clients.DB table includes a record with `LastName Anderson`, a search for `Ander` will be successful. That is, if `FindNearest()` fails to find a record whose `LastName` field is `Ander`, the search continues, and because `Ander` is a substring of `Anderson`, the search will be successful.

At the beginning of this procedure, you set the `Table` control's `IndexName` property to `ByLastName` because you needed to perform a search by the `LastName` field. Now that the search is completed, you need to set the `IndexName` property according to the status of the option buttons. You accomplish this with the following `if` statement:

```
if optCustNum.Checked = True then
   begin
   ClientsTable.IndexName := '';
   ClientsTable.Refresh;
   end;
```

If the Customer Number radio button is currently selected, you must return the order to the primary index as follows:

```
ClientsTable.IndexName := '';
ClientsTable.Refresh;
```

However, if the Last Name radio button is currently selected, it means that the Clients.DB table is ordered by the `LastName` field, and so there is no need to set the `IndexName` property because it is already set to `ByLastName`.

Summary

In this chapter, you implemented a form used for displaying the Clients.DB table. The user can insert new records to the table, delete records from the table, and search for records in the table.

As you saw in this chapter, you can let the user use the `Navigator` control, and you can implement custom-made buttons that emulate the `Navigator` control buttons.

You also used the `DBText` and `DBEdit` controls to edit and view fields from the Clients.DB table.

Q&A

Q The first record of the Clients.DB table was set to 10000. This means that the last record with five digits is 99999. Should I use five digits for the CustNum field, four digits, or maybe six digits?

A It depends on the particular applications you're developing. As stated in this chapter, the purpose the CustNum field serves is for each customer to have a unique customer number. You cannot use CustNum as the counter of the Clients.DB table.

There is, however, one additional purpose that CustNum can serve: it indicates the order by which the records were entered into the Clients.DB table. For example, record 33000 was entered after record 22000 because CustNum is a field of type Autoincrement.

Some companies take advantage of the Autoincrement nature of the CustNum field and start a new sequence of CustNum every year. For example, if on January 1, 1996, the CustNum field is set to 9610000, on January 1, 1997, the CustNum field is set to 9710000, and so on, you can determine the year in which a customer was entered to the table simply by examining the customer number.

Q The Search mechanism of the Clients program uses the FindNearest procedure (not the FindKey() that was used in Chapter 7, "Searching For and Validating Data"). Why?

A When searching with FindKey(), the search is performed by comparing the record's field contents with the parameter supplied to FindKey(). FindKey() returns True provided that the string matches the field value. If you have a field with the value Robin in it, for instance, the search for Robi with FindKey(['Robi'] will not yield a successful match.

The Clients.DB could have many records in it. The user can search, for example, for r (or R), and if there are any records that have a LastName field starting with the characters r or R, FindNearest() places the current record at the first record whose LastName field starts with r or R. The user can then proceed with the search by scrolling the Grid control.

Similarly, the user can search for Ro, and the FindNearest() places the current record at the first record whose LastName field starts with the characters ro.

In fact, you can place a series of pushbuttons. The leftmost button has the caption A on it. The next button will be a button with the caption B, and so on. When the user clicks the A button, the following code is executed:

```
ClientsTable.FindNearest(['a']);
```

When the user clicks the B button, the following code is executed, and so on:

```
ClientsTable.FindNearest(['b']);
```

This is a way to immediately place the current record position at the records that start with the character the user clicks.

Quiz

1. The DBText control is used for _____.

2. Placing a DBEdit control and setting its ReadOnly property to False has the same effect as placing a DBText control:

   a. True.

   b. False.

Exercises

1. The Clients program lets the user edit only the LastName and the FirstName fields. Enhance the program so that it also lets the user edit the City field.

2. Currently, the Clients program lets the user use the Delete and the Add New Customer buttons. How do you remove the Navigator control?

Answers to Quiz

1. The DBText control is used for displaying a field value that you don't want the user to be able to edit.

2. a.

Answers to Exercises

1. To complete the frmClients form, you must add more DBEdit controls, one for each of the remaining fields. For example, to be able to edit the City field, you must do the following:

   ☐ Enlarge the size of the frmClients form so there is free space in which to place additional controls.

   ☐ Place a DBEdit control in the frmClients form.

   ☐ Set the following properties for the DBEdit control you just placed:

   ```
   Name        DBEditCity
   DataSource  ClientsDataSource
   DataField   City
   ```

☐ Place a Label control from the Standard page above the DBEditCity control, and set its properties as follows:

Name	lblCity
Caption	City

If you think you need the practice, place DBEdit controls for the other fields as well.

2. You don't have to remove the Navigator control. You simply can make its Visible property equal to False. If you really dislike the Navigator control, you can delete it from the form.

Alternatively, you can implement a checkbox from the Standard page that has the following properties:

Name	chkWithNavigator
Caption	&With Navigator

You then can attach code to the OnClick event of the checkbox that determines the Check property of the checkbox. If the Check property of the checkbox is equal to True, set the Navigator control's Visible property to True.

If the checkbox Check property is equal to False, set the Navigator control's Visible property to False.

If you remove the Navigator control from the form, you must implement your own custom buttons allowing the user to perform the same operations that the Navigator control performs (for example, Next, Previous, Delete, and so on).

9

Lookups and Lists

In the previous chapter, you learned how to create a data-entry form, a form that enables the user to enter data into the Clients.DB table. In this chapter, you learn about lists and lookup tables as well as how to incorporate them into your data-entry forms.

Lists and Lookup Tables

There are two ways to save the user the trouble of typing.

- By using lists
- By using lookup tables

You want to save the user the trouble of typing because this makes the process of entering data to the data-entry form easier. Furthermore, if the user selects the data (from a list, for example), the user cannot make typing errors.

The MyList Program

The MyList.EXE program demonstrates how a list is used in a data-entry form.

Let's say that the Clients.DB table includes the `ClientType` field. This field can contain one of the following values:

```
Company
Individual
Government
```

When creating a record for the customer in the Clients.DB table, the `ClientType` field is filled with one of these three client types. Of course, there are other possible client types, such as School, City, State, and so on. The data-entry form you're creating must provide the user with a list of common client types that are appropriate to the particular application you're developing. The list should contain only the most likely client types. When entering the client type data, the user simply selects the appropriate item from a list. Nevertheless, your data-entry form also should enable the user to type the client type if it does not appear in the pre-prepared list.

☐ Use Database Desktop to add the `ClientType` field to the Clients.DB table as follows:

```
Field Name    ClientType
Type          Alpha
Size          10
Key           No
```

After adding this field, the Clients.DB table structure should be as shown in Table 9.1 (see Figure 9.1).

☐ Terminate the Database Desktop program.

Table 9.1. The structure of the Clients.DB table.

Field Name	Type	Size	Key
CustNum	Autoincrement	n/a	Yes
LastName	Alpha	30	No
FirstName	Alpha	20	No
Street	Alpha	40	No
City	Alpha	30	No
State	Alpha	10	No
AreaCode	Alpha	3	No
Phone	Alpha	8	No
ZipCode	Alpha	5	No
ClientType	Alpha	10	No

Figure 9.1.
The Clients.DB structure of after adding the `ClientType` *field.*

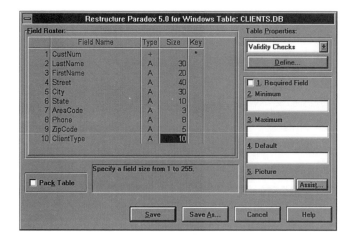

Creating the MyList Project

Create the MyList project by following these steps:

☐ Start Delphi.

☐ Select New Project from the File menu.

☐ Select the `Form1` form, select Save File As from the File menu, and save the file as CMyList.Pas in the C:\DProg\Ch09 directory.

☐ Select Save Project As from the File menu, and save the project file as MyList.Dpr in the C:\DProg\CH09 directory.

☐ Set the Form1 properties as follows:

```
Name      frmMyList
Caption   The MyList Program
```

The table you use in the MyList program is the Clients.DB table.

☐ Place a Table control from the Data Access page in the frmMyList form.

☐ Set the Table control properties as follows:

```
Name           ClientsTable
DatabaseName   MYWORK (or C:\Dprog\Work)
TableName      Clients.DB
```

☐ Place a DataSource control from the Data Access page in the frmMyList form.

☐ Set the DataSource control properties as follows:

```
Name      ClientsDataSource
DataSet   ClientsTable
```

☐ Place a Navigator control from the Data Controls page in the frmMyList form.

☐ Set the Navigator control properties as follows:

```
Name         ClientsNavigator
DataSource   ClientsDataSource
```

Placing *DBEdit* Controls in the Form

Place the two DBEdit controls shown in Figure 9.2 in the frmMyList form.

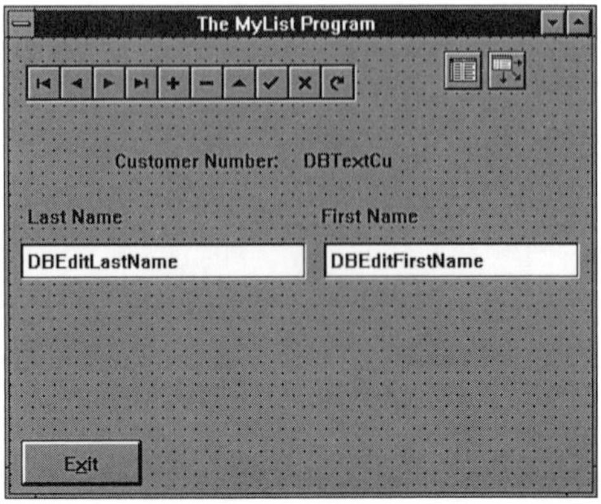

Figure 9.2.

The frmMyList form with two DBEdit controls and one DBText control in it (design mode).

☐ Place a DBEdit control from the Data Controls page in the frmMyList form, and set its properties as follows:

Name	DBEditLastName
DataSource	ClientsDataSource
DataField	LastName

☐ Place a Label control from the Standard page above the DBEditLastName control, and set the Label control properties as follows:

Name	lblLastName
Caption	Last Name

☐ Place a DBEdit control from the Data Controls page in the frmMyList form, and set its properties as follows:

Name	DBEditFirstName
DataSource	ClientsDataSource
DataField	FirstName

☐ Place a Label control from the Standard page above the DBEditFirstName control, and set the Label control properties as follows:

Name	lblFirstName
Caption	First Name

Placing a *DBText* Control in the Form

Place a DBText control in the frmMyList form, as shown in Figure 9.2.

☐ Place a DBText control from the Data Controls page in the frmMyList form, and set its properties as follows:

Name	DBTextCustNum
DataSource	ClientsDataSource
DataField	CustNum

☐ Place a Label control from the Standard page to the left of the DBTextCustNum control, and set the Label control properties as follows:

Name	lblCustNum
Caption	Customer Number

The *FormCreate* Procedure

Now add the code that opens the Clients.DB table in the `FormCreate` procedure.

☐ Add the following code to the `FormCreate` procedure:

```
procedure TfrmMyList.FormCreate(Sender: TObject);
begin

ClientsTable.Open;

end;
```

Implementing an Exit Button

Implement the Exit button of the `frmMyList` form.

☐ Place a pushbutton from the Standard page in the `frmMyList` form, and set the pushbutton properties as follows:

```
Name      cmdExit
Caption   E&xit
```

☐ Attach code to the `OnClick` event of the `cmdExit` button.

After attaching the code, the `cmdExitClick` procedure should appear as follows:

```
procedure TfrmMyList.smdExitClick(Sender: TObject);
begin

frmMyList.Close;

end;
```

☐ Select Save Project from the File menu.

☐ Execute the MyList program.

The MyList program window appears as shown in Figure 9.3.

☐ Experiment with the MyList program. For example, use the `Navigator` control to move from record to record, and note that the `DBText` and `DBEdit` controls display the values of the different records of the Clients.DB table.

☐ Click the Exit button to terminate the MyList program.

Figure 9.3.
The MyList program with its DBText *and* DBEdit *controls.*

Placing a *DBText* Control for the *ClientType* Field

Place in the frmMyList form a DBText control that holds the ClientType field data.

☐ Place a DBText control from the Data Controls page in the frmMyList form.

☐ Set the DBText control properties as follows:

```
Name        DBTextClientType
DataSource  ClientsDataSource
DataField   ClientType
```

☐ Place a Label control from the Standard page to the left of the DBTextClientType control, and set the Label control properties as follows:

```
Name     lblClientType
Caption  Client Type:
```

Your frmMyList form should now appear as shown in Figure 9.4.

Figure 9.4.

The frmMyList *from with the* DBTextClientType *control (design mode).*

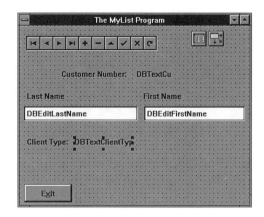

Placing a *DBComboBox* Control in the Form

In the previous step, you placed a DBText control for the ClientType field (not a DBEdit control). Why? Because you don't want the user to type the client type. Instead, you want the user to select the client type from a pre-prepared list.

☐ Place a DBComboBox control from the Data Controls page in the frmMyList form. The icon DBComboBox control in the Data Controls page is shown in Figure 9.5.

Figure 9.5.

The DBComboBox *control icon in the Data Controls page.*

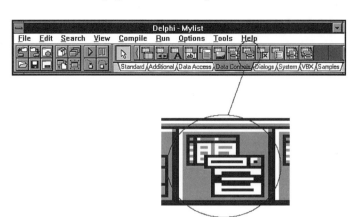

☐ Set the properties of the DBComboBox control as follows:

```
Name        DBComboBoxClientType
DataSource  ClientsDataSource
DataField   ClientType
```

The `frmMyList` form should now appear as shown in Figure 9.6.

Figure 9.6.
The `frmMyList` with the `DBComboBox` control (design mode).

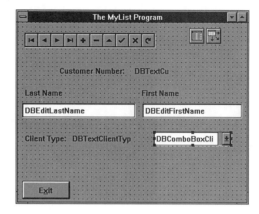

☐ Select Save Project from the File menu.

☐ Execute the MyList program.

The MyList window appears.

☐ Click the down-arrow icon that appears to the right of the `DBComboBox` control.

As shown in Figure 9.7, a list drops down, but it's empty because you have not yet prepared the list.

Figure 9.7.
The MyList program with the `DBComboBoxClientType` control in it.

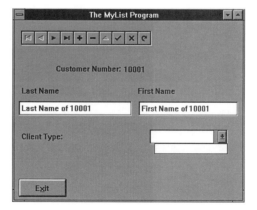

Later in this chapter, you add items to the `DBComboBox` control list. In the meantime, you can type a value in the combobox. That is, the `DBComboBox` enables the user either to select an item from the dropdown list or to type a value in the combobox.

☐ Type **General** in the combobox, and then click the Navigator control's Refresh button.

As you can see, the DBTextClientType control now displays the value General. In other words, whatever you typed in the combobox was assigned to the ClientType field of the current record in the Clients.DB table.

☐ Experiment with the DBComboBoxClientType, and then click the Exit button to terminate the MyList program.

Adding a List to the *DBComboBox* Control

In the previous section, the DBComboBox control didn't have any items in it. Now you need to add items to the DBComboBox control list.

☐ In the Object Inspector window, click the three-dots icon that appears to the right of the DBComboBoxClientType control's Items property.

Delphi responds by displaying the String list editor window shown in Figure 9.8.

Figure 9.8.
The String list editor window.

The String list editor window is used for entering the list that appears in the DBComboBox control.

☐ Type several items in the String list editor window. When adding a new line (a new item), press the Enter key.

For example, type the following items in the String list editor window, and press Enter after each one:

```
Individual
Company
Government
```

☐ Click the OK button of the String list editor window.

> **Note:** The Save button of the String list editor window enables you to save the listing. So the next time you implement a DBComboBox control, you can click the Load button and load a list that you previously saved.

☐ Select Save Project from the File menu.

☐ Execute the MyList program.

☐ Select an item from the list of the DBComboBox (see Figure 9.9).

Figure 9.9.
The combobox contains the client types you entered with the String list editor.

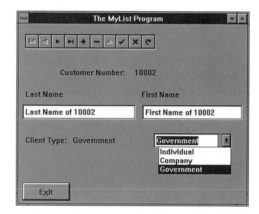

As you can see, the list of the DBComboBox contains the items that you entered to the String list editor window.

☐ Experiment with the MyList program, and then click its Exit button to terminate it.

> **Note:** The DBTextClientType control you placed in the form is not required. The only reason you were instructed to place this control in the form is so you'll understand that the DBComboBox control indeed placed the data in the Clients.DB table ClientType field.
>
> Perform the following experiment to see why the DBComboBoxClientType is the only control you need in the frmMyList form for the ClientType field.
>
> ☐ Place the current record pointer at the first record, using the leftmost button of the Navigator control.

☐ Now that the record pointer is on the first record of the Clients.DB table, type **General** in the DBComboBox.

☐ Use the Navigator control to move to the next record, and select Individual from the DBComboBox.

☐ Use the Navigator control to move to the next record, and select Company from the DBComboBox.

☐ Use the Navigator control to move to the next record, and select Government from the DBComboBox.

The following data is now in the Clients.DB table ClientType field:

Record	Data in ClientType Field
1	General
2	Individual
3	Company
4	Government

☐ Now use the Navigator control to place the record pointer on the first record, and verify that the DBComboBox control displays General in its editbox.

☐ Use the Navigator control to place the record pointer on the second record, and verify that the DBComboBox control displays Individual in its editbox.

☐ Use the Navigator control to place the record pointer on the third record, and verify that the DBComboBox control displays Company in its editbox.

☐ Use the Navigator control to place the record pointer on the fourth record, and verify that the DBComboBox control displays Government in its editbox.

As you can see, the DBComboCox has two functions: It enables the user to set the ClientType field data, and it displays the ClientType field data.

☐ Experiment with the MyList program, and then click its Exit button to terminate it.

Lookup Tables

In the following sections, you implement a program called MyLookup that demonstrates the use of lookup tables.

Suppose you have a table called SalesPer.DB. This table contains data about the sales people of a company. In the project that you implement, you need the SalesPer.DB table.

☐ Use Database Desktop to create a table called SalesPer.DB, and save the table in the C:\DProg\Work directory. The SalesPer.DB table structure is shown in Table 9.2 (see Figure 9.10).

Table 9.2. The structure of the SalesPer.DB table.

Field Name	Type	Size	Key
SalesPersonNum	Numeric	n/a	Yes
LastName	Alpha	40	No
First	Name	30	No

Figure 9.10.
The SalesPer.DB table structure.

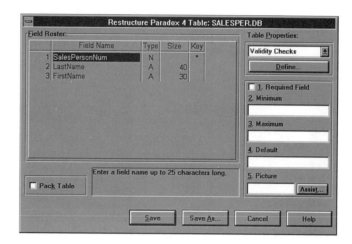

The MyLookup program you implement next needs to have a few records in the SalesPer.DB table. Go ahead and enter a few records to the SalesPer.DB table.

☐ Use Database Desktop to fill a few records in the SalesPer.DB table.

Suppose further that once a salesperson solicited a new customer, it is the responsibility of that salesperson to enter a new record for that customer in the Clients.DB table. Because the salesperson brought in the client, he or she earns a commission on any purchases the client makes. The bottom line is that each record in the Clients.DB table has a salesperson associated with it.

Thus, you need to add the SalesPersonNum field to the Clients.DB table.

☐ Use Database Desktop to add the SalesPersonNum field (a numeric field) to the Clients.DB table.

The Clients.DB structure should now appear as shown in Figure 9.11.

Figure 9.11.
The Clients.DB table structure with the SalesPersonNum *field added to the table.*

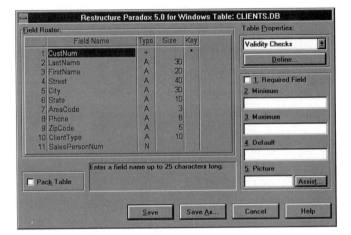

Note: The Clients.DB table should not contain redundant fields. This means that it is enough to have the SalesPersonNum field in the Clients.DB table. It is redundant to have the salesperson's name in the Clients.DB table because the last name can be extracted from the SalesPer.DB table.

The idea of the MyLookup program is to keep very strict data integrity on the SalesPersonNum field of the Clients.DB table. Commissions are paid to salespeople based on the purchases that the clients make, and so it is very important that the Clients.DB table have only valid data in the SalesPersonNum field.

Implementing the MyLookup Project

Now you're ready to implement the MyLookup program. It illustrates how to implement lookup mechanisms in your data-entry forms.

☐ Select New Project from the File menu.

☐ Select the Form1 form, select Save File As from the File menu, and save Form1 as CLookup.Pas in the C:\DProg\Ch09 directory.

☐ Select Save Project As from the File menu, and save the project as MyLookup.Dpr in the C:\DProg\Ch09 directory.

☐ Set the Form1 Name property to frmMyLookup, and then implement the frmLookup form according to the information presented in Table 9.3. When you finish implementing the form, it should look like the one shown in Figure 9.12.

Table 9.3. The `frmMyLookup` form properties.

Object	Property	Setting
Form	Name	frmMyLookup
	Caption	The MyLookup Program
Table	Name	ClientsTable
	DatabaseName	C:\DProg\Work
	TableName	Clients.DB
DataSource	Name	ClientsDataSource
	DataSet	ClientsTable
Table	Name	SalesperTable
	DatabaseName	C:\DProg\Work
	TableName	Salesper.DB
DataSource	Name	SalesperDataSource
	DataSet	SalesperTable
Navigator	Name	ClientsNavigator
	DataSource	ClientsDataSource
DBText	Name	DBTextCustNum
	DataSource	ClientsDataSource
	DataField	CustNum
Label	Name	lblCustNum
	Caption	Customer Number:
DBEdit	Name	DBEditLastName
	DataSource	ClientsDataSource
	DataField	LastName
Label	Name	lblLastName
	Caption	Last Name
DBEdit	Name	DBEditFirstName
	DataSource	ClientsDataSource
	DataField	FirstName

continues

Table 9.3. continued

Object	Property	Setting
Label	Name	lblFirstName
	Caption	First Name
Pushbutton	Name	cmdExit
	Caption	E&xit

Figure 9.12.
The frmLookup *form (design mode).*

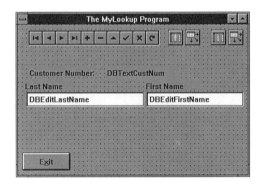

The *FormCreate* Procedure Code

☐ Attach code to the OnCreate event of the frmMyLookup form. After attaching the code, the FormCreate procedure should appear as follows:

```
procedure TfrmMyLookup.FormCreate(Sender: TObject);
begin

ClientsTable.Open;
SalesperTable.Open;

end;
```

Attaching Code to the Exit Button's *OnClick* Event

☐ Attach code to the OnClick event of the cmdExit button.

After attaching the code, the cmdExitClick procedure should appear as follows:

```
procedure TfrmMyLookup.cmdExitClick(Sender: TObject);
begin
```

```
frmMyLookup.Close;
```

end;

Although you aren't finished implementing the MyLookup program, let's see if everything is working as expected.

☐ Select Save Project from the File menu.

☐ Execute the MyLookup program.

The MyLookup program window appears as shown in Figure 9.13.

9

Figure 9.13.
The MyLookup program.

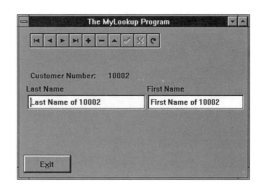

☐ Move from record to record, and note that, as you move, the Customer Number, Last Name, and First Name, of the Clients.DB current record are displayed.

☐ Experiment with the MyLookup program, and then click its Exit button to terminate it.

Updating the *SalesPersonNum* Field of Clients.DB

Recall that one of the fields of the Clients.DB table is the SalesPersonNum field. As stated, SalesPersonNum plays an important role in calculating commissions, and so now you'll implement a mechanism that makes it impossible to enter invalid data into the SalesPersonNum field of Clients.DB.

Now place a DBLookupList control in the frmMyLookup form. This control displays the values of the LastName field of SalesPer.DB. The user selects a salesperson from the list. Because the list comes directly from SalesPer.DB, the user's selection must be valid!

Recall that Clients.DB does not have a field containing the salesperson's LastName. Clients.DB has a SalesPersonNum field, and this field contains the salesperson's number.

The DBLookupList control places in the Clients.DB table's SalesPersonNum field the value corresponding to the user's selection. For example, suppose that in the SalesPer.DB table you have the following record:

```
SalesPersonNum    1001
LastName          Anderson
FirstName         Jim
```

Suppose further that the user selects Anderson from the DBLookupList list. As a result, the SalesPersonNum field of the Clients.DB table is automatically filled with the value 1001.

☐ Place a DBLookupList control from the Data Controls page in the frmMyLookup form. The DBLookupList control icon on the Data Controls page is shown in Figure 9.14.

Figure 9.14.

The DBLookupList control icon on the Data Controls page.

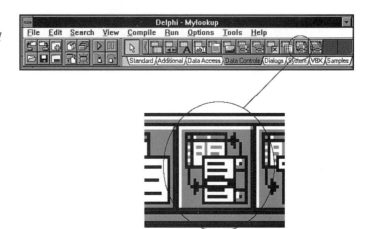

☐ Set the DBLookupList control properties as follows:

```
Name              DBLookupListSalesPer
DataSource        ClientsDataSource
DataField         SalesPersonNum
LookupSource      SalesperDataSource
LookupDisplay     LastName
LookupField       SalesPersonNum
```

Here's a review of the properties you set for the DBLookupList control.

You set the DBLookupList control's Name property to DBLookupListSalesPer because this control serves as a lookup mechanism from the SalesPer.DB table. As you know, you can set the Name property to any name you like. However, the rest of the DBLookupList control properties are important.

You set the `DBLookupList` control `DataSource` property to `ClientsDataSource` because this `DBLookupList` control places data in one of the Clients.DB table fields.

You set the `DataField` of the `DBLookupList` control to `SalesPersonNum` because this `DBLookupList` control places data in the Clients.DB table `SalesPersonNum` field.

You set the `DBLookupList` control `LookupSource` property to `SalesperDataSource` because this `DBLookupList` control displays in it items appearing in the SalesPer.DB table.

You set the `DBLookupList` control `LookupDisplay` property to `LastName` because you want the `DBLookupList` control to display the SalesPer.DB table `LastName` field.

You set the `DBLookupList` control `LookupField` property to `SalesPersonNum` because you want the `DBLookupList` control to extract information from the SalesPer.DB table `SalesPersonNum` field.

> **Note:** At first glance, it looks as if setting the `DBLookupList` control properties is a complicated task. However, think of the alternative: Writing code that accomplishes the same task is far more complicated.

☐ Place a `Label` control from the Standard page above the `DBLookupList` control, and set the `Label` control properties as follows:

```
Name       lblSalesPersonLastName
Caption    Sales person last name:
```

The label you placed explains to the user that the list contains the salespersons' last names.

The last controls that you place display the Clients.DB table's `SalesPersonNum` field. Because this field is filled automatically by the `DBLookupList` control, you use the `DBText` control to display this field. Place this control for the sole purpose of displaying the Clients.DB table's `SalesPersonNum` field contents—to prove to yourself that the `SalesPersonNum` field was filled with the correct data.

☐ Place a `DBText` control from the Data Controls page in the `frmMyLookup` form, and set its properties as follows:

```
Name         DBText
DataSource   ClientsDataSource
DataField    SalesPersonNum
```

☐ Place a Label control above the DBText control that you placed, and set the properties of the Label control as follows:

Name	lblSalesPersonNum
Caption	(SalesPersonNum from Clients.DB)

Your frmMyLookup form should now appear as shown in Figure 9.15.

Figure 9.15.
The frmMyLookup *form (design mode).*

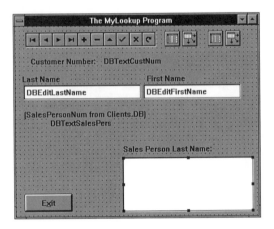

☐ Select Save Project from the File menu.

☐ Execute the MyLookup program.

The program window appears as shown in Figure 9.16.

Figure 9.16.
The MyLookup program with the DBLookupList *control in it.*

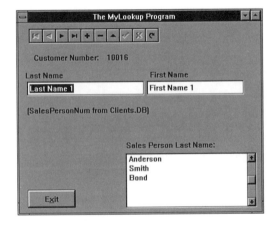

☐ Click a salesperson's name from the list, and then click the Navigator control's Refresh button.

MyLookup responds by filling the Clients.DB SalesPersonNum field with the salesperson number of the item that you clicked. You can see that indeed this is what occurred because the DBText control now displays the salesperson number.

☐ Use the Navigator control to move to second record in Clients.DB, and click an item in the DBLookupList control. Click the Refresh button to actually fill the SalesPersonNum field.

The SalesPersonNum value of the item that you clicked is assigned to the Clients.DB table SalesPersonNum field.

☐ Continue to fill other SalesPersonNum fields. Don't forget to click the Navigator control's Refresh button to actually fill the SalesPersonNum field.

☐ Click the leftmost button of the Navigator control to set the Clients.DB record pointer to the first record, and then move to other records.

As you move from record to record, note that the DBLookupList control highlights the LastName value of the salesperson corresponding to the Clients.DB current record. In other words, the DBLookupList control serves as both a tool to enter valid data to the SalesPersonNum field as well as a tool to display the LastName field of SalesPer.DB that corresponds to the current record in Clients.DB

☐ Experiment with the MyLookup program, and then click its Exit button to terminate the program.

Refreshing

As you saw in the previous steps, you have to click the Navigator control's Refresh button to actually fill the Clients.DB table SalesPersonNum field. It would be nice to eliminate the need to click this button so that whenever the user selects an item in the DBLookupList control, the Refresh action occurs automatically.

☐ Attach code to the OnClick event of the DBLookupList control. After attaching the code, the DBLookupListSalesPersonNum procedure should look as follows:

```
procedure TfrmMyLookup.DBLookupListSalesPersonNumClick(Sender: TObject);
begin

ClientsTable.Refresh;

end;
```

The code you typed executes the Refresh method whenever the user clicks an item in the DBLookupList control.

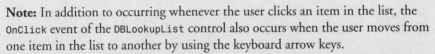
Note: In addition to occurring whenever the user clicks an item in the list, the OnClick event of the DBLookupList control also occurs when the user moves from one item in the list to another by using the keyboard arrow keys.

Generally speaking, whenever you want to determine whether a particular event has occurred, insert code that indicates the event occurred in the corresponding procedure. For example, modify the DBLookupListSalesPersonNumClick procedure so that it appears as follows:

```
procedure TfrmMyLookup.DBLookupListSalesPersonNumClick(Sender: TObject);
begin

MessageBeep(1);
ClientsTable.Refresh;

end;
```

In this procedure, there is a beep whenever the OnClick event occurs.

Of course, after verifying for yourself that the event occurs, you have to delete the MessageBeep statement.

If you prefer, use the MessageDlg statement to display a messagebox as a visual indication that the event occurs instead of the MessageBeep() that gives you an audio indication.

☐ Execute the MyLookup program, and verify that every time you click an item in the DBLookupList control, the Clients.DB SalesPersonNum field is filled with a value corresponding to the clicked item in the DBLookupList control. You do not have to click the Navigator control's Refresh button to update the Clients.DB table because you added code that accomplishes the refreshing.

☐ Experiment with the MyLookup program. In particular, note that moving from one item in the list to another by using the keyboard arrow keys has the same effect as clicking an item in the list.

☐ Click the Exit button to terminate the MyLookup program.

Enhancing the MyLookup Program

The DBLookupList control is useful only if the list it contains doesn't include too many items. For example, if the list contains thousands of items, the user must scroll the list many times until the item is found. This, of course, doesn't make the DBLookupList control useful.

Suppose that the list in the DBLookupList control contains 10 items (10 salespersons). In this case, it's reasonable to expect the user to locate the salesperson's name on the list. However,

suppose there are two Andersons on the list: Anderson Jim and Anderson Alice. How does the operator know which Anderson to select?

You can solve this problem by displaying additional information in the list of the DBLookupList control as follows:

☐ Double-click the SalesPer.DB table's Table control.

Delphi responds by displaying the Fields Editor window.

☐ Click the Add button to list all the SalesPer.DB table fields, and then click the OK button.

Now each field of the SalesPer.DB table has a corresponding field object in the frmMyLookup form (SalesperTableLastName, SalesperTableFirstName, and SalesperTabelSalesPersonNum).

However, you want to add a calculated field.

☐ Click the Define button of the Fields Editor window.

Delphi responds by displaying the Define window, which enables you to define a calculated field.

☐ Set the name of the calculated field to **LastFirst**. Set the field type to **StringField**, make sure that the Calculated checkbox is checked, and then close the Define window.

The frmMyLookup form now contains the SalesPerTableLastFirst field object.

You named this calculated field LastFirst because you want this calculated field to contain information from the LastName field as well as from the FirstName field. However, you can name this field anything you like.

☐ Attach code to the OnCalcFields event of the SalesperTable object. After attaching the code, the SalesperTableCalcFields procedure should look as follows:

```
procedure TfrmMyLookup.SalesperTableCalcFields(DataSet: TDataset);
begin

SalesperTableLastFirst.Value :=
   SalesperTableLastName.Value +
   ', ' +
   SalesperTableFirstName.Value;

end;
```

The code you typed sets the Value property of the calculated field to a value composed of three strings:

```
SalesperTableLastFirst.Value :=
   SalesperTableLastName.Value +
   ', ' +
   SalesperTableFirstName.Value;
```

The DBLookupList control displays the contents of the field mentioned in the DBLookupList control LookupDisplay property. Currently, the DBLookupList control is set to LastName. This means that the lookup list currently displays a list of the LastName field from the SalesPer.DB table.

☐ Set the LookupDisplay property of the DBLookupList control to **LastFirst**.

So, the DBLookupList control now displays the values of the LastFirst calculated field.

Because the LastFirst field is a long string, you have to set the SalesPerTableLastFirst object's Size property to a larger number.

☐ Set the Size property of the SalesPerTableLastFirst object to **80**.

☐ Use the mouse to make the DBLookupList control wider.

☐ Select Save Project from the File menu.

☐ Execute the MyLookup program.

☐ Verify that the DBLookupList control list is composed of the LastName, a comma, and then the FirstName.

☐ Click the Exit button to terminate the MyLookup program.

> **Note:** *Referential integrity* is a concept resembling the lookup table concept. See Question 1 and Exercise 3 of this chapter for discussions about referential integrity.

Summary

In this chapter, you learned how to use the DBComboBox control as a tool for displaying field data. This control also enables the user either to select an item from a list or to type the data in the combobox.

You also learned how to use the DBLookupList control. As you saw, by setting several properties of this control, you can make this control a tool for looking into a table field and filling another table's field—hence the name *lookup*.

Q&A

Q I've heard the term *referential integrity.* Is referential integrity the same as lookup tables?

A Referential integrity is not the same as lookup tables. To understand referential integrity, consider the Clients.DB table that contains the SalesPersonNum field. As discussed in this chapter, this field contains the salesperson's ID number, and it's very important that this number be a valid number (one that exists in the SalesPer.DB table).

In the MyLookup program, you ensured that the Clients.DB SalesPersonNum field had a valid value because you used the DBLookupList control to fill the SalesPersonNum field directly from the SalesPer.DB table.

An alternative way to ensure that the Clients.DB SalesPersonNum field has a valid value (one that exists in SalesPer.DB) is to establish a referential-integrity relationship between SalesPer.DB and Clients.DB. After establishing the relationship, the user is not able to enter a value for the SalesPersonNum field that doesn't exist in the SalesPer.DB table. (You then can use the DBLookupList control as in the MyLookup program to let the user enter data into the Clients.DB SalesPersonNum field). The fact that you established referential integrity means that even you (using, for example, Database Desktop) are not able to enter invalid data into the SalesPersonNum field.

For example, if you try to enter a non-unique value for the Clients.DB CustNum field (from Database Desktop or from a program that you write with Delphi), you receive an error message: Key Violation. The uniqueness of a key field is embedded in the tables. Likewise, if you establish a referential-integrity relationship and later enter data that violates the referential integrity (from Database Desktop or from within your Delphi program), you are prompted with an error message.

Exercise 3 of this chapter outlines the procedure of establishing referential integrity with Database Desktop.

Q The MyList program uses the DBComboBox control as well as the DBText control. This chapter said that the DBText control is not really needed (because the DBComboBox displays the ClientType field data). Is it a good idea to include the DBText control for the same field of the DBComboBox?

A As you can see, the DBText can't hurt the operation because the user can't edit the DBText control. In some situations, it's helpful to have the DBText control because your users may not be accustomed to seeing a combobox that serves as both displaying the current record's data and accepting data. Nevertheless, you can train your user to know that the combobox is used for both displaying and modifying data.

Quiz

1. The DBComboBox control lists items that were created by _____.

2. The user can select an item from the list of the DBComboBox control as well as enter data that isn't included in the list of the combobox:

    a. True.

    b. False.

Exercises

1. Modify the MyList program so that when the user changes the value of the ClientType, the PC beeps.

2. In the MyLookup program, the DBLookupList control lists the values of the LastName and FirstName from the SalesPer.DB table. Modify the code of the program so the list also contains the SalesPersonNum field value.

3. Establish a referential-integrity relationship between the Clients.DB table and the SalesPer.DB table. The referential integrity should be based on the SalesPersonNum field.

Answers to Quiz

1. The DBComboBox control list items created by the programmer using the String list editor window.

2. a.

Answers to Exercises

1. Whenever the user changes the DBComboBox control editbox value, the DBComboBoxClientType control Change event occurs.

    ☐ Attach code to the Change event of the DBComboBox ClientType control. After attaching the code, the DBComboBoxClientTypeChange procedure should look as follows:

    ```
    procedure TfrmMyList.DBComboBoxClientTypeChange(Sender: TObject);
    begin

        MessageBeep(1);

    end;
    ```

2. Currently, the code attached to the `SalesperTable` control `OnCalcFields` event is as follows:

```
procedure TfrmMyLookup.SalesperTableCalcFields(DataSet: TDataset);
begin

SalesperTableLastFirst.Value :=
   SalesperTableLastName.Value +
   ', ' +
   SalesperTableFirstName.Value;

end;
```

Change the code of this procedure to the following:

```
SalesperTableLastFirst.Value :=
   SalesperTableSalesPersonNum.AsString +
   ', ' +
   SalesperTableLastName.Value +
   ', ' +
   SalesperTableFirstName.Value;
```

Now each item in the list of the `DBLookupList` control is composed of the `SalesPersonNum` field, a comma, the `LastName` field, a comma, and the `FirstName` field.

Note that `AsString` is used because you have to convert `SalesPersonNum` from a number to a string.

3. The SalesPer.DB table is called the *Parent table* because this table has unique values for the `SalesPersonNum` field. The Clients.DB table is called the *Child table* because there could be many records with the same `SalesPersonNum`.

☐ Start Database Desktop.

☐ Select Restructure from the Database Desktop Utilities menu.

> *Database Desktop responds by displaying a window that enables you to open a table.*

☐ Select the Clients.DB table.

> *Database Desktop responds by displaying the Clients.DB structure.*

☐ Set the Table Properties combobox to **Referential Integrity**.

☐ Click the Define button.

> *Database Desktop responds by displaying the Referential Integrity window.*

☐ Select the SalesPer.DB item from the right list, and click the button that has a left-pointing arrow.

☐ Select the `SalesPersonNum` from the left list, and then click the button that has a right-pointing arrow.

> *The Referential Integrity window should now look as shown in Figure 9.17.*

Figure 9.17.
The Referential Integrity window of Database Desktop.

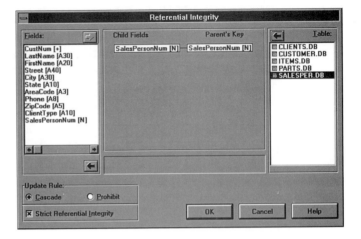

☐ Click the OK button.

> *Database Desktop responds by displaying a dialog box that asks you to type a name for the Referential Integrity.*

☐ Type `ClientsSalesPer` as the name of the Referential Integrity, close the dialog box, and then click the Save button of the Restructure window.

To see the Referential Integrity in action, do the following:

☐ Display the Clients.DB table so you can edit records in it (don't forget to select Edit Data from the View menu).

☐ Add a new record to the Clients.DB table.

☐ Fill the `LastName` and `FirstName` fields of the new record.

☐ Fill the `SalesPersonNum` field with a value that doesn't exist in the SalesPer.DB table.

When you try to move to another record, Database Desktop refuses to accept the value, and you see the message: `Missing Master Record`. The master table (SalesPer.DB) doesn't have a record that has its `SalesPersonNum` field equal to the value you entered for the Clients.DB `SalesPersonNum` field.

☐ Fill a value in the Clients.DB `SalesPersonNum` field that exists in the SalesPer.DBtable, and then move to another record.

The value you entered to the `SalesPersonNum` field is accepted.

Similarly, if you try to fill the Clients.DB table `SalesPerNum` field with invalid data (a value that doesn't exist in SalesPer.DB) from within your Delphi programs, you get an error message.

Queries and Ranges

Whenever you displayed table data in previous chapters, you let the user browse through the entire table and display any of the table records. Sometimes, however, you want the user to be able to view or edit only records containing a certain value in a certain field. In this chapter, you learn how to accomplish this.

The OnlyJim Program

The OnlyJim.EXE program demonstrates how you can display a selected group of records from the Clients.DB table. In particular, you display only these records whose FirstName field is equal to Jim.

Creating the OnlyJim Project Form

To create the OnlyJim project's main form, follow these steps.

☐ Start Delphi.

☐ Select a New Project from the File menu.

☐ Select Database Form Expert from the Help menu.

   Delphi responds by displaying the first window of Database Form Expert.

In previous chapters, you selected the Create a form using TTable objects option button in the first window of the Database Form Expert. Database Form Expert then places a TTable component in the form. For this program, however, you select the Create a Form using TQuery objects option button. Database Form Expert places a TQuery component in the form instead of a TTable component.

☐ Select the Create a Form using TQuery objects option button, select the Create a simple form option button (see Figure 10.1), and then click the Next button.

   Database Form Expert responds by displaying the next window in which Database Form Expert lets you select a table.

☐ Select the Clients.DB table from the C:\DProg\Work directory.

   Delphi responds by displaying a window enabling you to select Clients.DB table fields.

☐ Make sure all the fields on the left list are selected, and then click the button with the right-pointing double arrow on it.

   Delphi responds by moving all the fields from the left list to the right list.

☐ Click the Next button.

   Delphi responds by displaying the window enabling you select to the layout of the data.

Figure 10.1.
*Setting the first window of
Database Form Expert.*

☐ Select the Grid option button, and then click the Next button.

Delphi responds by displaying the last window of the Database Form Expert session.

☐ Make sure that the Create main form checkbox is selected, and then click the Create
button.

Database Form Expert responds by creating the Form2 form (see Figure 10.2).

Figure 10.2.
*The Form2 form generated
by Database Form Expert.*

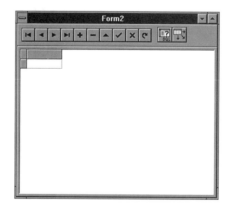

Unlike on previous Form2 forms generated by Database Form Expert, the Table component is
not used. In previous Form2 forms, Database Form Expert placed a Table component and a
DataSource component in Form2. Now, because you requested it during the Database Form
Expert session, a TQuery component and a DataSource component were placed in Form2.

☐ Make sure that Form2 is selected, and select Save File As from the File menu.

☐ Save Form2 as CJim.Pas in the C:\DProg\Ch10 directory.

☐ Select Remove File from the File menu, and remove the Form1 form from the project.
When Delphi asks if you want to save Form1, click the No button.

☐ Select Save Project from the File menu, and save the project as OnlyJim.Dpr in the C:\DProg\Ch10 directory.

Implementing an Exit Button

Here's how you implement an Exit button.

☐ Set the `Align` property of the `Grid` control to `clNone`, and size the `Grid` control so there's a free area in `Form2` where you can place a pushbutton.

☐ Place a pushbutton from the Standard page in `Form2`.

☐ Set the properties of the Exit button as follows:

```
Name      cmdExit
Caption   E&xit
```

☐ Attach code to the `OnClick` event of the `cmdExit` button.

After attaching the code the `cmdExitClick` procedure should look as follows:

```
procedure TForm2.cmdExitClick(Sender: TObject);
begin

Application.Terminate;

end;
```

☐ Set the `Name` property of `Form2` to `frmOnlyJim`.

☐ Set the `Caption` property of `Form2` to `The OnlyJim program`.

Note: When you attached code to the `cmdExitClick` procedure, the name of the corresponding procedure is

`TForm2.cmdExitClick()`

Delphi precedes the name of the procedure with the name of the form in which the Exit button resides.

Once you change the name of the form to `frmOnlyJim`, Delphi automatically changes the names of the procedures so the name is preceded by `TfrmOnlyJim` as in the following:

```
procedure TfrmOnlyJim.cmdExitClick(Sender: TObject);
begin
```

```
        Application.Terminate;

end;
```

The `frmOnlyJim` form should now look as shown in Figure 10.3.

Figure 10.3.
*The `frmOnlyJim` form
(design mode).*

☐ Select Save Project from the File menu.

☐ Execute the OnlyJim program.

The window of the OnlyJim program appears as shown in Figure 10.4.

Figure 10.4.
*The OnlyJim program
window.*

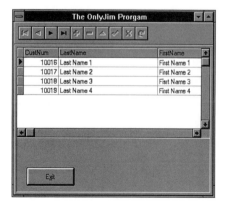

As you can see, all the records of Clients.DB are displayed. As of now, you haven't established any query that filters out records from the Clients.DB table.

☐ Click the Exit button to terminate the OnlyJim program.

Establishing a SQL Query

Now you'll set the properties of the `Query` control so it allows the user to browse only through Clients.DB table records having their `FirstName` field equal to `Jim`.

☐ Set the `Active` property of the `Query` control to `True`.

Because you haven't set the query request, no records are filtered yet.

☐ Click the SQL property of the `Query` control.

Delphi responds by displaying the String list editor window, as shown in Figure 10.5.

Figure 10.5.

The String list editor window.

The String list editor window contains code that Database Form Expert wrote for you.

```
Select
  clients."CustNum",
  clients."LastName",
  clients."FirstName",
  clients."Street",
  clients."City",
  clients."State",
  clients."AreaCode",
  clients."Phone",
  clients."ZipCode",
  clients."ClientType",
  clients."SalesPersonNum"
From "c:\dprog\work\clients.db"
As clients
```

☐ Add the following line after the last line in the String list editor window:

```
  where FirstName = "Jim"
```

Now the String list editor should contain the following:

```
Select
  clients."CustNum",
```

```
    clients."LastName",
    clients."FirstName",
    clients."Street",
    clients."City",
    clients."State",
    clients."AreaCode",
    clients."Phone",
    clients."ZipCode",
    clients."ClientType",
    clients."SalesPersonNum"
From "c:\dprog\work\clients.db"
As clients
where FirstName = "Jim"
```

Note: As you can see from the preceding statement, you do not terminate lines with a semicolon, and you use double quotes (not single quotes).

☐ Click the OK button of the String list editor window.

☐ Select Save Project from the File menu.

☐ Execute the OnlyJim program.

If you have records with FirstName equal to Jim, these records appear in the Grid control. If you don't have any records with FirstName equal to Jim, the Grid control does not list any records.

☐ Experiment with the OnlyJim program. Use Database Desktop (or any of the programs you implemented in previous chapters) to change the FirstName field of several records to Jim. Then execute the OnlyJim program and verify that the Grid control displays only those records having Jim in their FirstName field.

☐ Click the Exit button to terminate the OnlyJim program.

What Is a SQL Statement?

SQL stands for Structured Query Language. SQL, which is pronounced *sequel*, is a programming language that enables you to access data in tables. For example, in the OnlyJim program, the statement in the String list editor window is a SQL statement.

The beauty of SQL is that it is independent from the type of computer you're using as well as from the type of programming language you're using. For example, SQL is widely used in mainframe computers, mini-computers, and PCs. Also, SQL is used in Delphi and almost any other programming language dealing with databases. In essence, SQL is a universal database language.

The *RequestLive* Property of the *Query* Control

The default setting of the Query control RequestLive property is False, which means that during the execution of the OnlyJim program, the user cannot edit the Clients.DB table data.

To enable the user to edit the Clients.DB table data, follow these steps:

☐ Set the RquestLive property of the Query control to True.

☐ Select Save Project from the File menu.

☐ Execute the OnlyJim program, and verify that you can edit the Clients.DB table data.

☐ If no records appear in the Grid control (which means there are no records with FirstName equal to Jim), the Grid control displays one empty record, which you can fill. If you fill the FirstName field with Jim, the record is displayed. However, if you fill FirstName with a name other than Jim, that record is removed from the list because the SQL query is in effect. Likewise, if you have any Jim records listed, you can change the FirstName to another name and store that change in the database table. However, because the grid list is determined by the SQL query and the changed name doesn't fit the query, the modified record will disappear from the Grid display.

☐ Experiment with the OnlyJim program, and then terminate it by clicking its Exit button.

Static and Dynamic Queries

The OnlyJim program illustrates the use of a *static query*. That is, you set the query at design time, and this query is effective during the program execution. The word static means that you cannot modify the setting of the query during runtime.

Making the Query Active or Inactive at Runtime

You can make the query inactive by setting its Active property to False, as follows:

```
Query1.Active := False;
```

Place a checkbox in the OnlyJim program form.

☐ Place a checkbox from the Standard page in the form, and set the checkbox properties as follows:

```
Name        chkQueryOn
Caption     &Query On
Checked     True
```

After placing the checkbox, the form of the OnlyJim program should look as shown in Figure 10.6.

Figure 10.6.

The OnlyJim program with the Query On checkbox in it.

☐ Attach code to the OnClick event of the chkQueryOn checkbox.

After adding the code, the chkQueryOnClick procedure should look as follows:

```
procedure TfrmOnlyJim.chkQueryOnClick(Sender: TObject);
begin

if chkQueryOn.Checked = True then
   begin
   Query1.Active := True;
   end
else
   begin
   Query1.Active := False;
   end;

end;
```

The code that you typed uses an if...else statement to examine the checkbox's Checked property. If the checkbox is checked, the Query is made active:

```
Query1.Active := True;
```

If the checkbox is not checked, the checkbox is made inactive:

```
Query1.Active := False;
```

☐ Select Save Project from the File menu.

☐ Execute the OnlyJim program, and experiment with the Query On checkbox.

☐ Click the Exit button of the OnlyJim program to terminate the program.

The SetQuery Program

The OnlyJim program illustrates how a *static query* is implemented. The SetQuery program you're about to implement demonstrates how a *dynamic query* is implemented. A dynamic query is a query you modify during program execution. For example, you can set the query so the Grid control displays only the records having their LastName field equal to Smith. If, during program execution, you want to display only these records that have their LastName field equal to Anderson, you can do so with a dynamic SQL statement.

Creating the SetQuery Project

To create the project of the SetQuery program, follow these steps:

☐ Use Database Form Expert to create a form that

- Uses the Clients.DB table residing in the C:\Dprog\Work directory.
- Is a simple form
- Contains a TQuery object
- Uses all the fields of the Clients.DB table.
- Uses the Grid layout option.

Database Form Expert creates Form2 with the TQuery control in it.

☐ Select the Form2 form created by Database Form, select Save File As from the File menu, and save Form2 as CQuery.Pas in the C:\DProg\Ch10 directory.

☐ Select Remove File from the File menu, and remove Form1 from the project.

☐ Select Save Project As from the File menu, and save the project as SetQuery.Dpr in the C:\DProg\Ch10 directory.

☐ Set the Grid control Align property to clNone, and then size the Grid control so there will be a free area where you can place controls in Form2.

☐ Set the properties of Form2 as follows:

```
Name      frmSetQuery
Caption   The SetQuery Program
```

Implementing an Exit button

Implement an Exit button as follows:

☐ Place an Exit button in the frmSetQuery form.

☐ Set the properties of the Exit button as follows:

```
Name        cmdExit
Caption     E&xit
```

☐ Attach code to the OnClick event of the Exit button.

After attaching the code, the cmdExitClick procedure should look as follows:

```
procedure TfrmSetQuery.cmdExitClick(Sender: TObject);
begin

Application.Terminate;

end;
```

The *FormCreate* Procedure

The Name property assigned by Database Form Expert is Query1. Change the Name property of Query1.

☐ Set the Name property of Query1 to LastNameQuery.

☐ Search the entire CQuery.Pas file for the text *Query1*.

The text *Query1* appears once, in the FormCreate procedure, as follows:

```
procedure TfrmSetQuery.FormCreate(Sender: TObject);
begin

  Query1.Open;

end;
```

☐ In the FormCreate procedure, replace the word *Query1* with LastNameQuery as follows:

```
procedure TfrmSetQuery.FormCreate(Sender: TObject);
begin

  LastNameQuery.Open;

end;
```

Defining SQL Parameters

Set the initial setting of the LastNameQuery control.

☐ Set the Active property of the LastNameQuery control to True.

☐ Select the SQL property of the LastNameQuery object in the Object Inspector window, and then click the three dots that appear to the right of the SQL property.

Delphi responds by displaying the String list editor window.

☐ After the last line in the String list editor window, type

```
where LastName = :TheLastName
```

Now the statement in the String list editor window looks as follows:

```
Select
  clients."CustNum",
  clients."LastName",
  clients."FirstName",
  clients."Street",
  clients."City",
  clients."State",
  clients."AreaCode",
  clients."Phone",
  clients."ZipCode",
  clients."ClientType",
  clients."SalesPersonNum"
From "c:\dprog\work\clients.db"
As clients
where LastName = :TheLastName
```

The SQL statement you typed is similar to the SQL statement you used in the OnlyJim program. However, in the OnlyJim program you typed

```
where FirstName = 'Jim'
```

which means that only those records whose FirstName field is equal to Jim are selected.

In this program, you typed the statement

```
where LastName = :TheLastName
```

which means that only those records whose LastName field is equal to TheLastName are selected. TheLastName is a variable that is called a *SQL parameter*. If TheLastName parameter is equal to Anderson, only those records whose LastName field is equal to Anderson are displayed.

At this point, the parameter TheLastName is not defined. Here's how you define the TheLastName parameter.

☐ Right click the LastNameQuery control.

Delphi responds by displaying a menu.

☐ Select the Define Parameters from the menu.

Delphi responds by displaying a window that enables you to define the TheLastName variable (see Figure 10.7).

☐ Set the parameter of the SQL query as follows:

```
Data    type String
Value   Anderson
```

Figure 10.7.
*The window that Delphi
displays for defining SQL
parameters.*

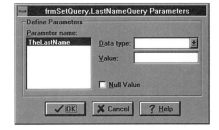

After setting the above settings, the window that defines the query parameter looks as shown in
Figure 10.8.

Figure 10.8.
*Defining the TheLastName
SQL parameter.*

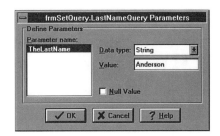

☐ Click the OK button of the window that defines the TheLastName SQL parameter.

☐ During the operation in which you define the SQL parameter, Delphi may have set the
Active property of the LastNameQuery control back to False, and so make sure that the
Active property is set to True.

☐ Set the RequestLive property of the LastNameQuery control to True so you'll be able to
edit the Clients.DB records during runtime.

☐ Select Save Project from the File menu.

☐ Execute the SetQuery program.

The SetQuery window appears as shown in Figure 10.9. If you have any records with the
LastName field equal to Anderson, they appear in the Grid control.

☐ Experiment with the SetQuery program. In particular, modify the LastName of a new
record to Anderson, and note that this record is displayed in the Grid control. If you
modify the LastName field of an existing record appearing in the Grid control from
Anderson to another last name, the record is removed from the Grid control.

☐ Click the Exit button to terminate the SetQuery program.

Figure 10.9.

The SetQuery program.

Modifying the SQL Condition During Runtime

Here's a review of the current status of the SetQuery program.

You set a SQL statement in the String list editor window that established a SQL statement where all the records whose LastName field matches the TheLastName parameter are selected.

You declared a variable (the parameter TheLastName) by right-clicking the LastNameQuery control and selecting Define Parameters from the menu that pops up. You defined the TheLastName parameter as a string, and the value that you set for TheLastName was Anderson.

When you executed the SetQuery program, only those records with the LastName field equal to Anderson are displayed in the Grid control.

Now you're ready to enhance the SetQuery program so that during runtime you can change the value of TheLastName parameter. For example, you set TheLastName to Smith, and this causes the Grid control to display only those records with the LastName field equal to Smith.

☐ Place a pushbutton from the Standard page in the frmSetQuery form.

☐ Set the properties of the pushbutton as follows:

```
Name      cmdSetQuery
Caption   &Set Query
```

☐ Add the word *Dialogs* to the list of uses at the beginning of the CQuery.Pas file. The uses section should now look as follows:

```
uses
   SysUtils, WinTypes, WinProcs, Messages, Classes, Graphics,
   Controls, StdCtrls, Forms, DBCtrls, DB, DBGrids, DBTables,
   Grids, ExtCtrls,
   Dialogs;
```

You need `Dialogs` in the uses section because you're going to use the `InputBox` function.

☐ Attach code to the `OnClick` event of the `cmdSetQuery` button. After attaching the code, the `cmdSetQueryClick` procedure should look as follows:

```
procedure TfrmSetQuery.cmdSetQueryClick(Sender: TObject);
var

LastNameString: String;

begin


LastNameString :=
   InputBox ('Set the LastName field',
             'Enter Last Name:',
             '');

LastNameQuery.DisableControls;

  try

     LastNameQuery.Active := False;

     LastNameQuery.Params[0].AsString :=
              LastNameString;

     LastNameQuery.Active := True;

  finally

     LastNameQuery.EnableControls;

  end;

end;
```

In this code, you declared a var section in the procedure.

```
procedure TfrmSetQuery.cmdSetQueryClick(Sender: TObject);
var

LastNameString: String;

begin
...
```

The `LastNameString` variable that you declared in the var section is used to hold the string that the user types into an input box.

You then display an input dialog box, and the string the user types in the input dialog box is stored as the `LastNameString` variable.

```
LastNameString :=
   InputBox ('Set the LastName field',
             'Enter Last Name:',
             '');
```

You then "disable" the Query component:

```
LastNameQuery.DisableControls;
```

This prevents the Query component from notifying its dependent data-aware controls (DBgrids, DBEdits, and so on) when the current record in the query changes. This allows you to perform multi-record batch operations on a query (or table) very quickly because the form doesn't have to redraw the data-aware controls every time the current record changes during the batch operation. In this exercise, DisableControls is used to eliminate screen flicker as the query is closed, changed, and respopened. You should always call EnableControls after a call to DisableControls, or your form will be left in a paralyzed state.

A try...finally block is then executed as follows:

```
try

    LastNameQuery.Active := False;

    LastNameQuery.Params[0].AsString :=
                LastNameString;

    LastNameQuery.Active := True;

finally

    LastNameQuery.EnableControls;

end;
```

The code between finally and end is always executed, and so no matter what happens during the execution of the statements between the try and the finally, you enable the Query component as follows:

```
LastNameQuery.EnableControls;
```

The code between try and finally sets the Active property of the LastNameQuery Query control to False because you can't change the value of a SQL query parameter while the Query component is active.

```
LastNameQuery.Active := False;
```

You then assign the string input by the user to the parameter of the SQL query, as follows:

```
LastNameQuery.Params[0].AsString :=
        LastNameString;
```

The TheLastName parameter is the only parameter the SQL query has; it's considered parameter 0. If you had a second SQL query parameter, it would be parameter 1, and so on.

Because the TheLastName parameter is now equal to the string the user typed in the input box, you can activate the LastNameQuery control.

```
LastNameQuery.Active := True;
```

Why did you type the SQL setting in a try...finally block? To guarantee that the LastNameQuery is restored to its normal (enabled) state when this procedure exits. First, LastNameQuery.DisableControls disables the data refresh of all controls that rely on the query. Next, the program enters the protection of a try block. If an error occurs during execution of the statements between try and finally, the procedure will abort, and later an error message will be displayed to the user. However, because LastNameQuery.EnableControls is in the finally part, it will execute as any exception aborts the procedure, and so the disabled LastNameQuery will be re-enabled (all controls that rely on the query will once again receive data-refresh notifications). The finally part will execute if an exception occurs, and it will execute if no exception occurs; so, no matter what happens in the try part, the LastNameQuery will be restored to its normal operating state before execution leaves this procedure.

☐ Select Save Project from the File menu.

☐ Execute the SetQuery program.

☐ Click the Set Query button, type a last name in the input box, and then click the OK button of the input box.

> *The SetQuery program responds by displaying all records (if any) that have their* LastName *field equal to the string that you typed in the input box.*

☐ Experiment with the SetQuery program, and then click the Exit button to terminate the program.

Setting a Range of Records

The OnlyJim and SetQuery programs demonstrate how to select records that comply with certain conditions.

Sometimes you would want to only display a range of records. The SetRange program demonstrates how you accomplish this.

Creating the Form of the SetRange Project

Use Database Form Expert to create a form.

☐ Use Database From Expert to create a form as follows:

- Use the Simple form option.
- Use the TTable object option (not the TQuery option).
- Use the Clients.DB table from the C:\DProg\Work directory.

- Include all the fields of the Clients.DB table.
- Use the Grid option.

Database Form Expert generated the Form2 form with the Table1 Table component in it.

☐ Select Form2, select Save File As from the File menu, and save Form2 as CRange.Pas in the C:\DProg\Ch10 directory.

☐ Select Remove File from the File menu, and remove Form1 from the project.

☐ Select Save Project As from the File menu, and save the project as SetRange.Dpr in the C:\DProg\Work directory.

Implementing an Exit Button

Implement an Exit button in Form2, as follows:

☐ Set the Align property of the Grid control to clNone, and then size the Grid control to make room for an Exit button.

☐ Place a pushbutton (from the Standard page) in Form2, and set its properties as follows:

```
Name       cmdExit
Caption    E&xit
```

☐ Attach code to the OnClick event of the cmdExit button.

After attaching the code, the cmdExitClick procedure should look as follows:

```
procedure TForm2.cmdExitClick(Sender: TObject);
begin

Application.Terminate;

end;
```

☐ Select Save Project from the File menu.

☐ Execute the SetRange program, and verify that everything is working as expected. During the execution of the SetRange program, take note of the CustNum field. In the next section, you'll write code that displays only those records that have their CustNum field in a certain range. Write down a range of records that will be used. For example, if you see the following records, the range you display could be 18002 to 18004:

```
CustNum
=======
18000
18001
18002
18003
18004
18005
```

☐ Click the Exit button to terminate the SetRange program.

Adding Field Objects

You'll now add field objects (a field object for each of the fields of the Clients.DB table).

☐ Double-click the Table1 component.

Delphi responds by displaying the Field editor window.

☐ Click the Add button.

Delphi responds by filling the Fields editor window with the names of the fields of the Clients.DB table.

☐ Click the OK button, and then close the Field editor window.

If you examine the Object Inspector window, you'll see that each field of the Clients.DB table now has a field object (for example, Table1CustNum).

Implementing a Range Button

Implement a Range button so that when the user clicks the button, the SetRange program will display only those records whose CustNum fields are between a certain range.

☐ Place a pushbutton (from the Standard page) in Form2, and set the properties of the pushbutton as follows:

```
Name      cmdSetRange
Caption   &Set Range
```

☐ Attach code to the OnClick event of the cmdSetRange button.

After attaching the code, the cmdSetRangeClick procedure should look as follows:

```
procedure TForm2.cmdSetRangeClick(Sender: TObject);
begin

  Table1.SetRange([10017],[10021]);

end;
```

This code will limit the table to records having a customer number between (and including) 10017 and 10021.

You also can specify selection ranges that do not include one or both of the endpoints, although this requires a little more code. To select customer numbers starting with 10017 and running up to (but not including) 10021, you could write the cmdSetRangeClick as follows:

```
procedure TForm2.cmdSetRangeClick(Sender: TObject);
begin

Table1.DisableControls;

try
    Table1.SetRangeStart;
    Table1CustNum.Value := 10017;
    Table1.KeyExclusive := True;

    Table1.SetRangeEnd;
    Table1CustNum.Value := 10021;
    Table1.KeyExclusive := False;

    Table1.ApplyRange;

finally

    Table1.EnableControls;

end;

end;
```

The code you typed disables the controls:

```
Table1.DisableControls;
```

Then, a try block is executed:

```
try
    Table1.SetRangeStart;
    Table1CustNum.Value := 10017;
    Table1.KeyExclusive := True;

    Table1.SetRangeEnd;
    Table1CustNum.Value := 10021;
    Table1.KeyExclusive := False;

    Table1.ApplyRange;
```

The first record that will be in the range is the record with CustNum field equal to 10017:

```
Table1.SetRangeStart;
Table1CustNum.Value := 10017;
```

You then set the KeyExclusive property to True:

```
Table1.KeyExclusive := True;
```

This means that the record with CustNum equal to 10017 is excluded from the range.

You then set the last record in the range as record with CustNum equal to 10021:

```
Table1.SetRangeEnd;
Table1CustNum.Value := 10021;
```

And the record with `CustNum` equal to `10021` (if any) is included in the range:

```
Table1.KeyExclusive := False;
```

Because you disabled the controls, the code under the `finally` enables the controls (whether or not there was a runtime error during the execution of the `try` block):

```
finally

   Table1.EnableControls;

end;
```

☐ Select Save Project from the File menu.

☐ Execute the SetRange program, click the Set Range button, and verify that the `Grid` control displays only the records that are within the range you specified in the code of the `cmdSetRangeClick` procedure.

If there are no records in this range, the `Grid` control will not display any records.

☐ Click the Exit button to terminate the SetRange program.

Note: For range selections to work on PC database tables (dBASE and Paradox tables), you must have an index on the field(s) you want to use to select the range. When selecting ranges in SQL database tables, indexes are not strictly required but are highly recommended for performance reasons.

Summary

In this chapter, you learned to implement a program (OnlyJim.EXE) that uses the static SQL technique. When implementing static SQL, during design time, you set the static SQL statements.

You also learned how to define a SQL parameter, set its initial value, and modify the value of the SQL parameter during runtime. As demonstrated with the SetQuery.EXE program, you can let the user select records that comply with certain conditions.

You also learned how to set the range of records so that only those records in the table that comply with the range conditions are selected.

Q&A

Q **The static SQL query does not let the user choose the specifications of the SQL query. Is there any practical use for static SQL queries?**

A Yes. For example, you can create small utility programs that displays certain records of a certain table. As you saw, it takes little time to implement such programs. Such utilities can be used for situations where there is a need to display records that comply with a certain condition, and you do not want the user to be able to view other records of the table, and you do not want the user to be able to set a different query.

Q **Do I have to use the `try...finally` block?**

A No. For example, comment out the `try`, `finally`, and the `end` that appears after the `finally`, as follows:

```
procedure TfrmSetQuery.cmdSetQueryClick(Sender: TObject);
var
LastNameString: String;

begin

LastNameString :=
   InputBox ('Set the LastName field',
             'Enter Last Name:',
             '');

LastNameQuery.DisableControls;

  {try}
     LastNameQuery.Active := False;

     LastNameQuery.Params[0].AsString :=
              LastNameString;

     LastNameQuery.Active := True;
  {finally}

     LastNameQuery.EnableControls;
  {end;}

end;
```

The above code will work fine (try it).

However, suppose that something goes wrong during the execution of the statements. You disabled the controls, with the statement

```
LastNameQuery.DisableControls;
```

If an exception occurs later in this procedure, the procedure will abort.

But guess what? The `LastNameQuery` control is still disabled! None of the data-aware controls linked to the `LastNameQuery` will receive data-refresh notifications, which essentially means your form will be paralyzed. By using the `try...finally` block,

the code under `finally` will be executed in any case (even if an exception occurs). Thus, the data-aware controls linked to the query will once again receive data-refresh notifications from the query, and the program can continue executing normally.

Quiz

1. Static SQL queries enable the user to change the setting of the SQL query during runtime:

   a. True.

   b. False.

2. You can change the `Active` property of the static SQL query during runtime:

   a. True.

   b. False.

10

Exercise

The range of records of the SetRange program is "hard coded" (that is, the range is specified in the code of the program). Modify the SetRange program so that the range can be specified by the user.

Answers to Quiz

1. b.

2. a.

Answer to Exercise

Add controls in the `Form2` form as follows:

☐ Place a pushbutton (from the Standard page) in `Form2`, and set the properties of the pushbutton as follows:

```
Name        cmdStart
Caption     &Start
```

☐ Place a pushbutton (from the Standard page) in `Form2`, and set the properties of the pushbutton as follows:

```
Name        cmdLast
Caption     &Last
```

☐ Add the Dialogs keyword to the uses section of the CRange.Pas file (because you're going to use the InputBox function).

☐ Under the var section of the CRange.Pas file, add the declarations of two general variables. After adding the declarations, the var section should look as follows:

```
var
  Form2: TForm2;
  gFirstString: String;
  gLastString: String;
```

Here, you declared the gFirstString and gLastString variables. Because you declared these variables at the beginning of the CRange.Pas file, they are accessible from any procedure of Form2.

☐ Attach code to the OnClick event of the cmdFirst button.

After you attach the code, the cmsFirstClick procedure should look as follows:

```
procedure TForm2.cmdFirstClick(Sender: TObject);
begin

gFirstString :=
  InputBox ('First Record',
            'Enter Customer Number:',
            '');

end;
```

The code you typed takes a string from the user and assigns the string to the gFirstString variable.

☐ Attach code to the OnClick event of the cmdLast button.

After you attach the code, the cmdLastClick procedure should look as follows:

```
procedure TForm2.cmdLastClick(Sender: TObject);
begin

gLastString :=
  InputBox ('Last Record',
            'Enter Customer Number:',
            '');

end;
```

The code you typed takes a string from the user and assigns the string to the gLastString variable.

☐ If you want to include the endpoints in the range, you can just modify the cmdSetRangeClick procedure to look like this:

```
procedure TForm2.cmdSetRangeClick(Sender: TObject);
begin

  Table1.SetRange([gFirstString],[gLastString]);

end;
```

If you want to tinker with the endpoint inclusion (in this case, include the range start and exclude the range end), modify the `cmdSetRangeClick` procedure so it will look as follows:

```
procedure TForm2.cmdSetRangeClick(Sender: TObject);
begin

Table1.DisableControls;

try
   Table1.SetRangeStart;
   Table1CustNum.AsString := gFirstString;
   Table1.KeyExclusive := True;

   Table1.SetRangeEnd;
   Table1CustNum.AsString := gLastString;
   Table1.KeyExclusive := False;

   Table1.ApplyRange;

finally

   Table1.EnableControls;

end;
```

The code you typed sets the beginning of the range as follows:

```
Table1.SetRangeStart;
Table1CustNum.AsString := gFirstString;
```

That is, the user's input `gFirstString` is assigned as the beginning of the range.

Similarly, the end of the range is set as follows:

```
Table1.SetRangeEnd;
Table1CustNum.AsString := gLastString;
```

☐ Select Save Project from the File menu.

☐ Execute the SetRange program.

The window of the SetRange program should appear as shown in Figure 10.10.

Figure 10.10.

The SetRange program with its First and Last buttons.

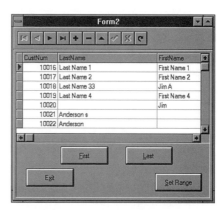

271

☐ Click the First button, and then type a customer number. This customer number serves as the beginning of the range.

☐ Click the Last button, and then type a customer number. This customer number serves as the end of the range.

☐ Click the Set Range button.

The SetRange program now displays only those records that comply with the range you specified.

☐ Experiment with the SetRange program, and then click its Exit button to terminate it.

Multiple Forms
and Printing
Forms

In previous chapters, you implemented projects that included only one form. In this chapter, you'll implement a project composed of several forms. You'll also learn about important topics such as printing and bookmarking.

The Need for a Multiple-Form Project

Typically, a database project consists of various programs. For example, one program enables the user to view records of a certain table, another enables the user to view records of another table, another enables the user to enter and modify records, and so on. Because all these programs use the same database (the same group of tables), it's convenient to create one program that serves as the front-end for all the other programs. Doing so enables the user to move from one program to another easily.

The AddView.EXE program demonstrates how to implement a multiple-form project. The AddView program enables the user to enter new records to the Clients.DB table, as well as to view the Parts.DB table. For example, if a customer inquires about a part number, the user doesn't have to quit the current program and start a new program that displays the Parts.DB table records.

The AddView program uses the Clients.DB and Parts.DB tables.

☐ Make sure that the C:\DProg\Work directory includes the Clients.DB and Parts.DB tables, and that the structures of the Clients.DB and Parts.DB tables are as shown in Tables 11.1 and 11.2.

Table 11.1. The Clients.DB table structure.

Field Name	Type	Size	Key
CustName	Autoincrement	n/a	Yes
LastName	Alpha	30	No
FirstName	Alpha	20	No
Street	Alpha	40	No
City	Alpha	30	No
State	Alpha	10	No
AreaCode	Alpha	3	No
Phone	Alpha	8	No
ZipCode	Alpha	5	No
ClientType	Alpha	10	No
SalesPersonNum	Numeric	n/a	No

Table 11.2. The Parts.DB table structure.

Field Name	Type	Size	Key
PartNum	Numeric	n/a	Yes
Description	Alpha	40	No
QtyInStock	Numeric	n/a	No
SellingPrice	Numeric	n/a	No

Creating the AddView Project

Create the AddView project by following these steps:

☐ Start Delphi.

☐ Select New Project from the File menu.

When creating a new project, an empty Form1 form is created. Form1 serves as the project's main form. After starting the AddView program, the user sees Form1.

☐ Select Form1, select Save File As from the File menu, and save Form1 as CAllApps.Pas in the C:\DProg\Ch11 directory.

☐ Select Save Project As from the File menu, and save the project as AddView.Dpr in the C:\DProg\Ch11 directory.

As stated, Form1 serves as the main form. Now customize this form.

☐ Set the Name property of Form1 to frmAllApps.

☐ Implement the frmAllApps form according to Table 11.3. When you finish implementing the form, it should look as shown in Figure 11.1.

Table 11.3. The frmAllApps Form Properties.

Object	Property	Setting
Form	Name	frmAllApps
	Caption	The AddView Program
Push Button	Name	cmdExit
	Caption	E&xit
Push Button	Name	cmdClients
	Caption	&Add/View Clients
Push Button	Name	cmdParts
	Caption	&View Parts

Figure 11.1.
The frmAllApps *Form*
(design mode).

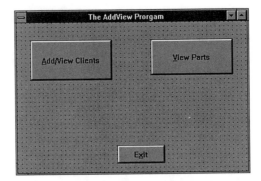

Note: If you have a high resolution monitor and you use large fonts for your screen display, you'll need to set an additional property for each form used in the sample programs for this book so that forms will display properly. If you don't set this property, the contents of the forms scale up proportionally but the form border stays the same, which produces a form with only part of its control surface showing. For each form, you need to set the AutoScroll property to False, which scales the form to a readable size.

Implementing the Exit Dialog Box

During execution of the AddView program, a user might click the Exit button unintentionally. To address this possibility, it's a good idea to implement a dialog box that asks users whether or not they really want to exit the program.

☐ Attach code to the OnClick event of the Exit button.

After attaching the code, the cmdExitClick procedure should appear as follows:

```
procedure TfrmAllApps.cmdExitClick(Sender: Tobject);
begin

  Close;

end;
```

☐ Attach code to the onCloseQuery event of the form.

After attaching the code, the cmdFormCloseQuery procedure should appear as follows:

```
procedure TfrmAllApps.cmdFormCloseQuery(Sender: TObject;
  var CanClose: Boolean);
```

```
var
UserChoiceWord: Word;

begin

UserChoiceWord :=
  MessageDlg ('Are you sure you want to exit?',
              mtConfirmation,
              [mbYes,mbNo]
              0) ;

CanClose := (UserChoiceWord = mrYes) ;

end;
```

The added code declares a local variable.

```
var
UserChoiceWord: Word;
```

Then, a message box is displayed. The message box contains Yes and No buttons (see the third parameter of the MessageDlg function).

```
UserChoiceWord :=
  MessageDlg ('Are you sure you want to exit',
              mtConfirmation,
              [mbYes,mbNo],
              0);
```

The user selection is stored in the UserChoiceWord variable. For example, if the user clicked the Yes button, the UserChoiceWord variable is equal to mrYes.

Next, the UserChoiceWord variable is examined to determine what value to assign to the CanClose Boolean parameter.

```
CanClose := (UserChoiceWord = mrYes) ;
```

If the user clicked the Yes button, CanClose will get the value True. If the user clicked the No button, UserChoiceWord will equal mrNo, and CanClose will get the value False. If CanClose is set to True, the form is allowed to close, and the application terminates. If CanClose is set to False, the form-close operation is ignored, and the application continues to run.

☐ Execute the AddView program, and verify that the Exit button works as expected. After clicking the Exit button, the dialog box shown in Figure 11.2 appears.

Figure 11.2.
*The dialog box that
AddView displays after
clicking the Exit button.*

☐ While the dialog box of Figure 11.2 is displayed, attempt to click in the frmAllApps form.

The program refuses to switch to the frmAllApps form. Why? Because the message box is a *modal window*. A modal window means that you cannot switch to other windows in the same application before you close the modal window.

☐ Experiment with the Exit button, and then terminate the program.

Adding Forms to the Project

Two more forms should be added to the project.

☐ Select New Form from the File menu.

Delphi responds by displaying the Browse Gallery window shown in Figure 11.3.

Figure 11.3.
The Browse Gallery window.

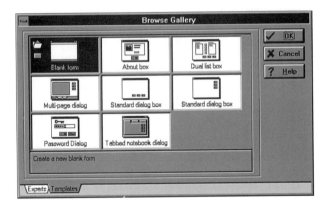

As you can see in Figure 11.3, the Browse Gallery window enables you to select different types of forms.

☐ Select the Blank form, and then click the OK button.

Delphi responds by adding a new form to the project. Currently, the project contains two forms: frmAllApps and Form1 (which is the new form that you just added with the Browse Gallery window).

☐ Select New Form from the File menu again.

Delphi responds by re-displaying the Browse Gallery window as shown in Figure 11.3.

☐ Select the Blank form, and then click the OK button.

Delphi responds by adding a new form to the project. Currently, the project contains three forms: frmAllApps, Form1, and Form2 (which is the new form that you just added with the Browse Gallery window).

☐ Select the Form1 form, select Save File As from the File menu, and save Form1 as CClients.Pas in the C:\DProg\Ch11 directory.

☐ Select the Form2 form, select Save File As from the File menu, and save Form2 as CParts.Pas in the C:\DProg\Ch11 directory.

☐ Set the Name property of Form1 to **frmClients**.

☐ Set the Caption property of frmClients to **Clients**.

☐ Set the Name property of Form2 to **frmParts**.

☐ Set the Caption property of frmParts to **Parts**.

Adding Close Buttons to the Forms

Add Close buttons to the frmClients and frmParts forms by following these steps:

☐ Place a pushbutton from the Standard page in the frmClients form.

☐ Set the properties of the pushbutton as follows:

```
Name      cmdClose
Caption   &Close
```

☐ Attach code to the OnClick event of the cmdClose button.

After attaching the code, the cmdCloseClick event should appear as follows:

```
procedure TfrmClients.cmdCloseClick(Sender: TObject);
begin

Close;

end;
```

The added code closes the frmClients form.

Add a Close button to the frmParts form by following these steps:

☐ Place a pushbutton in the frmParts form, and set the properties of the pushbutton as follows:

```
Name      cmdClose
Caption   &Close
```

☐ Attach code to the OnClick event of the cmdClose button of the frmParts form.

After attaching the code, the cmdCloseClick procedure of the frmParts form should appear as follows:

```
procedure TfrmParts.cmdCloseClick(Sender: TObject);
begin

Close;

end;
```

Displaying the Clients and Parts Forms

To display the Clients and Parts forms, you need to attach code to the OnClick events of the cmdClients and cmdParts buttons of the frmAllApps form.

☐ Attach code to the cmdClients button of the frmAllApps form.

After attaching the code, the cmdClientsClick procedure should appear as follows:

```
procedure TfrmAllApps.cmdClientsClick(Sender: TObject);
begin

frmClients.ShowModal;

end;
```

The added code displays the frmClients form as a modal window, and so you won't be able to switch to the frmAllApps form while the frmClients form is displayed.

If you compile the AddView program now, you will get a compiling error because the CAllApps.Pas unit doesn't know that the CClients.Pas unit exists.

☐ In the uses section at the beginning of the CAllApps.Pas file, add code.

After adding the code, the uses section of the CAllApps.Pas file should appear as follows:

```
uses
  SysUtils, WinTypes, WinProcs, Messages, Classes, Graphics,
  Controls, Forms, Dialogs, StdCtrls,
  CClients, CParts;
```

CAllApps.Pas now recognizes the CClients.Pas and CParts.Pas units.

☐ Attach code to the OnClick event of the cmdParts button of the frmAllApps form.

After adding the code, the cmdPartsClick procedure should appear as follows:

```
procedure TfrmAllApps.cmdPartsClick(Sender: TObject);
begin

frmParts.ShowModal;

end;
```

The added code displays the frmClients form as a modal window.

☐ Select Save Project from the File menu.

☐ Execute the AddView program.

The frmAllApps form appears as shown in Figure 11.4.

Figure 11.4.
The AddView program window.

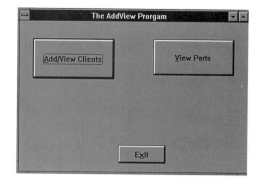

☐ Click the Add/View Clients button.

The frmClients form appears as shown in Figure 11.5.

Figure 11.5.
The Clients window.

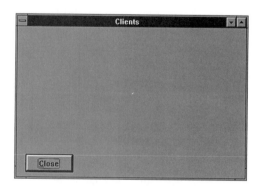

☐ Click the Clients window's Close button to close the window.

The AddView program again displays the main form (Figure 11.4).

☐ Click the Parts button.

The frmParts form appears as shown in Figure 11.6.

Figure 11.6.
The Parts window.

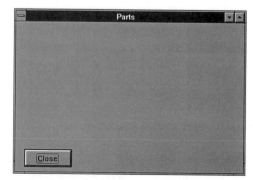

☐ Click the Parts window's Close button to close the window.

The AddView program again displays the main form (Figure 11.4).

☐ Experiment with the program, and then click its Exit button to terminate it.

Displaying Forms As Non-Modal Windows

The frmClients and frmParts forms were displayed as modal windows using the following code:

```
frmClients.ShowModal;
```

Alternatively, you can display a form as a *non-modal window*.

☐ Modify the code in the frmAllApps form's cmdClientsClick procedure as follows:

```
procedure TfrmAllApps.cmdClientsClick(Sender: TObject);
begin

{frmClients.ShowModal;}

frmClients.Show;

end;
```

In this code, you commented out the statement that displays the frmClients as a modal window, and you added a statement that displays the frmClients form as a non-modal window by using the Show method.

☐ Select Save Project from the File menu.

☐ Execute the AddView program.

☐ Click the Add/View Clients button.

The frmClients form appears as a non-modal window.

☐ Click in the frmAllApps window.

Because the frmClients form is a non-modal window, the program enables you to switch to the frmAllApps window.

☐ Click the Add/View Clients button again.

The Clients window becomes the active window again.

☐ Experiment with the program, and then click the Exit button to terminate the program.

> **Note:** Depending on the particular application you're developing, you may decide that it's convenient to display the different forms as either modal or non-modal windows.
>
> For example, suppose the Clients form is used for extracting a client's phone number. While making a phone call to the client, the user inquires about a certain part number. The user can switch to the Parts window, locate the part number, and inform the client about the part's price and availability. Because the client may have additional questions about the part, it's easier for the user to have the Clients and the Parts windows displayed as non-modal windows because switching between the windows is easier to do.

Implementing the Clients Form

Now you're ready to proceed with the implementation of the `frmClients` and `frmParts` forms as you did in previous chapters.

Place some controls in the `frmClients` form.

☐ Place a `Table` component from the Data Access page in the `frmClients` form.

☐ Set the properties of the `Table` component as follows:

```
Name            ClientsTable
DatabaseName    MYWORK (or C:\DProg\Work)
TableName       Clients.DB
```

☐ Place a `DataSource` component from the Data Access page in the `frmClients` form.

☐ Set the properties of the `DataSource` component as follows:

```
Name       ClientsDataSource
DataSet    ClientsTable
```

☐ Place a `Navigator` control from the Data Controls page in the `frmClients` form.

☐ Set the properties of the `Navigator` control as follows:

```
Name          ClientsDBNavigator
DataSource    ClientsDataSource
```

☐ Attach the following code to the `FormCreate` procedure of the `frmClients` form:

11

```
procedure TfrmClients.FormCreate(Sender: TObject);
begin

ClientsTable.Open;

end;
```

The added code opens the Clients.DB table.

☐ Place a `Grid` control from the Data Controls page in the `frmClients` form, and set the
properties of the `Grid` control as follows:

```
Name          ClientsDBGrid
DataSource    ClientsDataSorce
```

The `frmClients` form should now appear as shown in Figure 11.7.

Figure 11.7.
*The frmClients form
(design mode).*

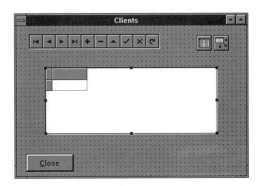

☐ Select Save Project from the File menu.

☐ Execute the AddView program.

☐ Click the Add/View Clients button, and verify that the Clients window displays the
Clients.DB table data.

☐ Terminate the AddView program.

Implementing the Parts Form

To add controls to the `frmParts` form, follow these steps.

☐ Place a `Table` component from the Data Access page in the `frmParts` form.

☐ Set the properties of the `Table` component as follows:

```
Name           PartsTable
DatabaseName   MYWORK (or C:\DProg\Work)
TableName      Parts.DB
```

☐ Place a DataSource component from the Data Access page in the frmParts form.

☐ Set the properties of the DataSource component as follows:

Name	PartsDataSource
DataSet	PartsTable

☐ Place a Navigator control from the Data Controls page in the frmParts form.

☐ Set the properties of the Navigator control as follows:

Name	PartsDBNavigator
DataSource	PartsDataSource

☐ Attach the following code to the FormCreate procedure of the frmParts form:

```
procedure TfrmParts.FormCreate(Sender: TObject);
begin

PartsTable.Open;

end;
```

The added code opens the Parts.DB table.

☐ Place a Grid control from the Data Controls page in the frmParts form, and set the properties of the Grid control as follows:

Name	PartsDBGrid
DataSource	PartsDataSource

The frmParts form should now appear as shown in Figure 11.8.

Figure 11.8.
The frmParts form (design mode).

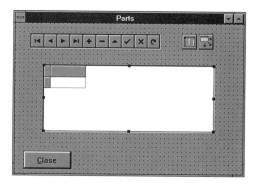

☐ Select Save Project from the File menu.

☐ Execute the AddView program.

☐ Click the Parts button, and verify that the Parts window displays the Parts.DB table data.

☐ Terminate the AddView program.

Printing Your Forms

You can print your forms, and thus make a hard copy. In this section, you implement Print buttons that enable your user to print forms.

☐ Place a pushbutton from the Standard page in the frmClients form.

☐ Set the properties of the button as follows:

```
Name      cmdPrint
Caption   &Print
```

☐ Attach code to the OnClick event of the cmdPrint button.

After attaching the code, the cmdPrintClick procedure of the frmClients form should appear as follows:

```
procedure TfrmClients.cmdPrintClick(Sender: TObject);
begin

Print;

end;
```

The added code executes the Print method of the frmClients form.

☐ Select Save Project from the File menu.

☐ Execute the AddView program. Click the Add/View button.

AddView responds by displaying the Clients window.

☐ Prepare your printer to print, and then click the Print button.

AddView responds by printing the frmClients from.

☐ Terminate the AddView program.

In a similar manner, you can attach a Print button to the frmParts form.

☐ Place a pushbutton in the frmParts form, set the Name property of the button to cmdPrint, set the Caption property of the button to &Print, and type the following code in the cmdPrintClick procedure of the frmParts form:

```
procedure TfrmParts.cmdPrintClick(Sender: TObject);
begin

Print;

end;
```

☐ Save your project, execute the AddView program, and verify that the Print button of the frmParts form prints the Parts form.

☐ Terminate the AddView program.

Creating Bookmarks

While browsing through tables, you can create a bookmark. For instance, suppose that the Parts.DB table includes thousands of records, and the user of the AddView program is trying to locate a certain part for a client. Naturally, you have to enhance the frmParts form to enable the user to easily search for a part number. For example, you have to implement a Search button and maybe permit the user to search for a part number by different keys (by PartNum, by Description, and so on). The topics of searching and ordering the tables by different keys were discussed in previous chapters. However, even with the various Search mechanisms you provide, the Search operation is time consuming. During a conversation between the user and the client, the client may ask the user to search first for part number 1001, then for part number 1075, and finally require additional information on part 1001, for which the user already searched.

It's a good idea to provide the user with a mechanism for marking a certain record (just like a bookmark of a book).

To implement a Mark button that marks the current record of the Parts.DB table, follow these steps.

☐ In the public section at the end of the TfrmParts class declaration, add the declaration of the gMarkedRecord variable.

After adding the declaration, the TfrmParts class declaration should appear as follows:

```
TfrmParts = class(TForm)
    cmdClose: TButton;
    PartsTable: TTable;
    PartsDataSource: TDataSource;
    PartsDBNavigator: TDBNavigator;
    PartsDBGrid: TDBGrid;
    cmdPrint: TButton;
    procedure cmdCloseClick(Sender: TObject);
    procedure FormCreate(Sender: TObject);
    procedure cmdPrintClick(Sender: TObject);
  private
    { Private declarations }
  public
    { Public declarations }
    gMarkedRecord: TBookmark;
  end;
```

The added variable is of type TBookmark and is designed to hold the location of a record. Declaring the gMarkedRecord in the public section of the form class declaration means that this variable is accessible from any method in the frmParts form, and if multiple frmParts forms are open, each will have its own bookmark. This sample program doesn't open multiple copies of the frmParts form, but it's good programming style to keep variables related to a form inside the form itself.

☐ Place a pushbutton from the Standard page in the frmParts form.

☐ Set the properties of the button as follows:

```
Name     cmdMark
Caption  &Mark
```

☐ Attach code to the OnClick event of the cmdMark button of the frmParts form.

After attaching the code, the cmdMarkClick procedure in the frmParts form should appear as follows:

```
procedure TfrmParts.cmdMarkClick(Sender: TObject);
begin

gMarkedRecord := PartsTable.GetBookmark;

end;
```

The added code assigns to the gMarkedRecord variable the pointer to the current record in the Parts.DB table.

Place another button in the frmParts form, the Go To Bookmark button.

☐ Place a pushbutton from the Standard page in the frmParts form.

☐ Set the properties of the button as follows:

```
Name     cmdGoToBookmark
Caption  &Go To Bookmark
```

☐ Attach code to the OnClick event of the cmdGoToBookmark button.

After attaching the code, the cmdGoToBookmarkClick procedure of the frmParts form should appear as follows:

```
procedure TfrmParts.cmdGoToBookmarkClick(Sender: TObject);
begin

PartsTable.GotoBookmark(gMarkedRecord);

end;
```

The added code uses the GotoBookmark method to place the current record pointer on the record whose pointer is stored in the gMarkedRecord variable.

The frmParts form should now appear as shown in Figure 11.9.

☐ Select Save Project from the File menu.

☐ Execute the AddView program.

☐ Click the Parts button.

AddView responds by displaying the Parts window.

Figure 11.9.
The frmParts form with its Mark and Go To Bookmark buttons (design mode).

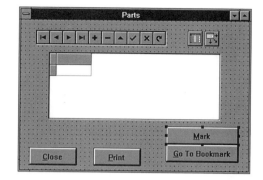

Browse through the Parts.DB table, and then click the Mark button. Take note of the record that was selected when you clicked the Mark button.

☐ Place the current record on a different record of the Parts.DB table.

☐ Click the Go To Bookmark button.

The program responds by placing the current record pointer on the record that was selected when you clicked the Mark button.

☐ Experiment with the AddView program, and then click its Exit button to terminate the program.

The program runs as expected, but it contains a subtle bug. A bookmark is a dynamically allocated structure. You can allocate multiple bookmarks for a table, each referring to a different record and each consuming a small amount of memory. Have you spotted the bug? If not, here's a hint: GetBookmark allocates memory for the bookmark structure. Where does the code free that memory allocation? It doesn't, and that's the bug: the program contains a memory leak, albeit a small one. Every time you click the Go To Bookmark button, a new bookmark is allocated and assigned to the gMarkedRecord variable, but the previous bookmark assigned to gMarkedRecord is not released.

To fix this memory leak, you need to release the previous bookmark before allocating a new one. Bookmarks are relesed by calling the FreeBookmark method of the Table component. Modify the cmdMarkClick method so it looks like this:

```
procedure TfrmParts.cmdMarkClick(Sender: TObject);
begin

if Assigned(gMarkedRecord) then
  PartsTable.FreeBookmark(gMarkedRecord);

gMarkedRecord := PartsTable.GetBookmark;

end;
```

The `if` statement makes sure that `FreeBookmark` is called only when `gMarkedRecord` actually contains a value. The first time the user clicks on the Mark button, `gMarkedRecord` won't contain a bookmark (it will be *nil*). Before deallocating any resource, it's a good idea to make sure you actually have something to deallocate.

This change to the code will ensure that the previous bookmark, if any, will be freed before the next bookmark is allocated. But what if the user runs the program, clicks on the Mark button (allocating a bookmark), and then terminates the program? The bookmark will be allocated, but never freed. To free the bookmark when the form is destroyed, we need to add some code to the Parts form's `OnDestroy` event.

☐ Attach code to the `OnDestroy` event of the `frmParts` form.

Edit the `FormDestroy` method so it looks like this:

```
procedure TfrmParts.FormDestroy(Sender: TObject);
begin

if Assigned(gMarkedRecord) then
begin
  PartsTable.FreeBookmark(gMarkedRecord);
  gMarkedRecord := nil;
end;

end;
```

This checks to see if the `gMarkedRecord` variable contains a bookmark, and if it does, it frees the bookmark and assigns `nil` to the `gMarkedRecord` variable. `Nil` is a special Pascal language constant which indicates that the `gMarkedRecord` variable refers to nothing.

☐ Execute the AddView program, and confirm that the visible operation of the program has not changed.

Summary

In this chapter, you learned how to implement a project containing multiple forms. You learned that a window can be displayed as either a modal or non-modal window.

You learned how to implement a Print button that causes the program to print the form, and you implemented the Mark and Go To Bookmark buttons, mechanisms that place the current record pointer on a marked record.

Q&A

Q **Should I display the forms as modal or non-modal windows?**

A It depends on the particular application that you are developing. As discussed in this chapter, making the windows non-modal makes the switching between forms easier. But remember that letting the user display too many windows could cause confusion, and thus, could make your program difficult to use.

Q **Does the Print button have any practical use?**

A Yes. For example, you can implement a program that displays application forms. The user types the name and other information on an application, and then clicks the Print button to generate a hard copy of the application form. Of course, you have to design the form so that it looks like an application form (for example, use DBEdit controls, Labels with the name of the company, and so on). In one operation, the user enters a new record in a table containing information about applicants, and with one click of a button, a hard copy of an application form is printed.

Q **What other uses does the bookmark have?**

A In the AddView program, the bookmark mechanism was implemented so the user can utilize this feature.

You can utilize the bookmark feature in your programs as follows:

☐ Establish a bookmark on the current record.

☐ Perform some calculations requiring the record pointer to move to other records. For example, if you perform a search operation, the current record pointer changes.

☐ At the end of the calculations, you can return the current record pointer to the bookmark by using the GotoBookmark method.

Quiz

1. A modal window does not let the user switch to another window of the same application while the modal window is displayed.

    a. True.

    b. False.

2. A form containing the Table component can be displayed in modal as well as non-modal form.

    a. True.

    b. False.

3. While displaying a modal window, the user can switch to a window of another application.
    a. True.
    b. False.

Exercise

The AddView program implements a Mark button and a Go To Bookmark button. Implement another button that removes the bookmark. **Hint:** Use the FreeBookmark method.

Answers to Quiz

1. a.
2. a.
3. a.

Answer to Exercise

You can release the bookmark by executing the FreeBookmark method.

☐ Place a pushbutton from the Standard page in the frmParts form.

☐ Set the properties of the button as follows:

Name	cmdFreeBookmark
Caption	&Release Bookmark

☐ Attach code to the OnClick event of the cmdFreeBookmark button.

After attaching the code, the frmParts form cmdFreeBookmarkClick procedure should appear as follows:

```
procedure TfrmParts.cmdReleaseBookmarkClick(Sender: TObject);
begin

PartsTable.FreeBookmark(gMarkedRecord);

end;
```

Note that if you release the bookmark by clicking the Release Bookmark button and then click the Go To Bookmark button, an error message is displayed. This is because you executed the GotoBookmark method when no bookmark was set.

You can avoid the error message by inserting code in the cmdGoToBookmarkClick button that first checks whether a bookmark exists, as follows:

```
procedure TfrmParts.cmdGoToBookmarkClick(Sender: TObject);
begin

if Assigned(gMarkedRecord) then
    PartsTable.GotoBookmark(gMarkedRecord);

end;
```

The GoToBookmark method is executed provided that the gMarkedRecord variable has been assigned a bookmark. The expression if Assigned(gMarkedRecord then is equivalent to if gMarkedRecord <> nil then.

You also will get a runtime error if you click the Release Bookmark button twice because the program cannot free a resource that is nil or has already been freed. You have to modify the cmdReleaseBookmarkClick Procedure so that it appears as follows:

```
procedure TfrmParts.cmdReleaseBookmarkClick(Sender: TObject);
begin

if Assigned(gMarkedRecord) then
begin
  PartsTable.FreeBookmark(gMarkedRecord);
  gMarkedRecord := nil;
end;

end;
```

Whenever the user clicks the Release Bookmark button now, if a bookmark has been allocated, it's released and the gMarkedRecord variable is set to nil.

Whenever the user clicks the Go To Bookmark button, the GotoBookmark method is not executed if gMarkedRecord is equal to nil.

Graphics and
Memos with Delphi

In previous chapters, you designed tables that had numeric and alphanumeric fields in them. In this chapter, you learn how to handle tables with Graphics and Memo fields in them. You also learn how to move between records in the tables from within the code of your Delphi programs.

Graphics and Memo Fields

Use Database Desktop to create a table called Anim.DB. As you'll see later in this chapter, the Anim.DB table is used for animation.

☐ Use Database Desktop to create the Anim.DB table according to Table 12.1, and save the table in the C:\DProg\Work directory. The Structure window of the Anim.DB table in Database Desktop is shown in Figure 12.1.

Table 12.1. The Anim.DB table structure.

Field Name	Type	Size	Key
FrameNum	Numeric	n/a	Yes
FramePicture	Graphics	n/a	No
FrameMemo	Memo	200	No

Figure 12.1.
The Anim.DB structure window.

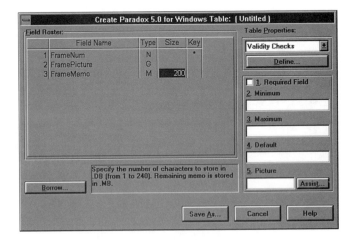

Creating the FillAnim Project

Create the FillAnim.EXE program project. This program enables you to fill the records of the Anim.DB table.

☐ Start Delphi.

☐ Select New Project from the File menu.

☐ Select the Form1 form, select Save File As from the File menu, and save Form1 as CFill.Pas in the C:\DProg\Ch12 directory.

☐ Select Save Project As from the File menu, and save the project as FillAnim.Dpr in the C:\DProg\Ch12 directory.

Implementing the FillAnim Program Form

Implement the FillAnim.EXE program form, as follows:

☐ Set the Name property of Form1 to **frmFillAnim**.

☐ Set the Caption property of the frmFillAnim form to **The FillAnim Program**.

☐ Place a Table component from the Data Access page in the frmFillAnim form.

☐ Set the properties of the Table component as follows:

```
Name            AnimTable
DatabaseName    MYWORK (or C:\DProg\Works)
TableName       Anim.DB
```

☐ Place a DataSource component from the Data Access page in the frmFillAnim form.

☐ Set the properties of the DataSource component as follows:

```
Name       AnimDataSource
DataSet    AnimTable
```

☐ Place a DBEdit control from the Data Controls page in the frmFillAnim form.

☐ Set the properties of the DBEdit control as follows:

```
Name          FrameNumDBEdit
DataSource    AnimDataSource
DataField     FrameNum
```

☐ Place a Label control from the Standard page in the frmFillAnim form.

☐ Set the properties of the Label control as follows:

```
Name       lblFrameNumber
Caption    Frame Number
```

12

☐ Place a `Navigator` control from the Data Controls page in the `frmFillAnim` form.

☐ Set the properties of the `Navigator` control as follows:

Name	AnimDBNavigator
DataSource	AnimDataSource

☐ Attach code to the `OnCreate` event of the `frmFillAnim` form.

After attaching the code, the `FormCreate` procedure of the `frmFillAnim` form should appear as follows:

```
procedure TfrmFillAnim.FormCreate(Sender: TObject);
begin

AnimTable.Open;

end;
```

The code that you typed opens the Anim.DB table.

Implementing an Exit Button

Now implement an Exit button.

☐ Place a pushbutton from the Standard page in the `frmFillAnim` form.

☐ Set the properties of the button as follows:

Name	cmdExit
Caption	E&xit

☐ Attach code to the `OnClick` event of the `cmdExit` button.

After attaching the code, the `cmdExitClick` procedure should appear as follows:

```
procedure TfrmFillAnim.cmdExitClick(Sender: TObject);
begin

Close;

end;
```

The `frmFillAnim` form should now appear as shown in Figure 12.2.

Although you haven't completed implementing the `FillAnim` program, execute it, and verify that everything is working as expected.

☐ Select Save Project from the File menu.

☐ Execute the FillAnim program.

Figure 12.2.
The frmFillAnim form (design mode).

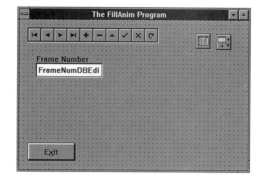

The window of the FillAnim program appears as shown in Figure 12.3. The fact that the some of the buttons of the Navigator control are available is an indication that the Anim.DB table is open.

Figure 12.3.
The FillAnim program window.

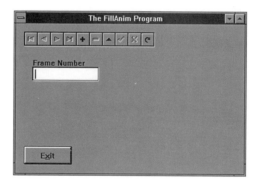

☐ Click the Exit button to terminate the program.

Using the *DBMemo* and *DBImage* Controls

When you designed the Anim.DB table, you created the FramePicture and FrameMemo fields. The FramePicture field contains the BMP picture of the record, and the FrameMemo field contains text.

Figure 12.4 shows the DBImage control icon on the Data Control page, and Figure 12.5 shows the DBMemo control icon on the Data Controls page. The DBImage control serves as the control that holds the contents of the Graphics fields, and the DBMemo control serves as the control that holds the contents of the Memo fields.

Figure 12.4.

The DBImage control icon on the Data Controls page.

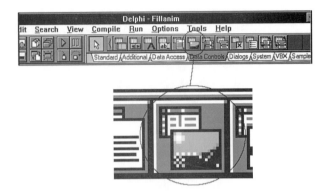

Figure 12.5.

The DBMemo control icon on the Data Controls page.

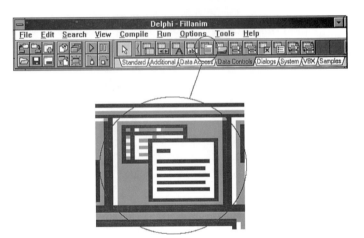

☐ Place a DBMemo control from the Data Controls page in the frmFillAnim form.

☐ Set the properties of the DBMemo control as follows:

Name	FrameDBMemo
DataSource	AnimDataSource
DataField	FrameMemo

The frmFillAnim form should now appear as shown in Figure 12.6.

Although you haven't completed implementing the FillAnim program, let's see the DBMemo control in action.

☐ Select Save Project from the File menu.

☐ Execute the FillAnim program.

☐ Fill the FrameNum field of the first record of Anim.DB with 1.

Figure 12.6.
The frmFillAnim *form with the* DBMemo *control in it (design mode).*

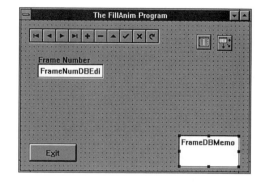

☐ Switch to any program that lets you copy text into the Clipboard. For example, start Notepad or Word for Windows.

☐ Type something with Notepad (or another program), and then copy the text to the Clipboard. To do this, highlight the text you typed, and select Copy from the Edit menu.

The Clipboard now contains the text you typed. In the next step, you paste the text into the DBMemo control.

☐ Switch back to the FillAnim program, select the DBMemo control, and press Ctrl+v.

The contents of the Clipboard are now in the DBMemo control. In other words, you filled the FrameMemo field of the current record.

☐ Experiment with the FillAnim program by adding new records to the Anim.DB table, filling the FrameNum field, and then pasting text from the Clipboard into the FrameMemo field.

☐ Terminate the FillAnim program by clicking its Exit button.

Note: An alternative way to edit the Memo field contents is as follows:

☐ Make sure that the DBMemo control ReadOnly property is set to False (the default setting).

☐ Set the DBMemo control ScrollBars property to ssBoth.

During runtime, you can now edit the Memo field text.

The FrameMemo field was introduced in the FillAnim program for the sole purpose of demonstrating the DBMemo control.

The *AutoDisplay* Property of the *DBMemo* Control

If the FrameMemo field has a lot of text in it, browsing through the Anim.DB table is very slow because a lot of text must be loaded whenever the user moves from record to record.

This is why the DBMemo control's AutoDisplay property is so important. To see the AutoDisplay property in action,

☐ Set the AutoDisplay property to False.

☐ Execute the FillAnim program.

☐ Browse through the Anim.DB table by using the Navigator control.

As you browse through the records, note that you cannot see the FrameMemo field contents. To see the contents, you must double-click the DBMemo control.

☐ Experiment with the FillAnim program, and then click its Exit button to terminate the program.

As it turns out, the MyAnim program (an animation program that you write later in this chapter) does not need the DBMemo control.

☐ Select the DBMemo control, and then press the Delete key to remove the control from the frmFillAnim program.

Placing the *DBImage* Control

Now you place the DBImage control in the frmFillAnim form.

☐ Place the DBImage control from the Data Controls page in the frmFillAnim form.

☐ Set the properties of the DBImage control as follows:

```
Name          FramePictureDBImage
DataSource    AnimDataSource
DataField     FramePicture
```

☐ Use the mouse to enlarge the DBImage control.

The frmFillAnim form should now appear as shown in Figure 12.7.

Figure 12.7.
The frmFillAnim *with the* DBImage *control in it (design mode).*

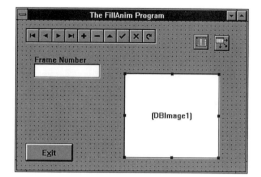

> **Note:** Just like the DBMemo control, the DBImage control has the AutoDisplay property. Setting this property to False means that to view the contents of the FramePicture field, the user must double-click the DBImage control.
>
> Leave the AutoDisplay property of the DBImage control set at its default setting, which is True.

☐ Select Save Project from the File menu.

☐ Execute the FillAnim program.

☐ Start the Paintbrush program.

☐ Draw something with Paintbrush, and save your drawing as a BMP file.

☐ Use the Paintbrush tools to copy the picture you drew to the Clipboard. Use the tool appearing on the first row on the right column of the Paintbrush toolbox to enclose the picture, and then select Copy from the Paintbrush Edit menu.

Now the picture is in the Clipboard.

☐ Switch back to the FillAnim program, click in the DBImage control, and then press Ctrl+v.

The Clipboard contents are pasted to the DBImage control, and so the current displayed record has the picture in its FramePicture field.

☐ Experiment with the FillAnim program by filling other records of the Anim.DB table.

☐ Use the Navigator control to delete all the records of the Anim.DB table.

12

The *DBImage* Control's *Stretch* Property

The DBImage control's Stretch property stretches the picture it contains so that it fits in the DBImage control. This means that if the picture is too large to fit in the control, the DBImage control will shrink the picture appropriately.

☐ Set the Stretch property of the DBImage control to True.

☐ Enlarge the frmFillAnim form and the DBImage control.

The frmFillAnim form should now appear as shown in Figure 12.8.

Figure 12.8.
Enlarging the DBImage control (design mode).

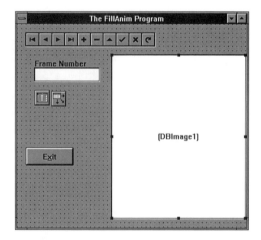

Filling the Anim.DB Table

You're ready now to fill the Anim.DB table with various BMP pictures.

In the C:\DProg\BMP directory, you find several BMP files.

☐ Fill the records of the Anim.DB table (using the FillAnim program) as outlined in Table 12.2. For example, in the first record of Anim.DB fill the FrameNum with 1. Then load the C:\DBProg\BMP\Dance01.BMP picture with Paintbrush, use the Paintbrush tools to copy the picture to the Clipboard, switch back to the FillAnim program, click in the DBImage control, and press Ctrl+v.

The contents of the Clipboard (which currently contains the Dance01.DMP picture) is pasted to the Anim.DB table `FramePicture` field.

Table 12.2. The Anim.DB table records

Record	FrameNum	FramePicture
1	1	Dance00.BMP
2	2	Dance01.BMP
3	3	Dance02.BMP
4	4	Dance03.BMP
5	5	Dance04.BMP

☐ Use the `Navigator` control to move from record to record, and verify that the five records contain the data and pictures shown in Table 12.2.

The FillAnim program windows showing the five records of the Anim.DB table are shown in Figures 12.9 through 12.13.

☐ Terminate the FillAnim Program.

Figure 12.9.
Record 1 of Anim.DB.

Figure 12.10.
Record 2 of Anim.DB.

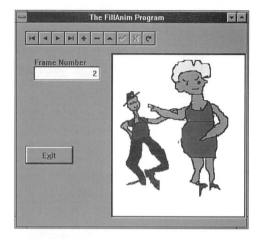

Figure 12.11.
Record 3 of Anim.DB.

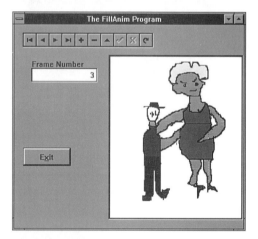

Figure 12.12.
Record 4 of Anim.DB.

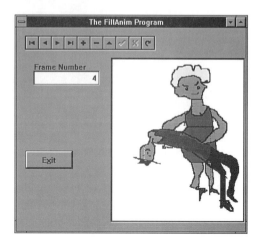

Figure 12.13.
Record 5 of Anim.DB.

Creating the MyAnim Project

Your next mission is to create the MyAnim program, a program that displays animation.

You may argue that by clicking the Next button in the FillAnim program's Navigator control, you can see the animation (a couple dancing), but the MyAnim program that you now write automates the process. That is, you design the MyAnim program so the program automatically moves the record pointer from record to record. Also, the MyAnim program displays the animation in an endless loop. After showing the five frames of the animation, the MyAnim program starts the show all over again.

☐ Make sure that the FillAnim project is saved because, as you'll soon see, the MyAnim project uses the files from the FillAnim project.

☐ Select New Project from the File menu.

Select the Form1 form, select Save File As from the File menu, and save Form1 as CMyAnim.Pas in the C:\DProg\Ch12 directory.

☐ Select Save Project from the File menu, and save the project as MyAnim.Dpr in the C:\DProg\CH12 directory.

☐ Set the properties of Form1 as follows:

```
Name       frmMyAnim
Caption    The MyAnim Program
```

☐ Place a pushbutton from the Standard page in the frmMyAnim form.

☐ Set the properties of the pushbutton as follows:

```
Name       cmdFillAnim
Caption    &Fill Anim.DB
```

☐ Attach code to the OnClick event of the cmdFillAnim button.

After attaching the code, the cmdFillAnimClick procedure of the frmMyAnim form should appear as follows:

```
procedure TfrmMyAnim.cmdFillANimClick(Sender: TObject);
begin

frmFillAnim.ShowMoadl;

end;
```

The code that you typed displays the frmFillAnim form (a form you implemented earlier in this chapter) as a modal window.

Of course, if you now execute the MyAnim program, you get a compiler error because the frmMyAnim form doesn't know about the frmFillAnim form's existence.

☐ Select Project Manager from the View menu.

Delphi responds by displaying the Project Manager window, and as you can see from Figure 12.14, only the frmMyAnim (CMyAnim.Pas) appears in the window.

Figure 12.14.
The Project Manager window (only one form exists in the project).

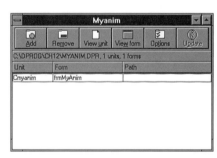

To add the frmMyAnim form to the MyAnim project, use the following steps:

☐ Select Add File from the File menu, and select the file C:\DProg\Ch12\CFill.Pas.

☐ Select Project Manager from the View menu.

Delphi responds by displaying the Project Manager window shown in Figure 12.15, and as you can see, there are now two forms in the project:

```
frmFillAnim (CFill.Pas)
frmMyAnim (CMyAnim.Pas)
```

Figure 12.15.
The Project Manager window with two forms in it.

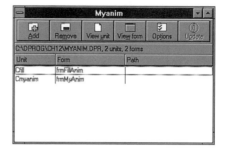

Now the project has two forms in it, but which form is executed when the MyAnim program is executed? You can click the Project Manager's Option button to display the Project Options window, which tells you which is the main form:

☐ Click the Options button of the Project Manager window.

  Delphi responds by displaying the Project Options window, as shown in Figure 12.16.

Figure 12.16.
The Project Options window.

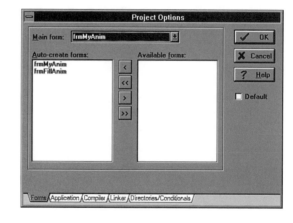

In Figure 12.16, the frmMyAnim form is shown as the main form, so when executing the MyAnim program, the frmMyAnim form is displayed.

☐ Close the Project Options window and then close the Project Manager window.

The project now includes two forms, but the frmMyAnim form still doesn't know about the frmFillAnim form. If you now execute the MyAnim program, you still get a compiler error.

☐ In the uses section at the beginning of the MyAnim.Pas file, add **CFill** as follows:

```
uses
  SysUtils, WinTypes, WinProcs, Messages, Classes, Graphics,
  Controls, Forms, Dialogs, StdCtrls,
  CFill;
```

☐ Select Save Project from the File menu.

☐ Execute the MyAnim program.

The window shown in Figure 12.17 appears.

Figure 12.17.

The MyAnim program.

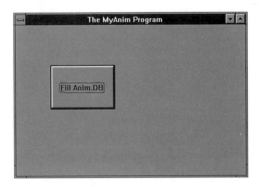

☐ Click the Fill Anim.DB button.

The `frmFillAnim` form appears.

The user can now fill records in the Anim.DB table. (You already filled the records of the Anim.DB table according to Table 12.2.)

☐ Click the Exit button of the `frmFillAnim` form.

The `frmMyAnim` form appears again.

☐ Terminate the MyAnim program by clicking the minus-sign (–) icon appearing on the upper-left corner of its window, and then select Close from the system menu that pops up.

Let's review the major steps you've accomplished so far:

☐ At the beginning of this chapter, you created the FillAnim program, which enables you to fill records in the Anim.DB table.

☐ You then created a new project, the MyAnim project. The MyAnim program uses the `frmFillAnim` form you created earlier. In other words, without changing a single line of code in the `frmFillAnim` form, you use this form in another project.

Implementing an Exit Button

Implement an Exit button in the `frmMyAnim` form.

☐ Place a pushbutton from the Standard page in the `frmMyAnim` form.

☐ Set the properties of the pushbutton as follows:

```
Name        cmdExit
Caption     E&xit
```

☐ Attach code to the OnClick event of the cmdExit button.

After attaching the code, the cmdExitOnClick procedure should appear as follows:

```
procedure TfrmMyAnim.cmdExitClick(Sender: TObject);
begin

Application. Terminate;

end;
```

Note: The cmdExitClick procedure of the frmFillAnim form includes the statement

Close;

which means that the frmFillAnim form is closed, and the program returns to the frmMyAnim form that serves as the program's main form.

However, in the cmdExitClick procedure of the frmMyAnim form's cmdExit button, you execute the following statement, which terminates the program:

Application.Terminate;

☐ Select Save Project from the File menu.

☐ Execute the MyAnim program and verify that the Exit buttons work as expected.

Implementing the *frmShow* Form

So far, you have two forms in the MyAnim project:

frmMyAnim (CMyAnim.Pas)	This serves as the main form.
frmFillAnim (CFill.Pas)	This serves as the form to fill records in the Anim.DB table.

Now add a third form to the project.

☐ Select New Form from the File menu.

Delphi responds by displaying the Browse Gallery window, as shown in Figure 12.18.

☐ Select Blank Form, and then click the OK button.

Delphi responds by adding the Form1 form to the project.

12

Figure 12.18.
The Browse Gallery window.

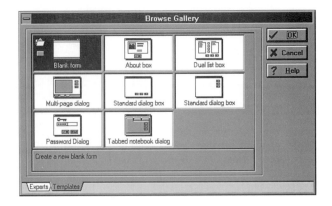

☐ Select Form1, select Save File As from the File menu, and save the Form1 as CShow.Pas in the C:\DProg\Ch12 directory.

☐ Set the properties of Form1 as follows:

    Name   frmShow
    Caption   The Animation Show

☐ Place a pushbutton from the Standard page in the frmShow form.

☐ Set the properties of the pushbutton as follows:

    Name   cmdExit
    Caption   E&xit

The frmShow form now appears as shown in Figure 12.19.

Figure 12.19.
The frmShow form (design mode).

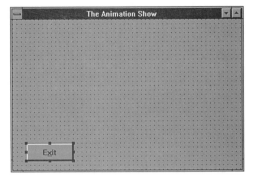

☐ Attach code to the OnClick event of the Exit button of the frmShow form.

After attaching the code, the `cmdExitClick` procedure of the `frmShow` form should appear as follows:

```
procedure TfrmShow.cmdExitClick(Sender: TObject);
begin

Close;

end;
```

Add a second pushbutton to the `frmMyAnim` form:

☐ Place a pushbutton from the Standard page in the `frmMyAnim` form.

☐ Set the properties of the pushbutton as follows:

```
Name        cmdShow
Caption     &Show
```

The `frmMyAnim` form should now appear as shown in Figure 12.20:

Figure 12.20.

The frmMyAnim *form (design mode).*

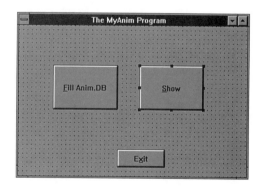

☐ Attach code to the `OnClick` event of the `cmdShow` button of the `frmMyAnim` form.

After attaching the code, the `cmdShowClick` procedure of the `frmMyAnim` form should appear as follows:

```
procedure TfrmMyAnim.cmdShowClick(Sender: TObject);
begin

frmShow.ShowModal;

end;
```

The code you typed displays the `frmShow` form as a modal window.

The project now contains three forms, but the `frmMyAnim` form does not know of the existence of the `frmShow` form (CShow.Pas). You now add **CShow** to the uses section of the `frmMyAnim` form.

☐ In the uses section, at the beginning of the CMyAnim.Pas file, add **CShow** as follows:

```
uses
    SysUtils, WinTypes, WinProcs, Messages, Classes, Graphics,
    Controls, Forms, Dialogs, StdCtrls,
    CFill,
    CShow;
```

☐ Select Save Project from the File menu.

☐ Execute the MyAnim program.

The MyAnim program window appears.

☐ Click the Show button.

MyAnim responds by displaying the frmShow form, as shown in Figure 12.21.

Figure 12.21.

The frmShow form.

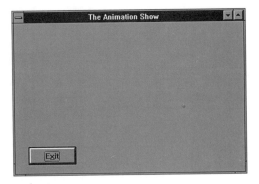

☐ Click the Exit button of the frmShow form.

The program returns to the main form (frmMyAnim).

☐ Experiment with the MyAnim program, and then terminate the program.

Implementing the Animation Show

Everything is now ready for the implementation of the animation show. You implemented the frmMyAnim form, which serves as the program's main form. The user can click the Fill Anim.DB button to fill the Anim.DB table records, and click the Show button to display the frmShow form. All you have to do now is add the code to the frmShow form that displays the animation show.

☐ Place a pushbutton from the Standard page in the frmShow form and set its properties as follows:

```
Name        cmdStartShow
Caption     &Start Show
```

☐ Place a pushbutton from the Standard page in the frmShow form and set its properties as follows:

```
Name         cmdStopShow
Caption      Sto&p Show
```

☐ Place a Table component from the Data Access page in the frmShow form, and set its properties as follows:

```
Name          AnimTable
DatabaseName  MYWORK (or C:\DProg\Work)
TableName     Clients.DB
```

☐ Place a DataSource component from the Data Access page in the frmShow form, and set its properties as follows:

```
Name      AnimTable
DataSet   AnimTable
```

☐ Place a DBImage control from the Data Controls page in the frmShow form, and set its properties as follows:

```
Name         FramePistureDBImage
DataSource   AnimDataSource
DataField    FramePicture
Stretch      True
```

☐ Enlarge the size of the frmShow form, and then enlarge the frmShow form's DBImage control.

The frmShow form should now appear as shown in Figure 12.22.

Figure 12.22.
The frmShow with its Data Controls.

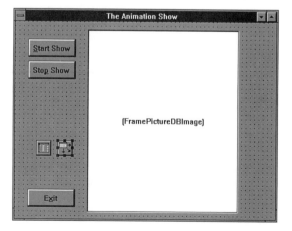

☐ Attach code to the OnCreate event of the frmShow form.

After attaching the code, the FormCreate procedure of the frmShow form should appear as follows:

```
procedure TfrmShow.FormCreate(Sender: TObject);
begin

AnimTable.Open;

end;
```

The code you typed opens the Anim.DB table.

Although you haven't completed the program, execute it.

☐ Select Save Project from the File menu.

☐ Execute the MyAnim program.

☐ Click the Show button.

The frmShow form appears as shown in Figure 12.23.

Figure 12.23.

The picture of the first record of the Anim.DB table appears in the frmShow window.

Of course, if you now click the Start Show button, nothing happens because you haven't yet attached any code to it.

Note that when clicking the main form's Show button (the frmMyAnim form), the frmShow appears with the picture of the first record in it. This is because when you open a table (as you did in the FormCreate procedure of the frmShow form), the Anim.DB table is opened, and the record pointer points to the first record.

Using the *Timer* Control

Now you place a Timer control in the frmShow form. The Timer control icon on the System page is shown in Figure 12.24.

Figure 12.24.
The Timer *control icon on the System page.*

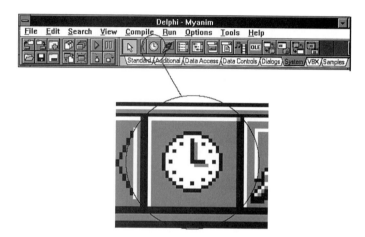

☐ Place a Timer control from the System page in the frmShow form.

☐ Set the properties of the Timer control as follows:

```
Name       tmrSpeed
Enabled    False
Interval   250
```

The frmShow should now appear as shown in Figure 12.25.

Figure 12.25.
The frmShow *form with the* Timer *control in it.*

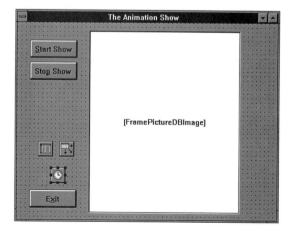

The OnTimer event of the Timer control periodically occurs automatically. For example, you set the Interval property of the tmrSpeed Timer control to 250. This means that every 250 milliseconds, the tmrSpeedTimer procedure is automatically executed.

☐ Attach code to the OnTimer event of the tmrSpeedTimer procedure of the frmShow form.

After attaching the code, the tmrSpeedTimer procedure should appear as follows:

```
procedure TfrmShow.tmrSpeedTimer(Sender: TObject);
begin

AnimTable.MoveBy(1);

if AnimTable.EOF then
   begin
   AnimTable.First;
   end;

end;
```

The code you typed advances the record pointer to the next record.

```
AnimTable.MoveBy(1);
```

You could have used the Next method to advance to the next record, but we want to illustrate the use of the MoveBy() method for moving the record pointer. For example, to move two records forward, use the statement

```
AnimTable.MoveBy(2);
```

To move two records backward, use the following statement:

```
AnimTable.MoveBy(-2);
```

An if statement is then executed.

```
if AnimTable.EOF then
   begin
   AnimTable.First;
   end;
```

The if condition is satisfied if the record pointer is at the end of the table. Every 250 milliseconds, the record pointer is advanced by one record. If you look at the record pointer, its values are as follows:

```
Record 1
Record 2
Record 3
Record 4
Record 5
```

On the next execution of the tmrSpeedTimer procedure, the record pointer is again advanced by one, and this puts the record pointer at EOF (end of file). This means that the if statement is satisfied, and the record pointer is placed at the first record:

```
AnimTable.First;
```

Putting it all together, the record pointer points to the following records:

```
Record 1
Record 2
Record 3
Record 4
Record 5
Record 1
Record 2
Record 3
Record 4
Record 5
...
```

If you now execute the MyAnim program and click the Show button, you will not see the animation because you set the Enabled property of the tmrSpeed Timer control to False. This means that the tmrSpeedTimer procedure is not executed.

To make the tmrSpeedTimer procedure execute every 250 milliseconds, you must set the Enabled property of the tmrSpeed Timer control to True.

You now attach code to the cmdStartClick procedure. This code enables the tmrSpeed Timer control whenever the user clicks the Start button.

Attaching Code to the Start Button

☐ Attach code to the OnClick event of the cmdStart button of the frmShow form.

After attaching the code, the cmdStartClick procedure should appear as follows:

```
procedure TfrmShow.cmdStartShowClick(Sender: TObject);
begin

tmrSpeed.Enabled := True;

end;
```

The code you typed sets the Enabled property of the tmrSpeed control to True, and so once the user clicks the Start button, the tmrSpeedTimer procedure is automatically executed every 250 milliseconds.

☐ Select Save Project from the File menu.

☐ Click the Show button of the frmMyAnim form.

MyAnim responds by displaying the frmShow *form.*

☐ Click the Start button.

The program responds by displaying the animation show.

☐ Click the Exit button of the frmShow form, and then click the Exit button of the frmMyAnim program to terminate the program.

Attaching Code to the Stop Show Button

Attach code to the Stop button of the frmShow form as follows:

☐ Attach code to the OnClick event of the frmShow form's cmdStop button.

After attaching the code, the cmdStopClick procedure should appear as follows:

```
procedure TfrmShow.cmdStopShowClick(Sender: TObject);
begin

tmrSpeed.Enabled := False;
AnimTable.First;

end;
```

The code you typed sets the Enabled property of the tmrSpeed Timer control to False.

```
tmrSpeed.Enabled := False;
```

The animation show is stopped because the tmrSpeedTimer procedure is no longer executed.

You placed the current record pointer on the first record,

```
AnimTable.First;
```

and so when the user clicks the Stop Show button, the animation show is stopped, and the picture of the first record is displayed.

☐ Select Save Project from the File menu.

☐ Execute the MyAnim program.

☐ Click the Show button.

☐ Click the Start Show button.

The animation show starts.

☐ Click the Stop button.

The animation show is stopped.

☐ Experiment with the MyAnim program, and then terminate the MyAnim program.

Summary

In this chapter, you learned how to design a table containing Memo and Graphics fields. You also learned how to implement a program (the FillAnim.EXE program) that fills the Memo and Graphics fields by using Delphi's DBMemo and DBImage controls.

The MyAnim program you implemented demonstrates how to use the frmFillAnim form that you implemented in the FillAnim program, and without modifying a single line of code in the frmFillAnim form, you used the frmFillAnim form for the implementation of the MyAnim program, which is a multiple form program.

The MyAnim program demonstrates how to use the MoveBy() method to move from record to record, and how to use the EOF to determine whether the table's end of file (EOF) is encountered.

Q&A

Q How many characters can the Memo field contain?

A In Windows 3.1, the Memo field can contain 32KB (where one byte holds one character). The contents of the Memo field are stored on the hard disk as a file. While browsing through the table, the program extracts the text from the file and places it in the DBMemo control.

Q In Question/Answer 1, it is stated that the DNMemo control can hold 32KB, but when I designed the Anim.DB table with Database Desktop, I was instructed by Database Desktop and Table 12.1 to set the FrameMemo field size to 200. Why?

A You set the FrameMemo field size to 200. This means that the first 200 characters of the text contained in FrameMemo field reside in the Anim.DB table. When browsing through the table, the first 200 characters are loaded fast, just like an Alpha field of a table.

Quiz

1. The `AutoDisplay` property of the `DBMemo` and `DBImage` control is used so that _____.

2. The `DBImage` control has an `AutoDisplay` property:

   a. True.

   b. False.

3. The `EOF` is used for _____.

4. The `MoveBy` method is used for _____.

Exercises

1. Perform the following steps:

   ☐ Execute the MyAnim program.

   ☐ Click the Show button.

   ☐ Start the show (by clicking the Start Show button).

   ☐ Click the Exit button of the `frmShow` form.

   ☐ Click the Start Show button again.

   The `frmShow` form appears, and the animation is in progress.

   Terminate the program, and then modify the program so that once the `frmMyAnim` form is closed, and when starting the show again, the user must click the Start button to start the show.

2. Do you like the speed at which the animation is performed? Enhance the MyAnim program so that the user can set the speed at which the animation show is performed.

Answers to Quiz

1. The `AutoDisplay` property of the `DBMemo` and `DBImage` control is used so that browsing through the table records is accomplished quickly even if the corresponding `DBMemo` or `DBImage` control files are large.

2. a.

3. The `EOF` is used for determining whether the record pointer points to the end of file of the table.

4. The `MoveBy` method is used for moving the record pointer.

Answers to Exercises

1. Here's what to do.

   ☐ Add code to the cmdExitClick procedure of the frmShow form.

   After adding the code, the `frmShow` form `cmdExitClick` procedure should appear as follows:

   ```
   procedure TfrmShow.cmdExitClick(Sender: TObject);
   begin

   tmrSpeed.Enabled := False;
   AnimTable.First;
   Close;

   end;
   ```

   The code that you added sets the `Enabled` property of the `Timer` control to `False`, and then the record pointer is placed on the first record. In other words, before you closed the `frmShow` form, you performed the same operations that the Stop button performs.

2. Now place a scroll bar and two `Label` controls in the `frmShow` form, as shown in Figure 12.26.

Figure 12.26.

The `frmShow` *form with the scroll bar and two* `Label` *controls in it.*

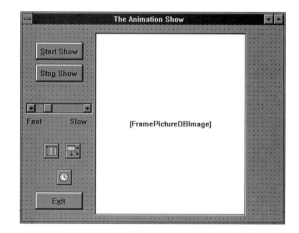

12

   ☐ Place a scroll bar from the Standard page in the `frmShow` form.

   ☐ Place a `Label` control from the Standard page on the left side of the scroll bar.

   ☐ Place a `Label` control from the Standard page on the right side of the scroll bar.

☐ Set the properties of the scroll bar as follows:

```
Name        hsbSpeed
Min         50
Max         1000
Position    250
```

☐ Set the properties of the Label control that you placed on the left side of the scroll bar as follows:

```
Name        lblSlow
Caption     Slow
```

☐ Set the properties of the Label control that you placed on the right side of the scroll bar as follows:

```
Name        lblFast
Caption     Fast
```

☐ Attach code to the OnChange event of the scroll bar.

After attaching the code, the hsbSpeedChange procedure should appear as follows:

```
procedure TfrmShow.hsbSpeedChange(Sender: TObject);
begin

tmrSpeed.Interval := hsbSpeed.Position;

end;
```

The code you typed sets the Timer control's Interval property according to the scroll bar's Position property.

When the user changes the scroll bar's position, the hsbSpeedChange procedure is executed. The code that you typed in this procedure sets the Timer control Interval property according to the new position of the scroll bar.

☐ Select Save Project from the File menu.

☐ Execute the MyAnim program.

☐ Click the Show button.

☐ Click the Start Show button.

☐ Change the scroll bar position and note that the animation speed is changed accordingly.

☐ Experiment with the MyAnim program, and then terminate the program.

13

VBX and Sound in Your Delphi Program

Users will expect your Delphi programs to be sophisticated, state-of-the-art technology software. You can create sophisticated, impressive Delphi programs by adding sound capability. Thus, in addition to displaying a message telling the user to do something, your program also can play an audio message for the user. In this chapter, you'll learn how to implement sound playing from within your programs. The program you'll implement plays a speech through the PC speaker, so even if you or your users don't have a sound card, you still can play audio prompts.

Sound Capabilities

Nowadays, almost every vendor ships PCs with multimedia capabilities. In this section, you examine your PC's multimedia capabilities. Don't worry; even if you don't have a sound card, you can write Delphi programs that play sound (speech and music) through the PC speaker.

One of the programs shipped with Windows is the Media Player program. Media Player usually resides in the Windows Program Manager Accessories group. Figure 13.1 shows the Media Player program icon.

Figure 13.1.

The Media Player program icon in the Accessories group.

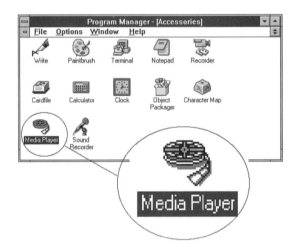

You now use Media Player to determine your PC's multimedia capabilities.

☐ Start the Media Player program.

The Media Player program window appears as shown in Figure 13.2.

☐ Select the Device menu.

The Device menu appears as shown in Figure 13.3.

Figure 13.2.
The Media Player program.

Figure 13.3.
Media Player's Device menu.

The Device menu shown in Figure 13.3 contains the items described in Table 13.1. Your Device menu may contain more or fewer items. These items appear on the Device menu provided that you installed the required hardware and software.

For example, to be able to play movie AVI files, you must first install the AVI drivers (your PC must be a 386 or better, and your monitor must be VGA or better). To see the Sound item in the Media Player Device menu, you need to install a sound card and the sound card drivers that come with it. Most sound cards are capable of handling WAV files as well as MIDI files, and so when you complete installation of the Sound card, the Media Player Device menu includes the Sound item as well as the MIDI Sequencer item. Most CD-ROM drives are designed to handle CD-ROM data (a CD-ROM that contains programs), as well as CD-ROM Audio (a CD-ROM that can be purchased at music stores). Again, once you install the CD-ROM drive and its drivers, the CD Audio item appears in the Media Player Device menu.

Table 13.1. Device menu items for a PC on which the required software and hardware are installed.

Menu Item	Meaning
Video for Windows	The PC on which this Media Player program was executed is capable of playing movie AVI files.
MIDI Sequencer	The PC on which this Media Player program was executed is capable of playing MIDI files. MIDI files are synthesized sound files.
Sound	The PC on which this Media Player program was executed is capable of playing WAV files. It also is capable of recording WAV files. WAV files are recorded sound files.
CD Audio	The PC on which this Media Player program was executed is capable of playing CD-ROM discs containing digital sound tracks—the kind of CD you would find at a music store. Most computer CD-ROM drives also can play audio CDs.

13

> **Note:** If you install a sound card and you don't see the Sound item in the Media Player Device menu, something went wrong during the sound-card installation. Even if the programs that come with your sound card are working well, you must see the Sound item (and the MIDI item if your sound card is capable of playing MIDI files) in the Device menu. Why? Because when the Device menu includes these items, *any* Windows application can use these multimedia devices.

By inspecting the Media Player Device menu, you can immediately determine the multimedia capabilities of your PC.

Playing Through the PC Speaker

One multimedia capability that every PC has is the capability of playing sound (speech and music) through the PC speaker.

To play through the PC speaker, you don't have to install any drivers. The PC Speaker item doesn't appear in the Media Player Device menu. (Note that every PC has the ability to play through the PC speaker.)

Now you're ready to implement a program that plays WAV files through the PC speaker.

Creating the Kennedy Project

The Kennedy.EXE program plays a famous speech by former President John F. Kennedy.

☐ Start Delphi.

☐ Select New Project from the File menu.

☐ Select the Form1 form, select Save File As from the File menu, and save Form1 as CKennedy.Pas in the C:\DProg\Ch13 directory.

☐ Select Save Project As from the File menu, and save the project as Kennedy.Dpr in the C:\DProg\Ch13 directory.

☐ Set the properties of Form1 as follows:

```
Name      frmKennedy
Caption   The Kennedy Program
```

Implementing an Exit Button

Implement an Exit button for the form.

☐ Place a pushbutton from the Standard page in the frmKennedy form.

☐ Set the properties of the pushbutton as follows:

```
Name      cmdExit
Caption   E&xit
```

☐ Attach code to the OnClick event of the cmdExit button.

After attaching the code, the cmdExitClick procedure should appear as follows:

```
procedure TfrmKennedy.cmdExitClick(Sender: TObject);
begin

Close;

end;
```

☐ Select Save Project from the File menu.

☐ Execute the Kennedy program, and verify that its Exit button works as expected.

The Kennedy.DB Table

The Kennedy program uses a table called Kennedy.DB. Create the Kennedy.DB table by following these steps.

☐ Use Database Desktop to create the Kennedy.DB table according to Table 13.1, and save the Kennedy.DB table in the C:\DProg\Work directory. The Kennedy.DB table structure window is shown in Figure 13.4.

Table 13.1. The Kennedy.DB table structure.

Field Name	Type	Size	Key
SpeechSection	Numeric	n/a	Yes
From	Numeric	n/a	No
To	Numeric	n/a	No
SpeechText	Alpha	200	No

Figure 13.4.

The Kennedy.DB table structure.

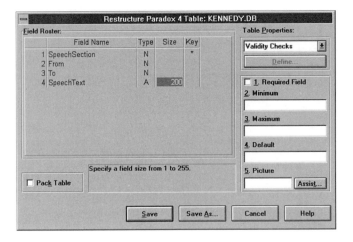

☐ Use Database Desktop to fill the records of the Kennedy.DB table with the data, as follows:

Record 1

SpeechSection	1
From	0
To	3000
SpeechText	So my fellow Americans

Record 2

SpeechSection	2
From	3001
To	7000
SpeechText	Ask not what your country can do for you

Record 3

SpeechSection	3
From	7000
To	11900
SpeechText	Ask what you can do for your country

The SpeechSection field contains the section number. As you can see from the preceding data, the WAV file was broken into three sections. The first section is from location 0 to 3000 milliseconds. The first section contains the phrase So my fellow Americans.

☐ Terminate Database Desktop, and switch back to the Kennedy project.

The data you entered into the Kennedy.DB table can be extracted from the WAV file as follows:

☐ Start the Media Player program.

☐ Select Open from the File menu of Media Player, and load the \DProg\WAV\8Kenned3.WAV file.

☐ Click the Play button of the Media Player program (the leftmost button).

As the Media Player plays the 8Kenned3.WAV file, the Media Player moves a file pointer indicating the current position of the played WAV file. After practicing with Media Player for a while, you'll see that the phrase So my fellow Americans is between the 0-millisecond and 3000-millisecond (three-second) position of the WAV file. The phrase Ask not what your country can do for you is between the 3001-millisecond and 7000-millisecond range of the WAV file, and the phrase Ask what you can do for your country is between the 7001-millisecond and 11900-millisecond range.

Placing an *Image* Control in the *frmKennedy* Form

To place an Image control in the frmKennedy form, follow these steps.

☐ Place an Image control from the Additional page in the frmKennedy form. The Image control icon on the Additional page is shown in Figure 13.5.

Figure 13.5.
The Image *control icon on the Additional page.*

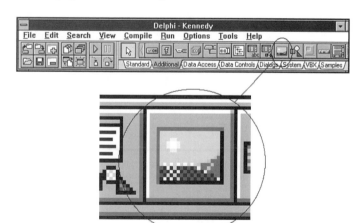

13

Your frmKennedy form should now appear as shown in Figure 13.6.

Figure 13.6.

The frmKennedy *form with the* Image *control in it.*

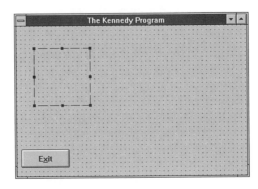

☐ Set the Name property of the Image control to **imgKennedy**.

Next, set the Picture property of the Image control.

☐ Click the three dots to the right of the Image control's Picture property cell in the Object Inspector window.

Delphi responds by displaying the Picture Editor window, as shown in Figure 13.7.

Figure 13.7.

The Picture Editor window.

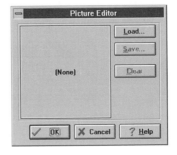

☐ Click the Load button of the Picture Editor window.

Delphi responds by displaying a Load Picture dialog box that enables you to load a picture.

☐ Load the \DProg\BMP\Kennedy.BMP picture.

Your Picture Editor window should now appear as shown in Figure 13.8.

Figure 13.8.
The Picture Editor window with the Kennedy.BMP picture in it.

☐ Click the OK button of the Picture Editor window.

Your frmKennedy form should now contain the Kennedy picture in it.

The reason you see only a portion of the Kennedy.BMP picture in the imgKennedy control is that the default Stretch property of the Image control is set to False.

☐ Set the Stretch property of the imgKennedy control to True, and then enlarge the imgKennedy control.

As you enlarge the Image control, the Kennedy.BMP picture is stretched to fill the entire area of the Image control. Your frmKennedy form should now appear as shown in Figure 13.9.

Figure 13.9.
The frmKennedy form with the Kennedy.BMP picture set as the Picture property of the imgKennedy Image control.

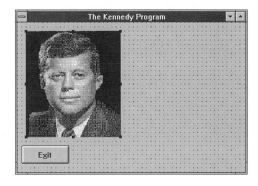

☐ Although you haven't finished writing the Kennedy program, verify that everything is working as expected so far.

☐ Select Save Project from the File menu.

☐ Execute the Kennedy program.

☐ Click the Exit button to terminate the program.

Placing Data Controls in the *frmKennedy* Form

To place Data controls in the frmKennedy form, follow these steps.

☐ Place a Table control from the Data Access page in the frmKennedy form.

☐ Set the properties of the Table control as follows:

```
Name            KennedyTable
DatabaseName    MYWORK (or C:\DProg\Work)
TableName       Kennedy.DB
```

☐ Place a DataSource control from the Data Access page in the frmKennedy form.

☐ Set the properties of the DataSource control as follows:

```
Name       KennedyDataSource
DataSet    KennedyTable
```

Attaching Code to the *OnCreate* Event of the *frmKennedy* Form

☐ Attach code to the OnCreate event of the frmKennedy form.

After attaching the code, the FormCreate procedure should appear as follows:

```
procedure TfrmKennedy.FormCreate(Sender: TObject);
begin

KennedyTable.Open;

end;
```

The added code opens the Kennedy.DB table.

Placing a *DBText* Control in the *frmKennedy* Form

Place a DBText control in the frmKennedy form by following these steps.

☐ Place a DBText control from the Data Controls page in the frmKennedy form.

☐ Set the properties of the DBText control as follows:

Name	KennedyDBText
DataSource	KennedyDataSource
DataField	SpeechText

☐ Enlarge the DBText control.

The frmKennedy form should now appear as shown in Figure 13.10.

Figure 13.10.
The frmKennedy *form with its* DBText *control.*

☐ Select Save Project from the File menu.

☐ Execute the Kennedy program.

The window shown in Figure 13.11 appears. As you can see, the DBText control displays in it the SpeechText field of the Kennedy.DB table's first record.

☐ Click the Exit button to terminate the Kennedy program.

Figure 13.11.
The DBText *control displays the* SpeechText *field contents of the Kennedy.DB table's first record.*

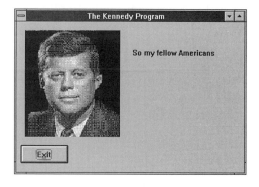

What Is a VBX Control?

Take a look at the various pages of controls of Delphi (for example, the Standard page, the Additional page, the Data controls page, and the Data Access page). Delphi is equipped with quite a few controls. You can build powerful programs with these controls. However, what if the particular feature you're trying to implement in the program isn't available? That is, what if Delphi does not come with the control you need? In this case, you'll have to use a VBX control. A VBX control enables you to expand the capabilities of Delphi.

One of the control pages of Delphi is the VBX page, which is shown in Figure 13.12.

Figure 13.12.
The VBX page.

As you can see in this figure, Delphi has several VBX controls on its VBX page. Next, you'll add a new VBX control to the VBX page that enables you to play sound files through the PC speaker.

Installing VBX controls

Many third-party vendors (those other than Borland International) design and sell VBX controls that enable you to expand the capability of Delphi. This is one of the main advantages of a modular programming language such as Delphi. A modular programming language enables you to use components developed by others. Thus, for a reasonable price, you can obtain controls that will add to Delphi the capabilities you need for your programs.

☐ Make sure that the C:\Windows\System directory contains the TegoMM.VBX file. If you don't have this file in that directory, copy it there from the \DProg\VBX directory of the book's CD-ROM.

Note: The TegoMM.VBX file provided on the book's CD-ROM is the limited version of the control. You can purchase the full version of the control directly from TegoSoft, Inc. See the Special Offer at the end of this book.

☐ Select Save Project from the File menu.

☐ Select New Project from the File menu.

☐ Select Install Component from the Options menu.

Delphi responds by displaying the Install Components window, as shown in Figure 13.13.

Figure 13.13.
The Install Components window enables you to install a VBX control.

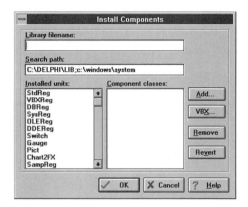

☐ Click the VBX button of the Install Components window.

>   *Delphi responds by displaying a window that enables you to select the VBX file.*

☐ Select the TegoMM.VBX file from your C:\Windows\System directory, and then click the OK button.

>   *Delphi responds by displaying the Install VBX window, as shown in Figure 13.14.*

Figure 13.14.
The Install VBX window.

☐ Click the OK button of the Install VBX window.

☐ Click the OK button of the Install Component window.

That's it! You now can play sound files.

Access Delphi's VBX page again (see Figure 13.15) so you can verify that it includes the TegoMM.VBX control.

☐ Select Open Project from the File menu, and load the Kennedy.Dpr project from the C:\DProg\Ch13 directory.

Figure 13.15.

The VBX page includes the TegoMM.VBX control.

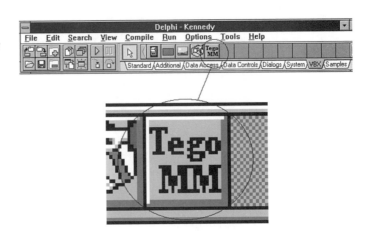

Placing the Multimedia Control in the *frmKennedy* Form

Place the TegoMM.VBX Multimedia control from the VBX page in the frmKennedy form so that the Kennedy program can play sound files.

☐ Place the TegoMM.VBX Multimedia control from the VBX page in the frmKennedy form.

Your frmKennedy form should now appear as shown in Figure 13.16. (You may have to increase the size of the form to make room for the multimedia control.) Later in this chapter, you'll add a Start button to the form.

Figure 13.16.

The frmKennedy form with the TegoMM.VBX Multimedia control in it (design mode).

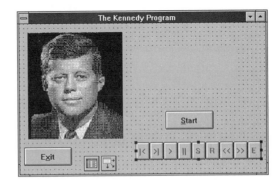

Look at the Name property that Delphi set for the Multimedia control. The Name property is set to Tegomm1, which is the name you'll use in the following sections when you write code.

Playing Sound Through the PC Speaker

In the FormCreate procedure, add code that opens a sound session.

After adding the code, the FormCreate procedure should appear as follows:

```
procedure TfrmKennedy.FormCreate(Sender: TObject);
begin

KennedyTable.Open;

Tegomm1.Visible := False;
Tegomm1.DeviceType := 'PCSpeaker';
Tegomm1.FileName := '8Kenned3.WAV';
Tegomm1.Command := 'Open';

end;
```

The code you added sets the Multimedia control's Visible property to False.

```
Tegomm1.Visible := False;
```

This means that during runtime, the Multimedia control is invisible.

The next statement sets the DeviceType of the Multimedia control to PCSpeaker.

```
Tegomm1.DeviceType := 'PCSpeaker';
```

Now the Multimedia control is set to play sound files (WAV files).

The next statement you added sets the FileName property of the Multimedia control to the name of the WAV file.

```
Tegomm1.FileName := '8Kenned3.WAV';
```

This statement assumes that the WAV file resides in the same directory from which the Kennedy.EXE program is executed, and so you need to make sure that the 8Kenned3.WAV file resides in the C:\DProg\Ch13 directory.

The last statement you added executes the Open command, which opens a WAV session.

```
Tegomm1.Command := 'Open';
```

You set the Visible property of the Tegomm1 object to False because there is no need to see the Multimedia control during runtime in the Kennedy program.

However, for the sake of testing your work, perform this experiment: In the FormCreate procedure, change the statement that sets the Visible property of the Tegomm1 control from False to True.

13

The `FormCreate` procedure should now appear as follows:

```
procedure TfrmKennedy.FormCreate(Sender: TObject);
begin

KennedyTable.Open;

Tegomm1.Visible := True;
Tegomm1.DeviceType := 'PCSpeaker';
Tegomm1.FileName := '8Kenned3.WAV';
Tegomm1.Command := 'Open';

end;
```

☐ Select Save Project from the File menu.

☐ Execute the Kennedy.EXE program.

The window of the Kennedy program appears with the `Multimedia` control in it.

☐ Click the Play button (the third button from the left of the `Multimedia` control).

The Kennedy program responds by playing a speech by President Kennedy.

☐ To hear the speech again, click the Rewind button (the leftmost button on the `Multime-dia` control), and then click the Play button.

During playback of the speech, you can Stop playback (the fifth button from the left) or Pause playback (the fourth button from the left).

☐ Experiment with the Kennedy program, and then click its Exit button to terminate it.

Implementing the Synchronization

Now you're ready to implement synchronized animation. While playback is in progress, the played phrases are displayed on the screen.

☐ In the `FormCreate` procedure, set the `Visible` property of the `Tegomm1` form's `Multimedia` control back to `False`.

The `FormCreate` procedure should now appear as follows:

```
procedure TfrmKennedy.FormCreate(Sender: TObject);
begin

KennedyTable.Open;

Tegomm1.Visible := False;
Tegomm1.DeviceType := 'PCSpeaker';
Tegomm1.FileName := '8Kenned3.WAV';
Tegomm1.Command := 'Open';

end;
```

Add field objects to the frmKennedy form by following these steps.

☐ Double-click the KennedyTable control.

   Delphi responds by displaying the Fields editor window.

☐ Click the Add button of the Fields editor window, make sure that all the fields are selected, and then click the OK button.

If you look at the Object Inspector window now, you'll see that each Kennedy.DB table field has a corresponding field object (for example, KennedyTableFrom, KennedyTableTo, and so on).

☐ Close the Fields editor window.

☐ Set the Visible property of the KennedyDBText control to False.

As you'll soon see, you set the Visible property of the KennedyDBText control to True only during playback.

☐ Place a pushbutton from the Standard page in the frmKennedy form.

☐ Set the properties of the pushbutton as follows:

```
Name      cmdStart
Caption   &Start
```

☐ Attach code to the OnClick event of the cmdStart button.

After attaching the code, the cmdStartClick procedure should appear as follows:

```
procedure TfrmKennedy.cmdStartClick(Sender: TObject);
begin

KennedyDBText.Visible := True;
KennedyDBText.Refresh;
Tegomm1.From := KennedyTableFrom.AsInteger;
frmKennedy.Tegomm1.pTo := KennedyTableTo.AsInteger;
Tegomm1.Command := 'Play';

KennedyTable.Next;
KennedyDBText.Refresh;
Tegomm1.From := KennedyTableFrom.AsInteger;
Tegomm1.pTo := KennedyTableTo.AsInteger;
Tegomm1.Command := 'Play';

KennedyTable.Next;
KennedyDBText.Refresh;
Tegomm1.From := KennedyTableFrom.AsInteger;
frmKennedy.Tegomm1.pTo := KennedyTableTo.AsInteger;
Tegomm1.Command := 'Play';

KennedyTable.First;
KennedyDBText.Visible := False;

end;
```

13

The added code sets the `Visible` property of the `DBText` control to `True`.

```
KennedyDBText.Visible := True;
```

When the user clicks the Start button, the `DBText` control becomes visible.

Then the `DBText` control is refreshed by this statement:

```
KennedyDBText.Refresh;
```

The `KennedyDBText` control now displays the contents of the current record. Because the record pointer points to the first record in the Kennedy.DB table when the Kennedy program starts, the `KennedyDBText` control displays the contents of the `SpeechText` field in the Kennedy.DB table's first record.

The `From` property of the `Multimedia` control is updated with the `From` field of the Kennedy.DB table because when you created the field objects with the Field editor, you created the `KennedyTableFrom` object for the `From` field.

```
Tegomm1.From := KennedyTableFrom.AsInteger;
```

In this statement, you assigned the value of the Kennedy.DB `From` field to the `From` property of the `Multimedia` control.

Similarly, the contents of the `To` field in the Kennedy.DB table are assigned to the `To` property of the `Multimedia` control.

```
Tegomm1.pTo := KennedyTableTo.AsInteger;
```

In this statement, you assigned the value of the `To` field to the `pTo` property because `To` is a keyword in Delphi. You can realize this by typing the following statement:

```
frmKennedy.Tegomm1.To
```

Delphi displays the `To` in a bold font. The bottom line is that even though the `Multimedia` control has the `To` property, Delphi does not let you use the `To` property directly. Delphi does, however, let you access the `To` property of the `Multimedia` control by calling it `pTo`. When you installed the TegoMM.VBX control, Delphi checked the control, and in the C:\Windows\System directory, you'll find the file TegoMM.Pas, which was prepared by Delphi at the time you installed the TegoMM.VBX control. If you search for `To` in this file, you'll see that Delphi replaced `To` with `pTo`.

The next statement you added plays the WAV file through the PC speaker.

```
Tegomm1.Command := 'Play';
```

What is played? The `Multimedia` control plays the WAV file (specified in the Multimedia control's `FileName` property from the location specified by the `Multimedia` control's `From` property up to the location specified by the `Multimedia` control's `To` property.

Putting it altogether, the first section of the WAV file is played, and the DBText control displays the contents of the SpeechText field.

Then, the record pointer is advanced by one to record number 2.

```
KennedyTable.Next;
```

The DBText control is refreshed so it displays record number 2's SpeechText field contents.

```
KennedyDBText.Refresh;
```

The From and pTo properties of the Multimedia control are updated.

```
Tegomm1.From := KennedyTableFrom.AsInteger;
frmKennedy.Tegomm1.pTo := KennedyTableTo.AsInteger;
```

Finally, the second section of the WAV file is played.

```
Tegomm1.Command := 'Play';
```

In a similar manner, the third section of the WAV file is played.

```
KennedyTable.Next;
KennedyDBText.Refresh;
Tegomm1.From := KennedyTableFrom.AsInteger;
frmKennedy.Tegomm1.pTo := KennedyTableTo.AsInteger;
Tegomm1.Command := 'Play';
```

Now that the WAV file is played in its entirety, the record pointer is placed on the first record.

```
KennedyTable.First;
```

The KennedyDBText control is then made invisible.

```
KennedyDBText.Visible := False;
```

☐ Select Save Project from the File menu.

☐ Execute the Kennedy program.

The Kennedy program window appears, as shown in Figure 13.17. As you can see, the DBText control is invisible.

☐ Click the Start button.

The Kennedy program plays Kennedy's speech and displays the spoken words as the speech is played. For example, when the phrase Ask what you can do for your country is played, the window shown in Figure 13.18 is displayed.

13

Figure 13.17.
The Kennedy program window.

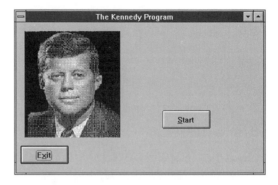

Figure 13.18.
When the phrase Ask what you can do for your country *is played, the window shown is displayed.*

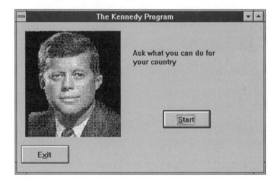

☐ Experiment with the Kennedy program, and then click its Exit button to terminate it.

Note: During playback of the sound file, the mouse cursor is an hour glass. You cannot use the mouse during playback. However, the TegoMM.VBX control contains additional properties that enable you to use the mouse during playback. For example, you can set additional Multimedia control properties so that while playback is in progress, the mouse cursor is not an hour glass, and you can use the mouse to click other buttons. A full description of all the properties of the TegoMM.VBX Multimedia control is supplied with the full version of the control. See the Special Offer at the end of this book.

Summary

In this chapter, you created the Kennedy.DB table and filled its records with information about the 8Kenned3.WAV file. You broke the WAV file into three sections, and each record of the Kennedy.DB table describes a section of the WAV file.

You also implemented the Kennedy.EXE program, which plays the WAV file according to the records of the Kennedy.DB table. By doing so, you implemented a synchronized animation with the spoken words also displayed on the screen. Because Delphi offers easy-to-use database programming tools, it's often useful to use Delphi for implementing programs that are not strictly database programs, such as clients, invoices, and so on.

You also learned what a VBX control is, how to install the VBX control, and how to use the VBX control from within your Delphi programs.

Q&A

Q Should I use Delphi for implementing programs that are not strictly database applications?

A As was demonstrated with the Kennedy.EXE program, by using database technology, you can implement sophisticated programs with great ease using Delphi because Delphi offers powerful tools that enable you to save and extract data from tables. The data can be clients, invoices, and so on, but it also can be small tables used for multi-media applications, games (for saving and extracting the player scores), and a variety of other applications.

Q What is the origin of VBX controls?

A Originally, VBX controls were designed for Visual Basic. However, VBX controls can be used by many other programming languages (for example, Delphi, Visual C++, Borland C++, and many others).

Q I have a sound card installed in my PC, and the software that comes with the sound card works well. However, the Media Player Device menu does not have the Sound item in it. Why?

A Something went wrong during the installation of your sound card. In any case, if you want *any* Windows application to be able to utilize your sound card, you must be able to see the Sound item in the Media Player Device menu.

13

Quiz

1. When a certain VBX control has a property that is used also as a keyword in Delphi, Delphi cannot use this property:

    a. True

    b. False

2. How can you tell if a property of a VBX control is a keyword in Delphi?

Exercise

Enhance the Kennedy program so that it allows the user to play any desired section in the WAV file.

Answers to Quiz

1. b. Delphi changes the name of the property so that you can use it. For example, the `Multimedia` control has the `To` property, but `To` is a keyword in Delphi. Thus, from within your Delphi programs, you have to refer to the `Multimedia` control `To` property as the `pTo` property.

2. When you type the statement in Delphi, a keyword is displayed in a bold font.

Answer to Exercise

Here is one way to implement the enhancement.

☐ Place a scroll bar from the Standard page in the form. This scroll bar serves as the `FromScrollBar`.

☐ Place another scroll bar from the Standard page in the form. This scroll bar serves as the `ToScrollBar`.

☐ Place a pushbutton from the Standard page in the form. This pushbutton serves as the Play button.

During runtime, the user will set the `FromScrollBar` position to the `Multimedia` control's `From` property. Attach code to the `OnChange` event of `FromScrollBar` that sets the `From` property of the `Multimedia` control to the `Position` property of the `FromScrollBar` control as follows:

```
Tegomm1.From := FromScrollBar.Position;
```

Similarly, you have to attach code to the `OnChange` event of the `ToScrollBar` as follows:

```
Tegomm1.pTo := ToScrollBar.Position;
```

Finally, attach code to the `cmdPlay` button that issues the `Play` command as follows:

```
Tegomm1.Command := 'Play';
```

Writing Multimedia Database Applications with Delphi (Part 1)

In the previous chapter, you learned how to examine your PC's multimedia capabilities. In this chapter and the next, you'll implement a program, the MM.EXE program, which uses multimedia technologies.

During the implementation of the MM.EXE program, you'll apply database topics that were presented earlier in this book, and you'll learn how to use additional data controls that Delphi offers (DBRadioGroup, for example).

Creating the MM.DB Table

First, create the MM.DB table (MM stands for *multimedia*).

☐ Use Database Desktop to design the MM.DB table according to the structure shown in Table 14.1, and save MM.DB in the C:\DProg\Work directory. The MM.DB table's structure window is shown in Figure 14.1.

Table 14.1. The MM.DB table structure.

Field Name	Type	Size	Key
ShowNum	N	n/a	Yes
Device	A	20	No
FileName	A	255	No

Figure 14.1.
The MM.DB table structure.

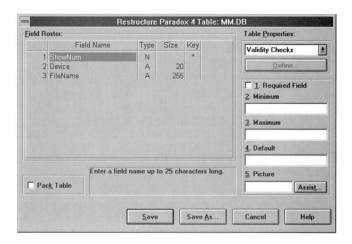

The ShowNum is a unique number assigned to a multimedia show. The multimedia show could utilize a variety of multimedia devices. The Device field indicates the name of the multimedia device. The FileName field contains the name of the multimedia file.

SAMS

Sams
Learning
Center

SAMS
PUBLISHING

Creating the MM Project

Create the MM project by following these steps:

☐ Start Delphi.

☐ Select New Project from the File menu.

☐ Select Form1, select Save File As from the File menu, and save Form1 as CMM.Pas in the C:\DProg\Ch14 directory.

☐ Select Save Project As from the File menu, and save the project file as MM.Dpr in the C:\DProg\Ch14 directory.

☐ Set the properties of Form1 as follows:

```
Name      frmMM
Caption   The Multimedia Program
```

The frmMM form serves as the main form. You display other forms by clicking various buttons on the frmMM form.

Implementing the Exit Button of the *frmMM* Form

Implement the Exit button of the frmMM form. Because the frmMM form serves as the main form of the MM.EXE program, clicking the Exit button causes program termination.

☐ Place a pushbutton from the Standard page in the frmMM form, and set the pushbutton properties as follows:

```
Name      cmdExit
Caption   E&xit
```

☐ Attach code to the OnClick event of the cmdExit button.

After attaching the code, the cmdExitClick procedure should appear as follows:

```
procedure TfrmMM.cmdExitClick(Sender: TObject);
begin

Application.Terminate;

end;
```

Now implement a pushbutton that displays another form.

☐ Place a pushbutton from the Standard page in the frmMM form.

14

☐ Set the pushbutton properties as follows:

```
Name      cmdFillMM
Caption   MM.DB
```

Once the user clicks the cmdFillMM button, another form appears enabling you to fill the MM.DB table records.

Implementing the *frmFillMM* Form

The frmFillMM form is used for editing the MM.DB table. As stated in the previous section, when the user clicks the cmdFillMM button, the frmFill form appears.

☐ Select New Form from the File menu.

Delphi responds by displaying the Browse Gallery window.

☐ In the Browse Gallery window, select Blank form and then click the OK button.

Delphi responds by adding a blank Form1 to the project.

☐ Select Form1, select Save File As from the File menu, and save Form1 as CFillMM.Pas in the C:\DProg\Ch14 directory.

☐ Set the new Form1 form properties as follows:

```
Name      frmFillMM
Caption   Edit MM.DB
```

☐ Attach code to the cmdFillMM button of the frmMM form.

After attaching the code, the cmdFillMMClick procedure of the frmMM form should appear as follows:

```
procedure TfrmMM.cmdFillMMClick(Sender: TObject);
begin

frmFillMM.ShowModal;

end;
```

If you execute the MM program now, you'll get a compile error because you didn't yet include the CFillMM.Pas file in the uses section of the frmMM form.

☐ Add CFillMM to the uses section of the frmMM form.

After adding CFillMM to the uses section at the beginning of the CMM.Pas file, the uses section should appear as follows:

```
uses
  SysUtils, WinTypes, WinProcs, Messages, Classes,
  Graphics, Controls,Forms, Dialogs, StdCtrls,
  CFillMM;
```

☐ Select Save Project from the File menu.

☐ Execute the MM program.

☐ Click the MM.DB button.

> *The* `frmFillMM` *form appears.*

☐ Close the `frmFillMM` form by clicking the minus-sign (–) icon that appears on the upper-left corner of the window, and then select Close from the system menu that pops up.

☐ Click the Exit button of the `frmMM` form to terminate the program.

Editing the MM.DB Table

You're ready now to place various controls in the `frmFillMM` form that enable you to edit the MM.DB table.

☐ Place a pushbutton from the Standard page in the `frmFillMM` form.

☐ Set the pushbutton properties as follows:

Name	cmdExit
Caption	E&xit

☐ Attach code to the `cmdExit` button of the `frmFillMM` form.

After attaching the code, the `cmdExitClick` procedure of the `frmFillMM` form should appear as follows:

```
procedure TfrmFillMM.cmdExitClick(Sender: TObject);
begin

Close;

end;
```

☐ Place a `Table` control from the Data Access page in the `frmFillMM` form.

☐ Set the `Table` control properties as follows:

Name	MMTable
DatabaseName	MYWORK (or C:\DProg\Work)
TableName	MM.DB

14

☐ Place a DataSource control from the Data Access page in the frmFillMM form.

☐ Set the DataSource control properties as follows:

```
Name        MMDataSource
DataSet      MMTable
```

☐ Place a Navigator control from the Data Controls page in the frmFillMM form.

☐ Set the Navigator control properties as follows:

```
Name        MMDBNavigator
DataSource   MMDataSource
```

☐ Attach code to the OnCreate event of the frmFillMM form.

After attaching the code, the FormCreate procedure of the frmFillMM form should appear as follows:

```
procedure TfrmFillMM.FormCreate(Sender: TObject);
begin

MMTable.Open;

end;
```

Next, add three DBEdit controls to the frmFillMM form.

☐ Place a DBEdit control from the Data Controls page in the frmFillMM form, and set the DBEdit control properties as follows:

```
Name        ShowNumDBEdit
DataSource   MMDataSource
DataField    ShowNum
```

☐ Place a DBEdit control from the Data Controls page in the frmFillMM form, and set the DBEdit control properties as follows:

```
Name        DeviceNumDBEdit
DataSource   MMDataSource
DataField    Device
```

☐ Place a DBEdit control from the Data Controls page in the frmFillMM form, and set the DBEdit control properties as follows:

```
Name        FileNameNumDBEdit
DataSource   MMDataSource
DataField    FileNameDevice
```

Place three Label controls from the Standard page in the frmFillMM form by following these steps:

☐ Place a `Label` control from the Standard page in the `frmFillMM` form to the left of the `ShowNumDBEdit` control, and set the properties of the `Label` control as follows:

```
Name        lblShowNum
Caption     Show Number:
```

☐ Place a `Label` control from the Standard page in the `frmFillMM` form, which is to the left of the `DeviceNumDBEdit` control, and set the `Label` control properties as follows:

```
Name        lblDevice
Caption     Device:
```

☐ Place a `Label` control from the Standard page in the `frmFillMM` form, which is to the left of the `FileNameDBEdit` control, and set the `Label` control properties as follows:

```
Name        lblFileName
Caption     FileName:
```

Your `frmFillMM` form should now appear as shown in Figure 14.2.

Figure 14.2.

The `frmFillMM` *form (design mode).*

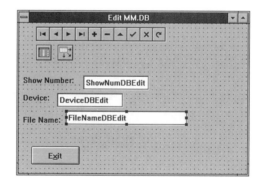

☐ Select Save Project from the File menu.

☐ Execute the MM program.

☐ Click the MM.DB button.

> *The MM program responds by displaying the* `frmFillMM` *form.*

Use the `Navigator` control and the `DBEdit` controls to add the following record to the MM.DB table:

Record 1

```
ShowNum     101
Device      AviVideo
FileName    C:\DProg\Avi\Bush.AVI
```

☐ Click the Post button on the Navigator control, and then terminate the program.

The Device field contents determine which multimedia device is used for playing the show. For example, if you set the Device field of the first record of MM.DB to AviVideo, that record represents a movie.

Using the *DBRadioGroup* Control

The possible values for the Device field are

```
WaveAudio
AviVideo
PCSpeaker
Sequencer
```

To make entering the Device value easier, implement a better way for entering the Device field values.

☐ Delete the DeviceDBEdit control.

☐ Delete the lblDevice control.

☐ Place a DBRadioGroup control in the frmFillMM form. The DBRadioGroup control icon on the Data Controls page is shown in Figure 14.3.

Figure 14.3.
The DBRadioGroup control icon on the Data Controls page.

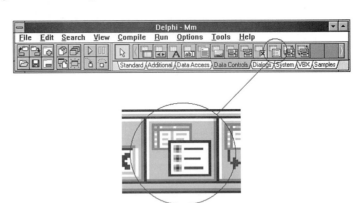

☐ Set the DBRadioGroup control properties as follows:

```
Name           DeviceDBRadioGroup
DataSource     MMDataSource
DataField      Device
Caption        Device
```

Setting the Caption property to Device places the text *Device* in the control frame.

☐ In the Object Inspector, click the three dots appearing to the right of the Items property of the DeviceDBRadioGroup control.

Delphi responds by displaying the String list editor window. You use the String list editor window to define the radio buttons appearing in the DeviceDBRadioGroup control.

☐ In the String list editor window type the following:

```
WaveAudio
AviVideo
PCSpeaker
Sequencer
```

Your String list editor window should now appear as shown in Figure 14.4. The CD Audio device is not listed because it is not relevant to the MM program.

Figure 14.4.

The String list editor window of the DeviceDBRadioGroup control.

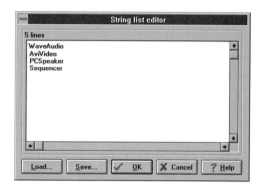

☐ Click the OK button of the String list editor window.

☐ Select Save Project from the File menu.

☐ Execute the MM program.

☐ Click the MM.DB button.

The window shown in Figure 14.5 appears.

Note that because you previously set the first record's Device field to AviVideo, the DeviceDBRadioGroup control has its AviVideo option selected. In other words, the DBRadioGroup control serves as a tool to enter data in a field as well as for displaying field data.

Figure 14.5.
The frmFillMM form displaying the first record of MM.DB.

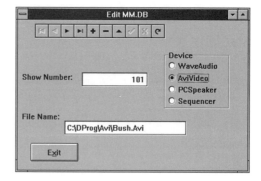

Note: The DBRadioGroup control displays one of its radio buttons as selected, provided that the field the radio button represents contains one of the values appearing in the String list editor window (Figure 14.4).

For example, if the Device field contains the AVIVideo string, none of the radio buttons is selected because the capitalization of the button name and the contents of the field differ. In other words, case is important. If, on the other hand, the Device field contains the AviVideo string, the AviVideo radio button is selected.

☐ Use the frmFillMM form to add five more records to the MM.DB table.

Record 2

ShowNum	102
Device	AviVideo
FileName	C:\DProg\Avi\Reagan.AVI

Record 3

ShowNum	103
Device	AviVideo
FileName	C:\DProg\Avi\Movie.AVI

Record 4

ShowNum	104
Device	AviVideo
FileName	C:\DProg\Avi\Einstein.AVI

Record 5

Device	AviVideo
FileName	C:\DProg\Avi\Kennedy.AVI

☐ Use the Navigator control to browse from record to record and to make sure that the records contain the data you entered. In particular, make sure that the DeviceDBRadioGroup control shows the AviVideo radio button selected.

☐ Terminate the MM program.

Implementing the *frmShow* Form

Now you'll add the frmShow form, a form that selects a show from the MM.DB table and plays the show.

☐ Select New Form from the File menu, and then select Blank Form from the Browse Gallery window.

> *Delphi responds by adding a form Form1 to the project.*

☐ Select Form1, select Save File As from the File menu, and save Form1 as CShow.Pas in the C:\DProg\Ch14 directory.

☐ Set the Form1 properties as follows:

Name	frmShow
Caption	Show

Next, implement the frmShow form's Exit button.

☐ Place a pushbutton from the Standard page in the frmShow form.

☐ Set the pushbutton properties as follows:

Name	cmdExit
Caption	E&xit

☐ Attach code to the OnClick event of the pushbutton.

After attaching the code, the cmdExitClick procedure of the frmShow form should appear as follows:

```
procedure TfrmShow.cmdExitClick(Sender: TObject);
begin

Close;

end;
```

14

Displaying the *frmShow* Form

Place a pushbutton in the frmMM form. When the user clicks this button, the frmShow form is displayed.

☐ Place a pushbutton from the Standard page in the frmMM form.

☐ Set the pushbutton properties as follows:

```
Name      cmdShow
Caption   &Show
```

☐ Attach code to the OnClick event of the cmdShow button.

After attaching the code, the cmdShowClick procedure of the frmMM form should appear as follows:

```
procedure TfrmMM.cmdShowClick(Sender: TObject);
begin

frmShow.ShowModal;

end;
```

☐ In the uses section of the CMM.Pas file, add the CShow word.

After adding CShow to the uses section of the frmMM form, the uses section should appear as follows:

```
uses
  SysUtils, WinTypes, WinProcs, Messages, Classes,
  Graphics, Controls, Forms, Dialogs, StdCtrls,
  CFillMM,
  CShow;
```

☐ Select Save Project from the File menu.

☐ Execute the MM program, click the Show button, and verify that the frmShow form is displayed.

☐ Close the frmShow form, and then terminate the MM program.

Adding Controls to the *frmShow* Form

To add controls to the frmShow form, follow these steps.

☐ Place a RadioGroup control from the Standard page in the frmShow form.

☐ Set the RadioGroup control properties as follows:

```
Name      radDevice
Caption   Multimedia
```

Your frmShow form should now appear as shown in Figure 14.6.

Figure 14.6.
The frmShow *from with the* RadioGroup *control in it (design mode).*

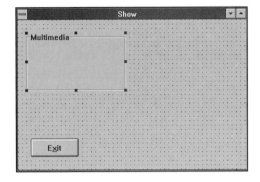

☐ Place four radio buttons from the Standard page in the radDevice RadioGroup control of the frmShow form. You might have to increase the size of the RadioGroup control.

☐ Select Save Project from the File menu.

☐ Execute the MM program, click the Show button, and then verify that only one radio button at a time can be selected.

☐ Terminate the MM program.

Setting the Properties of the Radio Buttons

The four radio buttons of the frmShow form are used for selecting the type of multimedia show. For example, when users select the Movie radio button, they can select a movie show. When users select the Sound radio button, they can select a Sound show, and so on.

Set the properties of the four radio buttons.

☐ Set the properties of the radio button of the frmShow form according to Table 14.2.

Table 14.2. The frmShow form radio button properties.

Object	Property	Setting
RadioButton	Name	optWAV
	Caption	&Sound
	Checked	False
RadioButton	Name	optAvi
	Caption	&Movie
	Checked	True

Table 14.2. continued

Object	Property	Setting
RadioButton	Name	optPCSpeaker
	Caption	&PC Speaker
	Checked	False
RadioButton	Name	optSequencer
	Caption	&MIDI
	Checked	False

The frmShow form should now appear as shown in Figure 14.7.

Figure 14.7.
The frmShow form with its four radio buttons (design mode).

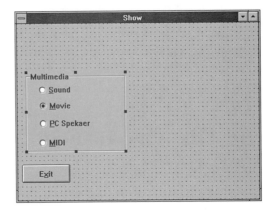

Establishing a SQL Relationship (Corresponding to the Radio Buttons)

Now you need to establish a SQL relationship corresponding to the status of the radio buttons. For example, if users select the Movie radio button, only those records in MM.DB that have their Device field equal to AviVideo should be selected.

☐ Place a Query control from the Data Access page in the frmShow form, and set its Name property to MMQuery.

☐ Place a DataSource control from the Data Access page in the frmShow form, and set its properties as follows:

```
Name      MMDataSource
DataSet   MMQuery
```

☐ In the Object Inspector, click the three dots to the right of the MMQuery object's SQL property cell.

Delphi responds by displaying the String list editor window.

☐ Type the following in the Strong list editor window:

```
Select
  MM."ShowNum",
  MM."Device",
  MM."FileName"
From "c:\dprog\work\mm.db"
As MM
where Device = :DeviceName
```

The preceding statement is a SQL statement that selects those fields from the MM.DB table whose field contents equal the value of the DeviceName. In the next section, you'll define the DeviceName parameter.

☐ Click the OK button of the String list editor window.

Defining the *DeviceName* Parameter

In the previous section, you typed a SQL statement that uses the DeviceName parameter. Now you can define the Device parameter.

☐ Right click the MMQuery control.

Delphi responds by displaying a menu.

☐ Select the Define Parameters item from the menu that pops up.

Delphi responds by displaying a window that enables you to define the parameter.

That is, you wrote a SQL statement that uses the DeviceName parameter so that when you right-click the Query control and select the Define Parameters item, a window is displayed. This window enables you to define the parameters that appear in the SQL statement.

☐ Define the DeviceName parameter as follows:

```
DataType    String
Value       AviVideo
```

The window that enables you to define the SQL parameters should now appear as shown in Figure 14.8.

☐ Click the OK button of the window that enables you to define the SQL parameters.

☐ In the FormCreate procedure of the frmShow form, add code that opens the MMQuery control and sets the Active property of the MMQuery control to True.

14

Figure 14.8.

Defining the DeviceName *parameter.*

After adding the code, the frmShow form's FormCreate procedure should appear as follows:

```
procedure TfrmShow.FormCreate(Sender: TObject);
begin

MMQuery.Open;
MMQuery.Active := True;

end;
```

To move from record to record in the MM.DB table, place a Navigator control in the frmShow form.

☐ Place a Navigator control from the Data Controls page in the frmShow form.

☐ Set the Navigator control properties as follows:

```
    Name          MMDBNavigator
    DataSource    MMDataSource
```

Displaying Record Contents

You now can place a DBGrid control in the frmShow form to display the MM.DB table records that comply with the SQL statement. Alternatively, you can display DBText controls that display the MM.DB table contents.

Place two DBText controls in the frmShow form. Each DBText control corresponds to an MM.DB table field.

☐ Place a DBText control from the Data Controls page in the frmShow form.

☐ Set the DBText control properties as follows:

```
    Name          ShowNumDBText
    DataSource    MMDataSOurce
    DataField     ShowNum
```

☐ Place a `Label` control from the Standard page to the left of the `DBText` control, and set the `Label` control properties as follows:

```
Name        lblShowNum
Caption     Show Number:
```

☐ Place a `DBText` control from the Data Controls page in the `frmShow` form.

☐ Set the `DBText` control properties as follows:

```
Name        FileNameDBText
DataSource  MMDataSOurce
DataField   FileName
```

☐ Place a `Label` control from the Standard page above the `DBText` control, and set the `Label` control properties as follows:

```
Name        lblFileName
Caption     FileName:
```

The `frmShow` form should now appear as shown in Figure 14.9.

Figure 14.9.

The `frmShow` *with its* `DBText`
controls (design mode).

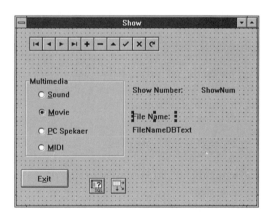

☐ Select Save Project from the File menu.

☐ Execute the MM program, and then click the Show button.

The window shown in Figure 14.10 appears.

☐ Use the `Navigator` control to move from record to record in the MM.DB table and verify that the `frmShow` form displays the contents of the MM.DB table. You previously set the `Device` field of all the records in MM.DB to `AviVideo`. The initial setting of the SQL

14

statement is to display those records of MM.DB with `Device` fields equal to `AviVideo`. Thus, when you execute the MM program, the `frmShow` form can display all the MM.DB records.

Figure 14.10.
The `frmShow` window during runtime.

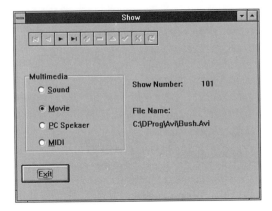

☐ Experiment with the MM program, and then terminate it.

What Next?

The radio buttons you placed in the `frmShow` form do not function yet because you didn't attach code to them. In the next chapter, you continue implementing the MM program and then display the selected show.

Summary

In this chapter, you started implementing the MM program. You implemented a main form (`frmMM`), a form that enables the user to fill the records of the MM.DB table (`frmFillMM`), and a form that enables the user to display all the records whose `Device` field is equal to `AviVideo`. In the next chapter, you continue implementing the MM program. In particular, you write code that actually performs the selected show.

Q&A

Q **Should I use the DBRadioGroup control to enable the user to enter data into a table's records?**

A If the field is supposed to have only a few values, such as the Device field of the MM.DB table, the DBRadioGroup control is an ideal tool for displaying and editing the field. Note, however, that if the number of possible valid values for the field is large, it isn't convenient to use the DBRadioGroup control.

Q **When implementing the frmShow form, I didn't use Database Form Expert. Rather, I manually set the properties of the MMQuery and DataSource controls. Any reason?**

A In previous chapters (see Chapter 10, "Queries and Ranges"), you did use the Database Form Expert to place a Query control and a DataSource control as well as to set the properties of these controls. As you saw in this chapter, it doesn't take long to manually perform the same operations that Database Form Expert performs for you.

Quiz

1. You define the radio buttons appearing in the DBRadioGroup control by _____.
2. Upon starting the MM program and clicking the Show button, the Show window enables you to browse through all the records of the MM.DB table because _____.

Exercise

The SQL statement is set to select all the MM.DB table records that have the Device field set to AviVideo. Modify the SQL statement so it selects all the records that have the Device field set to WaveAudio.

Answers to Quiz

14

1. You define the radio buttons appearing in the DBRadioGroup control by clicking the three dots to the right of the Items property in the Object Inspector window, and then typing in the String list editor window that pops up.
2. When you start the MM program and click the Show button, the Show window enables you to browse through all the MM.DB table records because the SQL is set to display all the MM.DB table records that have their Device fields equal to AviVideo. Currently, all the MM.DB table records have their records with the Device field equal to AviVideo.

Answer to Exercise

The procedure is as follows:

☐ Right-click the MMQuery control to display a menu.

☐ Select Define Parameters from the menu that pops up to display the window that enables you to define the parameters.

☐ Set the Value box of the window that enables you to define the SQL parameter to WaveAudio.

When you execute the MM program and click the Show button, you do not see any records, because the MM.DB table currently does not contain any records with the Device field equal to WaveAudio.

☐ Before terminating Delphi, make sure to return the MM program to its original state, where the initial SQL statement selects the records with Device fields equal to AviVideo. In the next chapter, you continue to implement the MM program, and we assume that the initial SQL statement selects the records with Device fields equal to AviVideo.

3

On Day 15, "Writing Multimedia Database Applications with Delphi (Part 2)," you complete implementing the MM.EXE program that you started to implement on Day 14.

Delphi is a useful tool for generating any Windows application, from the simple to the sophisticated. On Day 16, "3D Virtual Reality with Delphi," you create a Delphi program that uses 3D Virtual Reality technology and learn how to take advantage of the database features of Delphi to create some powerful 3D, virtual-reality games.

On Day 17, "Preparing Reports," you start learning about the important topic of generating reports.

On Days 18 and 19, "Preparing Reports from More than One Table" and "Preparing Reports with Calculated Fields, and More," you continue with the study of generating reports. In particular, you learn how to create reports that are made from more than one table, how to sort reports, how to group the records of a report, how to create report variables, and how to let the user specify what records will appear in the report.

On Day 20, "Derived Fields and Derived Columns in Reports," you learn how to create columns in your reports whose values are calculated based on other columns in the report. You also learn how to place a derived field in the footer or header area of the report.

On your final day, Day 21, "Other Report Formats," you learn how to generate reports using different formats than what you've learned so far. You also learn how to generate reports for mass mailing, such as invoices and statements, where each statement is printed on a separate page and stuffed into an envelope.

Writing Multimedia Database Applications with Delphi (Part 2)

In the previous chapter, you started to implement the MM.EXE program, a program that enables the user to play multimedia shows with Delphi. In this chapter, you finish writing the MM.EXE program.

Dynamic SQL Statements

When starting the MM program and clicking the Show button, the frmShow form appears. The SQL statement that you implemented selected all records having the Device field equal to AviVideo. Now you'll add code to set the SQL statement according to the radio button that is selected in the Multimedia group of radio buttons in the frmShow form. It's possible to modify the SQL statement during runtime because, in the previous chapter, you implemented the SQL statement as a dynamic SQL statement. To modify the statement during runtime, you use a parameter (DeviceName) to implement the SQL statement.

When the user selects the Sound radio button of the frmShow form, the program selects only those records with Device fields equal to WaveAudio.

☐ Attach code to the OnClick event of the frmShow form's optWAV radio button.

After attaching the code, the optWAVClick procedure of the frmShow form should appear as follows:

```
procedure TfrmShow.optWAVClick(Sender: TObject);
begin

MMQuery.DisableControls;

try

   MMQUery.Active := False;
   MMQuery.Params[0].AsString := 'WaveAudio';
   MMQuery.Active := True;

finally

   MMQuery.EnableControls;

end;

end;
```

The code begins by disabling the controls with the following line:

```
MMQuery.DisableControls;
```

Then a try...finally block is executed. Even if there is a runtime error during the execution of the procedure, the code after the finally statement is executed. In any case, the controls are enabled because the statement after finally enables the controls.

```
finally

   MMQuery.EnableControls;

end;
```

The code after the `try` sets the `Active` property of the `MMQuery` control to `False`.

```
MMQUery.Active := False;
```

After the `Active` property of the `Query` control is set to `False`, you can modify the SQL statement's parameter.

```
MMQuery.Params[0].AsString := 'WaveAudio';
```

Now that the query object's parameter value is modified, you can set the query's `Active` property back to `True`.

```
MMQuery.Active := True.
```

Attaching Code to the Movie Radio Button's *Click* Event

In the previous section, you attached code that is executed whenever the user selects the Sound radio button. The code creates an SQL statement that selects only those records with `Device` fields equal to `WaveAudio`. In this section, you attach code to the `OnClick` event of the `frmShow` form's `optAvi` radio button. This code sets the SQL statement so that only those records with the `Device` field equal to `AviVideo` are selected.

☐ Attach code to the `OnClick` event of the `frmShow` form's `optAvi` radio button.

After attaching the code, the `optAviClick` procedure should appear as follows:

```
procedure TfrmShow.optAviClick(Sender: TObject);
begin

MMQuery.DisableControls;

try

   MMQUery.Active := False;
   MMQuery.Params[0].AsString := 'AviVideo';
   MMQuery.Active := True;

finally

   MMQuery.EnableControls;

end;

end;
```

The added code is similar to the code you added in the `optWAVClick` procedure. The only difference is that you are now selecting only those records with `Device` fields equal to `AviVideo`.

```
MMQuery.Params[0].AsString := 'AviVideo';
```

☐ Select Save project from the File menu.

Testing the Dynamic SQL Statement

Execute the MM.EXE program to test your work.

☐ Execute the MM program.

☐ Click the Show button.

The Show window appears.

☐ Use the `Navigator` control to move from record to record in the MM.DB table.

As you can see, you can browse through all the records of MM.DB because currently the SQL statement is set to select the records with `Device` fields equal to `AviVideo`.

☐ Click the Sound radio button of the `frmShow` form.

Because there are no records with `Device` fields equal to `WaveAudio`, no records are selected.

☐ Click the Movie button again.

As you can see, you now can browse through the records of MM.DB.

☐ Experiment with the MM program, and then click the Show window's Exit button.

The `frmMM` form (the main form) appears again.

☐ Click the MM.DB button.

The program displays the `frmFillMMform` that enables you to fill records in the MM.DB table.

☐ Add records to the MM.DB table as follows:

Record 6

ShowNum	106
Device	WaveAudio
FileName	C:\DProg\WAV\8Kenned3.WAV

Record 7

ShowNum	107
Device	WaveAudio
FileName	C:\DProg\WAV\Picki2M6.WAV

Record 8

ShowNum	108
Device	WaveAudio
FileName	C:\DProg\WAV\Regga2M6.WAV

Record 9

ShowNum	109
Device	WaveAudio
FileName	C:\DProg\WAV\Strol2M3.WAV

Note: Make sure that the filenames you are entering into the record's FileName fields exist in your hard disk C:\DProg\WAV directory. Later in this chapter, you execute code that assumes these files exist in the directory mentioned in the FileName fields.

☐ Use the Navigator control to browse through the MM.DB table records.

☐ Click the Exit button of the frmFillMM form.

The frmMM form appears.

☐ Click the Show button to display the Show button.

☐ Experiment with the Sound and Movie radio buttons of the frmShow form, and verify that when the Movie radio button is selected, only the records with Device fields equal to AviVideo are selected. Verify, too, that when the Sound button is selected, only those records with the Device field equal to WaveAudio are selected.

☐ Terminate the MM.EXE program.

Playing Movies

So far, you've attached code only to the OnClick event of the frmShow form's Movie and Sound radio buttons. Later in this chapter, you'll attach code to the other radio buttons of the frmShow

form, but for now, you'll just implement a multimedia button. When the user clicks the multimedia button's Play button, the current record's file is played. If, for example, the current record is an AVI file, the corresponding movie is played.

> **Note:** In the following step, you're instructed to place the Multimedia control TegoMM.VBX from the VBX page in the frmShow form.
>
> If your VBX page does not include the Multimedia VBX control, add the TegoMM.VBX control to the VBX page as outlined in Chapter 13, "VBX and Sound in Your Delphi Program."

☐ Place a Multimedia control in the frmShow form.

Your frmShow form should now appear as shown in Figure 15.1.

Figure 15.1.

The frmShow *form with the* Multimedia *control in it (design mode).*

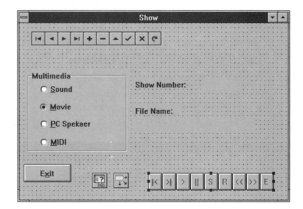

Note that the default name Delphi assigned to the Multimedia control's Name property is Tegomm1. You'll use this name when you write code in the next sections.

Adding Object Fields

In previous chapters, you added a Table component and then added object fields to the form by double-clicking the Table component, and then adding field objects from the Field editor window.

The frmShow form includes the MMQuery control. It doesn't include a Table component. Because you'll write code that uses the value of the MM.DB table fields in the next sections, you need to create field objects now. As it turns out, you create field objects from the Query component in the same way that you create field objects from the Table component.

☐ Double click the MMQuery control.

Delphi responds by displaying the Field editor window.

☐ Click the Add button, make sure that all the MM.DB table fields are selected, and then click the OK button.

☐ Close the Fields editor window.

☐ Take a look at the Object Inspector window. The combobox listing the frmShow form objects includes the field objects: MMQueryShowNum, MMQueryDevice, and MMQueryFileName. You can now read the values of the MM.DB fields by using these field objects.

Setting the *Multimedia* Control

When displaying the frmShow form, the form's FormCreate procedure is executed. This is a good point to insert code that sets the Multimedia control properties.

☐ In the FormCreate procedure, add code that sets the Multimedia control properties.

After adding the code, the FormCreate procedure of the frmShow form should appear as follows:

```
procedure TfrmShow.FormCreate(Sender: TObject);
begin

MMQuery.Open;
MMQuery.Active := True;

Tegomm1.DeviceType := MMQueryDevice.Value;
Tegomm1.FileName := MMQueryFileName.Value;
Tegomm1.Command := 'Open';

end;
```

The added code sets the Multimedia control DeviceType property to the current record's Device field value.

```
Tegomm1.DeviceType := MMQueryDevice.Value;
```

If, for example, the current record has AviVideo in its Device field, the Multimedia control's DeviceType property is set to AviVideo, which means that the Multimedia control is set to play movies.

The next statement sets the Multimedia control's FileName property to the current record's FileName field value.

```
Tegomm1.FileName := MMQueryFileName.Value;
```

Finally, the Open command is issued to the Multimedia control.

```
Tegomm1.Command := 'Open';
```

The `Multimedia` control is now set to play the file specified in its `FileName` property.

Note: You can examine the `Error` property of the `Multimedia` control to check whether the multimedia session was opened successfully. If, after issuing the `Open` command, the `Multimedia` control's `Error` property is not equal to 0, an error occurred during execution of the `Open` command. Examine the Error property as follows:

```
if Tegomm1.Error <> 0 then
    begin
    MessageDlg (Tegomm1.ErrorMessage,
                mtError,
                [mbOK],
                0);
    end;
```

The `if` statement is executed to determine the `Multimedia` control `Error` property. If the `Error` property is not equal to 0, the `MessageDlg` statement is executed. As you can see from the first parameter of the `MessageDlg` function, the `Multimedia` control's `ErrorMessage` property is a string explaining the nature of the error.

Note: If an error occurs during the execution of the `Open` command, all the `Multimedia` control buttons are dimmed.

For example, an error could occur when trying to open a movie session because the AVI drivers are not installed either because the `DeviceType` property was assigned with an incorrect string or because the file specified in the `FileName` property of the `Multimedia` control does not exist.

Opening a WAV Session

When the user selects the `frmShow` Sound radio button, the program displays the records with `Device` fields equal to `WaveAudio`. In this section, you add code to the `OnClick` event of the `frmShow` form `optWAV` radio button. This code opens a WAV session for the WAV file of the current record.

☐ Add code to the `OnClick` event of the `frmShow` form's `optWAV` button.

After you add the code, the `frmShow` form's `optWAVClick` procedure should appear as follows:

```
procedure TfrmShow.optWAVClick(Sender: TObject);
begin

MMQuery.DisableControls;
try
   MMQUery.Active := False;
   MMQuery.Params[0].AsString := 'WaveAudio';
   MMQuery.Active := True;
finally
   MMQuery.EnableControls;
end;

Tegomm1.DeviceType := MMQueryDevice.Value;
Tegomm1.FileName := MMQueryFileName.Value;
Tegomm1.Command := 'Open';

end;
```

The new code sets the `Multimedia` control's `DeviceType` property to the current record's `Device` field value.

```
Tegomm1.DeviceType := MMQueryDevice.Value;
```

Because the user clicks the Sound radio button, the records with `Device` fields equal to `WaveAudio` are selected. The preceding statement produces the following effect:

```
Tegomm1.DeviceType := 'WaveAudio';
```

The `Multimedia` control's `FileName` property is set to the value of the current record's `FileName` field.

```
Tegomm1.FileName := MMQueryFileName.Value;
```

Finally, the `Open` command is issued to the `Multimedia` control.

```
Tegomm1.Command := 'Open';
```

Attaching Code to the Movie Radio Button's *OnClick* Event

When displaying the `frmShow` form, the `Multimedia` control opens an AviVideo session because you opened an AviVideo session in the `frmShow` form's `FormCreate` procedure.

In the previous section, you added code to the `optWAVClick` procedure, which opens a WaveAudio session.

If the user then selects the `optAvi` radio button, your code has to again open an AviVideo session. Thus, you have to add code to the `optAviClick` procedure.

☐ Add code to the optAviClick procedure.

After adding the code, the optAviClick procedure should appear as follows:

```
procedure TfrmShow.optAviClick(Sender: TObject);
begin

MMQuery.DisableControls;
try
   MMQUery.Active := False;
   MMQuery.Params[0].AsString := 'AviVideo';
   MMQuery.Active := True;
finally
   MMQuery.EnableControls;
end;

Tegomm1.DeviceType := MMQueryDevice.Value;
Tegomm1.FileName := MMQueryFileName.Value;
Tegomm1.Command := 'Open';

end;
```

Because the user selected the Movie radio button, the SQL statement selects the records with Device fields equal to AviVideo, and an AviVideo session is opened for the current record.

Attaching Code to the *OnClick* Event of the *Navigator* Control

Whenever the user moves from record to record, the Multimedia control must open a session for the new record. In the frmShow form, you can move from the current record to another record by clicking the radio buttons. For example, if the Sound radio button is currently selected, and the user clicks the Movie radio button, the current record is changed to a record with the Device field equal to AviVideo. Also, if the Movie radio button is currently selected, and the user clicks the Sound radio button, the current record is changed to a record with the Device field equal to AviVideo. In the preceding section, you attached code that opens WaveAudio or AviVideo sessions to the OnClick event of the Sound and Movie radio buttons.

However, the user can move from record to record also by clicking the Navigator control buttons, and so you must attach code to the Navigator control's and OnClick event. This code opens a session for the new current record.

☐ Attach code to the Navigator control's OnClick event.

After you attach the code, the MMDBNavigatorClick procedure should appear as follows:

```
procedure TfrmShow.MMDBNavigatorClick(Sender: TObject;
  Button: TNavigateBtn);
begin

Tegomm1.DeviceType := MMQueryDevice.Value;
Tegomm1.FileName := MMQueryFileName.Value;
```

```
Tegomm1.Command := 'Open';
```

end;

As the user moved to a new record by clicking the `Navigator` control, a multimedia session is opened for the new record.

☐ Select Save Project from the File menu.

☐ Execute the MM program and click the Show button.

The `frmShow` form appears.

☐ Select the Sound radio button.

Move from record to record, click the `Multimedia` control Play button to listen to the current record's WAV file. The `Multimedia` control Play button is the third button from the left on the `Multimedia` control. The WAV file is played through the sound card.

If the `Multimedia` control buttons are dimmed, it's because the MM.DB table data in the current record is incorrect. Make sure that the WAV file name in the MM.DB table records are typed correctly and that the WAV files reside in the C:\DProg\WAV directory.

☐ Click the Movie radio button to select the Movie records.

☐ Use the `Navigator` control to move from record to record, and play the movies by clicking the `Multimedia` control Play button.

Note: Some of the buttons on the `Multimedia` control are applicable for only a certain multimedia device.

For example, the Play button is used by all the multimedia devices, but the Eject button (the rightmost button on the `Multimedia` control) is available only when playing CD Audio.

The second and third buttons from the right on the `Multimedia` control are available only for AviVideo.

☐ Click the second and third buttons from the right of the `Multimedia` control.

As you can see, these buttons enable you to advance the movie frame by frame. The third button from the left moves the movie back one frame, and the second button from the left moves the movie forward one frame.

When you play a WAV file, the second and third buttons from the right on the `Multimedia` control are dimmed because these buttons are not applicable for a WAV file.

> **Note:** Because the `Multimedia` control is visible in the MM.EXE program, you can use its buttons.
>
> However, you can make the `Multimedia` control invisible by setting its `Visible` property to `False` in the `frmShow` form's `FormCreate` procedure. Instead of using the `Multimedia` control buttons, you can place your own pushbuttons from the Standard page and attach code to the `OnClick` events of these buttons. For example, you can place a pushbutton in the `frmShow` form and type the following statement in the pushbutton's `cmdPlayClick` procedure:
>
> ```
> Tegomm1.Command := 'Play';
> ```

☐ Experiment with the MM.EXE program, and then terminate it.

Implementing the MIDI Feature

The `Multimedia` control is also capable of playing MIDI files (synthesized sound files), and so you'll implement the MIDI feature of the MM.EXE program in this section.

☐ Execute the MM program.

☐ Click the MM.DB button because you are now going to add new records to the MM.DB table.

☐ Add the following records to the MM.DB table:

Record 10

ShowNum	110
Device	Sequencer
FileName	C:\DProg\MIDI\Bourbon6.MID

Record 11

ShowNum	111
Device	Sequencer
FileName	C:\DProg\MIDI\Pickin6.MID

Record 12

ShowNum	112
Device	Sequencer
FileName	C:\DProg\MIDI\Strolli6.MID

☐ Make sure that you typed the names of the MIDI files correctly and that the MIDI files exist in the C:\DProg\MIDI directory.

☐ Terminate the MM program.

Establishing SQL Statements for Selecting the MIDI Records

Implement the SQL statement that selects only the MIDI records (MM.DB table records with the Device field equal to Sequencer) as follows:

☐ Attach code to the OnClick event of the frmShow form's optMIDI radio button.

After attaching the code, the optSequencerClick procedure of the frmShow form should appear as follows:

```
procedure TfrmShow.optSequencerClick(Sender: TObject);
begin

MMQuery.DisableControls;
try
   MMQUery.Active := False;
   MMQuery.Params[0].AsString := 'Sequencer';
   MMQuery.Active := True;
finally
   MMQuery.EnableControls;
end;

Tegomm1.DeviceType := MMQueryDevice.Value;
Tegomm1.FileName := MMQueryFileName.Value;
Tegomm1.Command := 'Open';

end;
```

The code you added is similar to the code you attached to the OnClick event of the Movie and Sound radio buttons. A SQL statement is established to select MM.DB table records with the Device field equal to Sequencer.

```
MMQuery.DisableControls;
try
   MMQUery.Active := False;
   MMQuery.Params[0].AsString := 'Sequencer';
   MMQuery.Active := True;
finally
   MMQuery.EnableControls;
end;
```

Then, a MIDI session is opened for the current record.

```
Tegomm1.DeviceType := MMQueryDevice.Value;
Tegomm1.FileName := MMQueryFileName.Value;
Tegomm1.Command := 'Open';
```

☐ Select Save Project from the File menu.

☐ Execute the MM program, click the Show button, and play the MIDI files.

☐ Terminate the MM program.

Implementing the PC Speaker Feature

Implement the PC Speaker feature by following these steps:

☐ Execute the MM program.

☐ Click the MM.DB button because you are now going to add a record to the MM.DB table.

☐ Fill a new record in the MM.DB table as follows:

Record 13

ShowNum	113
Device	PCSpeaker
FileName	C:\DProg\WAV\8Kenned3.WAV

☐ Terminate the MM program.

> **Note:** Most sound cards are capable of playing WAV files recorded as mono or as stereo, as well as WAV files recorded as 8-bit or 16-bit sound. The PC speaker, however, can play WAV files recorded as 8-bit mono files only.
>
> Because the 8Kenned3.WAV file is an 8-bit mono WAV file, you can play this WAV file through the PC speaker.

Attaching Code to the Speaker Radio Button's *OnClick* Event

You now attach code to the OnClick event of the frmShow form's Speaker radio button.

☐ Attach code to the OnClick event of the frmShow form's optPCSPeaker radio button.

After attaching the code, the frmShow form's optPCSpeakerClick procedure appears as follows:

```
procedure TfrmShow.optPCSpeakerClick(Sender: TObject);
begin

MMQuery.DisableControls;
try
   MMQUery.Active := False;
   MMQuery.Params[0].AsString := 'PCSpeaker';
   MMQuery.Active := True;
finally
   MMQuery.EnableControls;
end;

Tegomm1.DeviceType := MMQueryDevice.Value;
Tegomm1.FileName := MMQueryFileName.Value;
Tegomm1.Command := 'Open';

end;
```

The added code sets the SQL statement to select only those records from the MM.DB table with the Device fields equal to PCSpeaker.

```
MMQuery.Params[0].AsString := 'PCSpeaker';
```

☐ Select Save Project from the File menu.

☐ Execute the MM program.

☐ Click the Show button.

The frmShow form appears.

☐ Click the PC Speaker radio button.

As you can see, the frmShow form lets you view only one record in the MM.DB table because only one record has the Device field equal to PCSpeaker.

☐ Click the Multimedia control's Play button to play the WAV file through the PC speaker.

☐ Experiment with the MM program, and then terminate it.

Summary

In this chapter, you finished implementing the MM.EXE program. During program implementation, you used various Delphi database features. You executed dynamic SQL statements, you used the DBRadioGroup control, you attached code to the DBNavigator control's OnClick event, and you created field objects from the Query component.

Q&A

Q I want to build a full WAV editor program that enables the user to copy, cut, and paste WAV sections, increase/decrease the volume, add echo, and manipulate the WAV file in some other ways. Is it possible to accomplish this with the `Multimedia` control and Delphi?

A Yes, and Delphi is an ideal programming language to accomplish these tasks. The TegoMM.VBX control has many other properties and methods that enable you to accomplish these tasks. For example, you can record your own voice, and then you can use the `Multimedia` control to modify the characteristics of the WAV file so that it sounds like a different person. (For the full version of the TegoMM.VBX control, see the Special Offer at the end of this book.)

Q I want to use Delphi to build an encyclopedia-type application. Any suggestions?

A Delphi is an ideal candidate for this purpose. An encyclopedia application is an application that basically contains a lot of data in tables. Using Delphi, you can implement various search mechanisms that enable the user to search for topics. Some of the topics include shows, such as movies, animation, and sound. Whenever a topic has a certain show associated with it, you can display the `Multimedia` control and let the user view or hear the show.

Quiz

1. To play a movie AVI file with the `Multimedia` control, the following statements have to be executed: _____.

2. To play a WAV file with the `Multimedia` control, the following statements have to be executed: _____.

3. To play a MIDI file with the `Multimedia` control, the following statements have to be executed: _____.

Exercise

Implement the CD Audio feature. **Hint:** To play a CD Audio, use the following statements:

```
Tegomm1.DeviceType := 'CDAudio';
Tegomm1.Command := 'Open';
```

Answers to Quiz

1. To play a movie AVI file called MyMovie.AVI with the `Multimedia` control, the following statements must be executed:

```
Tegomm1.DeviceType := 'AviVideo';
Tegomm1.FileName := 'C:\DProg\Avi\MyMovie.AVI';
```

2. To play a WAV file called MyWAV.WAV with the `Multimedia` control, the following statements must be executed:

```
Tegomm1.DeviceType := 'WaveAudio';
Tegomm1.FileName := 'C:\DProg\Avi\MyWAV.WAV';
```

3. To play a MIDI file called MyMIDI.MID with the `Multimedia` control, the following statements must be executed:

```
Tegomm1.DeviceType := 'Sequencer';
Tegomm1.FileName := 'C:\DProg\Avi\MyMIDI.MID';
```

Answer to Exercise

Unlike with other multimedia devices, it doesn't make sense to add records to the MM.DB table with the `Device` field equal to `CDAudio`.

You can, however, place a pushbutton from the Standard page in the `frmShow` form, set the pushbutton's `Name` property to `cmdCD`, set the `Caption` property to `&CD`, and attach the following statements to the `OnClick` event:

```
Tegomm1.DeviceType := 'CDAudio';
Tegomm1.Command := 'Open';
```

The `Multimedia` control then lets the user play the CD audio tracks, move from track to track on the CD, and so on.

At the time the `Open` command is issued to the `Multimedia` control, a CD Audio must be inserted in the CD-ROM drive. Thus, you should display a message box to the user (using the `MessageDlg` function) telling the user to insert a CD Audio in the CD-ROM drive. Once the user clicks the message box's OK button, issue the `Open` command to the `Multimedia` control.

3D Virtual Reality
with Delphi

As stated in the Introduction, you can write some very powerful state-of-the-art-technology Windows programs with Delphi. In this chapter, you learn how to write a 3D virtual reality Delphi program by using a powerful VBX control—the 3D Virtual Reality VBX control. As you soon discover, writing a 3D virtual reality Delphi program by using the 3D Virtual Reality VBX control is very easy. You can, for example, write a 3D Virtual Reality game program, and then take advantage of Delphi's database features to keep players' scores, and to set other parameters of the game.

What Is a 3D Virtual Reality Program?

As implied by its name, a 3D virtual reality program is one that simulates a 3D (three-dimensional) environment. The user uses the mouse or keyboard to "travel" in a 3D environment, and feels as if he or she is moving in a 3D environment. The program enables the user to move in the 3D environment and to interact with various objects (stationery objects as well as moving objects) that are in the environment.

Depending on the user's actions, the program displays the objects in different ways. For example, when the user moves toward a wall, it appears to be closer. When the user moves away from the wall, it appears further away.

Once you finish writing the graphics aspect of a virtual reality program, you can make the program feel more "real" by adding sound to the program. For example, when the user shoots a monster, the program plays the sound of a shooting gun, and if the user hits the monster, the program plays sound of a screaming monster. You can add sound to the 3D virtual reality program by using the Multimedia VBX control discussed in previous chapters.

You might think that writing a 3D virtual reality program with Delphi requires a lot of code writing. However, as you soon see, writing a complete 3D virtual reality program by using the 3D Virtual Reality VBX control requires very little code.

Note: Expensive 3D virtual reality equipment is made of the following components:

- A set of goggles through which the user sees the 3D environment. While the 3D virtual reality program is running, the user wears these goggles and sees the 3D environment. The goggles are made of two tiny TV screens. Using the goggles makes the program more realistic than using a monitor or a TV set to view the graphics.

- Headphones through which the user hears the sounds of the 3D environment.

- Sensors that are attached to various points on the user's body. These sensors relay information to the program about the user's movements, and depending on the user's actions, the program displays the appropriate graphics through the goggles and plays the appropriate sounds through the headphones. For example, if the user moves his head to the left, the sensors would relay this information to the program, and the program would display the appropriate 3D view through the goggles.

Alternatively, a 3D virtual reality program can use standard PC devices:

- Instead of using special goggles, the program can display the 3D environment graphics on the PC monitor.

- Instead of playing sound through headphones, the program can play sound through the PC's sound card.

- Instead of using sensors for detecting the user's actions, the program can detect them through the keyboard, the mouse, or a joystick.

What Is the 3D Virtual Reality VBX Control?

The 3D Virtual Reality VBX control enables you to write a 3D virtual reality program that displays a 3D environment and lets the user move in the 3D picture. As the user moves in the 3D environment, depending on the user's movements, the Floor VBX control displays the appropriate 3D views.

The 3D Virtual Reality VBX control enables you to design your own 3D pictures (with walls, floors, and rooms). The control enables you to design a two-dimensional (2D) representation of the 3D floor with a text editor. The control then uses your 2D design to display the corresponding 3D pictures.

The 3D Virtual Reality VBX control also includes a sprites mechanism that enables you to add stationary objects (such as chairs and tables) as well as moving objects (such as dogs, cats, and monsters) to the 3D pictures. Your program lets the user interact with the sprites. For example, if the user bumps into a chair, the program can move the chair.

The 3D Virtual Reality VBX control utilizes *WinG* technology. WinG (pronounced "Win Gee") is a technology that enhances the standard graphics capabilities of Windows. It performs graphics operations in a high-performance manner.

Because the 3D Virtual Reality VBX control utilizes WinG technology, before you can execute and write programs using the 3D Virtual Reality VBX control, you must first install WinG in your Windows system.

Here is how you install WinG into your PC.

☐ Copy all the files residing in the \DProg\WinG directory of the accompanying CD to your \Windows\System directory.

That's it! Your PC can now utilize WinG technology.

Note: The My3DVR.EXE program uses the Tego3DVR.VBX control. Thus, you have to copy the Tego3DVR.VBX control to your \Windows\System directory.

☐ Copy the Tego3DVR.VBX file from the \DProg\VBX directory of the accompanying CD-ROM to your \Windows\System directory.

The My3DVR.EXE Program

In the following sections, you write a program called My3DVR.EXE that illustrates how to use the 3D Virtual Reality VBX control.

Before you start writing the My3DVR.EXE program by yourself, let's first execute a copy of the program that resides on the accompanying CD.

Note: Remember, before you can execute the My3DVR.EXE program, you must copy the WinG files into your \Windows\System directory.

☐ Insert the CD into your CD-ROM drive.

☐ Execute the My3DVR.EXE program from the CD. The My3DVR.EXE program resides in the \DProg\Ch16 directory of the CD.

The main window of the My3DVR.EXE program appears, as shown in Figure 16.1.

As you can see, the My3DVR.EXE program placed you in a virtual 3D room. You are currently facing the exit door.

Figure 16.1.
*The My3DVR.EXE
program main window.*

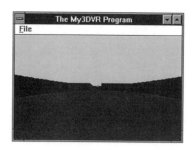

16

You can use the right-arrow key and left-arrow keys to rotate. When you press the right-arrow key, you rotate clockwise, and when you press the left-arrow key, you rotate counter-clockwise. To see the right- and left-arrow keys in action, do the following:

☐ Press the left-arrow key several times.

As you can see, every time you press the left-arrow key, you rotate counter-clockwise (approximately six degrees). Figures 16.2 and 16.3 show two snapshots of your 3D view as you rotate counter-clockwise in the room. After pressing the left-arrow key a few times, you return to your original position.

Figure 16.2.
*Rotating counter-clockwise
(snapshot 1).*

Figure 16.3.
*Rotating counter-clockwise
(snapshot 2).*

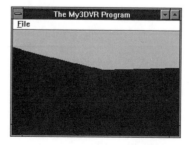

> **Note:** The left- and right-arrow keys enable you to rotate in the room. When you press the left- and right-arrow keys, you aren't moving forward or backward, you are only rotating.

☐ Press the left-arrow key, but do not release it.

As you can see, pressing the left-arrow key without releasing it makes you continuously rotate counter-clockwise.

After continuously rotating counter-clockwise, you may feel a little dizzy, and so rotate clockwise now.

☐ Press the right-arrow key several times (or keep pressing the key down without releasing it).

As you can see, pressing the right-arrow key makes you rotate clockwise.

So far, you've rotated only around the point where you are standing. As you've seen, the right- and left-arrow keys enable you to change your viewing direction.

To move forward or backward in the same direction you're currently facing (your viewing direction), you must use the up-arrow and down-arrow keys. The up-arrow key moves you forward in the current viewing direction. The down-arrow key moves you backward in the current viewing direction.

To see the up-arrow and down-arrow keys in action, do the following:

☐ Use the left-arrow key to change your viewing direction until you are facing one of the corners of the room.

You now can get closer to the corner by pressing the up-arrow key.

☐ Press the up-arrow key several times.

As you can see, every time you press the up-arrow key, you get closer to the corner.

In a similar manner, you can use the down-arrow key to move backward in the current viewing direction. That is, when you press the down-arrow key you move in reverse.

> **Note:** To continue moving forward in the current viewing direction, you can continuously press the up-arrow key. That is, press the up-arrow key and don't release it.

> To continue moving backward in the current viewing direction, you can continu-
> ously press the down-arrow key. That is, press the down-arrow key and don't
> release it.

You should know that you are not alone on the floor. Two more persons are on the floor. One
person, a jogger, keeps running in the main hall of the floor, and another person, a woman, is
exercising in another room on the floor. You'll soon have a chance to meet these people, but
before you move to other rooms on the floor, take a look at Figure 16.4. This is a 2D map of
the floor you're moving in.

Figure 16.4.
A 2D map of the floor of the
My3DVR.EXE program.

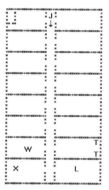

As shown in Figure 16.4, the floor of the My3DVR.EXE program consists of 16 rooms. The
room in the upper-left corner of the floor has a small sub-room in it (in the upper-left corner
of the room). The exit doors of each of the 16 rooms connect to the main hall of the floor.

Figure 16.4 includes several uppercase letters on the floor. These letters represent various points
on the floor that have objects (moving objects and stationary objects). Here is a description of
each of these points.

Point X is the starting point. Point W represents a woman who is exercising. Point J, with the
down arrow next to it, represents a jogger who runs across the hall. The two T points represent
two trees. Point L represents a light fixture (chandelier) attached to the ceiling.

> **Note:** When you write your own 3D virtual reality program, the design of the floor
> (or floors) of the program is an important part of the development. For example,
> you can develop a 3D virtual reality game where the object of the game is to figure
> out the floor's map. Once the user is able to figure out the map (by traveling in it),
> the user can score more points.

As you see later in this chapter, designing a floor for the 3D Virtual Reality control is easy.

Now that you're familiar with the My3DVR.EXE program's floor map, let's travel around the floor.

☐ Use the arrow keys to move toward the exit door.

As you get closer to the exit door, you start seeing more clearly the inside of the room on the other side of the hall. For example, you can see that it has a light fixture (chandelier) attached to the ceiling.

☐ Exit to the hall, and turn left so you're facing the far end of the hall.

Figure 16.5 shows the 3D view when you're facing the far end of the hall.

Figure 16.5.

Facing the far end of the hall.

A jogger is in the main hall of the floor. As shown back in Figure 16.4, the jogger runs from the far end of the hall toward the point where you're now standing. Once the jogger reaches the other side of the hall, the program places him back at the far end of the hall, and he runs in the same direction again.

Once the jogger is close to you, you can see the details of his appearance. For example, you can see that he's wearing sunglasses, is in a good mood (he's smiling), and is wearing a short-sleeved shirt. You can even see the five fingers of his right hand.

The picture of the jogger is a sprite picture that contains transparent regions. For example, the region between the legs of the jogger's image is a transparent region. Thus, through this area, you can see whatever is behind the jogger.

The jogger's movement is an animation consisting of two frames. In each of his movements, he has a different foot and a different hand in the forward direction. One time, his left foot is forward on the floor while his right foot is in the air, and the next time, his right foot is forward

on the floor while his left foot is in the air. The two pictures (frames) composing the jogger's animation are shown in Figure 16.6.

Figure 16.6.
The two frames of the jogger's animation (when the jogger moves toward you).

Frame 1 of the jogger animation when the jogger moves towards you.

Frame 2 of the jogger animation when the jogger moves towards you.

Once the jogger passes you by, you can make a 180-degree turn by pressing the left-arrow key or the right-arrow key so you can see the back of the jogger as he runs away from you. Figures 16.7 and 16.8 show two snapshots of the jogger as he runs away.

Figure 16.7.
The jogger running away from you (snapshot 1).

Figure 16.8.
The jogger running away from you (snapshot 2).

The animation of the jogger's movement as he moves away from you is also made of two frames, as shown in Figure 16.9.

Figure 16.9.

The two frames of the jogger's animation.

Frame 1 of the
jogger animation
when the jogger moves
away from you.

Frame 2 of the
jogger animation
when the jogger moves
away from you.

As shown back in Figure 16.4, (the 2D map of the floor), the second room from the bottom-left corner of the floor has a point marked W, which represents the woman who is exercising. Let's go to the room where the woman is exercising:

☐ Move into the room where the woman is exercising.

Figures 16.10 and 16.11 show two snapshots of the exercising woman as you are getting closer to her.

Figure 16.10.

Moving toward the exercising woman (snapshot 1).

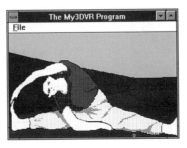

Figure 16.11.

Moving toward the exercising woman (snapshot 2).

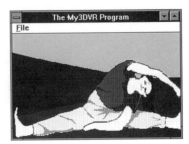

The movement of the exercising woman is an animation consisting of two frames, as shown in Figure 16.12.

Figure 16.12.

The two frames of the exercising woman animation.

Frame 1 of the exercising woman.

Frame 2 of the exercising woman.

16

The My3DVR.EXE program can be enhanced so the woman's animation consists of more frames. This way, the woman's movement is smoother. For simplicity's sake, we included only two frames for the woman's animation.

So far, you've seen the jogger and the exercising woman. There are still three more sprites you can inspect: two trees and a light fixture (a chandelier).

☐ Move into the room containing the two trees. As shown back in Figure 16.4, the second room from the lower-right corner of the floor has two points marked T, each of which represents the location of a tree.

Figures 16.13 and 16.14 show two snapshots of the trees as you move closer to them.

Figure 16.13.

Moving toward the two trees (snapshot 1).

Figure 16.14.

Moving toward the two trees (snapshot 2).

As you can see, each tree is located in a different corner of the room.

The last sprite in the floor that you haven't inspected closely yet is the light fixture. As shown previously in Figure 16.4, the lower-right room has a point marked L, which is where the light fixture is located.

☐ Move into the room where the light fixture is located.

Figures 16.15 shows a snapshot of the 3D view as you get closer to the light fixture.

Figure 16.15.
Moving toward the light fixture.

The light fixture is an example of a *soft sprite*, which is a sprite you can walk through. On the other hand, the jogger sprite, the woman sprite, and the tree sprites are *hard sprites*. You can't walk through hard sprites. Once you reach a hard sprite, you have to walk around it.

The light fixture sprite was made a soft sprite because you should be able to walk through it. Once you are exactly under the light fixture, you don't see it.

As you see later when you write the My3DVR.EXE program code, making a sprite either soft or hard is easy.

The My3DVR.EXE program has a File menu (see Figure 16.16). When the user selects Exit from the File menu, the program is terminated. When the user selects About from the Help menu, the About message box is displayed.

Figure 16.16.
The File menu of the My3DVR.EXE program.

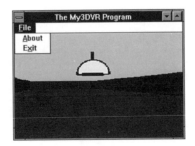

☐ Keep experimenting with the My3DVR.EXE program by moving to various rooms.

> **Note:** In the preceding steps, you were instructed to move in the floor by using the four arrow keys.
>
> Another way to move in the floor is by dragging the mouse.
>
> Dragging the mouse to the left and right is equivalent to pressing the right- and left-arrow keys. It changes your viewing direction.
>
> Dragging the mouse up and down is equivalent to pressing the up- and down-arrow keys. It moves you forward or backward in the current viewing direction.
>
> Because the mouse is more sensitive than the keyboard, using the mouse for moving inside the floor isn't as easy as using the arrow keys. However, when you use the mouse, you can move faster.

☐ Terminate the My3DVR.EXE program by selecting Exit from its File menu.

Now that you know what the My3DVR.EXE program is supposed to do, let's start writing this program.

Adding the Tego3DVR.VBX Control to the VBX Page

Because the My3DVR program uses the Tego3DVR.VBX control, you must first add this VBX control to Delphi's VBX page.

☐ Make sure that the Tego3DVR.VBX control resides in the \Windows\System directory. You can copy this file from the \DProg\VBX directory of the accompanying CD.

☐ Select Install Components from the Tools menu.

   Delphi responds by displaying the Install Components dialog box.

☐ Click the VBX button of the Install Components dialog box.

   Delphi responds by displaying the Install VBX File dialog box.

☐ Select the Tego3DVR.VBX file from the \Windows\System directory.

Your Install VBX File dialog box should now appear as shown in Figure 16.17.

Figure 16.17.
The Install VBX File dialog box.

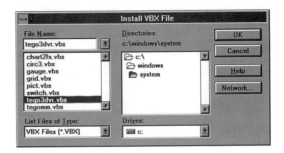

☐ Click the OK button of the Install VBX File dialog box.

Delphi responds by displaying the Install VBX dialog box shown in Figure 16.18.

Figure 16.18.
The Install VBX dialog box.

☐ Click the OK button of the Install VBX dialog box.

Delphi responds by again displaying the Install Components dialog box.

☐ Click the OK button of the Install Components dialog box.

Delphi responds by asking you if you want to save the current unit.

☐ Click the No button.

Delphi responds by installing the VBX and then recompiling and reloading the Delphi component library (a process that may take a few seconds).

☐ Take a look at the VBX page of Delphi. As shown in Figure 16.19, the Tego3DVR.VBX control is displayed as one of the VBX icons.

Figure 16.19.
The Tego3DVR.VBX control icon on the VBX page.

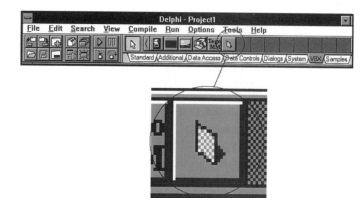

The Visual Implementation of the My3DVR Program

You now visually implement the My3DVR program.

☐ Select New Project from the File menu.

☐ Make sure that Form1 is selected, select Save File As from the File menu, and save the form as C:\DProg\Ch16\C3DVR.Pas.

☐ Select Save Project As from the File menu, and save the project as C:\DProg\Ch16\My3DVR.Dpr.

☐ Set the Name property of the form to **frmMy3DVR**.

☐ Set the Caption property of the form to **The My3DVR Program**.

☐ Set the BorderStyle property of the frmMy3DVR form to **bsSingle**.

☐ Place a Virtual Reality control (the Tego3DVR.VBX control from the VBX page) in the frmMy3DVR form.

☐ Make sure that the Name property of the Virtual Reality control is Tego3DVR1.

☐ Place a Timer control from the System page in the frmMy3DVR form.

☐ Set the Name property of the Timer to **tmrTimer**.

☐ Set the tmrTimer control interval to **400**.

☐ Place a MainMenu control from the Standard page in the frmMy3DVR form.

☐ In the Object Inspector window, click the three dots to the right of the Items property of the MainMenu control.

Delphi responds by displaying a window that lets you set the menu items.

☐ Use the mouse to select the leftmost menu item on the menu bar, and set its Caption property to **&File**.

☐ Set the Caption properties of the About and Exit menu items (below the File menu) so that the File menu looks as follows:

```
&File
&About...
E&xit
```

The menu items appear as shown in Figure 16.20.

Figure 16.20.
Setting the menu items (design time).

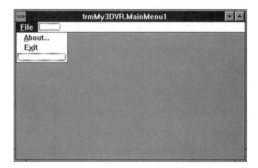

The completed frmMy3DVR form should look like the one shown in Figure 16.21.

Figure 16.21.
The frmMy3DVR *form (design mode).*

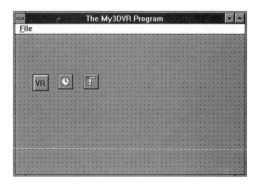

☐ Save your work by selecting Save Project from the File menu.

The visual implementation of the form of the My3DVR program is complete.

Preparing a Floor File (FLR File) for the My3DVR Program

Before you start writing the My3DVR program code, you first must prepare a *floor file*. A floor file is a text file containing a 2D representation of a floor. Once you finish preparing the floor file, you can use the 3D Virtual Reality control to write a program that displays the floor file in 3D and enables the user to move in the 3D floor. That is, your program converts the 2D drawing to a 3D drawing.

A floor file typically has the file extension .FLR. Because floor files are regular text files, you can use any text editor to create and edit them.

To see how a floor file looks, do the following:

☐ Use any text editor to open the floor file FLOOR50.FLR that is included on the accompanying CD. (The FLOOR50.FLR floor file resides inside the \DProg\Ch16 directory of the accompanying CD.)

> **Note:** Because floor files are regular text files, you can use any text editor to create and edit them. For example, you can use the Notepad program or the Write program. Both Notepad and Write are shipped with Windows. The Notepad and Write icons are in the Program Manager Accessories group.

Figures 16.22 and 16.23 show the Notepad program with the FLOOR50.FLR file open. We display the FLOOR50.FLR file contents in two figures because the contents don't fit on one Notepad screen. To see the bottom section of the FLOOR50.FLR file with Notepad, you have to scroll the file contents.

Figure 16.22.

Viewing the top section of the FLOOR50.FLR file with Notepad.

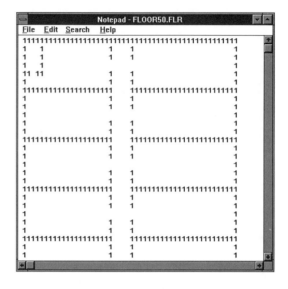

Figure 16.23.

Viewing the bottom section of the FLOOR50.FLR file with Notepad.

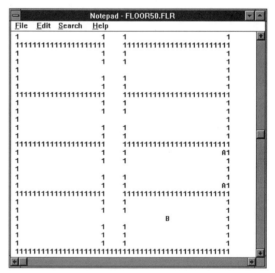

As you can see, a floor file is very simple. The 1 character represents a solid cell in the floor, and the space character (blank) represents an empty cell.

Note: When you view a floor file with a word processor such as Word for Windows, you should set the font to a fixed-pitch font, such as Courier or Courier New. This is necessary because you want all the characters of the FLR file (the 1s and the spaces) to be the same width. When you save the FLR file, save it as a Text file.

16

The following three examples illustrate how to create floor files.

Example 1

To create a floor file representing a floor with a width of 15 cells, a height of 10 cells, and only one room, you must type the following text in the floor file:

```
111111111111111
1             1
1             1
1             1
1             1
1             1
1             1
1             1
1             1
111111111111111
```

Example 2

The following text represents a floor with a width of 20 cells, a height of 10 cells, and two rooms:

```
11111111111111111111
1                  1
1                  1
1                  1
11111111  1111111111
1                  1
1                  1
1                  1
11111111111111111111
```

As you can see, there is an opening between the two rooms. The opening is necessary because we want the user to be able to move from room to room. Of course, the preceding text is not the only way to create two rooms. You can rearrange the locations and sizes of the rooms in any way you wish.

> **Note:** The Floor VBX control enables you to place new cells or to remove cells from the floor during runtime from within your program. This feature of the 3D Virtual Reality control enables you to write game programs that have secret openings. When the user hits a secret cell, your program can remove the cell so the user is able to move into a secret room.

Example 3

The following text represents a floor with a width of 20 cells, a height of 15 cells, and four rooms:

```
11111111111111111111
1       1          1
1       1          1
1       1          1
1       1          1
1111  11111111  1111
1       1          1
1       1          1
1       1          1
11111111111111111111
```

In addition to 1s and spaces, a floor file may also contain non-numeric characters (for example, A, B, C, a, b, c, and so on). These characters represent sprites. The pictures of these sprites are set from within your program during runtime. For example, your program may set the A sprite to a picture of a chair. Thus, all cells in the floor file containing the letter A display a chair.

Now that you know how a floor file is constructed, inspect the Floor50.FLR file with your text editor (see Figures 16.22 and 16.23). When you inspect the Floor50.FLR file, notice the following:

- The Floor50.FLR file width is 50 cells, and the height is also 50 cells.
- The floor file contains 16 rooms. Each of these rooms is connected to the main hall.
- The upper-left room contains a small sub-room.
- The lower-right room contains the letter B in the middle of the room (see Figure 16.23). The B represents a sprite. As you see later in this chapter, the code you write defines sprite B as a picture of a light fixture. Thus, when the user moves into the bottom-left room, he sees a light fixture in the middle of the room.
- The room above the lower-right room contains the letter A in two corners (see Figure 16.23). The A represents a sprite. As you see later in this chapter, the code you write defines sprite A as a picture of a tree. Thus, when the user moves into the room containing the two A sprites, he sees two trees.

In the following sections, you write the My3DVR program code. This code uses the FLOOR50.FLR floor file. You need to copy the FLOOR50.FLR file from the accompanying CD to your hard disk:

☐ Copy the FLOOR50.FLR file from the \DProg\Ch16 directory of the accompanying CD to your C:\DProg\CH16 directory.

The My3DVR program uses various sprites. Each sprite is composed of various BMP files. As you soon see, the My3DVR.EXE program assumes that the BMP files reside in the same directory where the My3DVR.EXE program resides, and so you must copy the BMP files to the C:\DProg\Ch16 directory.

☐ Copy all the BMP files from the \DProg\Ch16 directory of the accompanying CD to the C:\DProg\Ch16 directory.

Declaring Global Variables

The My3DVR program uses various global variables. Declare these global variables now.

☐ At the beginning of the C3DVR.Pas file, add variable declarations to the var section.

After declaring the variables, the var section appears as follows:

```
var
  frmMy3DVR: TfrmMy3DVR;
  gPrevX: Integer;
  gPrevY: Integer;
  gMouseButtonIsDown: Boolean;
  gExerciseFrame: Integer;
  gJoggerY: Integer;
  gJoggerFrame: Integer;
```

☐ Save your work by selecting Save Project from the File menu.

Attaching Code to the Exit Menu Item's *Click* Event

Add code to the Exit menu item as follows:

☐ Attach code to the OnClick event of the Exit menu item.

After attaching the code, the Exit1Click() procedure appears as follows:

```
procedure TfrmMy3DVR.Exit1Click(Sender: TObject);
begin

Application.Terminate;

end;
```

☐ Save your work by selecting Save Project from the File menu.

The code you typed terminates the program.

Attaching Code to the *OnClick* Event of the About Menu Item

When the user selects About from the File menu, the program displays an About message box. Write the code that accomplishes this task.

☐ Attach code to the OnClick event of the About menu item.

After attaching the code, the About1Click() procedure appears as follows:

```
procedure TfrmMy3DVR.About1Click(Sender: TObject);
var
Msg: String;
CR: String;

begin

CR := Chr(13) + Chr(10);

{ Prepare the message of the About message box.}
Msg := 'This program was written with Delphi ';
Msg := Msg + 'using the TegoSoft 3D Floor VBX control.';
Msg := Msg + CR + CR;
Msg := Msg + 'For more information about the ';
Msg := Msg + 'TegoSoft VBX Control Kit, contact TegoSoft ';
Msg := Msg + 'at:';
Msg := Msg + CR + CR;
Msg := Msg + 'TegoSoft Inc.' + CR;
Msg := Msg + 'P.O. Box 389' + CR;
Msg := Msg + 'Bellmore, NY 11710 ';
Msg := Msg + CR + CR;
Msg := Msg + 'Phone: (516)783-4824 ';

{ Display the About message box.}
MessageDlg (Msg, mtConfirmation, [mbOK], 0);

end;
```

☐ Save your work by selecting Save Project from the File menu.

The code you typed uses MessageDlg() to display an About message box. The message is the string Msg.

Attaching Code to the *frmMy3DVR* Form's *FormCreate()* Procedure

The FormCreate() procedure of the frmMy3DVR form is executed when starting the program. It's a good place to write various initialization code.

The code you attach now to the FormCreate() procedure opens the FLOOR50.FLR floor file.

☐ Attach code to the frmMy3DVR form's OnCreate event.

After attaching the code, the FormCreate() procedure appears as follows:

```
procedure TfrmMy3DVR.FormCreate(Sender: TObject);

var
OpenResult: Integer;
OpenResultString: String;
Msg: String;

begin

{Make the Tego3DVR1 control invisible.}
Tego3DVR1.Visible := False;

{Open the FLOOR50.FLR file.}
Tego3DVR1.FileName := 'FLOOR50.FLR';
Tego3DVR1.hWndDisplay := frmMy3DVR.Handle;
Tego3DVR1.NumOfRows := 50;
Tego3DVR1.NumOfCols := 50;

Tego3DVR1.Command := 'Open';

{If FLR file could not be opened, terminate
the program}
OpenResult := Tego3DVR1.ErrorCode;
If OpenResult <> 0 Then
    begin
    MessageDlg(
      Format('Unable to open file: %s'#13#10'Error Code: %d',
      [Tego3DVR1.FileName, OpenResult]), mtError, [mbOK], 0);
    Application.Terminate;
    end;

{Set the initial user's position and viewing angle.}
Tego3DVR1.PixelPosX := 4 * Tego3DVR1.CellWidth;
Tego3DVR1.PixelPosY := 4 * Tego3DVR1.CellWidth;
Tego3DVR1.Angle := 0;

{Set the StepSize property to 50.}
```

16

```
Tego3DVR1.StepSize := 50;

{Set the colors of the walls, ceiling, and floor.}
Tego3DVR1.WallColorA := 7;     { White }
Tego3DVR1.WallColorB := 4;     { Red   }
Tego3DVR1.CeilingColor := 11; { Light Cyan }
Tego3DVR1.FloorColor := 2;     { Green }
Tego3DVR1.StripeColor := 0;    { Black }

{ Load the sprites. }
Tego3DVR1.SpritePath := '';
Tego3DVR1.SpriteNumber := 65;
Tego3DVR1.SpriteFileName := 'TREE.BMP';
Tego3DVR1.SpriteNumber := 66;
Tego3DVR1.SpriteFileName := 'LIGHT.BMP';
Tego3DVR1.SpriteNumber := 67;
Tego3DVR1.SpriteFileName := 'EX1.BMP';
Tego3DVR1.SpriteNumber := 68;
Tego3DVR1.SpriteFileName := 'EX2.BMP';
Tego3DVR1.SpriteNumber := 69;
Tego3DVR1.SpriteFileName := 'JOG1.BMP';
Tego3DVR1.SpriteNumber := 70;
Tego3DVR1.SpriteFileName := 'JOG2.BMP';
Tego3DVR1.SpriteNumber := 71;
Tego3DVR1.SpriteFileName := 'JOG3.BMP';
Tego3DVR1.SpriteNumber := 72;
Tego3DVR1.SpriteFileName := 'JOG4.BMP';

{ Set sprite number 66 (the Light sprite)
  as a soft sprite.
  (i.e. the user can walk through this sprite). }
Tego3DVR1.SpriteNumber := 66;
Tego3DVR1.Command := 'SetSpriteSoft';

gMouseButtonIsDown := False;
gJoggerY := 0;

end;
```

☐ Save your work by selecting Save Project from the File menu.

You declared local variables in the var section of the procedure.

```
procedure TfrmMy3DVR.FormCreate(Sender: TObject);

var
OpenResult: Integer;
OpenResultString: String;
Msg: String;

begin

...

end;
```

The next statement you typed makes the virtual reality control invisible.

```
{Make the Tego3DVR1 control invisible.}
Tego3DVR1.Visible := False;
```

The following statements are responsible for opening the FLOOR50.FLR floor file:

```
{Open the FLOOR50.FLR file.}
Tego3DVR1.FileName := 'FLOOR50.FLR';
Tego3DVR1.hWndDisplay := frmMy3DVR.Handle;
Tego3DVR1.NumOfRows := 50;
Tego3DVR1.NumOfCols := 50;

Tego3DVR1.Command := 'Open';
```

The first statement,

```
Tego3DVR1.FileName := 'FLOOR50.FLR';
```

sets the FileName property of the 3D Virtual Reality control to the name of the FLOOR50.FLR floor file. The FileName property of the 3D Virtual Reality control specifies which floor file you want to open.

The second statement,

```
Tego3DVR1.hWndDisplay := frmMy3DVR.Handle;
```

sets the hWndDisplay property of the 3D Virtual Reality control to the frmMy3DVR form's window handle. The hWndDisplay property of the 3D Virtual Reality control specifies the window handle where the 3D graphics are displayed. Because you want the 3D graphics to be displayed in the frmMy3DVR form, you set the hWndDisplay property to the frmMy3DVR form's Handle property.

The next two statements set the NumOfRows and NumOfCols properties of the 3D Virtual Reality control to 50:

```
Tego3DVR1.NumOfRows := 50;
Tego3DVR1.NumOfCols := 50;
```

The NumOfRows property specifies the floor file height in cell units, and the NumOfCols property specifies the floor file width in cell units. (Recall that when you inspected the FLOOR50.FLR file, you saw that its width is 50 cells and its height is 50 cells).

Finally, the FLOOR50.FLR file is opened by issuing the Open command.

```
Tego3DVR1.Command := 'Open';
```

The Open command opens the floor file specified by the 3D Virtual Reality control's FileName property.

By examining the ErrorCode property, the result of the Open command can be inspected to see whether the 3D Virtual Reality control was able to open the floor file.

```
OpenResult := Tego3DVR1.ErrorCode;
```

If the floor file was opened successfully, the `ErrorCode` value (after issuing the `Open` command) is `0`. Otherwise, the `ErrorCode` value will be a nonzero integer that specifies an error code. Notice that in the preceding statement, the `ErrorCode` value is assigned to the `OpenResult` local variable.

The next block of statements evaluates the value of `OpenResult` to see if the floor file was opened successfully.

```
If OpenResult <> 0 Then
   begin
   Msg := 'Unable to open file: ' + Tego3DVR1.FileName;
   Msg := Msg + Chr(13) + Chr(10);
   Str(OpenResult, OpenResultString);
   Msg := Msg + 'Error Code: ' +  OpenResultString;
   MessageDlg (Msg, mtError, [mbOK], 0);
   Application.Terminate;
   end;
```

If the `Open` command failed, the condition of the preceding `If` statement is satisfied, and the statements after the `If` display an error message box and terminate the program.

> **Note:** To open a floor file, you first have to set the 3D Virtual Reality control `FileName`, `hWndDisplay`, `NumOfRows`, and `NumOfCols` properties, and then use the `Open` command.
>
> The `NumOfRows` and `NumOfCols` properties of the 3D Virtual Reality control must be set to the correct height and width of the floor file. If you do not set them to the correct values, the `Open` command fails.
>
> The result of the `Open` command specifies whether the command was successful. If the `ErrorCode` property is equal to `0`, the floor file was opened successfully. If the returned value is not `0`, the `Open` command failed.

The next three statements set the initial position and viewing direction of the user:

```
{Set the initial user's position and viewing angle.}
Tego3DVR1.PixelPosX := 4 * Tego3DVR1.CellWidth;
Tego3DVR1.PixelPosY := 4 * Tego3DVR1.CellWidth;
Tego3DVR1.Angle := 0;
```

The user's position is set by setting the 3D Virtual Reality control's `PixelPosX` and `PixelPosY` properties. The `PixelPosX` and `PixelPosY` properties determine the X,Y coordinates of the user's position in pixel units. The lower-left corner of the floor is at the X,Y coordinate 0,0. In the preceding code, both the `PixelPosX` property and `PixelPosY` properties are set to the following:

```
4 * Floor1.CellWidth
```

The 3D Virtual Reality control CellWidth property reports the width of one cell in pixels. Thus, the preceding code places the user at the cell that is fourth from the bottom of the floor and fourth from the left side of the floor. If you inspect the bottom section of the FLOOR50.FLR file (Figure 16.23), you see that the cell that is fourth from the bottom of the floor and fourth from the left of the floor is in the bottom-left room of the floor. When starting the program, the user will be inside the bottom-left room of the floor.

The 3D Virtual Reality control Angle property specifies the user's viewing direction in degrees. The Angle property can be set to an integer in the range of 0 through 360. When you want the user to face the right side of the floor, you have to set the Angle property to 0. In the preceding code, you set the Angle property to 0 because when starting the program, you want the user to face the exit door of the bottom-left room of the floor.

> **Note:** When starting the program, you must place the user somewhere in the floor by setting the PixelPosX and PixelPosY properties.
>
> Make sure that you place the user in an empty cell. You don't want to place the user in a wall.

You then set the StepSize property as follows so that when the user advances, each step is 50 pixels:

```
{Set the StepSize property to 50.}
Tego3DVR1.StepSize := 50;
```

The next statements you typed in the FormCreate procedure are

```
{Set the colors of the walls, ceiling, and floor.}
Tego3DVR1.WallColorA := 7;    { White }
Tego3DVR1.WallColorB := 4;    { Red  }
Tego3DVR1.CeilingColor := 11; { Light Cyan }
Tego3DVR1.FloorColor := 2;    { Green }
Tego3DVR1.StripeColor := 0;   { Black }
```

These statements set the colors of the walls, ceiling, and floor. The WallColorA property specifies the color of the vertical walls, the WallColorB property specifies the color of the horizontal walls, the CeilingColor property specifies the ceiling color, the FloorColor property specifies the floor color, and the StripeColor property specifies the color of the vertical stripes separating cells. Table 16.1 lists all the possible values you can specify for the color properties.

Table 16.1. The values that you can assign to the 3D Virtual Reality control color properties.

Value	Color
0	Black
1	Blue
2	Green
3	Cyan
4	Red
5	Magenta
6	Yellow
7	White
8	Gray
9	Light Blue
10	Light Green
11	Light Cyan
12	Light Red
13	Light Magenta
14	Light Yellow
15	Bright White

You then loaded the sprites as follows:

```
{ Load the sprites. }
Tego3DVR1.SpritePath := '';

Tego3DVR1.SpriteNumber := 65;
Tego3DVR1.SpriteFileName := 'TREE.BMP';

Tego3DVR1.SpriteNumber := 66;
Tego3DVR1.SpriteFileName := 'LIGHT.BMP';

Tego3DVR1.SpriteNumber := 67;
Tego3DVR1.SpriteFileName := 'EX1.BMP';

Tego3DVR1.SpriteNumber := 68;
Tego3DVR1.SpriteFileName := 'EX2.BMP';

Tego3DVR1.SpriteNumber := 69;
Tego3DVR1.SpriteFileName := 'JOG1.BMP';

Tego3DVR1.SpriteNumber := 70;
Tego3DVR1.SpriteFileName := 'JOG2.BMP';
```

```
Tego3DVR1.SpriteNumber := 71;
Tego3DVR1.SpriteFileName := 'JOG3.BMP';

Tego3DVR1.SpriteNumber := 72;
Tego3DVR1.SpriteFileName := 'JOG4.BMP';
```

The SpritePath property is set to null as follows:

```
Tego3DVR1.SpritePath := '';
```

When you executed the My3DVR program, you saw various sprites. Each sprite is a BMP file. The sprites' BMP files are assumed to reside in the current directory—the same directory as the My3DVR.EXE program, and so there's no need to specify a path. In future projects, you can place the BMP files in another directory, and set the SpritePath to the name of the directory where you placed the BMP files.

The floor file (see Figures 16.22 and 16.23) uses, for example, the A character as the symbol for tree sprites. You tell the 3D Virtual Reality control that the tree sprites are represented by A, which has the ASCII value of 65, as follows:

```
Tego3DVR1.SpriteNumber := 65;
Tego3DVR1.SpriteFileName := 'TREE.BMP';
```

The light fixture is denoted in the floor file as the B character (ASCII 66), and you correlate the BMP of the light fixture with B as follows:

```
Tego3DVR1.SpriteNumber := 66;
Tego3DVR1.SpriteFileName := 'LIGHT.BMP';
```

The animation showing the woman exercising is composed of two BMP frames: EX1.BMP and EX2.BMP.

You tell the 3D Virtual Reality control that 67 represents EX1.BMP, as follows:

```
Tego3DVR1.SpriteNumber := 67;
Tego3DVR1.SpriteFileName := 'EX1.BMP';
```

Tell the 3D Virtual Reality control that 68 represents EX2.BMP, as follows:

```
Tego3DVR1.SpriteNumber := 68;
Tego3DVR1.SpriteFileName := 'EX2.BMP';
```

Note that the floor text file does not include the character C (ASCII 67), and the floor text file does not include the character D (ASCII 68). As of yet, the 3D Virtual Reality control loaded the EX1.BMP and EX2.BMP files, but these files were not placed on the floor because the cell locations where the pictures should be placed are not mentioned in the floor file. Later in this chapter, you see how to specify the location in which to place these sprites. One way to specify the location of a sprite is by using the floor file, as you did with the trees and the light fixture. Another way to specify the sprites' location is from within your code, as you see later in this chapter.

The jogger's animation is composed of four BMP files (JOG1.BMP, JOG2.BMP, JOG3.BMP, and JOG4.BMP). You didn't specify the locations of these sprites in the floor file, so you must do so later in the program. For now, just load the BMP files of these sprites.

```
Tego3DVR1.SpriteNumber := 69;
Tego3DVR1.SpriteFileName := 'JOG1.BMP';

Tego3DVR1.SpriteNumber := 70;
Tego3DVR1.SpriteFileName := 'JOG2.BMP';

Tego3DVR1.SpriteNumber := 71;
Tego3DVR1.SpriteFileName := 'JOG3.BMP';

Tego3DVR1.SpriteNumber := 72;
Tego3DVR1.SpriteFileName := 'JOG4.BMP';
```

A sprite's default setting is that the user can't go through the sprite (it is not a soft sprite). However, because the light fixture is a soft sprite, you have to set it as a soft sprite, as follows:

```
{ Set sprite number 66 (the Light sprite)
  as a soft sprite.
  (i.e. the user can walk through this sprite). }
Tego3DVR1.SpriteNumber := 66;
Tego3DVR1.Command := 'SetSpriteSoft';
```

Later in this chapter, you use the gMouseButtonIsDown global variable as a flag indicating whether the mouse button is up or down. The following statement that you typed in the FormCreate() procedure initialized the gMouseButtonIsDown variable to False.

```
gMouseButtonIsDown := False;
```

When you start the program, the mouse button is assumed to be up.

The code you typed in the FormCreate procedure is responsible for opening the floor file. In the following section, you write the code that actually displays the 3D floor.

Attaching Code to the *frmMy3DVR* Form's *OnPaint* Event

The OnPaint event of the frmMy3DVR form occurs whenever there is a need to redraw the form (for example, when starting the program). Whenever there is a need to redraw the frmMy3DVR form, the program should draw the current 3D view of the floor. Here's how to write the code that accomplishes this task.

☐ Attach code to the OnPaint event of the frmMy3DVR form.

After you attach the code, the FormPaint() procedure appears as follows:

```
procedure TfrmMy3DVR.FormPaint(Sender: TObject);
begin

{ Display the 3D view. }
Tego3DVR1.Command := 'Display3D';

end;
```

☐ Save your work by selecting Save Project from the File menu.

The code you typed inside the FormPaint() procedure is made up of a single statement:

```
Tego3DVR1.Command := 'Display3D';
```

This statement displays the current 3D view of the floor by issuing the Display3D command. The Display3D command displays the current 3D view of the floor based on the values of the PixelPosX, PixelPosY, and Angle properties of the 3D Virtual Reality control. You initialized the PixelPosX, PixelPosY, and Angle properties in the FormCreate() procedure.

Follow these steps to see the code you've written so far in action:

☐ Execute the My3DVR program.

As you can see, the program displays a 3D view of the floor (Figure 16.24). The program placed you in the bottom-left room of the floor, and you're currently facing the exit door.

Figure 16.24.
The initial 3D view that the
My3DVR program displays.

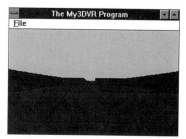

Of course, if you try to move in the floor by pressing the arrow keys, nothing happens because you haven't yet written the code that accomplishes this task.

☐ Terminate the My3DVR program by selecting Exit from its File menu.

In the following section, you write the code that enables the user to move in the floor.

Attaching Code to the *frmMy3DVR* Form's *OnKeyDown* Event

You're now ready to attach code to the OnKeyDown event of the frmMy3DVR form. This code enables the user to move in the 3D floor by using the left-, right-, up-, and down-arrow keys.

417

☐ Attach code to the OnKeyDown event of the frmMy3DVR form.

After you attach the code, the FormKeyDown() procedure appears as follows:

```
procedure TfrmMy3DVR.FormKeyDown(Sender: TObject;
        var Key: Word; Shift: TShiftState);

begin

case Key of

    37, 100:
        {Left key (37) or 4 key (100) was pressed.}
        Tego3DVR1.Angle := Tego3DVR1.Angle + 6;

    39, 102:
        {Right key (39) or 6 key (102) was pressed.}
        Tego3DVR1.Angle := Tego3DVR1.Angle - 6;

    38, 104:
        {Up key (38) or 8 key (104) was pressed.}
        Tego3DVR1.Command := 'Step';

    40, 98:
        {Down key (40) or 2 key (98) was pressed.}
        Tego3DVR1.Command := 'Back';

end;

{ Display the 3D view. }
Tego3DVR1.Command := 'Display3D';

end;
```

☐ Save your work by selecting Save Project from the File menu.

The FormKeyDown() procedure of the frmMy3DVR form is executed automatically whenever the user presses a key while the frmMy3DVR form is active. The FormKeyDown() procedure's Key parameter specifies which key the user pressed.

The code you typed in the FormKeyDown() procedure uses a case statement to evaluate the Key parameter.

```
case Key of

    37, 100:
        {Left key (37) or 4 key (100) was pressed.}
        Tego3DVR1.Angle := Tego3DVR1.Angle + 6;

    39, 102:
        {Right key (39) or 6 key (102) was pressed.}
        Tego3DVR1.Angle := Tego3DVR1.Angle - 6;

    38, 104:
        {Up key (38) or 8 key (104) was pressed.}
        Tego3DVR1.Command := 'Step';
```

```
40, 98:
     {Down key (40) or 2 key (98) was pressed.}
     Tego3DVR1.Command := 'Back';

end;
```

If the user pressed the left-arrow key (or the 4 key), the statement after the first Case is executed.

```
Tego3DVR1.Angle := Tego3DVR1.Angle + 6;
```

This statement increases the 3D Virtual Reality control's Angle property by 6 degrees. If the Angle property is set to a value greater than or equal to 360, the 3D Virtual Reality control automatically adjusts the Angle property's value to one in the range of 0 through 360. For example, if the current value of the Angle property is 358, the preceding statement sets the Angle property to 4 (358+6=364, and 364 degrees is the same as 4 degrees).

If the user pressed the right-arrow key (or the 6 key), the statement after the second Case is executed.

```
Tego3DVR1.Angle := Tego3DVR1.Angle - 6;
```

This statement decreases the 3D Virtual Reality control's Angle property by 6 degrees. If the Angle property is set to a value less than 0, the 3D Virtual Reality control automatically adjusts the Angle property value to one in the range of 0 through 360. For example, if the current value of the Angle property is 5, the preceding statement sets the property to 359 ($5 - 6 = -1$, and -1 degrees is the same as 359 degrees).

If the user pressed the up-arrow key (or the 8 key), the statement after the third Case is executed.

```
Tego3DVR1.Command := 'Step';
```

This statement issues the Step command to advance the user's position 50 pixels forward in the current viewing direction. In the FormCreate() procedure, you set the StepSize to 50 pixels as follows:

```
Tego3DVR1.StepSize := 50;
```

When you issue the Advance command, it moves the user position 50 pixels.

If the user pressed the down-arrow key (or the 2 key), the statement after the fourth Case is executed.

```
Tego3DVR1.Command := 'Back';
```

This statement issues the Back command to "advance" the user 50 pixels in the current viewing direction. That is, the user is moved 50 pixels backward (in reverse) in the current viewing direction.

The last statement you typed in the `FormKeyDown()` procedure is

```
{ Display the 3D view. }
Tego3DVR1.Command := 'Display3D';
```

This statement issues the `Display3D` command to display the new 3D view corresponding to the user's new position.

To see the code you attached to the `frmMy3DVR` form's `OnKeyDown` event in action, follow these steps:

☐ Execute the My3DVR program.

☐ Use the left-, right-, up-, and down-arrow keys to move to various locations on the floor and verify that the arrow keys work properly.

☐ Terminate the My3DVR program by selecting Exit from its File menu.

Attaching Code to the *frmMy3DVR* Form's *OnMouseUp*, *OnMouseDown*, and *OnMouseMove* Events

At this point, the user can move inside the 3D floor by using the arrow keys. Now you'll add code to the program so the user can use the mouse for moving in the 3D floor.

The code you attach to the `FormMouseMove()` procedure enables the user to move in the floor by dragging the mouse over the form.

Dragging the mouse to the left and right produces the same results as pressing the right- and left-arrow keys. It changes the viewing direction. Dragging the mouse up and down produces the same effects as pressing the up- and down-arrow keys. It moves the user forward or backward in the current viewing direction.

☐ Attach code to the `OnMouseDown` event of the `frmMy3DVR` form.

After you attach the code, the `FormMouseDown()` procedure appears as follows:

```
procedure TfrmMy3DVR.FormMouseDown(Sender: TObject; Button: TMouseButton;
        Shift: TShiftState; X, Y: Integer);

begin

gMouseButtonIsDown := True;

end;
```

The code you typed sets the global variable `gMouseButtonIsDown` to `True`.

☐ Attach code to the frmMy3DVR form's OnMouseUp event.

After you attach the code, the FormMouseUp() procedure appears as follows:

```
procedure TfrmMy3DVR.FormMouseUp(Sender: TObject; Button: TMouseButton;
        Shift: TShiftState; X, Y: Integer);

begin

gMouseButtonIsDown := False;

end;
```

The code you typed sets the global variable gMouseButtonIsDown to False.

The gMouseButtonIsDown variable now reflects the status of the mouse button. When the mouse button is pressed, the gMouseButtonIsDown variable is equal to True, and when the mouse button is not pressed, the gMouseButtonIsDown variable is equal to False.

☐ Attach code to the frmMy3DVR form's OnMouseMove event.

After you attach the code, the FormOnMouseMove() procedure appears as follows:

```
procedure TfrmMy3DVR.FormMouseMove(Sender: TObject; Shift: TShiftState;
        X, Y: Integer);

begin

{If none of the mouse buttons is pressed down,
 terminate this procedure.}
 If gMouseButtonIsDown = False then Exit;

{ Change the user's position according to the
 mouse movement. }
If Y < gPrevY Then Tego3DVR1.Command := 'Step';
If Y > gPrevY Then Tego3DVR1.Command := 'Back';
If X < gPrevX Then Tego3DVR1.Angle := Tego3DVR1.Angle + 3;
If X > gPrevX Then Tego3DVR1.Angle := Tego3DVR1.Angle - 3;

{ Display the 3D view. }
Tego3DVR1.Command := 'Display3D';

{ Update gPrevX and gPrevY for next time.}
gPrevX := X;
gPrevY := Y;

end;
```

☐ Save your work by selecting Save Project from the File menu.

In the var section of the C3DVR.Pas file, you declared the gPrevX and gPrevY global variables. These variables store the previous X and Y coordinates of the mouse cursor. In the FormMouseMove() procedure, you typed code comparing the current X and Y coordinates of the mouse cursor with the previous mouse coordinates, and accordingly, the user's position is changed (advanced, back, rotate clockwise, or rotate counter-clockwise).

An If statement is executed.

```
If gMouseButtonIsDown = False then Exit;
```

This If statement evaluates the value of gMouseButtonIsDown. If gMouseButtonIsDown is equal to False, none of the mouse buttons is currently pressed (the user is not dragging the mouse). If this is the case, the preceding If statement terminates the procedure. If, however, any of the mouse buttons is currently pressed (the user is dragging the mouse), the remaining statements in the procedure are executed.

The next block of code is a series of four If statements.

```
If Y < gPrevY Then Tego3DVR1.Command := 'Step';
If Y > gPrevY Then Tego3DVR1.Command := 'Back';
If X < gPrevX Then Tego3DVR1.Angle := Tego3DVR1.Angle + 3;
If X > gPrevX Then Tego3DVR1.Angle := Tego3DVR1.Angle - 3;
```

These If statements change the user's position in the 3D floor based on the new position of the mouse. If the user moved the mouse upward, gPrevY (the previous Y coordinate of the mouse) is less than the current Y position of the mouse. If this is the case, the first If condition is satisfied, and the following Step command is issued to move the user 50 pixels forward in the current viewing direction:

```
If Y < gPrevY Then Tego3DVR1.Command := 'Step';
```

If the user moved the mouse downward, gPrevY (the previous Y coordinate of the mouse) is greater than the current Y position of the mouse. If this is the case, the second If condition is satisfied, and the following statement is executed:

```
If Y > gPrevY Then Tego3DVR1.Command := 'Back';
```

This statement moves the user 50 pixels backward in the current viewing direction.

If the user dragged the mouse to the left, gPrevX (the previous X position of the mouse) is less than the current X position of the mouse. If this is the case, the third If condition is satisfied, and the following statement is executed:

```
If X < gPrevX Then Tego3DVR1.Angle := Tego3DVR1.Angle + 3;
```

This statement increases the Angle property of the 3D Virtual Reality control by 3 degrees.

If the user dragged the mouse to the right, gPrevX (the previous X position of the mouse) is greater than the current X position of the mouse. If this is the case, the fourth If condition is satisfied, and the following statement is executed:

```
If X > gPrevX Then Tego3DVR1.Angle := Tego3DVR1.Angle - 3;
```

This statement decreases the 3D Virtual Reality control `Angle` property by 3 degrees.

The next statement you typed in the `FormMouseMove()` procedure is

```
Tego3DVR1.Command := 'Display3D';
```

This statement issues the `Display3D` command to display the 3D view that corresponds to the user's new position.

Finally, the last two statements update the `gPrevX` and `gPrevY` global variables.

```
gPrevX := X;
gPrevY := Y;
```

Thus, on the next mouse movement, the `FormMouseMove()` procedure knows the previous X and Y positions of the mouse.

To see in action the code that you attached to the `OnMouseMove` event of the `frmMy3DVR` form, follow these steps:

☐ Execute the My3DVR program.

☐ Use the mouse to move to various locations on the floor.

☐ Terminate the My3DVR program by selecting Exit from its File menu.

About the Sprites

A sprite is a picture that has transparent sections. A sprite has two BMP files associated with it.

- The sprite's bitmap file.
- The sprite's mask bitmap file.

The sprite's bitmap file contains the picture of the sprite. The sprite's mask bitmap file specifies which sections of the sprite picture are transparent and which are not transparent.

The BMP files you create for the sprites of the 3D Virtual Reality control must be 256-color BMP files. You can convert any other types of BMP files into 256-color BMP files by using the Paintbrush program or similar painting programs. If you have Paintbrush, load your BMP picture with Paintbrush, select Save As from Paintbrush's File menu, and save the BMP as a 256-color BMP file.

As stated, each sprite's BMP file has a mask file associated with it. For example, the TREE.BMP file has the file MTREE.BMP file associated with it. The EX1.BMP file has the MEX1.BMP mask file associated with it. The EX2.BMP file has the MEX2.BMP mask file associated with it, and so on.

Your C:\DProg\Ch16 directory should contain the following BMP files:

EX1.BMP	Bitmap file of frame 1 of the Exercising Woman sprite.
EX2.BMP	Bitmap file of frame 2 of the Exercising Woman sprite.
JOG1.BMP	Bitmap file of frame 1 of the Jogger sprite when the jogger runs towards the user.
JOG2.BMP	Bitmap file of frame 2 of the Jogger sprite when the jogger runs towards the user.
JOG3.BMP	Bitmap file of frame 1 of the Jogger sprite when the jogger runs away from the user.
JOG4.BMP	Bitmap file of frame 2 of the Jogger sprite when the jogger runs away from the user.
LIGHT.BMP	Light Fixture sprite bitmap file.
MEX1.BMP	Mask bitmap file of frame 1 of the Exercising Woman sprite.
MEX2.BMP	Mask bitmap file of frame 2 of the Exercising Woman sprite.
MJOG1.BMP	Mask bitmap file of frame 1 of the Jogger sprite when the jogger runs towards the user.
MJOG2.BMP	Mask bitmap file of frame 2 of the Jogger sprite when the jogger runs towards the user.
MJOG3.BMP	Mask bitmap file of frame 1 of the Jogger sprite when the jogger runs away from the user.
MJOG4.BMP	Mask bitmap file of frame 2 of the Jogger sprite when the jogger runs away from the user.
MLIGHT.BMP	Light Fixture sprite mask bitmap file.
MTREE.BMP	Tree sprite mask bitmap file.
TREE.BMP	Tree sprite bitmap file.

Note that the name of the BMP mask file is identical to the name of the sprite's BMP file but with the M character preceding the filename (EX1.BMP and MEX1.BMP, for example). This means that you can't have a filename longer than seven characters for the sprite's BMP file. For example, if the sprite's BMP filename is 1234567.BMP, the name of the mask file for this BMP file is M1234567.BMP.

You can generate the mask files by using Paintbrush, as follows:

☐ Create the BMP file is used for the sprite. For example, create the MySpr.BMP file, save it as a 256-color BMP file. Set the size of the picture (using the Paintbrush Options menu) to a small size. Remember, the larger the sprite's BMP picture, the slower the program performs.

☐ Save the MySpr.BMP file also as MMySpr.BMP file (256-color BMP file).

☐ Fill the parts of the MMySpr.BMP pictures that you want to be transparent with black.

☐ Use the Paintbrush's erase color tool to erase all the other colors of the MMySpr.BMP picture.

Figure 16.25 shows the TREE.BMP file. After working on TREE.BMP, the MTREE.BMP picture is produced, as shown in Figure 16.26.

Figure 16.25.
The TREE.BMP picture.

As you can see from Figure 16.26, the white area is the opaque area, and the black area is the transparent area.

Figure 16.26.
The MTREE.BMP picture.

For another example, take a look at the Figures 16.27 and 16.28, which show the JOG1.BMP and MJOG1.BMP files.

Figure 16.27.
The JOG1.BMP file.

Figure 16.28.
The MJOG1.BMP file.

16

In the `FormCreate()` procedure, you loaded these BMP files.

> **Note:** When you define a sprite in the 3D Virtual Reality control, you have to
> specify only the sprite's bitmap file. The sprite's mask bitmap filename is always the
> sprite's bitmap filename prefixed with an M. For example, the statements
>
> ```
> Tego3DVR1.SpriteNumber := 69;
> Tego3DVR1.SpriteFileName := 'JOG1.BMP';
> ```
>
> define sprite number 69 of the 3D Virtual Reality control as the sprite whose BMP
> file is JOG1.BMP and whose mask BMP file is MJOG1.BMP.

At this point, the Jogger sprite and the Exercising Woman sprite do not appear on the floor.
That's because the FLOOR50.FLR file doesn't contain cells with the letters representing these
sprites. In the following section, you write code that animates the Jogger and Exercising Woman
sprites.

Animating the Jogger and Exercising Woman Sprites

Unlike the Tree sprite and the Light Fixture sprite, the Jogger and Exercising Woman sprites are moving sprites. When the user looks at these sprites, the sprites appear to be moving.

The illusion of a moving sprite is accomplished by animating several frames. The program displays several frames, one after the other. Each frame shows the character being animated in a slightly different position. For example, the two frames used for the animation of the Jogger when he moves towards the user were shown previously in Figure 16.6.

You're ready now to write the code responsible for the animation of the Jogger and Exercising Woman sprites. You attach the code that accomplishes these tasks to the Timer control's OnTimer event. Recall that during the visual implementation of the frmMy3DVR form you set the Timer control's Interval property to **400**, and so the code that you now attach to the Timer control's OnTimer event is executed every 400 milliseconds.

☐ Attach the following code to the tmrTimer control's OnTimer event.

After you attach the code, the tmrTimerTimer() procedure appears as follows:

```
procedure TfrmMy3DVR.tmrTimerTimer(Sender: TObject);

begin

{If the form is minimized, terminate this procedure.}
If frmMy3DVR.WindowState = wsMinimized Then Exit;

{ Display the next frame of the exercising woman
 (inside the cell at coordinate x=10, y=40).
 Frame 0 of the exercising woman is sprite
 number 67. And frame 1 of the exercising woman is
 sprite number 68. }
If gExerciseFrame = 0 Then
   begin
   gExerciseFrame := 1;
   SetCell (10, 40, 67);
   end
Else
   begin;
   gExerciseFrame := 0;
   SetCell (10, 40, 68);
   end;

{ Set the cell of the previous jogger position
 to an empty cell.}
If gJoggerY <> 0 Then SetCell(23, gJoggerY, 0);
```

```
{ If the jogger has reached the end of the hall,
  reset gJoggerY to 0. }
If gJoggerY = 48 Then  gJoggerY := 0;

{ Increment gJoggerY.}
gJoggerY := gJoggerY + 1;

{ Set JoggerFrame to the next frame number.}
If gJoggerFrame = 0 Then
   begin
   gJoggerFrame := 1;
   end
else
   begin
   gJoggerFrame := 0;
   end;

{ If the user is facing the jogger, show the front
 of the jogger (sprites 69 and 70). Otherwise, show
 the back of the jogger (sprites 71 and 72). }

 If Tego3DVR1.CellPosY >= gJoggerY Then
   begin
   If gJoggerFrame = 0 Then
      begin
      SetCell (23, gJoggerY, 69);
      end
   Else
      begin
      SetCell (23, gJoggerY, 70);
      end;
   end
Else
   begin
   If gJoggerFrame = 0 Then
      begin
      SetCell (23, gJoggerY, 71);
      end
   Else
      begin
      SetCell (23, gJoggerY, 72);
      end;
   end;

{ Display the 3D view.}
Tego3DVR1.Command := 'Display3D';

end;
```

☐ Select Save Project from the File menu to save your work.

Adding the *SetCell()* Procedure

Before going over the code you attached to the Timer control's OnTimer event, add a procedure to the frmMy3DVR form. The code you typed in the tmrTimerTimer() procedure uses the SetCell() procedure, and so you must now write the code of the SetCell() procedure.

☐ Type the following code in the C3DVR.Pas file:

```
procedure SetCell(X: Integer; Y: Integer; SpriteNumber: Integer);

begin

   frmMy3DVR.Tego3DVR1.CellX := X;
   frmMy3DVR.Tego3DVR1.CellY := Y;
   frmMy3DVR.Tego3DVR1.SpriteNumber := SpriteNumber;
   frmMy3DVR.Tego3DVR1.Command := 'SetCell';

end;
```

The code you typed is the SetCell() procedure that is being called from the tmrTimerTimer() procedure.

The SetCell() procedure has three parameters: X, Y, and SpriteNumber.

```
procedure SetCell(X: Integer; Y: Integer; SpriteNumber: Integer);

begin

...

end;
```

The SetSprite() procedure places a sprite on the 3D floor. Which sprite? The sprite whose SpriteNumber you supply as the SetCell() procedure's parameter. Where is the sprite placed? You supply the coordinates as the X and Y parameters of the SetCell() procedure.

The SetCell() procedure updates the CellX and CellY properties with the X and Y parameters that were supplied as the parameters of the SetCell() procedure.

```
frmMy3DVR.Tego3DVR1.CellX := X;
frmMy3DVR.Tego3DVR1.CellY := Y;
```

The SpriteNumber property is updated with the parameter that was supplied to the SetCell() procedure.

```
frmMy3DVR.Tego3DVR1.SpriteNumber := SpriteNumber;
```

Finally, the SetCell command is issued.

```
frmMy3DVR.Tego3DVR1.Command := 'SetCell';
```

Putting it all together, the SetCell() procedure lets you place any sprite in any location in the 3D picture.

☐ Save your work by selecting Save Project from the File menu.

Moving Sprites During Runtime

Now that you understand the propose of the SetCell() procedure, you can go over the tmrTimerTimer() procedure code. Again, the tmrTimerTimer() procedure is executed every 400 milliseconds. Basically, you use the SetCell() procedure to change the location of the sprites in the 3D floor. Besides changing the location of the sprites, you also change the picture of the sprite. Altogether, this gives the user the impression that the sprite objects are moving on the 3D floor.

In the var section of the C3DVR.Pas file, you declared three global variables: gExerciseFrame, gJoggerY, and gJoggerFrame.

These variables are declared as global so they won't lose their values when the tmrTimerTimer() procedure terminates. As you soon see, gExerciseFrame is used for storing the current frame number of the Exercising Woman animation. The gJoggerY variable is used for storing the jogger's current Y position as the jogger moves in the main hall. The gJoggerFrame variable is used for storing the current frame number of the Jogger animation. In the FormMouseMove() procedure, you also used the gPrevX and gPrevY global variables. You used global variables so you won't loose the previous coordinates of the mouse when the FormMouseMove() procedure terminates.

The first block of code in the tmrTimerTimer() procedure is an If...Else statement.

```
If gExerciseFrame = 0 Then
   begin
   gExerciseFrame := 1;
   SetCell (10, 40, 67);
   end
Else
   begin;
   gExerciseFrame := 0;
   SetCell (10, 40, 68);
   end;
```

This If...Else statement is responsible for animating the Exercising Woman sprite. In each iteration of the tmrTimerTimer() procedure (every 400 milliseconds), the preceding If...Else statement changes the value of the gExerciseFrame global variable. One time gExerciseFrame is set to 0; the next time (400 milliseconds later) it's set to 1; the next time it's set back to 0; and so on.

Depending on the current value of gExerciseFrame, the preceding If...Else statement displays a different sprite of the exercising woman. If gExerciseFrame is currently 0, the code after the If displays sprite number 67 in the cell with X,Y cell coordinates of 10,40:

```
SetCell (10, 40, 67);
```

If, however, the current value of gExerciseFrame is 1, the code after the Else displays sprite number 68 in the cell with X,Y cell coordinates of 10,40:

```
SetCell (10, 40, 68);
```

Thus, in every execution of the tmrTimerTimer() procedure, a different frame of the exercising woman is displayed in the cell with X,Y cell coordinates of 10,40. One time sprite number 67 is displayed; the next time sprite number 68 is displayed; the next time sprite number 67 is displayed again; and so on.

The code responsible for animating the Jogger sprites is as follows:

```
{ Set the cell of the previous jogger position
 to an empty cell.}
If gJoggerY <> 0 Then SetCell(23, gJoggerY, 0);

{ If the jogger has reached the end of the hall,
 reset gJoggerY to 0. }
If gJoggerY = 48 Then  gJoggerY := 0;

{ Increment gJoggerY.}
gJoggerY := gJoggerY + 1;

{ Set JoggerFrame to the next frame number.}
If gJoggerFrame = 0 Then
   begin
   gJoggerFrame := 1;
   end
else
   begin
   gJoggerFrame := 0;
   end;

{ If the user is facing the jogger, show the front
 of the jogger (sprites 69 and 70). Otherwise, show
 the back of the jogger (sprites 71 and 72). }

If Tego3DVR1.CellPosY >= gJoggerY Then
   begin
   If gJoggerFrame = 0 Then
      begin
      SetCell (23, gJoggerY, 69);
      end
   Else
      begin
      SetCell (23, gJoggerY, 70);
      end;
   end
```

```
Else
   begin
   If gJoggerFrame = 0 Then
      begin
      SetCell (23, gJoggerY, 71);
      end
   Else
      begin
      SetCell (23, gJoggerY, 72);
      end;
   end;
```

As you can see, the Jogger sprite's animation code is more involved than the animation code of the Exercising Woman sprite. That's because the jogger does not remain in the same cell. In addition to using a global variable that holds the current frame number for the Jogger animation (gJoggerFrame), the preceding code also uses the global variable gJoggerY, which is used for holding the jogger's current Y cell position.

In each iteration of the tmrTimerTimer() procedure, the Jogger's previous cell position is set to an empty cell, then gJoggerY is incremented, and the Jogger sprite is displayed in the new Y cell position. The X cell position of the Jogger is always the same (23).

Depending on the new Y position of the user, different sprites of the jogger are animated. If the Y cell position of the user is greater than the Y cell position of the jogger (that is, the user is facing the jogger), sprites 69 and 70 are animated (they show the jogger facing the user). If, however, the user's Y cell position is less than the jogger's Y cell position, (that is, the jogger is running away from the user), sprites 71 and 72 are animated (they show the jogger with his back to the user).

The last statement you typed in the tmrTimerTimer() procedure is

```
Tego3DVR1.Command := 'Display3D';
```

This statement issues the Display3D command to display the new 3D view that corresponds to the new status of the Exercising Woman and Jogger sprites.

Taking Advantage of the Delphi Database Features for Designing 3D Virtual Reality Games

As you can see, the fact that Delphi enables you to utilize VBX controls can make your programming life easy. For a reasonable price, you can use off-the-shelf VBX controls that let you design powerful Windows programs. As an example, you can design powerful Delphi game programs with the Tego3DVR.VBX control. When designing the game, set some game objectives, such as searching for a particular sprite, bumping into a sprite, and so on.

You then can take advantage of Delphi's database features to construct a scoring mechanism for the game so the scores can be saved into a table. Also, you can take advantage of the database features to save the current state of the game. In the case of the 3D virtual reality games, you can let the user pause the game and save the current `Angle`, `PixelPosX`, and `PixelPosY` values in a table. The next time the user starts the game, you can load the game status from the tables and set the 3D picture as it was when the user left the game.

Summary

In this chapter, you wrote a 3D virtual reality Delphi program called My3DVR.EXE that uses the Tego3DVR.VBX control. As you've seen, writing a program with the virtual reality VBX control is easy. Basically, all you have to do is design a 2D floor file (FLR file). The 3D Virtual Reality control converts your 2D FLR file to a 3D environment and enables the user to move in this environment.

As demonstrated by the My3DVR.EXE program, you can add sprites (stationary sprites and moving sprites) to the 3D picture. A sprite can be hard or soft. A soft sprite (such as the Light fixture sprite in the My3DVR.EXE program) is a sprite the user can walk through. A hard sprite (such as the Tree sprites in the My3DVR.EXE program) is a sprite the user can't walk through.

Q&A

Q What are the advantages of using Delphi for creating 3D virtual reality programs?

A Once you understand the basics of the 3D virtual reality control, you're limited only by your imagination. You can design some amazing games. You can change the colors of the rooms, sprites, ceiling, and floor during runtime. You can load new FLR files during runtime. You can place new sprites (stationary and animated sprites) in different places in the 3D picture, add sound to the program, and so on. As you can see, the 3D virtual game can be designed so it's a challenging and interesting game.

By using the Delphi database features, you can enhance the program. For example, you can design a table containing the path of an animated sprite. The sprite follows a predetermined path in the 3D picture. In the My3DVR program, the Jogger just jogs in a straight line across the hall, but you can set the jogger's path so he follows the cell coordinates that are stored in a table. In that `tmrTimerTimer()` procedure, you move the record pointer of the table storing the cell coordinates to the next record in that table. This way, the jogger follows a predetermined path, and you can move the jogger from room to room, across the hall, and so on.

434

Quiz

To be able to use the 3D virtual reality VBX control, you must copy certain files to the \Windows\System directory. The files that should be copied are _____.

Exercise

Add another object sprite to one of the rooms of the My3DVR program.

Answer to Quiz

To be able to use the virtual reality VBX control, you must copy certain files to the \Windows\System directory. The files that should be copied are

- The files provided in the \DProg\WinG directory of the accompanying CD.
- The Tego3DVR.VBX file provided in the \DProg\VBX directory of the accompanying CD.

Answer to Exercise

Place a character that is not used yet inside the 2D FLR file. This character represents the new sprite. Use Paintbrush to create the BMP 256-color picture, and then create the mask file as a 256-color BMP file. For example, create the sprite DOG.BMP and the MDOG.BMP. You should create the MDOG.BMP file with Paintbrush as outlined in this chapter.

In the `FormCreate()` procedure, load the sprite as follows:

```
Tego3DVR1.SpriteNumber := 73;
Tego3DVR1.SpriteFileName := 'DOG.BMP';
```

The preceding statement assumes that inside the 2D FLR file, you assigned the character I (whose ASCII is value is 73) to the sprite.

When you execute the program, you see the Dog sprite where it was placed in the 2D drawing.

You also can create additional frames for the sprite as well as animate the sprite by adding code to the `tmrTimerTimer()` procedure.

Preparing Reports

One of the most important tasks you'll have to perform in your database projects is designing reports, which is what you learn how to do in this chapter.

What Are Reports?

A *report* is a document that summarizes data. For example, a company may want to generate monthly reports that list all the names of the salespeople who exceeded their sales quotas.

Of course, you could write a Delphi program (using the know-how that you acquired in previous chapters) to write such a program by yourself—place the corresponding tables in a form and write code (or SQL statements) that selects only those records that meet certain criteria. However, the designers of Delphi included a powerful software utility that automates the report-generation process: ReportSmith.

Designing reports involves two basic steps:

- Defining the report contents (for example, which fields should appear in the report, and which fields should be summed).

- Determining the cosmetic aspects of the report (for example, the company logo as the report title, row and column alignment, and fonts used).

The ReportSmith program enables you to accomplish the task of preparing professional reports in a short time.

Note: During the course of your work with databases, you'll no doubt have to generate reports. Always consider using ReportSmith for report generation. Whatever ReportSmith can do, you could do by writing a Delphi program, but using ReportSmith will save you a lot of time.

Telling ReportSmith the Location of Your Data

The first thing you have to do when using ReportSmith to generate reports is to tell ReportSmith the location of the data and the type of data (for example, Paradox tables, or dBASE tables).

To tell ReportSmith the location and type of data that the report should use, follow these steps:

☐ Start the ReportSmith program. The ReportSmith program icon in the Delphi program group is shown in Figure 17.1.

Figure 17.1.
The ReportSmith program icon.

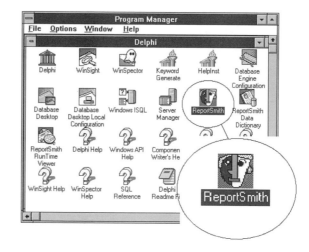

When starting ReportSmith, the Open Report dialog box appears as shown in Figure 17.2.

Figure 17.2.
When starting ReportSmith, the Open Report dialog box appears.

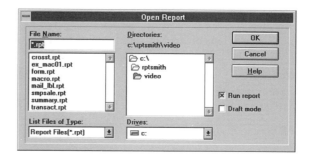

Note that the file extension of a report is *Rpt* as in MyReport.Rpt.

☐ At this point, you don't want to load a report, you just want to generate one, so click the Cancel button of the Open Report dialog box.

Before generating a report, you must tell ReportSmith where the data is located and the type of tables used in the report.

☐ Select Connections from the ReportSmith File menu.

ReportSmith responds by displaying the Connection dialog box shown in Figure 17.3.

Figure 17.3.

The Connection dialog box that appears after selecting Connections from the ReportSmith File menu.

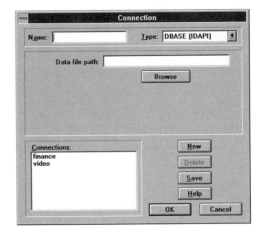

☐ Click the Browse button, and select the directory: C:\DProg\Work.

☐ In the Name editbox type **MyReport**.

☐ Select PARADOX (IDAPI) from the Type combobox in the Connections dialog box.

Your Connections dialog box should now look like the one shown in Figure 17.4.

Figure 17.4.

Setting the connection.

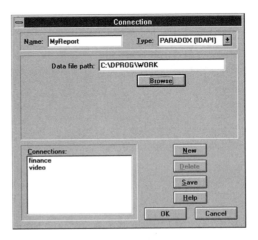

☐ Click the Save button of the Connection dialog box.

As shown in Figure 17.5, the MyReport connection now appears in the Connections dialog box Connections list.

Figure 17.5.
The MyReport connection now appears in the Connections list.

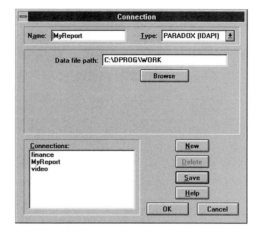

☐ Click the OK button.

You're now ready to generate your first report with ReportSmith.

Generating Your First Report

Before generating the report, take a look at the table that will be used for the report.

☐ Use Database Desktop to verify that the Clients.DB table resides in the C:\DProg\Work directory, and that the Clients.DB table structure is as shown in Table 17.1. The Clients.DB structure window is shown in Figure 17.6.

Table 17.1. The Clients.DB table structure.

Field Name	Type	Size	Key
CustName	Autoincrement	n/a	Yes
LastName	Alpha	30	No
FirstName	Alpha	20	No
Street	Alpha	40	No
City	Alpha	30	No
State	Alpha	10	No
AreaCode	Alpha	3	No
Phone	Alpha	8	No
ZipCode	Alpha	5	No
ClientType	Alpha	10	No
SalesPersonNum	Numeric	n/a	No

Figure 17.6.
The Clients.DB table structure.

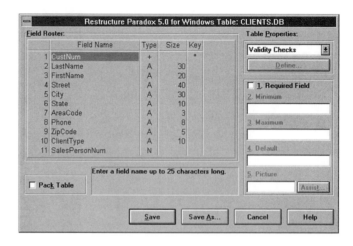

☐ Use Database Desktop to fill several of the Clients.DB table records. (The report you're going to generate uses Clients.DB, so fill at least three records in Clients.DB.)

☐ Terminate Database Desktop.

Now tell ReportSmith to generate a report based on Clients.DB.

☐ Select New from the ReportSmith File menu.

ReportSmith responds by displaying the Create a New Report dialog box shown in Figure 17.7.

Figure 17.7.
The Create a New Report dialog box.

As you can see from Figure 17.7, you can create Columnar reports (data is displayed in columns), Crosstab reports (like a spreadsheet), Form reports (records are displayed in a single form), and Label reports (records are prepared to be printed on a label).

☐ Select Columnar Report, and then click the OK button.

ReportSmith responds by displaying the Report Query - Tables dialog box shown in Figure 17.8.

Figure 17.8.
The Report Query - Tables dialog box.

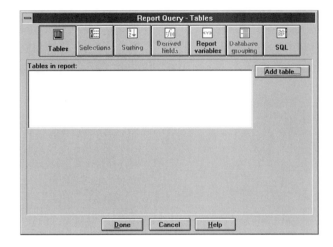

☐ Make sure that the Tables button is pressed, and then click the Add Table button.

> *ReportSmith responds by displaying the Select Table to Be Added dialog box (see Figure 17.9).*

Figure 17.9.
The Select Table To Be Added dialog box.

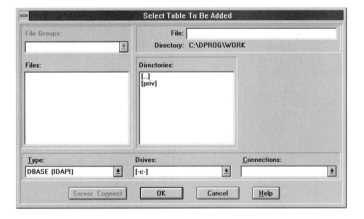

You use the Select Table To Be Added dialog box to tell ReportSmith the name of the tables that the report should use.

☐ Select the MyReport connection from the list of Connections (on the lower-right side of the Select Table To Be Added dialog box), and then select the Clients.DB table.

Your Select Table To Be Added dialog box now should look like the one shown in Figure 17.10.

Figure 17.10.
*Selecting the MyReport
connection and the
Clients.DB table.*

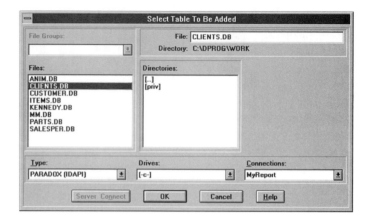

☐ Click the OK button of the Select Table To Be Added dialog box.

*ReportSmith responds by displaying the Report Query - Tables dialog box as shown in
Figure 17.11.*

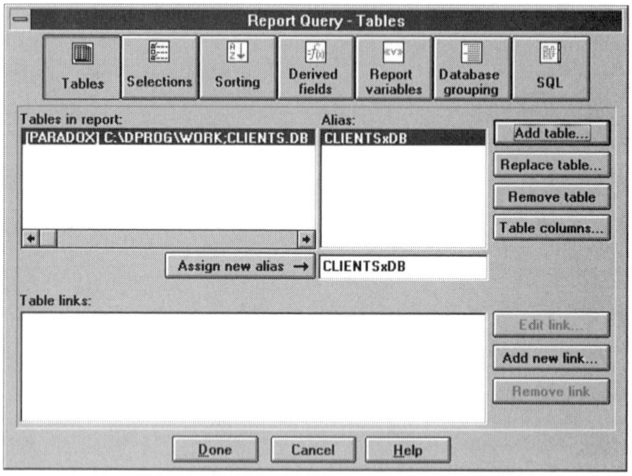

Figure 17.11.
*The Report Query - Tables
dialog box with the
Clients.DB table listed as
the table to be used for
the report.*

☐ Click the Done button.

That's it! ReportSmith prepared the report for you, and it is shown in Figure 17.12.

Figure 17.12.
The report that ReportSmith prepared.

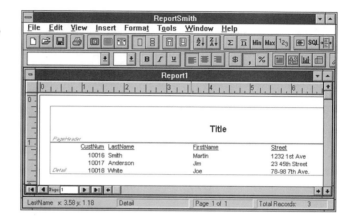

Saving the Report

Before looking at the report, save it.

☐ Select Save As from the ReportSmith File menu.

   ReportSmith responds by displaying a dialog box that enables you to save the report.

☐ Save the report as Client01.Rpt in the C:\DProg\Reports directory.

Viewing the Report

To view the report generated by ReportSmith, do the following:

☐ Use the scroll bar to scroll the report to the right and to the left.

Whatever can fit on a page (when the report is printed on paper) is enclosed with a rectangle. The Clients.DB table has many fields. When printing the report on 8 $^1/_2$×11-inch paper for example, only the first four columns will fit across the width of the paper. Thus, ReportSmith encloses the first four columns with a rectangle so you'll know that when you print the report, only the first four columns will appear on the page.

The best way to look at the report is to print it.

☐ Prepare your printer to print.

☐ Select Print from the File menu, and print the report.

   ReportSmith responds by printing the Client01.Rpt report.

There are many more things that you should do to customize the report. For example, the title of the report right now is "Title." Naturally, you'll want to replace that text with the actual report title. You also can modify the report by changing the fonts and the column headings. Actually, you can make the report as attractive as you want it to be.

Modifying the Appearance of the Client01.Rpt Report

Now that you have the Client01.Rpt report to work with, you're ready to customize the report so that it looks the way you want it to.

First, you'll modify the report title. The report is made of *objects*, and, typically, an object contains several other objects. You'll see how this works as you modify the report title.

☐ Click in the title area.

ReportSmith responds by selecting the title area. You can tell that the title area is selected because ReportSmith encloses the selected area with a rectangle that has small black handles on the sides (see Figure 17.13).

Figure 17.13.
The title area is selected.

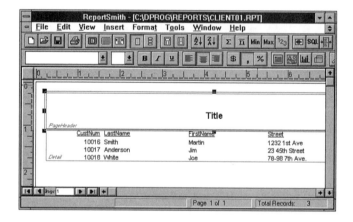

☐ Click on the word `Title`.

ReportSmith responds by enclosing the word `Title` with a rectangle (see Figure 17.14).

Figure 17.14.
The word Title *is selected.*

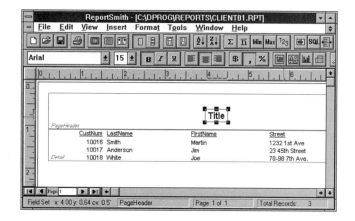

☐ Click again on the title text.

ReportSmith responds by letting you edit the word Title *(see Figure 17.15).*

Figure 17.15.
The text is ready to be edited.

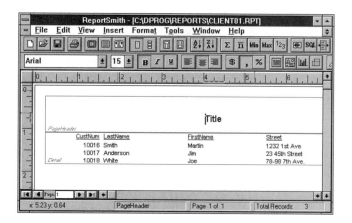

☐ Delete Title, and type **Report: Clients.DB**.

The report title now appears as shown in Figure 17.16.

Figure 17.16.
Changing the text of the report title.

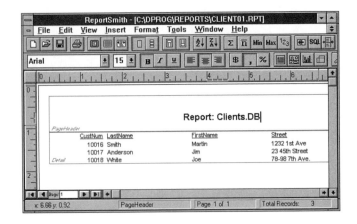

☐ Select Save As from the ReportSmith File menu to save your work.

Integrating a Report into a Delphi Program

There still is much to talk about concerning the various features of ReportSmith. However, before covering those topics, let's integrate the Client01.Rpt report into a Delphi program.

☐ Select Exit from the ReportSmith File menu to terminate the ReportSmith program.

☐ Start Delphi.

☐ Select New Project from the Delphi File menu.

☐ Set the Name property of Form1 to frmReports.

☐ Set the Caption property of the frmReports form to The Reports Program.

☐ Select the frmReports form, select Save File As from the File menu, and save the form as CReports.Pas in the C:\DProg\Ch17 directory.

☐ Select Save Project As from the File menu, and save the project as Reports.Dpr in the C:\DProg\Ch17 directory.

Implementing an Exit Button

Now you implement an Exit button in the frmReports form.

☐ Place a pushbutton from the Standard page in the frmReports form.

☐ Set the pushbutton properties as follows:

```
Name      cmdExit
Caption   E&xit
```

☐ Attach code to the OnClick event of the frmReports form cmdExit button.

After attaching the code, the cmdExitClick procedure appears as follows:

```
procedure TfrmReports.cmdExitClick(Sender: TObject);
begin

Application.Terminate;

end;
```

Placing a *TReport* Control in the Form

Now place a TReport control in the frmReports form. The TReport control icon on the Data Access page is shown in Figure 17.17. The TReport control enables you to incorporate a report into the form.

Figure 17.17.

The TReport control icon on the Data Access page.

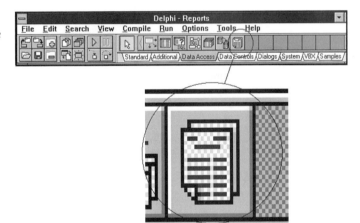

☐ Place a Report control from the Data Access page in the frmReports form.

☐ Set the Name property of the TReport control to Client01Report.

☐ Click the three dots to the right of the Client01Report control's ReportName property, and select the C:\DProg\Reports\Client01.Rpt file.

Placing a Print Report Button

You now place a Print Report button in the frmReports form.

☐ Place a pushbutton from the Standard page in the frmReports form.

☐ Set the pushbutton properties as follows:

```
Name       cmdPrintReport
Caption    &Print Report
```

Your frmReports form should now look like the one shown in Figure 17.18.

Figure 17.18.
The frmReports form (design mode).

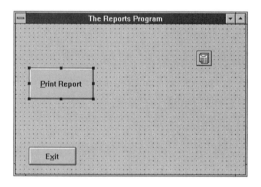

☐ Attach code to the OnClick event of the cmdPrintReport button.

After attaching the code, the cmdPrintReportClick procedure of the frmReports form is as follows:

```
procedure TfrmReports.cmdPrintReportClick(Sender: TObject);
begin

Client01Report.Run;

end;
```

The code you typed executes the report. Because you set the Report control's ReportName property to the Client01.Rpt report, clicking the Print Report button prints the Client01.Rpt report.

☐ Select Save Project from the Delphi File menu.

☐ Execute the Reports program.

The window shown in Figure 17.19 appears.

Figure 17.19.
The Reports program.

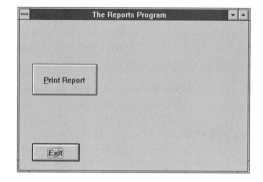

☐ Prepare your printer to print, and then click the Print Report button.

> *The Reports program responds by sending Client01.Rpt to the printer.*

Note that the program icon shown in Figure 17.20 appears. This icon is the ReportSmith runtime module's program icon—that is, the Reports program you created uses another program.

Figure 17.20.
The runtime ReportSmith program icon.

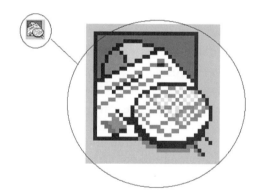

If you give the Reports.EXE program to someone else, the presence of the ReportSmith icon may confuse your users, and so it would be a good idea to unload the ReportSmith program as follows:

☐ Terminate the Reports program by clicking its Exit button.

☐ Set the AutoUnload property of the Client01Report control to True.

☐ Select Save Project from the Delphi File menu.

☐ Execute the Reports program.

☐ Click the Print Report button.

The Reports program responds by printing the Client01.Rpt report. Of course, ReportSmith's runtime module icon appears when the ReportSmith program prints the report. However, after the report is printed, the runtime module is unloaded because you set the AutoUnload property of the Report control to True.

☐ Click the Exit button of the Reports program to terminate the Reports program.

Summary

In this chapter, you started to learn how to use ReportSmith for generating reports. The Client01.Rpt report that you generated is a very simple report using a single table. You also created the Reports.EXE program that enables the user to print a report by clicking a button.

Q&A

Q Should I use ReportSmith, or should I write a Delphi program for generating a report?

A The reports that ReportSmith can generate are professional-looking reports. In most cases, you'll be able to generate a report with ReportSmith that complies with your report requirements, so it makes sense to save time and generate the report with ReportSmith rather than writing your own program.

Q When establishing the ReportSmith connections, I see that I have the choice to create a variety of connections. Which ones should I choose?

A In this chapter, you were instructed to create a connection to the C:\DProg\Work directory using Paradox tables. In this case, the tables are located on your PC's hard drive, and there are no additional complications. This simple connection is applicable if you are using Paradox tables residing on your local hard drive. Because this connection is the simple one, you should use it when practicing and learning ReportSmith. Once you understand what ReportSmith is all about and how to use it, you can establish other types of connections as applicable to the particular work you're performing.

Quiz

To execute ReportSmith from a Delphi program, you should use what statement?

Exercise

Use ReportSmith to generate another report from another table, and then print the report from within the Reports program.

Answer to Quiz

To execute ReportSmith from a Delphi program, you should use what statement?

```
Report1.Run;
```

This statement assumes that the Name property of the TReport control is set to Report1.

Answer to Exercise

17

Here are the steps for generating and printing the report:

☐ Start ReportSmith.

☐ Use the procedures outlined in this chapter to generate a simple report from any table residing in the C:\DProg\Work directory.

☐ Save the report in the C:\DProg\Reports directory.

☐ Terminate ReportSmith.

☐ Start Delphi.

☐ Load the Reports.Dpr project.

☐ Place another Report control (from the Data Access page) in the frmReports form.

☐ Set the Name property of the Report control. If you generated a report from the Customer.DB table, it is appropriate to set the Name property of the Report control to CustomerReport. However, you can set the Report control's Name property to any name that you wish.

☐ Set the Report control ReportName property to the name of the report that you generated with ReportSmith.

☐ Set the AutoUnload property of the Report control to True.

☐ Place a pushbutton from the Standard page in the frmReports form.

☐ Set the pushbutton's `Name` and `Caption` properties. For example, if you generated a report from the Customer.DB table, it is appropriate to set the properties of the pushbutton as follows:

```
Name      cmdPrintCustomerReport
Caption   Print &Customer Report
```

☐ Attach the following code to the `OnClick` event of the `cmdPrintCustomerReport` button:

```
CustomerReport.Run;
```

The preceding statement runs the report. (It also assumes that you set the `Report` control's `Name` property to `CustomerReport`.)

18

Preparing Reports from More than One Table

In the previous chapter, you learned how to generate a report (Client01.Rpt) from a single table (Clients.DB). In this chapter, you learn how to generate reports made from more than one table.

The Need to Generate Reports from Multiple Tables

The fundamental principle of database design is that a table never should contain redundant information. Consider the example of the Clients.DB and SalesPer.DB tables again.

The Clients.DB table contains information about the clients. One of the Clients.DB fields (see Table 17.1) is the SalesPersonNum field. This field contains the ID number of the salesperson who managed to solicit the client. Thus, all future sales that this client makes earn commission for the salesperson. In this example, the SalesPersonNum field of Clients.DB is a field that must be in the Clients.DB table.

☐ Start Database Desktop.

☐ Verify that the SalesPer.DB table structure is as shown in Table 18.1. The SalesPer.DB structure window is shown in Figure 18.1.

Table 18.1. The SalesPer.DB table structure.

Field Name	Type	Size	Key
SalesPersonNum	Numeric	n/a	Yes
LastName	Alpha	40	No
FirstName	Alpha	30	No

Figure 18.1.
The SalesPer.DB table structure.

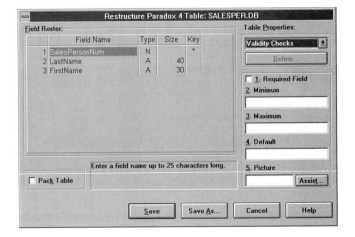

☐ You'll now use Database Desktop to fill several records of the SalesPer.DB and Clients.DB tables. Because the report that you are going to generate in this chapter uses the SalesPer.DB and the Clients.DB tables, make sure that you have records in the Clients.DB table with `SalesPersonNum` fields from the SalesPer.DB table. In particular, fill the Clients.DB table records and the SalesPer.DB table as follows:

Record 1

SalesPersonNum	2

Record 2

SalesPersonNum	3

Record 3

SalesPersonNum	3

☐ Delete all other records of Clients.DB.

☐ Use Database Desktop to update the SalesPer.DB table records as follows:

Record 1

SalesPersonNum	1

Record 2

SalesPersonNum	2

Record 3

SalesPersonNum	3

☐ Delete all other records in SalesPer.DB.

Let's review the status of the two tables.

The Clients.DB table has three records in it. The first record belongs to salesperson 2, and the next two clients belong to salesperson 3.

If you generate a report showing all the clients belonging to the salespersons, you find out the following:

- Salesperson 1 does not have any clients.
- Salesperson 2 has one client.
- Salesperson 3 has two clients.

As you can see, the SalesPer.DB table contains the `LastName` field (the salesperson's last name), but the Clients.DB table does not contain the salesperson's last name. Having the salesperson's

18

last name in the Clients.DB table amounts to having redundant information. Why? Because the LastName field can be extracted from the SalesPer.DB table. Who will extract the LastName field from SalesPer.DB? That's what reports are for! Suppose you want to display all the clients of SalesPersonNum 2. You can instruct ReportSmith to generate such a report. When instructing ReportSmith to generate the report, you can display the SalesPer.DB table LastName field.

Generating the SalesP01.Rpt Report

Generate the SalesP01.Rpt report, which is created from the SalesPer.DB table.

☐ Start ReportSmith.

ReportSmith displays a dialog box that enables you to load an existing report.

☐ Click the Cancel button (you don't want to load an existing report now).

☐ Select New from the ReportSmith File menu.

   ReportSmith responds by displaying the Create a New Report dialog box.

☐ Make sure that the Columnar Report button is pressed, and then click the OK button.

   ReportSmith responds by displaying the Query Report - Tables dialog box.

☐ Make sure that the Tables button is pressed, and then click the Add Table button.

   ReportSmith responds by displaying the Select Table To Be Added dialog box.

☐ Set the Connection to MyReport, select the SalesPer.DB table, and then click the OK button.

   ReportSmith responds by again displaying the Select Table To Be Added dialog box. Now the SalesPer.DB table appears in the dialog box.

☐ Click the Done button.

   ReportSmith responds by creating a report from the SalesPer.DB table.

☐ Select Save As from the File menu, and save the report as SalesP01.Rpt in the C:\DProg\Reports directory.

The SalesP01.Rpt report is shown in Figure 18.2.

Figure 18.2.

The SalesP01.Rpt report that ReportSmith generated from the SalesPer.DB table.

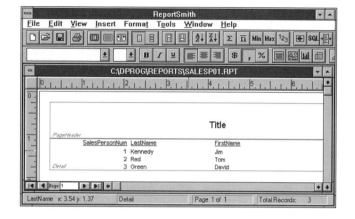

Merging Reports

Create one report created from the following two reports:

- The Client01.Rpt report you generated in Chapter 17, "Preparing Reports."
- The SalesP01.Rpt report you generated in the previous section.

☐ Select Open from the ReportSmith File menu.

ReportSmith responds by Displaying a dialog box that enables you to load an existing report.

☐ Select the Client01.Rpt report you created in Chapter 17.

Report Smith responds by loading the report, and now the ReportSmith desktop contains two windows. One window contains the Client01.Rpt report, and the other contains the SalesP01.Rpt report.

☐ Select Tile from the ReportSmith Window menu.

ReportSmith responds by tiling the windows, as shown in Figure 18.3.

Now you're ready to merge the two reports.

The column that both reports have in common is the SalesPersonNum column.

☐ Select the SalesPersonNum field in the Clients.DB table. You must scroll down the Client01.Rpt table until you see the column headings, scroll the report to the left until you see the SalesPersonNum column, and finally click the SalesPersonNum column heading.

Figure 18.3.
Tiling the two reports.

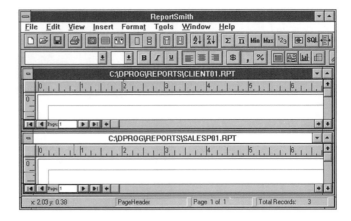

The Client01.Rpt report with its `SalesPersonNum` column selected is shown in Figure 18.4.

Figure 18.4.
Selecting the
`SalesPersonNum` *column*
in the Client01.Rpt
report.

☐ Select the `SalesPersonNum` field in the SalesP01.Rpt report.

The desktop of ReportSmith should now appear as shown in Figure 18.5.

☐ Make sure that the Client01.Rpt report is the active window, and then click the Merge button on the ReportSmith toolbar. The Merge button is shown in Figure 18.6.

ReportSmith responds by merging the Client01.Rpt and SalesP01.Rpt reports.

Figure 18.5.

The SalesPersonNum *column in the Client01.Rpt and SalesP01.Rpt reports are selected.*

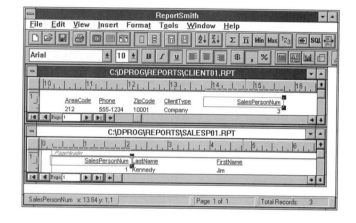

Figure 18.6.

The Merge button in the ReportSmith toolbar.

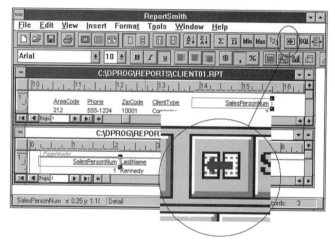

18

You don't need the SalesP01.Rpt report any more, so close it:

☐ Click the minus-sign (–) icon that appears on the upper-left corner of the SalesP01.Rpt window, and select Close from the system menu that pops up.

Before going over the merged report generated by ReportSmith, save the new report.

☐ Make sure that the window containing the merged report is selected, Select Save As from the ReportSmith File menu, and save the merged report as Client02.Rpt in the C:\DProg\Reports directory.

The merged report is shown in Figure 18.7.

Figure 18.7.
The Client02.Rpt merged report.

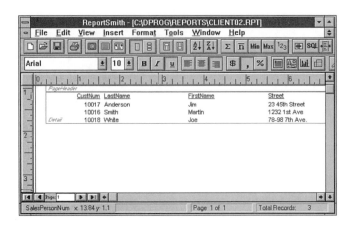

☐ Scroll the Client02.Rpt report to the left so that you see its first column as shown in Figure 18.7.

The CustNum fields are not ordered by CustNum because the report is ordered by the SalesPersonNum field.

☐ Scroll the report to the right so that you see the SalesPersonNum field.

As shown in Figure 18.8, the report is ordered by the SalesPersonNum field.

Figure 18.8.
The report is ordered by the SalesPersonNum field.

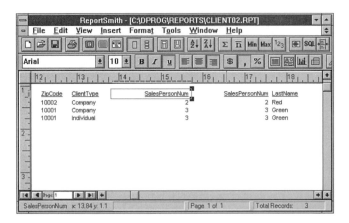

At the beginning of this chapter, you were instructed to fill the record of the Clients.DB and SalesPer.DB tables so that salesperson 1 does not have clients, salesperson 2 has one client, and salesperson 3 has two clients. Take a look at Figure 18.8; this is exactly what ReportSmith generated!

Adding Cosmetic Touches to the Merged Report

To make the merged report more aesthetically pleasing, you can add some cosmetic touches to it.

For one thing, the fields on the right side of the merged report have the following column headings:

```
SalesPersonNum
LastName
FirstName
```

When ReportSmith merged the two reports, it left the Client01.Rpt report columns in their original order, and then the SalesP01.Rpt report columns were added to the right of the Client01.Rpt report columns.

You know that the LastName and FirstName columns on the right of the merged report are the salesperson's last name and first name.

☐ Select the LastName column heading that came from the SalesP01.Rpt report.

ReportSmith responds by selecting the LastName column heading as shown in Figure 18.9.

Figure 18.9.
The LastName heading of the column from the SalesP01.Rpt report is selected.

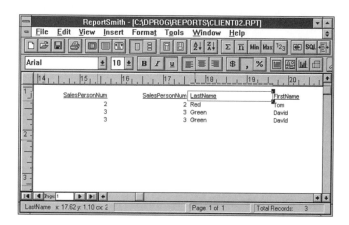

☐ Click again in the area of the LastName column heading, and change the column heading to **Salesperson Last Name**.

As shown in Figure 18.10, the column heading now makes it clear that this column contains the last names of the salespeople.

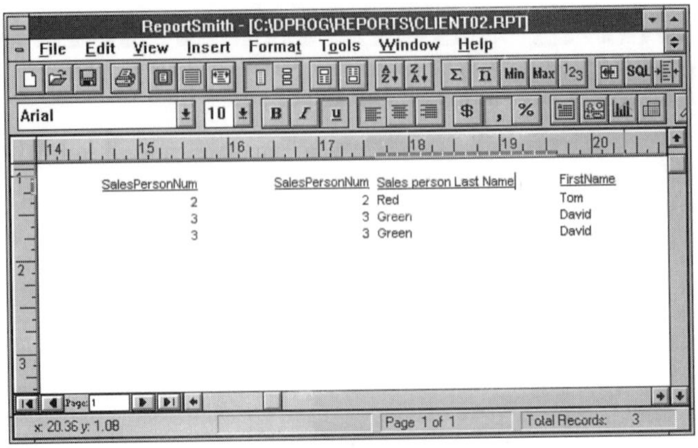

Figure 18.10.

The column heading of the salespeople's last names.

☐ Change the heading of the salesperson's `FirstName` column to: **`Salesperson First Name.`**

☐ Change the heading of the report to **`Report: Client02.Rpt.`**

Deleting Columns from the Report

Currently, there are too many columns in the report, and so you need to delete some of them.

The `SalesPersonNum` column appears twice (one from the Client01.Rpt report and one from the SalesP01.Rpt report). Delete one of these `SalesPersonNum` columns to eliminate the redundant information.

☐ Select one of the `SalesPersonNum` column headings, and then press the Delete key.

ReportSmith responds by deleting the column.

☐ The report should have only the following columns in it, and so delete all the other columns in the report except these:

```
CustNum
SalesPersonNum
Salesperson Last Name
Salesperson First Name
```

The Client02.Rpt report should now appear as shown in Figure 18.11.

☐ Select Save As from the File menu and save the report as Client02.Rpt in the C:\DProg\Reports directory.

☐ Select Print from the File menu to print the report.

☐ Select Close from the File menu to close the Client02.Rpt report.

Figure 18.11.
The Client02.Rpt report has only four columns.

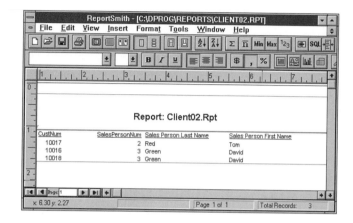

Another Way to Create a Merged Report

You created the Client02.Rpt report by first creating the Client01.Rpt report and then the SalesP01.Rpt report. Finally, you merged the two reports to create one merged report, Client02.Rpt.

An alternative way to create a report from two tables is as follows:

☐ Select New from the ReportSmith File menu.

ReportSmith responds by displaying the Create a New Report dialog box.

☐ Make sure the Columnar Report button is pressed, and then click the OK button.

ReportSmith responds by displaying the Report Query - Tables window.

☐ Click the Add Tables button.

ReportSmith responds by displaying a window that enables you to select a table.

☐ Select the Clients.DB table and then click the OK button.

ReportSmith again displays the Report Query - Tables window with the Clients.DB table listed.

☐ Click the Add Table button.

ReportSmith responds by again displaying a window that enables you to select a table.

☐ Select the SalesPer.DB table and then click the OK button.

The Report Query - Tables window now appears as shown in Figure 18.12.

Figure 18.12.
The Report Query - Tables window with two tables in it.

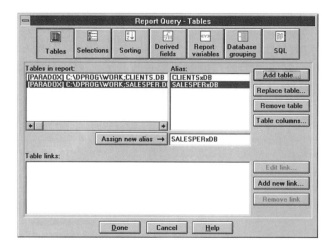

☐ Click the Add New Link button.

> *ReportSmith responds by displaying the Create New Table Link window, as shown in Figure 18.13.*

Figure 18.13.
The Create New Table Link window.

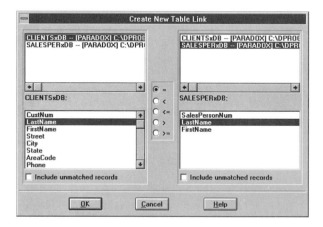

Creating a Table Link

Use the Create New Table Link window (Figure 18.13) to create a link between the Clients.DB table and the SalesPer.DB table.

☐ Select the Clients.DB table `SalesPersonNum` field, select the SalesPer.DB table `SalesPersonNum` field, and select the equal-sign (=) option button.

Your Create a New Table Link should now appear as shown in Figure 18.14.

Figure 18.14.
*The table link between
Clients.DB and
SalesPer.DB.*

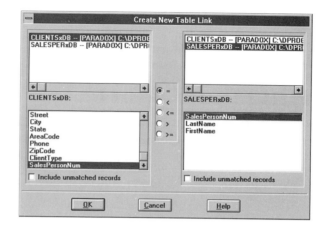

☐ Click the OK button.

> *ReportSmith responds by displaying the Report Query - Tables window, as shown in
> Figure 18.15.*

18

Figure 18.15.
*The Report Query - Tables
window with the link
between Clients.DB and
SalesPer.DB shown.*

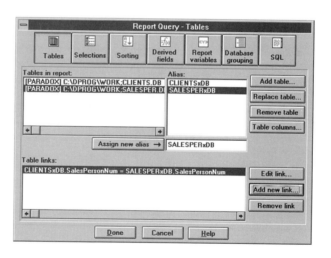

☐ Click the Done button.

That's it! ReportSmith creates a report that is identical to the Client02.Rpt report you created
at the beginning of this chapter.

☐ Scroll through the report to verify that the report consists of fields from both tables.

☐ Practice with the report by deleting columns, changing column headings, and changing
the report title.

☐ Select Close from the File menu to close the report. There is no need to save the report because it is identical to the Client02.Rpt report you generated at the beginning of this chapter.

Sorting the Report

ReportSmith is equipped with a variety of tools that enable you to manipulate data easily. For example, to see the sorting features of ReportSmith in action, follow these steps:

☐ Select Open from the ReportSmith File menu, and load the Client01.Rpt report from the C:\DProg\Reports directory. (You created this report on Day 17.)

The Client01.Rpt report appears, and as you can see, the table records are ordered by the CustNum field.

You can easily order the table by the LastName field as follows:

☐ Select the LastName heading (that is, click the LastName column heading).

The Client01.Rpt report should now appear as shown in Figure 18.16.

Figure 18.16.

Selecting the LastName *column header.*

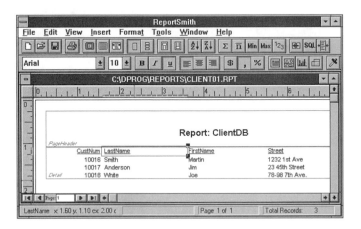

There are two sorting icons on the ReportSmith toolbar, as shown in Figure 18.17. The icon with the letter *A* on top and the letter *Z* on the bottom is the *ascending* button. The icon with *Z* on top and *A* on the bottom is the *descending* button.

Figure 18.17.
The Sorting icons on the ReportSmith toolbar.

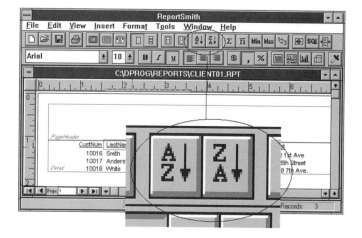

☐ While the LastName column is selected (as shown in Figure 18.16), click the ascending button.

ReportSmith responds by ordering the Client01.Rpt report by the LastName, as shown in Figure 18.18.

18

Figure 18.18.
The report is ordered by the LastName field.

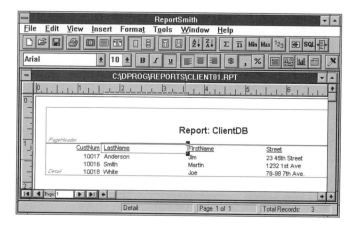

In Figure 18.16, the report is ordered by the CustNum field:

    10016
    10017
    10018

In Figure 18.18, however, the report is ordered by the LastName.

```
Anderson
Smith
White
```

☐ Make sure the LastName column heading is selected, and then click the descending button on the ReportSmith toolbar.

ReportSmith now orders the report by the LastName in descending order, as follows:

```
White
Smith
Anderson
```

An alternative way to sort the report is this:

☐ Select Sorting from the Tools menu.

The window shown in Figure 18.19 appears.

Figure 18.19.

After selecting Sorting from the Tools menu, the Report Query - Sorting window appears.

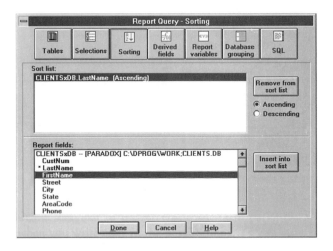

The report in this figure is ordered by the LastName field because the LastName field has the asterisk character (*) to its left.

To remove the asterisk, double-click the field in the Report Fields list; to place an asterisk, double-click the field again.

Note that you can drag a field from the Report fields list to the Sort list. Remove the asterisks from all the fields, and then use the mouse to drag a field from the Report fields list to the Sort list.

Typically, you sort a report such as the Client01.Rpt report by two fields: the LastName field and the FirstName field. If your report contained the following records, Anderson Tom and Anderson Tim, and you sorted the report in ascending order, the Anderson Tim record would appear before the Anderson Tom record.

Note: Once you sort a report, you can select Save As from the ReportSmith File menu to save the report by another name.

Grouping

Another important feature of ReportSmith is the Grouping feature. Recall that in the Client02.Rpt report, the records are ordered according to the SalesPersonNum field. The report lists the Clients.DB table records belonging to salesperson number 1 (if any), then the Clients.DB records belonging to SalesPersonNum 2, and so on.

You can group the report so that the group of records belonging to SalesPersonNum 1 are separated from the SalesPersonNum 2 group of records, and so on.

Here is how you group a report.

☐ Close all open reports on the ReportSmith desktop.

☐ Open the Client02.Rpt report that you created earlier in this chapter.

It makes sense to group the Client02.Rpt report by the SalesPersonNum column.

☐ Select the SalesPersonNum field.

Figure 18.20 shows the two Grouping icons on the ReportSmith toolbar.

☐ The Grouping icon on the left in Figure 18.20 groups the records and creates a header area above each group. The Grouping icon shown on the right in Figure 18.20 groups the records and creates a footer area below each group.

☐ While the SalesPersonNum column heading is selected, click the Grouping icon that creates a header area (the left icon shown in Figure 18.20).

The ReportSmith groups the records, as shown in Figure 18.21. There are no clients for SalesPersonNum 1, and so that SalesPersonNum does not have a group of records.

Figure 18.20.

The two Grouping icons on the ReportSmith toolbar.

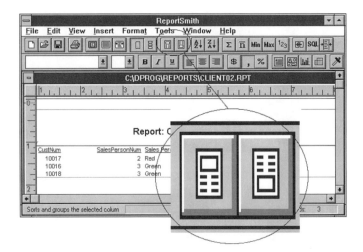

Figure 18.21.

The Client02.Rpt report is divided into groups.

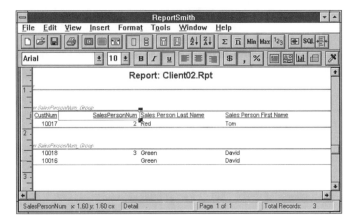

The SalesPersonNum 2 group of clients has one record, and SalesPersonNum 3 has three records.

Note that each group has a header area above it. Insert some information in the header area of each group.

☐ Click in the header area of the first group.

The Client02.Rpt report should now appear as shown in Figure 18.22.

☐ Select Field from the ReportSmith Insert menu.

ReportSmith responds by displaying the Insert Field dialog box.

Figure 18.22.
Selecting the header area.

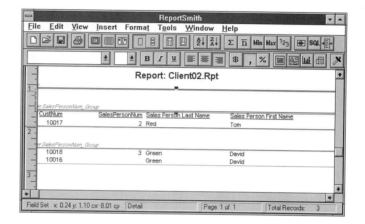

☐ Use the scroll bar of the Insert Field dialog box to scroll down the list of fields, and select the SalesPer.DB table `LastName` field, as shown in Figure 18.23.

Figure 18.23.
The Insert Field dialog box with the SalesPer.DB table `LastName` *field selected.*

☐ Click the Insert button of the Insert Field dialog box.

ReportSmith responds by changing the mouse cursor to an icon indicating that you are in Insert mode.

☐ Click in the Header area of the first group.

ReportSmith responds by inserting the `LastName` *field of the SalesPer.DB table in the header area, as shown in Figure 18.24.*

Figure 18.24.

The header area after inserting the SalesPer.DB table LastName *field.*

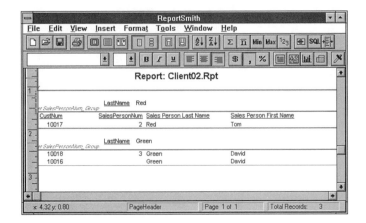

☐ Click the Done button of the Insert Field dialog box.

Look at the Client02.Rpt report. Each group header now has the name of its salesperson in it. (This means there's no need to display the LastName column of the SalesPer.DB table's LastName field in the report).

For now, save the report:

☐ Select Save As from the File menu, and save the report as Client03.Rpt in the C:\DProg\Reports directory. In Exercise 1 today, you make additional cosmetic changes to the Client03.Rpt report.

☐ Print the Client03.Rpt report, and then terminate the ReportSmith program.

Summary

In this chapter, you created a report from two tables. You learned two ways to create such a report. One way is to create two separate reports and then to merge the two reports. The other way is to create a report and to specify that the report is made out of two tables. When specifying the two tables, you have to tell ReportSmith which column is common to both reports.

You also learned how to order a report by different fields and how to group the records of a report.

Q&A

Q I want to include the `PhoneNumber` field for the salesperson's cellular phone. Should I include it in the Clients.DB table or the SalesPer.DB table?

A The `PhoneNumber` field (one that contains the salesperson's cellular phone number) should be a field in the SalesPer.DB table. This is the nature of the SalesPer.DB table! That is, each record of the SalesPer.DB table contains information regarding the salesperson.

Consider the alternative of placing the salesperson's phone number in the Clients.DB table. Because there could be many records in Clients.DB with the same `SalesPersonNum` field, the salesperson's phone number appears in many Clients.DB table records. If the phone number changes, you must go through the Clients.DB records and change it in *every* record in which this salesperson appears. If the salesperson has 1,000 clients, you must change the phone number in 1,000 Clients.DB table records. Besides making the process of maintaining the tables difficult, including a field containing the salesperson's number in the Clients.DB table is a waste of disk space.

Quiz

1. A new field should be added to the database. This new field (the `ContactDate` field) contains the first date on which the salesperson made contact with the client. The `ContactDate` field should be added to which table?

    a. The Clients.DB table.

    b. The SalesPer.DB table.

    c. A new table.

2. To order a report by a certain field in ReportSmith, you must _____.

Exercises

1. Create a program with a Print Report button. When the user clicks the Print Report button, the program should print the Client02.Rpt report that you created in this chapter.

2. Make additional cosmetic changes to the Client03.Rpt report that you created in this chapter.

Answers to Quiz

1. a. It doesn't make sense to add the ContactDate field to the SalesPer.DB table because a salesperson has many contact dates. That is, on a certain date the salesperson contacted client number 18000, on another date the same salesperson contacted client number 19000, and so on. Obviously, the ContactDate field should be added to the Clients.DB table. The ContactDate field represents the date on which the client was added to the Clients.DB table, and it is, therefore, a field belonging to the client.

2. To order a report by a certain field in ReportSmith, you must select the column heading and then click the sorting icon.

Answers to Exercises

1. Here is the procedure.

   ☐ Start Delphi, create a new project, save the Form1 form as a .Pas file, and save the Project file.

   ☐ Place a Report control from the Data Access page in Form1, and set the Report control properties as follows:

Name	Client03Report
AutoUnload	True
ReportName	C:\DProg\Reports\Client03.Rpt

   ☐ Place a pushbutton from the Standard page in the form, and set its properties as follows:

Name	cmdExit
Caption	E&xit

   Attach the following code to the cmdExit button's OnClick event:

   ```
   Application.Terminate;
   ```

   ☐ Place a pushbutton from the Standard page in the form, and set its properties as follows:

Name	cmdPrintReport
Caption	Print Client03.Rpt

   Attach the following code to the cmdPrintReport button's OnClick event:

   ```
   Client03Report.Run;
   ```

2. As you've probably guessed by now, ReportSmith enables you to design the report so that it looks any way you like it to look.

There are still a lot of things you can do to the Client03.Rpt report. Here are some of them:

☐ Start ReportSmith.

☐ Load the Client03.Rpt report.

☐ Click the LastName field in the header area of the first group, and then drag it to the right. (In the next step, you make the Label appearing to the left of the LastName field wider, so you need to make room for the label.)

☐ Click the text *LastName* appearing to the left of the LastName field in the header area. You are selecting a Label.

☐ Click again in the label so you can edit the label's contents.

☐ Change the text of the label from LastName to **Salesperson Last Name.**

☐ Deselect the Label. (To deselect an object in ReportSmith, you can right-click the label, and then select Deselect from the menu that pops up. Alternatively, select another object in the report.)

The Client03.Rpt report now looks as shown in Figure 18.25. Note that the changes you made in the header area of the first group appear in all the other groups.

Figure 18.25.
Setting the Label that appears to the left of the LastName field in the header area.

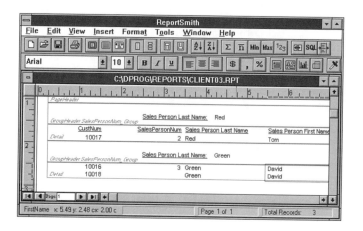

As stated in this chapter, you no longer need to display the salesperson's LastName column.

☐ Select the LastName column heading, and then press the Delete key.

You now can insert other fields into the Header area of the groups. For example, you can select Field from the Insert menu, select the SalesPer.DB table FirstName field, and insert this field into the header area of the groups. Then, delete the FirstName column of the SalesPer.DB table.

☐ Select the text *Report: Client02.Rpt* that appears in the report header, and change it to **Report: Client03.Rpt.**

Do you think it's appropriate to put a picture of the best salespeople as the header of the Client03.Rpt report? If so, perform the following steps:

☐ Select Picture from the Insert menu.

ReportSmith responds by displaying the window shown in Figure 18.26.

Figure 18.26.

The Picture window that is displayed after selecting Picture from the ReportSmith Insert menu.

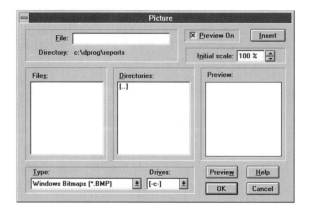

☐ Select the Dance00.BMP file from the C:\DPorg\BMP directory.

The Picture window should now appear as shown in Figure 18.27.

Figure 18.27.

Selecting the picture.

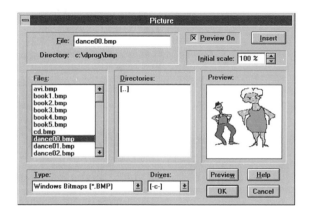

☐ Click the OK button in the Picture window.

☐ Click the mouse in the header area of the Report03.Rpt report.

*ReportSmith responds by inserting the picture Dance00.BMP in the header of the
report, as shown in Figure 18.28.*

Figure 18.28.
*The report header now
contains the picture.*

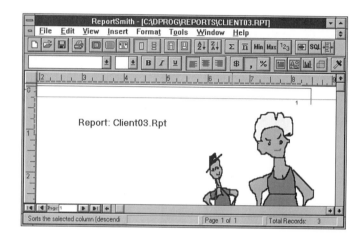

In a similar manner, you can insert the pictures of the salespeople in their header
groups.

You now can drag to the left the label that has the text `Client03.Rpt` in the report
header. You also can drag the Dance00.BMP picture to the left so that these objects fit
on an $8^1/_2 \times 11$ paper.

Preparing Reports with Calculated Fields, and More

In the previous chapter, you learned how to generate a report (Client02.Rpt) from two tables. As discussed throughout the book, when designing the tables, you should not include redundant fields. Eventually, you're going to use the collection of tables for creating a report, and this report will contain data extracted from various tables. The report should be designed so it is easy to read and understand. Thus, one major component of the report is its cosmetic touches.

Also, the report itself should contain "redundant" data. For example, when preparing invoices, the grand total should be calculated and printed in the report. That is, a grand total field in a table is considered redundant information (because the total field can be calculated), but when sending an invoice to a client, you do want to include the total field in the invoice.

In this chapter, you learn how to use ReportSmith for incorporating calculated fields in your reports as well as about other important ReportSmith topics.

The Need for Calculated Fields

A typical example of database work and database manipulation is shown through a program that prints invoices.

Naturally, the process of printing invoices can be accomplished in a variety of ways. However, keeping the principle of databases in mind (that is, there should not be any redundant fields in the tables), you can imagine that, basically, an invoice is a report.

One way to create an invoice printing mechanism is to have the following tables:

Clients.DB
Items.DB

The Clients.DB table is a table similar to the Clients.DB table that you used earlier in this book. The Items.DB table is also a table similar to the Items.DB table you used in previous chapters. Each record in the Items.DB table contains one item that the client purchased. You can add the InvoiceNumber field in the Clients.DB table. For example, if a client made a purchase of five items, the Items.DB table contains five records corresponding to this purchase. Each of these records has the same value for the InvoiceNumber field. If the same client made another purchase of three items on another date, there will be three additional records in the Items.DB table, and each of these records will have the same InvoiceNumber (which is different from the InvoiceNumber assigned to this client's first purchase).

At the end of the month, you can generate a report (using ReportSmith) listing all the Items.DB records having the same InvoiceNumber. This report is the invoice that you send to the client. Typically, you'll spend a significant amount of time on the appearance of the invoice—sizing the columns, setting different fonts for the column headings, setting the title, and so on.

When a report serves as an invoice, you need to add calculated fields to the invoice. For example, you'll have to add a calculated field for each item's total (multiplying the unit price by the quantity purchased), calculating the grand total, calculating sales tax, and so on.

Specifying the Records to Include in the Report

The ability to select the criteria of the records that should be included in a report is one of the most important features you'll use when preparing reports with ReportSmith. The report includes only those records complying with certain criteria.

The criteria selection is demonstrated with this example.

☐ Start ReportSmith.

☐ Load the Client02.Rpt report (you generated the Client02.Rpt report in the previous chapter).

As shown in Figure 19.1, the Client02.Rpt report has three records (clients) in it. One client belongs to SalesPersonNum 2 and two clients belong to SalesPersonNum 3.

Figure 19.1.
The Client02.Rpt report.

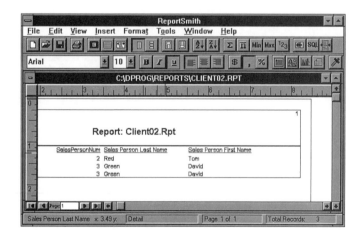

☐ Select the SalesPersonNum column heading, and then right-click the SalesPersonNum column heading (because you're now going to add a criteria to this field).

ReportSmith responds by displaying a menu.

☐ Select Selection Criteria from the menu.

ReportSmith responds by displaying the Field Selection Criteria dialog box, as shown in Figure 19.2.

Figure 19.2.
The Field Selection Criteria dialog box.

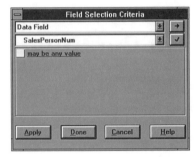

You use the Field Selection Criteria dialog box to specify the field criteria. Once you specify the criteria, only those records complying with the criteria are included in the report.

As you can see in Figure 19.2, the SalesPersonNum field can have any value.

☐ Click the text may be any value.

A list of possible criteria is dropped down as shown in Figure 19.3.

Figure 19.3.
A list of possible criteria for the SalesPersonNum field values.

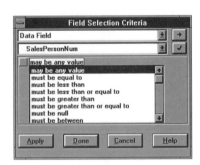

☐ Select the must be equal to item.

Your Field Selection Criteria dialog box should now appear as shown in Figure 19.4. The field criteria is such that only those records with the SalesPersonNum field equal to 0 are displayed.

Figure 19.4.

The criteria shown is that
`SalesPersonNum` *fields must*
be equal to 0*.*

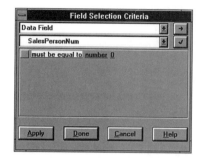

☐ Click the 0 that appears in the Field Selection Criteria dialog box, and type **3** instead of
the 0 (see Figure 19.5). Then click the Done button in the Field Selection Criteria
dialog box.

> *ReportSmith responds by including only those records having* `SalesPersonNum` *equal to 3*
> *(see Figure 19.6).*

Figure 19.5.

Setting the criteria so that
only those records with
`SalesPersonNum` *equal to 3*
are displayed in the report.

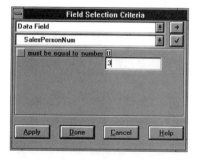

19

Figure 19.6.

Only those records with
`SalesPersonNum` *equal to 3*
are included in the report.

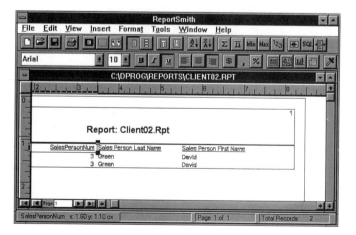

> **Note:** As you can see in Figure 19.3, you can select a different field in the Field Selection Criteria dialog box (via the combobox on the upper portion of the dialog box) and set different criteria. Setting the field criteria this way is easier than setting a SQL statement.

Incorporating Summary Fields into Your Report

You now learn how to create summary fields. The table you use in the following steps is the Items.DB table.

☐ Use Database Desktop to make sure that the Items.DB table residing in the C:\DProg\Work directory has the structure according to Table 19.1. The windows structure is shown in Figure 19.7.

Table 19.1. The Items.DB table structure.

Field Name	Type	Size	Key
ItemNum	Autoincrement	n/a	Yes
CustNum	Numer ic	n/a	No
PartNum	Numeric	n/a	No
QtySold	Numeric	n/a	No

Figure 19.7.
The Items.DB structure window.

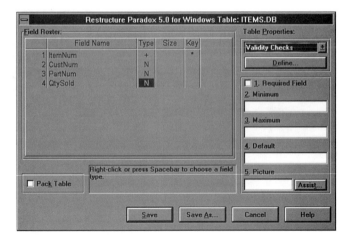

☐ Make sure that at least two records in the Items.DB table are items with `PartNum` equal to `102`.

☐ Terminate Database Desktop.

☐ Start ReportSmith.

☐ Select New from the ReportSmith File menu, and prepare a report for Clients.DB.

The report that ReportSmith prepares is shown in Figure 19.8.

Figure 19.8.

The report of the Items.DB table.

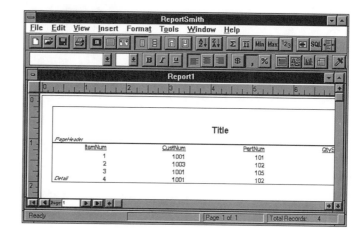

☐ Change the report title to `Report: Items02.Rpt`.

☐ Save the report as Items02.Rpt in the C:\DProg\Reports directory.

Setting Criteria

Suppose that you want to know how many items of part number 102 were sold. You can create criteria for the `PartNum` field as follows:

☐ Select the `PartNum` column heading, and then right-click the `PartNum` column heading.

   ReportSmith responds by displaying a menu.

☐ Select the Selection Criteria from the menu.

   ReportSmith responds by displaying the Field Selection Criteria.

☐ Set the criteria of the `PartNum` field to `must be equal to 102`.

The Field Selection Criteria window should now appear as shown in Figure 19.9.

Figure 19.9.
The PartNum *field of the* Items02.Rpt *report must be equal to* 102.

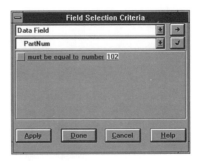

☐ Click the Done button of the Field Selection Criteria window.

Report Smith responds by including in the Client02.Rpt report only those records with PartNum *field equal to* 102 *(see Figure 19.10).*

Figure 19.10.
Only those records with PartNum *fields equal to* 102 *are included in the report.*

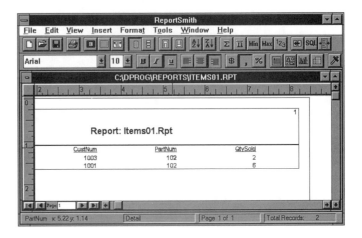

Creating a Summation Field

You now create a summation field that displays the sum of the QtySold field. In Figure 19.10, the report displays two records. The first record says that a quantity of 2 of part number 102 was sold to CustNum 1003, and the second record says that a quantity of 6 of part number 102 was sold to CustNum 1001. The total quantity of part number 102 that was sold is, therefore, 2+6=8.

Here is how you create a summation field for the QtySold column.

☐ Select Header/Footer from the Insert menu.

ReportSmith responds by displaying the Header/Footer dialog box.

☐ Set the Group Type to Footer as shown in Figure 19.11.

Figure 19.11.
*The Header/Footer
dialog box.*

☐ Click the OK button.

ReportSmith responds by inserting a footer in the report (see Figure 19.12).

Figure 19.12.
*A footer is inserted at the
bottom of the report.*

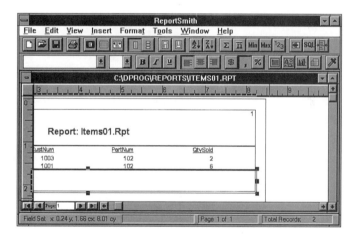

Now that you have a footer, you can insert a summation field in it.

Figure 19.13 shows the various summation operations you can perform.

☐ Select the QtySold column heading.

☐ Click the Sum icon (the leftmost icon shown in Figure 19.13).

*ReportSmith responds by inserting the summation field in the footer area as shown in
Figure 19.14. As shown in the figure, the summation field has the number 8 in it, which is
the sum of the QtySold fields of all records appearing in the report.*

Figure 19.13.

The summation icons on the ReportSmith toolbar.

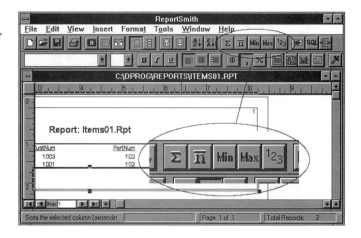

Figure 19.14.

A summation field for the QtySold column is inserted in the footer area.

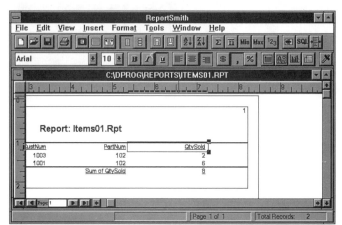

☐ Save the Items02.Rpt report.

Note: ReportSmith automatically placed a Label control to the left of the summation field (see Figure 19.14). The label text is

Sum of QtySold

You can change the label contents by selecting the label, clicking in the selected area, and typing new text in the label area. For example, friendlier text would be

Total items sold:

Creating an Average Field

As shown in Figure 19.13, you can create other types of summation fields. The leftmost icon, which you've used already, is the Summation icon, which sums column values. The second icon from the left is the Average icon, which averages column values.

☐ Click the Average icon.

ReportSmith inserts an average field in the footer area, as shown in Figure 19.15. The average of the QtySold column is (2+6)/2=4.

Figure 19.15.

The footer area now includes a summation field and an average field.

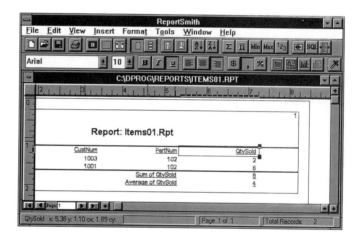

In a similar manner, you can select the QtySold column heading and click the Min icon (the third icon from the left in Figure 19.13) to insert a field that displays the minimum value in the QtySold column. As shown in Figure 19.16, the minimum of QtySold is two. There are two records, one with QtySold equal to 2 and the other record with QtySold equal to 6.

Figure 19.16 shows the result of clicking the Max icon (which causes ReportSmith to insert the value of the largest item in the QtySold column). In this figure, you also can see the result of clicking the 123 icon (the rightmost icon in Figure 19.13), which causes ReportSmith to display the total number of records in the column.

Figure 19.16.

Inserting various summation fields in the report footer.

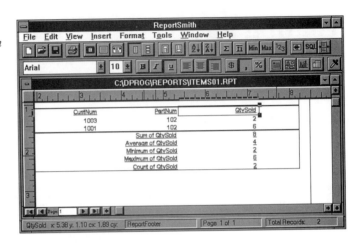

Using Report Variables

So far, you've learned how to generate reports based on the setting at design time. The user didn't need to indicate how the report should be generated.

ReportSmith also enables you to get users' input, and based on that input, you can generate the report. The user's input is stored as the report's variable. The concept of a report's variable is now demonstrated with an example.

☐ Close all reports from the ReportSmith desktop.

☐ Generate a report from the Items.DB table.

☐ Save the report as Items02.Rpt in the C:\DProg\Reports directory.

☐ Select Report Variables from the Tools menu.

> *ReportSmith responds by displaying the Report Variables window (see Figure 19.17). You now use the Report Variables window to define the report variables.*

☐ Fill the Name editbox of the Report Variables window with `PartNumVar`.

☐ Set the Type combobox of the Report Variables window to `Number` (because the report variable that you are now defining is numeric).

☐ Fill the Title editbox of the Report Variables window with `Part Number`.

Later, when the user is instructed (via a dialog box) to enter the part number of the records to be included in the report, the dialog box has the title `Part Number`.

☐ Fill the Prompt editbox of the Report Variables window with `Enter the Part Number to be included in the report`.

Figure 19.17.

The Report Variables window lets you define the report variables.

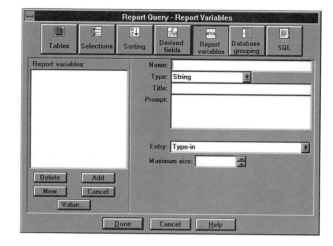

When the user is instructed later (via a dialog box) to enter the part number of the records to be included in the report, the dialog box displays the text that you typed in the Prompt editbox.

☐ Make sure that the Entry combobox is set to **Type-in**.

By setting the Entry to Type-in, you are indicating that the user has to type the value in a dialog box.

Your Report Variables window should now appear as shown in Figure 19.18.

Figure 19.18.

Defining the PartNumVar variable of the report.

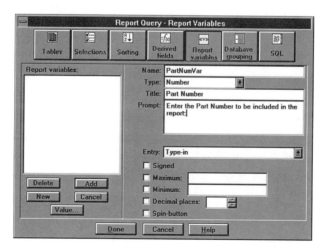

☐ Click the Add button of the Report Variables window.

ReportSmith responds by adding the PartNumVar variable to the Report variables list as shown in Figure 19.19.

Figure 19.19.

The PartNumVar *variable is added to the Report variables list.*

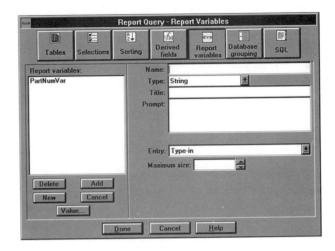

To see the dialog box that prompts the user to enter the part number, follow these steps:

☐ Click the PartNumVar item in the Report variables list, and then click the Value button.

ReportSmith responds by displaying the dialog box shown in Figure 19.20. This is the dialog box that the user sees when executing the report.

Figure 19.20.

The dialog box that the user sees when executing the report.

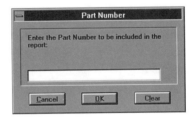

☐ Click the Cancel button of the dialog box.

Now that you've defined a report variable called PartNumVar, you can set a criteria based on the value of the PartNumVar variable.

☐ Click the Selections button of the Report Variables window.

ReportSmith responds by displaying the Selection window. You now use the Selections window to set the criteria.

☐ Click the button that has the number 1. on it.

ReportSmith responds by dropping down the list shown in Figure 19.21.

Figure 19.21.
Adding a selection criteria.

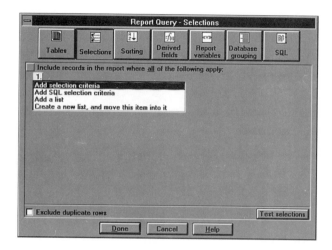

☐ Select the Add selection criteria item from the list.

> *ReportSmith responds by displaying a default criteria. You do not want to use the default criteria, and so you now customize the criteria.*

☐ Click the ITEMSxDB item to drop down a list containing the names of the Items.DB table fields (see Figure 19.22).

Figure 19.22.
Selecting the field on which the criteria is based.

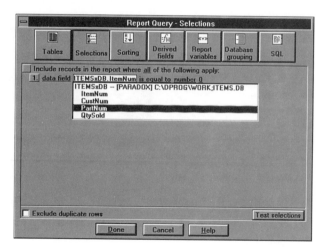

☐ Select the PartNum item from the list of fields.

☐ Click the word number appearing at the end of the criteria line.

> *ReportSmith responds by dropping down a list, as shown in Figure 19.23.*

Figure 19.23.
Selecting a report variable.

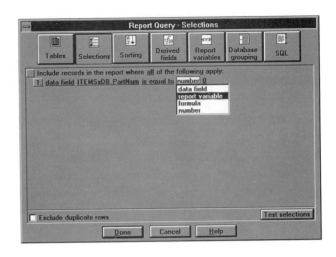

☐ Select the report variable item from the list.

Your Selections window should now appear as shown in Figure 19.24, which establishes the criteria. The report will include those records with PartNum fields equal to the value of the PartNumVar variable.

Figure 19.24.
The criteria statement is now ready to select those records with PartNum fields equal to the value of the PartNumVar variable.

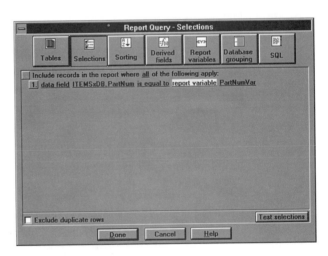

☐ Click the Done button.

If ReportSmith prompts you with a dialog box telling you that no rows were found, click the OK button of the dialog box.

☐ Select Save As from the File menu of ReportSmith, and save the report as Items02.Rpt in the C:\DProg\Reports directory.

☐ Close all reports on the ReportSmith desktop.

☐ Load the Items02.Rpt report.

ReportSmith responds by displaying a dialog box telling you to enter the part number.

☐ Type a part number that exists in the Items.DB table.

ReportSmith responds by generating a report that only includes those records with the `PartNum` field equal to the part number that you enter via the dialog box.

Every time the Items02.Rpt report is loaded, the user is prompted with a dialog box allowing the user to enter the part number.

Of course, typically you won't let the user use the ReportSmith program directly. Rather, you'll design a small Delphi program that includes the `Report` control. (See Exercise 1 at the end of this chapter.)

Letting the User Set the Report Variable from a List

In the previous section, you let the user enter the value of the report variable by displaying a dialog box, and then the user had to type the part number value.

ReportSmith also lets you create lists from which the user must select a value. This value is used as the setting of the report variable. Now you generate the Item03.Rpt report which demonstrates how you implement a list that lets the user select a value for the report variable.

☐ Close all reports on the ReportSmith desktop.

☐ Create a report from the Items.DB table, and save the report as Items03.Rpt in the C:\DProg\Reports directory.

☐ Select Report Variables from the ReportSmith Tools menu.

ReportSmith responds by displaying the Report Variables window.

☐ Set the Name editbox to `PartNumVar`.

The name of the report variable you're defining is now `PartNumVar`.

☐ Set the Type combobox to `Numeric` because the report variable that you are now creating is `Numeric`.

☐ In the Title editbox type `Part Number`.

The dialog box that prompts the user to enter the part number has the title `Part Number`.

☐ In the Prompt editbox, type `Select the part number:`

☐ Set the Entry combobox to `Choose from list`.

The user will be prompted to select a value from a list.

You now add three items to the list from which the user selects the part number.

☐ In the Allowed values editbox, type **101**, and then click the Add button of the Allowed values combobox. Type **102** in the editbox, and click the Add button again. The last item that you add to the list is 103—type **103** in the editbox and then click the Add button.

The Report Variables window should now appear as shown in Figure 19.25.

Figure 19.25.

Defining the PartNumVar *report variable.*

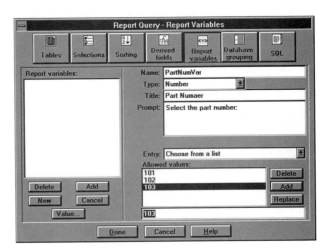

☐ Click the Add button of the Report variables list to add the PartNumVar variable to the list.

ReportSmith responds by adding the PartNumVar *variable to the Report variables list.*

☐ Click the PartNumVar items in the Report variables list.

The Report Variables list window should now appear as shown in Figure 19.26.

☐ Click the Value button to see how the user is asked to select a value for the part number.

ReportSmith responds by displaying the dialog box shown in Figure 19.27.

☐ Click the Cancel button of the dialog box that prompts the user to select a value for the part number.

Figure 19.26.

The PartNumVar *report variable defined in the Report variables window.*

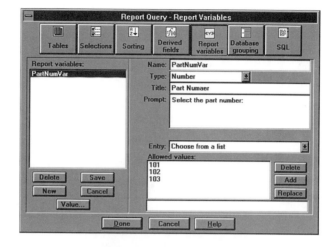

Figure 19.27.

The dialog box that asks the user to select a part number.

You now set the criteria by telling ReportSmith to display only those records with PartNum fields equal to the value of the PartNumVar variable.

☐ Click the Selections button of the Report Variables window.

ReportSmith responds by displaying the Selections window.

☐ Set the criteria as shown in Figure 19.28. (Click on the various words of the criteria statement, and select the appropriate item from the dropped list).

You set the criteria so that the Items.DB table PartNum field is equal to the SalesPartNum variable value.

Figure 19.28.

Setting the criteria based on the PartNumVar *variable.*

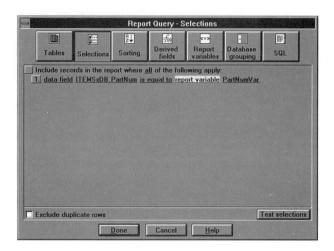

☐ Click the Done button.

If ReportSmith prompts you to select a value for the PartNum, select any value.

☐ Save the Items03.Rpt report, and then close the report.

☐ Load the Items03.Rpt report.

ReportSmith prompts you to select a part number from a list.

☐ Select a value from the list, and then click the OK button.

> *ReportSmith responds by generating the report with only those records with* PartNum *fields equal to the value that you selected.*

☐ Practice with the Items03.Rpt report by closing the report, loading the report again, and selecting a different value for the part number. Note that if there are no records with the part number you selected, the report contains no records.

Selecting a Value from a Table

In the previous section, you let the user select the value of the report variable by displaying a list that you prepared. An alternative way is to let the user select a value from one of the records of another table. To see this in action, prepare another report, Items04.Rpt, that lets the user select a part number from the Parts.DB table.

☐ Terminate the ReportSmith program.

☐ Use Database Desktop to make sure that the Parts.DB table in the C:\DProg\Work directory contains the information specified in Table 19.2. The structure window of Parts.DB is shown in Figure 19.29.

Table 19.2. The Parts.DB table structure.

Field Name	Type	Size	Key
PartNum	N	n/a	Yes
Description	A	40	No
QtyInStock	N	n/a	No
SellingPrice	N	n/a	No

Figure 19.29.
The Parts.DB structure window.

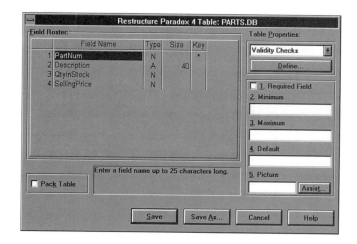

☐ Use Database Desktop to update the Items.DB records so that the Items.DB table includes records having PartNum fields that exist in the Parts.DB table.

☐ Terminate the Database Desktop program.

☐ Start ReportSmith.

☐ Create a report from the Items.DB table, and save the report as Items04.Rpt in the C:\DProg\Report directory.

You now create a report variable in the Items04.Rpt report. The report variable again represents the PartNum field. However, the user selects a value from the Parts.DB table records. This ensures that the user selects a valid part number.

☐ Select Report Variables from the ReportSmith Tools menu.

   ReportSmith responds by displaying the Report Variables window.

☐ Set the Name editbox of the Report Variables window to **PartNumVar**.

☐ Set the Type of the Report Variables window to Numeric.

☐ In the Title of the Report Variables window, type **Part Number**.

☐ In the Prompt editbox of the Report Variables window, type **Select a Part Number:**

☐ Set the Entry combobox of the Report Variables window to Choose from a table.

Tell ReportSmith from which table to extract the list of values for the PartNumVar variable.

☐ Click the Table button (on the lower-right portion of the Report Variables window), and select the Parts.DB table.

☐ Click the Fields button (on the lower-right portion of the Report Variables window), and select the PartNum fields (see Figure 19.30) from the dialog box. Close the dialog box.

Figure 19.30.
Setting the Display value
from field *and the* Use
value from field.

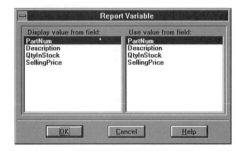

The Report variables window should now appear as shown in Figure 19.31.

Figure 19.31.
The Report Variables
window with the
PartNumVar *variable.*

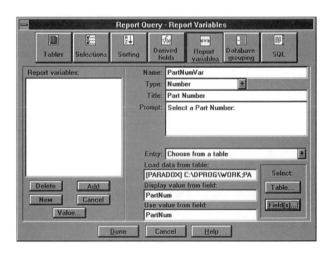

☐ Click the Add button to add the PartNumVar report variable to the Report variables list.

☐ Select the `PartNumVar` variable in the Report variables list, and click the Value button.

ReportSmith responds by displaying the dialog box shown in Figure 19.32. This is the dialog box that the user uses to select a part number. The values in the list are from the records of the Parts.DB table.

☐ Click the Cancel button of the Part Number list.

Figure 19.32.
The user selects a part number in this dialog box. The values in the list are from the Parts.DB table.

You established a report variable, and the user sets the report variable value from a list whose values come directly from the Parts.DB table. Now you set the criteria for the report.

☐ Click the Selection button.

ReportSmith responds by displaying the Selections window.

☐ Click the button that has the number 1 on it.

ReportSmith responds by dropping down a list as shown in Figure 19.33.

Figure 19.33.
The list of options to set criteria.

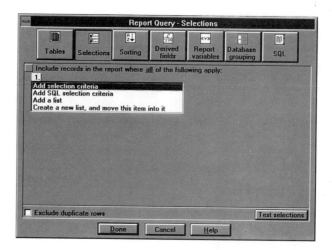

☐ Select the Add selection criteria from the list (see Figure 19.33).

ReportSmith displays a default statement for the criteria. Customize the statement as follows:

☐ Click the `ItemsxDb.ItemsNum` text, and select the `PartNum` item (see Figure 19.34).

Figure 19.34.
Selecting the field on which the criteria are based.

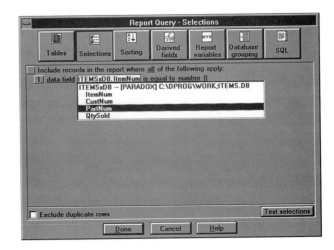

☐ Replace `data field` with **report variable**, as shown in Figure 19.35.

Figure 19.35.
Setting the criteria with the report variable.

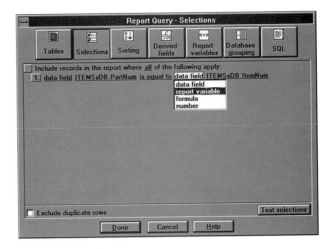

The final criteria statement is shown in Figure 19.36.

Figure 19.36.
The final criteria statement.

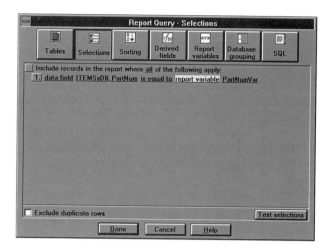

☐ Click the Done button of the Selections window.

If ReportSmith displays the dialog box that lets the user select a PartNum, select any part number, and then close the dialog box.

☐ Save the report as Items04.Rpt in the C:\DProg\Reports directory.

☐ Close all reports on the ReportSmith desktop.

☐ Load the Items04.Rpt report.

> *ReportSmith responds by displaying the list of PartNum fields from the Parts.DB table.*

☐ Select a PartNum from the list.

> *ReportSmith responds by creating a report containing only those records with the PartNum field equal to the value that you selected.*

☐ Close the Items04.Rpt report.

You can now load the Items04.Rpt again, and select a different value for the PartNum.

Summary

In this chapter, you learned how to create a selection criteria so that the report only includes those records meeting the field criteria that you specified.

You also learned how to create a summation field for a column (sum of values, average, minimum, maximum, and count of records).

You learned how to create a report variable and how to display a dialog box that lets the user update the report variable value. ReportSmith then creates a report based on the user's input. You learned to take user's input in the following ways:

- Allowing the user to type the report variable value.
- Allowing the user to select a value from a list.
- Allowing the user to select a value from a list. The list contains values that come from another table.

Q&A

Q Should I use ReportSmith for generating invoices, or should I write a Delphi program that generates invoices?

A Typically, if you can accomplish a certain task with ReportSmith, then this is the preferred way. As you saw, ReportSmith enables you to generate reports very easily. Sometimes, you need to combine a report and a Delphi program in a process such as printing invoices. For example, you may consider adding an additional field to the Items.DB table, the InvoiceDateSent field. This field represents the date on which the invoice was sent. You can write a Delphi program that fills the InvoiceDateSent field with the date on which the invoices were sent. At the end of the process of sending the printed invoices, you execute the Delphi program so those Clients.DB table records that were printed on an invoice and sent to the client are updated.

Quiz

1. To select only certain records in the report, you should _____.
2. Once you declare a report variable you should _____.
3. In this chapter, you learned how to update a report variable based on user's input by implementing the user's input mechanism in three ways. What are these three ways for implementing the user's input?

Exercise

Write a small Delphi program that lets the user print the Items02.Rpt report.

Answers to Quiz

1. To select only certain records in the report, you should use the Field Selection Criteria dialog box. To display the Field Selection Criteria dialog box, you can select the column heading of the field and then right-click the selected column heading. Alternatively, you can select Field Selection Criteria from the Tools menu.

2. Once you declare a report variable, you should click the Selection button and define the criteria.

3. The three ways are
   - Allow the user to type the report variable value.
   - Allow the user to select the report variable value from a list.
   - Allow the user to select a value from a table.

Answers to Exercises

1. Here's what to do.

   ☐ Terminate the ReportSmith program.

   ☐ Start Delphi.

   ☐ Create a new project.

   ☐ In Form1, place a Report control, an Exit pushbutton and a Print Report pushbutton.

   ☐ Set the Report control properties as follows:

   ```
   Name          Items02Report
   ReportName    C:\DProg\Reports\Items02.Rpt
   AutoUnload    True
   ```

   ☐ Save the Pas file of Form1, and save the project.

   ☐ Attach the following code to the OnClick event of the Exit button:

   ```
   Application.Terminate;
   ```

   ☐ Attach the following code to the OnClick event of the Print Report button:

   ```
   Items02Report.Run;
   ```

   ☐ Save your Work.

   When the user clicks the Print Report button, the program displays a dialog box asking the user to enter the Part Number, and then the report is printed.

Derived Fields
and Columns
in Reports

Derived Fields

In many reports, you'll want to generate derived fields. A *derived field* is a report column whose value is calculated based on other columns in the report. You also can place a derived field in the footer or header area of the report.

For example, you can create a derived field that displays the sales tax of an invoice. The value of the sales tax is calculated by summing the values contained in another column and then multiplying the result of the summation by the sales tax percentage.

As another example, consider an Items.DB table that contains the QtySold field. Based on the PartNum field, the selling price can be extracted from the Parts.DB table. You then can generate a derived field that calculates the total by multiplying the unit price by the value of the quantity.

Your objective now is to generate a report that calculates the total for an invoice item. You'll generate a report based on the Items.DB table records, and add a derived field containing the result of multiplying the selling price with the QtySold field. The selling price will be extracted from the Parts.DB table. You'll also generate a report, Items05.Rpt, that extracts the unit prices of the items.

Generating a Merged Table for the Items.DB-Parts.DB Tables

Before you can generate the Items05.Rpt report, you must first generate a merged table for the Items.DB-Parts.DB tables.

☐ Start ReportSmith.

☐ Select New from the ReportSmith File menu.

☐ Make sure that the Columnar Report button is pressed, and click the Add Table button.

ReportSmith responds by displaying a dialog box that enables you to select a table.

☐ Select the Items.DB table.

☐ Click the Add Table button again, and add the Parts.DB table.

Your Report Query - Tables window should look similar to the one shown in Figure 20.1.

Figure 20.1.

Creating a report from the Items.DB and Parts.DB tables.

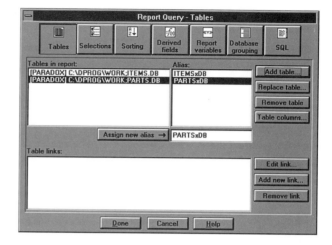

Creating a Link Between the Tables

Now you create a link between the Items.DB and Parts.DB tables.

☐ Click the Add new link button.

> *ReportSmith responds by displaying the Create New Table Link window.*

☐ Set the link between the Items.DB and Parts.DB tables as shown in Figure 20.2. Select PartNum in the list of Items.DB table fields, select the equal-sign (=) option button, and select PartNum from the list of Parts.DB table fields.

Your Create New Table Link window should now look like the one shown in Figure 20.2.

Figure 20.2.

Creating a link between the Items.DB and Parts.DB tables.

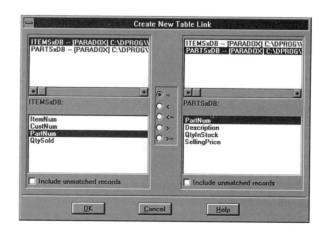

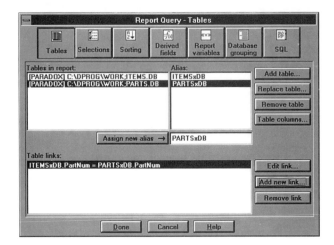
☐ Click the OK button of the Create New Table Link window.

> *ReportSmith responds by displaying the Report Query - Tables window as shown in Figure 20.3.*

Figure 20.3.

The Report Query - Tables window with the link between the Items.DB and Parts.DB tables shown.

☐ Click the Done button.

> *ReportSmith responds by generating the report (see Figure 20.4).*

☐ Change the title of the report to **Report: Items05.Rpt**.

☐ Select Save As from the File menu, and save the report as Items05.Rpt in the C:\DProg\Reports directory.

Figure 20.4.

The Items05.Rpt report.

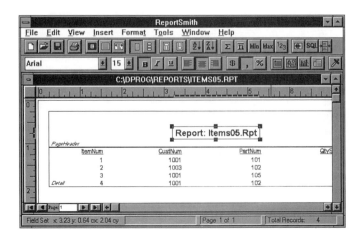

The reason you were instructed to create the Items05.Rpt report with the Parts.DB table in it is because you need to know the selling price. For example, you do not need to display the QtyInStock column, so delete it from the report.

☐ Delete the QtyInStock column.

☐ Delete the PartNum column that came from the Parts.DB table. The Items05.Rpt report has two PartNum columns, one from the Items.DB table and one from the Parts.DB table. You need only one PartNum column in the report.

☐ Delete the CustNum column.

Note: If Items05.Rpt is used as an invoice, you display the CustNum field in the invoice header, and you display only those Items.DB records that belong to a certain customer. You use the technique shown in Chapter 19, "Preparing Reports with Calculated Fields, and More," to generate criteria that displays only those Items.DB records that comply with CustNum equal to the customer to which you want to generate the invoice.

In any case, there is no need to display CustNum as a column appearing in every invoice item. Typically, you show the CustNum (as well as the name and address of the customer) only in the report header.

You'll usually want to show the Description field in an invoice. However, for simplicity, delete the Description field at this time.

☐ Delete the Description column.

The Items05.Rpt report should now look like the one shown in Figure 20.5.

☐ Select Save As from the ReportSmith File menu, and save the report as Items05.Rpt.

Figure 20.5.
The Items05.Rpt report after deleting several of its columns.

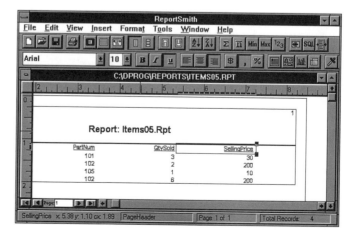

Creating the Total Column

In the preceding steps, you generated a report that includes the QtySold column from the Items.DB table and the SellingPrice column from the Parts.DB table.

You'll now create the TotalItem column, which displays the result of multiplying SellingPrice by QtySold. This column is a derived field.

☐ Select Derive Fields from the ReportSmith Tools menu.

ReportSmith responds by displaying the Derived Fields window shown in Figure 20.6.

Figure 20.6.

The Derived Fields window enables you to add a derived field.

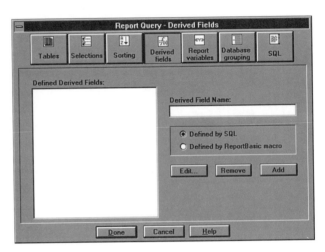

Use the Derived Fields window to derive the TotalItem column, which contains values that are the results of multiplying the SellingPrice by the QtySold.

☐ In the Derived Name Field editbox, type **TotalItem**.

☐ Make sure that the Defined by SQL option button is selected.

☐ Click the Add button.

ReportSmith responds by displaying the Edit Derived Field window shown in Figure 20.7.

☐ Select the QtySold item from the list of Items.DB table fields, and then click the Insert button.

ReportSmith responds by inserting the QtySold item in the Derived field formula as shown in Figure 20.8.

Figure 20.7.
The Edit Derived Field window.

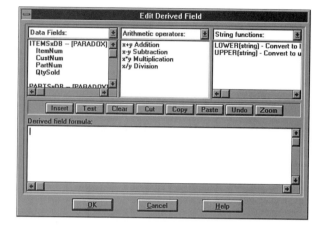

Figure 20.8.
The Edit Derived Field window after inserting the QtySold *item.*

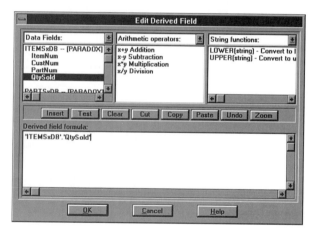

☐ Select the x*y Multiplication item from the Arithmetic operators list, and then click the Insert button.

ReportSmith responds by inserting the multiplication character (*) after the QtySold item.

So far, the derived field is QtySold*.

☐ Select the SellingPrice item from the list of Parts.DB table fields, and then click the Insert button.

ReportSmith responds by inserting the SellingPrice item in the Derived field formula as shown in Figure 20.9.

Figure 20.9.

The Edit Derived Field window after inserting the complete formula for calculating the TotalItem.

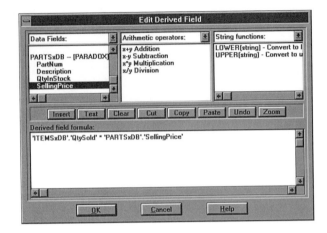

The derived field is now defined as follows:

```
QtySold*SellingPrice
```

☐ Click the OK button in the Edit Derived field window.

> *ReportSmith responds by again displaying the Derived Fields window (see Figure 20.10). As you can see, the TotalItem is listed in the Defined Derived Field list.*

Figure 20.10.

The TotalItem derived field as defined in the Derived Field window.

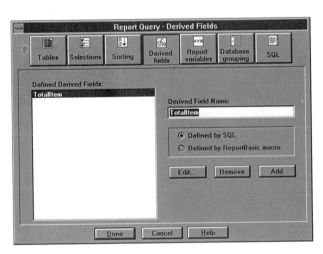

☐ Click the Done button of the Derived Fields window.

> *ReportSmith responds by adding the TotalItem column to the Items05.Rpt report, as shown in Figure 20.11.*

Figure 20.11.
The TotalItem *column
(a derived field) in the
Items05.Rpt report.*

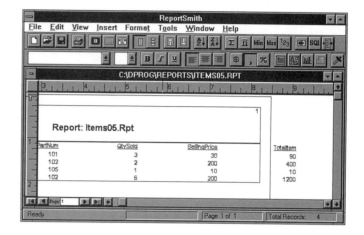

☐ Select Save As from the ReportSmith File menu to save the Items05.Rpt report.

Macro-Derived Fields

As shown earlier in Figure 20.10, the derived field that you generated is defined by SQL. An alternative way to generate derived fields is to use macro-derived fields, as we demonstrate next. Typically, you use the macro-derived fields when the calculations involve summation fields (and the value on which you are basing your calculation is not one of the table fields).

The Items05.Rpt report currently includes the TotalItem derived field. You'll now add another derived field, the SalesTax column. This column displays the sales tax, which we assume to be 10 percent. The derived SalesTax field should, therefore, be as follows:

```
          TotalItem
          =========
          90
          400
          10
          1200

  Total: 1700
SalesTax: 170
```

Because the sales tax is calculated based on the sum of the TotalItem column, first calculate the sum of the TotalItem column:

☐ Select Header/Footer from the Insert menu.

ReportSmith responds by displaying the Header/Footer dialog box.

☐ Set the Header/Footer dialog box as shown in Figure 20.12, and click the OK button.

ReportSmith responds by inserting a footer in the Items05.Rpt report.

517

Figure 20.12.
The Header/Footer dialog box.

☐ Select the TotalItem column, and then click the Summation icon on the ReportSmith toolbar.

> *ReportSmith responds by inserting a summation field in the Footer area (see Figure 20.13). As you can see, the Sum Of TotalItem (1700) is the sum of all the rows in the* TotalItem *column.*

Figure 20.13.
The Items05.Rpt report after adding the summation field for the TotalItem *column.*

Next, create a derived field based on a macro. As you'll soon see, the macro uses the value of the summation field.

☐ Select Derived Fields from the Tools menu.

> *ReportSmith responds by displaying the Derived Fields window as shown in Figure 20.10. Currently, there is one derived field in the report, the* TotalItem *column, which is a Defined-by-SQL derived field.*

☐ In the Derived Field Name editbox, delete the current text, and type **SalesTax**. This is the name of the new derived field that you're implementing now.

☐ Select the Defined by ReportBasic macro option button.

The Derived Fields window should look like the one shown in Figure 20.14.

Figure 20.14.
Setting the name for the
SalesTax *derived field.*
The SalesTax *derived field*
is defined as a Defined-by-
ReportBasic macro.

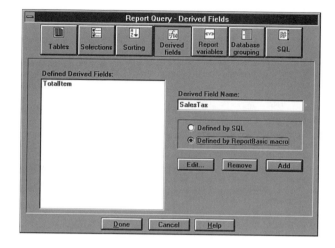

☐ Click the Add button.

> *ReportSmith responds by displaying the Choose a Macro dialog box.*

☐ In the Macro Name edit box, type **SalesTaxMacro**.

You're in the process of defining a macro called SalesTaxMacro that calculates the value of the SalesTax derived column. Your Choose A Macro window should look like the one shown in Figure 20.15.

Figure 20.15.
The Choose a Macro
dialog box.

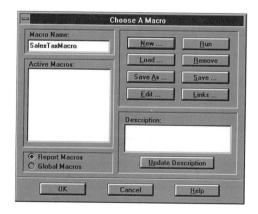

Now you're ready to write the code of the macro.

☐ Click the New button of the Choose A Macro dialog box.

> *Report Smith responds by displaying the Edit Macro window shown in Figure 20.16. As shown in Figure 20.16, ReportSmith typed the first and last lines of the macro for you.*

Your job is to type macro code between the first and last lines that will fill the SalesTax
derived column with the amount of sales tax.

Figure 20.16.

*The Edit Macro window.
ReportSmith typed the first
and last lines of the macro
for you.*

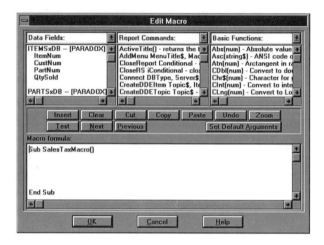

☐ Type macro code in the SalesTaxMacro.

After typing the code, the SalesTaxMacro macro should be as follows (see also Figure 20.17):

```
Sub SalesTaxMacro()

S = SumField$("TotalItem","Derived Field",0,"Sum")
S = S*0.1
DerivedField Str$(S)

End Sub
```

Figure 20.17.

*The Edit Macro window
with the complete*
SalesTaxMacro *in it.*

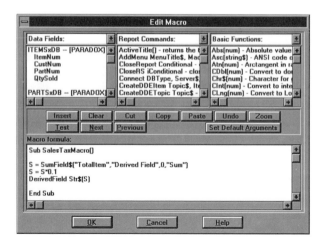

The code you typed uses the report macro code, not a regular Pascal code. For example, there are no semicolons at the end of each statement. You can click the Help button to learn about additional macro features.

The value that is the sum of all the TotalItem column entries is assigned to S:

```
S = SumField$("TotalItem","Derived Field",0,"Sum")
```

Then, S is multiplied by 0.1 (because 10 percent sales tax is used):

```
S = S*0.1
```

The derived field is assigned the value of S:

```
DerivedField Str$(S)
```

☐ Click the OK button of the Edit Macro window.

Report Smith responds by displaying the Choose a Macro window.

☐ Click the OK button of the Choose a Macro window.

ReportSmith responds by displaying the Derived Fields window (see Figure 20.18). As you can see from Figure 20.18, there are now two derived fields:

TotalItem   A derived field that you previously created using SQL.

SalesTax   A derived field that you created with a macro.

Figure 20.18.
The Derived Fields window with two derived fields in it.

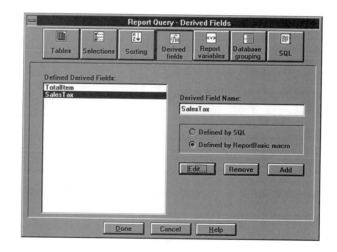

☐ Click the Done button of the Derived Fields window.

ReportSmith responds by displaying the Items05.Rpt report with SalesTax derived column as shown in Figure 20.19.

Figure 20.19.

The Items05.Rpt report with the SalesTax *derived column.*

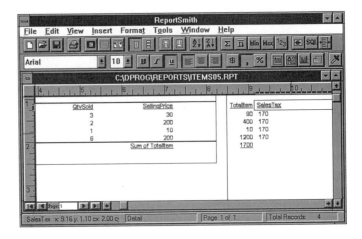

☐ Select Save As from the File menu to save the Items05.Rpt report.

As you can see in Figure 20.19, the SalesTax derived field is displayed as a column. Typically, you'll want to display the sales tax not as a column, but as a single field in the footer area. Here is how to accomplish this.

Look at Figure 20.20, which shows two of the icons on the ReportSmith toolbar. The left icon is the Column-editing icon, and the right icon is the Field-editing icon.

When you click on a report column, ReportSmith can select the entire column or individual rows in the column. To see this in action, follow these steps.

☐ Make sure that the Column icon (the left icon of Figure 20.20) is pushed down.

Figure 20.20.

The Column and Field editing icons on the ReportSmith toolbar.

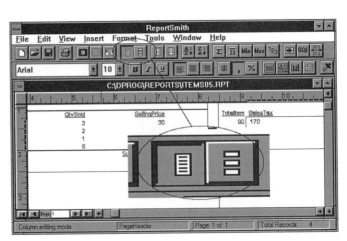

☐ Click on any row in the SalesTax column.

ReportSmith responds by selecting the entire SalesTax column, as shown in Figure 20.21.

Figure 20.21.
Selecting the entire
`SalesTax` *column.*

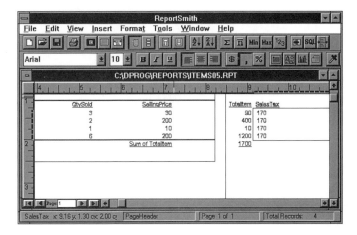

☐ Click the Field-editing icon on the ReportSmith toolbar (the right icon in Figure 20.20).

ReportSmith responds by selecting individual fields of the `SalesTax` *column as shown in Figure 20.22.*

Figure 20.22.
Selecting individual fields in
the `SalesTax` *column.*

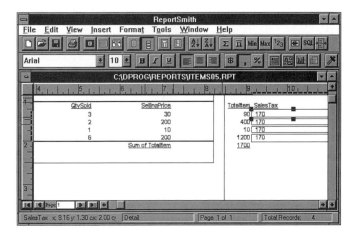

☐ Drag the `SalesTax` column to the footer area. While you drag the SalesTax column, the entire column is dragged, but only one row is dropped into the footer area.

The Items05.Rpt report should now look like the one shown in Figure 20.23.

Figure 20.23.

The Items05.Rpt report with the SalesTax derived field in its footer area.

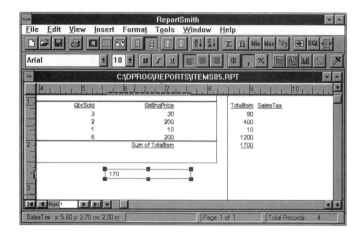

□ Select the SalesTax column heading and drag it to the left of the SalesTax derived field in the footer area.

The final footer area is shown in Figure 20.24.

Figure 20.24.

The Footer area of Items05.Rpt with the label and derived field of SalesTax.

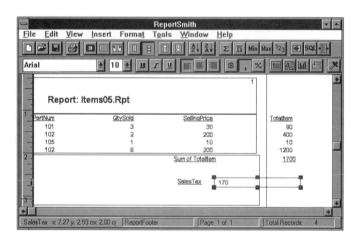

□ Select Save As from the File menu to save the Items05.Rpt report.

Summary

In this chapter, you learned how to create derived fields. A derived field is a field that represents values based on calculations made on other records. You also learned how to create SQL-derived fields and macro-derived fields.

Q&A

Q Should I use an SQL-derived field or a macro-derived field?

A As demonstrated in this chapter, sometimes, you'll need to calculate the value of a derived field based on a summary field. In that case, you'll have to calculate the value of the derived field by using the macro-derived-field method.

Quiz

1. To sum an entire column in a report, what do you use?

    a. A derived field.

    b. The summation icon on the toolbar of ReportSmith.

2. Before using the summation icon on the ReportSmith toolbar, you must _____.

Exercises

1. Oops! The governor just announced that the sales tax was reduced from 10 percent to 5 percent. Adjust the Items05.Rpt report accordingly.

2. In Exercise 1, you modified the sales-tax calculations so that 5 percent was used. However, the report doesn't enable the user to see what sales tax was used. Modify the report so that the user can tell what percentage sales tax was used for the calculations.

20

Answers to Quiz

1. b.

2. Before using the summation icon on the toolbar of ReportSmith, you must create a footer area by selecting Header/Footer from the Insert menu, and then select the column you want to sum.

Answers to Exercises

1. You must change the macro statement so that it calculates the SalesTax derived field using 5 percent sales tax.

   ☐ Select Derived Fields from the Tools menu.

   ReportSmith responds by displaying the Derived Field window.

   ☐ Select the SalesTax item, and then click the Edit button.

   ReportSmith responds by displaying the Choose a Macro window.

   ☐ Click the Edit button of the Choose a Marco window.

   ReportSmith responds by letting you edit the SalesTaxMacro that you previously typed.

   ☐ Change the macro so that 5 percent is used.

   After changing the macro, the SalesTaxMacro macro should be as follows:

   ```
   Sub SalesTaxMacro()

   S = SumField$("TotalItem","Derived Field",0,"Sum")
   S = S*0.05
   DerivedField Str$(S)

   End Sub
   ```

   ☐ Click the OK button of the Edit Macro window.

   ReportSmith responds by displaying the Choose a Macro window.

   ☐ Click the OK button of the Choose a Macro window.

   ReportSmith responds by displaying the Derived Fields window.

   ☐ Click the Done button

   ReportSmith generates the Items05.Rpt report using 5 percent as the sales tax.

2. The answer is as follows:

   ☐ Select the SalesTax label that appears to the left of the SalesTax derived field.

   ☐ Click in the selected SalesTax label so you can edit the label text.

   ☐ Change the label text to **Sales Tax (5%):**.

Other Report
Formats

In this chapter, you learn how to present reports in other formats. In pervious chapters, you created reports using the columnar format, where data is displayed in columns. However, as you see in this chapter, ReportSmith lets you prepare reports in other formats.

You also learn how to prepare the reports so that each group of records is printed on a separate page. This technique is used when preparing the hard copies for mailing statements and invoices.

Preparing a Crosstab Report

A Crosstab report is presented as a table similar to a spreadsheet. To prepare one, do the following:

☐ Select New from the ReportSmith File menu.

ReportSmith responds by displaying the Create a New Report window (see Figure 21.1).

Figure 21.1.
The Create a New Report window.

In previous chapters, you selected the Columnar Report. Select the Crosstab Report.

☐ Click the Crosstab Report button, and then click the OK button.

ReportSmith responds by displaying the Tables window (see Figure 21.2) which lets you select a table.

☐ Click the Add Table button, and then select the Items.DB table.

ReportSmith responds by displaying the Tables window with the Items.DB table in it.

☐ Click the Done button of the Tables window.

ReportSmith responds by displaying the Crosstab Report window (see Figure 21.3).

You use the Crosstab Report window to define the Crosstab report.

☐ In the Title editbox, type `Report: Items06.Rpt`.

☐ In the Description, type `This is the Items06.Rpt report.`

Figure 21.2.
The Tables window lets you select a table.

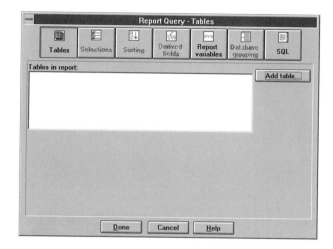

Figure 21.3.
The Crosstab Report window.

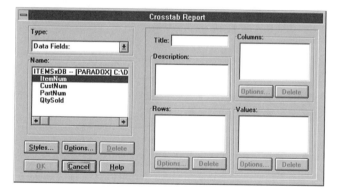

Define the columns, rows, and values of the Crosstab as follows:

☐ Use the mouse to drag the CustNum field to the Columns list.

☐ Use the mouse to drag the PartNum field to the Rows list.

☐ Use the mouse to drag the QtySold field to the Values list.

Your Crosstab Report window should now look as shown in Figure 21.4.

☐ Click the OK button of the Crosstab Report window, and then click in the report area.

   ReportSmith responds by preparing the report according to the way you specified it in the Crosstab Report window (see Figure 21.5).

☐ Select Save As from the File menu, and save the report as Items06.Rpt in the C:\DProg\Reports directory.

Figure 21.4.

The Crosstab Report window with its parameters defined.

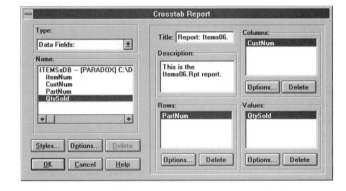

Figure 21.5.

The Items06.Rpt Crosstab report.

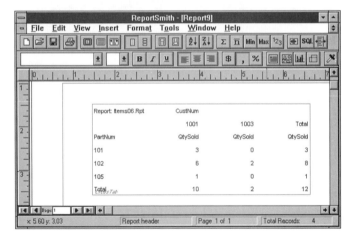

Take a look at the report in Figure 21.5. In many cases, such a report gives a better picture of the data. For example, by inspecting the Items06.Rpt report, you can see that customer 1001 purchased a total of 10 items. Three items are part number 101, six items are part number 6, and one item is part number 105.

You can use all the other features of ReportSmith that you learned in previous chapters and apply them to the Crosstab report. For example, the following steps show you how to display only that portion of the Crosstab containing information about part numbers greater than or equal to 102. This means you're filtering out part number 101 from the report shown in Figure 21.5.

☐ Select Selections from the Tools menu.

ReportSmith responds by displaying the window shown in Figure 21.6.

Figure 21.6.
The Selections window.

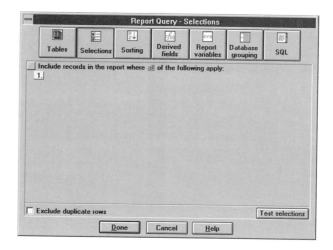

☐ Set the selection statement as shown in Figure 21.7. You are selecting only those records with `PartNum` fields equal to `102` or greater than `102`.

Figure 21.7.
Setting the selection so that only those records with PartNum fields equal to 102 or greater than 102 are selected.

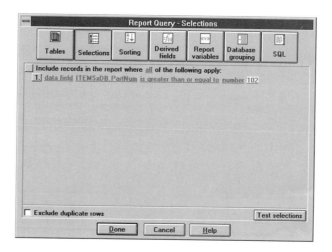

☐ Click the Done button.

21

ReportSmith responds by generating the report shown in Figure 21.8. As you can see, the report now contains only those records whose PartNum fields are equal to 102 or greater than 102.

Figure 21.8.

The report with records having PartNum *fields equal to 102 or greater than 102.*

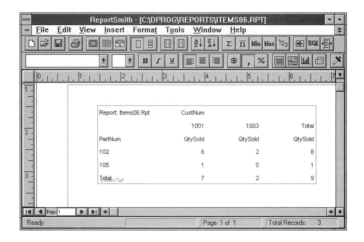

Converting a Columnar Report to a Crosstab

You learned a lot about the Columnar report in previous chapters. If you spent a lot of time creating a Columnar report (for example, creating derived fields, merging tables), you can convert the Columnar report to a Crosstab report and thus save all the work you invested in the Columnar report.

In the following steps, you create a Columnar report and then convert it to a Crosstab report.

☐ Close all reports on the ReportSmith desktop.

☐ Select New from the ReportSmith File menu.

   ReportSmith responds by displaying the Create a New Report dialog box.

☐ Make sure that the Columnar Report button is pressed, and then click the OK button.

☐ Click the Add Table button, select the Items.DB table, and then click the Done button.

   ReportSmith responds by creating a Columnar report.

☐ Change the title of the report to `Report: Items07.Rpt`.

☐ Select Save As from the File menu, and save the report as Items07.Rpt in the C:\DProg\Reports directory.

Now convert the Items07.Rpt Columnar report to a Crosstab report.

☐ Make sure that the Boundaries item of the View menu has a checkmark to its left.

When the Boundaries item of the View menu has a checkmark in it, you see the report with boundaries, as shown in Figure 21.9. When the Boundaries item of the View menu does not have a checkmark, you see the report without boundaries, as shown in Figure 21.10.

Figure 21.9.
The report with boundaries.

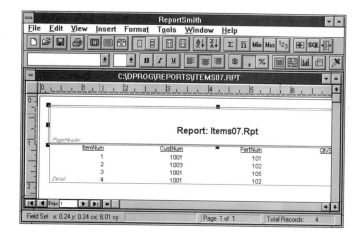

Figure 21.10.
The report without boundaries.

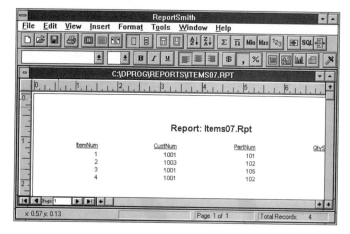

☐ Make sure that none of the objects in the report is selected, and then select Crosstab from the Tools menu.

> *ReportSmith responds by displaying the Crosstab toolbox (see Figure 21.11). As you place the mouse cursor on any of the Crosstab toolbox icons, the ReportSmith status bar displays a description of the icon.*

☐ Click the Modify Crosstab icon (the top icon shown in Figure 21.11).

> *ReportSmith responds by displaying the Crosstab Report window.*

Figure 21.11.
The Crosstab toolbox.

Set the columns, rows, and values of the crosstab.

☐ Use the mouse to drag the fields to the columns, rows, and values, as shown in Figure 21.12.

Figure 21.12.
Setting the column, row, and values of the Crosstab.

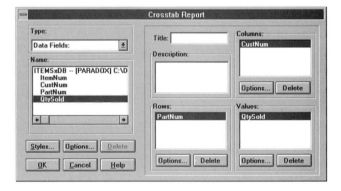

☐ Click the OK button of the Crosstab Report window, and then click the mouse in the header area of the report.

ReportSmith responds by placing a Crosstab (according the specifications that you set) in the header area as shown in Figure 21.13.

Now the report contains both a Detail section (the Columnar section of the report) as well as the Crosstab.

Hide the detail section of the report. The report includes only the crosstab.

☐ Select the Detail section (by clicking on the Detail section boundaries).

The report should now look as shown in Figure 21.14.

Figure 21.13.
The Crosstab in the header section of the report.

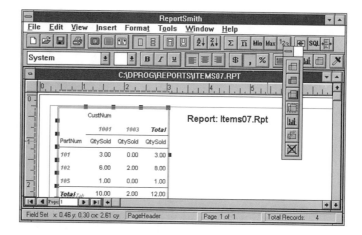

Figure 21.14.
Selecting the Detail section.

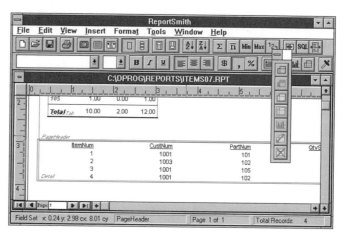

☐ Select Section from the Format menu.

   ReportSmith responds by displaying the Format Section dialog box.

☐ Make sure that the Format section dialog box is set as shown in Figure 21.15. The Detail section is selected, the Hide Section checkbox is checked, and then click the OK button.

   ReportSmith responds by hiding the Detail section, and so now the report looks as shown in Figure 21.16.

☐ Select Save As from the ReportSmith File menu to save the Items07.Rpt report.

21

Figure 21.15.

The Format Section dialog box.

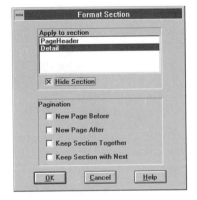

Figure 21.16.

The Items07.Rpt report with its Detail section hidden.

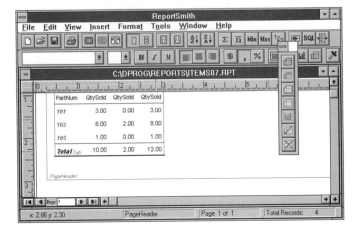

Printing Addresses

Mass mailing is the process of sending large amounts of mail. There are several ways to prepare mass mailings. One way is to use window envelopes.

A window envelope is one with an opening in it. The window enables the recipient's address to be seen through the window. For example, you can generate a report where each report represents an invoice. You print the name and address of the customer in a certain place on the invoice so that when the invoice is folded and inserted into the window envelope, the customer's address shows through the window. As you saw, ReportSmith lets you place the fields anywhere on the report.

In the next exercise, you'll link two tables:

Items.DB
Clients.DB

Before proceeding with the exercise, you must edit the values in the Items.DB table so there are records in Items.DB that belong to customers from the Clients.DB table.

☐ Execute the Database Desktop program, open the Clients.DB table, and take note of this table's CustNum fields.

☐ Use Database Desktop to open the Items.DB table, and make sure that the Items.DB table has several records in it that contain CustNum values appearing in the Clients.DB table. For example, if the Clients.DB table has records with CustNum equal to 10018, make sure that the Items.DB table has at least two records in it where CustNum is equal to 10018. Then, make sure that Items.DB has at least two additional records with another CustNum that appears in the Clients.DB table.

☐ Terminate the Database Desktop program.

☐ Close all reports on the ReportSmith desktop.

☐ Select New from the ReportSmith File menu.

ReportSmith responds by displaying the Create a New Report dialog box.

☐ Make sure that the Columnar Report button is pressed, and click the OK button.

☐ Click the Add Table button, and select the Items.DB table.

☐ Add the Clients.DB table to the report.

Your Tables window should now look as shown in Figure 21.17.

Figure 21.17.
The report is generated from the Items.DB and Clients.DB tables.

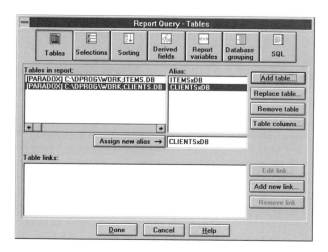

You now link the two tables as follows:

☐ Click the Add New Link button.

> *ReportSmith responds by displaying the Create New Table Link window.*

☐ Set the link between the Items.DB table and the Clients.DB table, as shown in Figure 21.18. Select the CustNum field from the Items.DB table, select the equal-sign (=) option button, and select the CustNum field from the Items.DB table.

Figure 21.18.
Linking the Items.DB and Clients.DB tables.

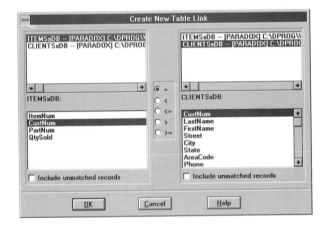

☐ Click the OK button of the Create New Link window.

> *ReportSmith responds by displaying the Tables window with the table link shown in it (see Figure 21.19).*

Figure 21.19.
The Tables window with the link between the tables shown.

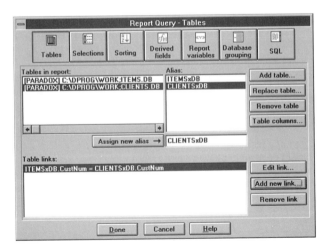

□ Click the Done button of the Tables window.

ReportSmith responds by generating the report.

□ Set the title of the report to **Report: Mail01.Rpt**.

□ Select Save As from the ReportSmith File menu, and save the report as Mail01.Rpt.

The report is shown in Figure 21.20. As you can see, there are two customers:

- `CustNum 10016`, which has two records in the Items.DB table.
- `CustNum 10017`, which also has two records in the Items.DB table.

Figure 21.20.
The initial state of the Mail01.Rpt report.

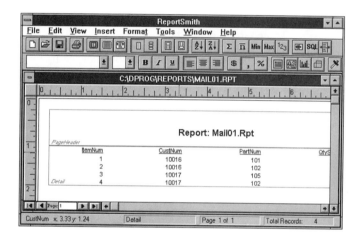

To generate a report that serves as a monthly statement or an invoice, you must separate the clients on the report and include various summation fields. The process of separating the clients is discussed in the following sections.

Separating the Clients

As shown in Figure 21.20, the report is just one big, long table at the moment. To generate an invoice, for example, you must separate the clients. The information about `CustNum 10016` must be printed and then stuffed into an envelope. The information about `CustNum 10017` has to be printed, and then stuffed into another envelope, and so on.

□ Select Report Grouping from the Tools menu.

ReportSmith responds by displaying the Define Group dialog box (see Figure 21.21). As shown in the figure, there is only one group now, the Entire Report Group.

Figure 21.21.

The Define Group dialog box.

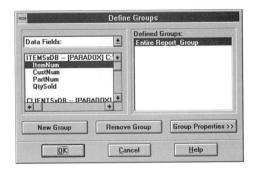

☐ Select the CustNum item from the list of fields, and then click the New Group button of the Define Group dialog box.

The Define Group dialog box should now look as shown in Figure 21.22.

Figure 21.22.

Defining the CustNum group.

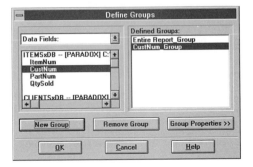

☐ Click the OK button of the Define Group dialog box.

ReportSmith responds by grouping the report records according to the CustNum field, as shown in Figure 21.23.

Your objective is to send a letter (an invoice or a statement) to CustNum 10016, another letter to CustNum 10017, and so on. To do this, you must insert a header and a footer in each group. The header contains the name and address of the client (which you place in such a way that the name and address shows through the opening of a window envelope). Typically, in the footer area you insert summation fields, such as the total due, the sales tax, and a statement that makes your customer feel good, such as, "We enjoy serving you."

☐ Select Header/Footer from the Insert menu.

ReportSmith responds by displaying the Header/Footer dialog box, as shown in Figure 21.24.

Figure 21.23.

The report records are grouped by the CustNum field.

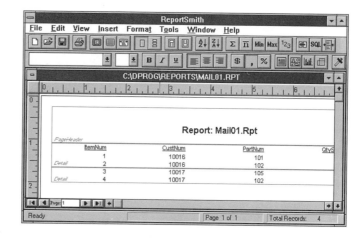

Figure 21.24.

The Header/Footer dialog box.

Note that one of the groups in the Group Name list is the CustNum_Group (because you previously grouped the report by CustNum).

☐ Select the CustNum_Group item, place a checkmark in the Header checkbox (because you want each group to have a header). Also place a checkmark in the Footer checkbox (because you want each group to have a footer area).

The Header/Footer dialog box should now look as shown in Figure 21.25.

Figure 21.25.

The Header/Footer setting for inserting a header and a footer for each group of the report.

☐ Click the OK button of the Header/Footer dialog box.

> *ReportSmith responds by inserting a header and a footer in each of the groups (see Figure 21.26).*

Figure 21.26.
Each group has a header and a footer.

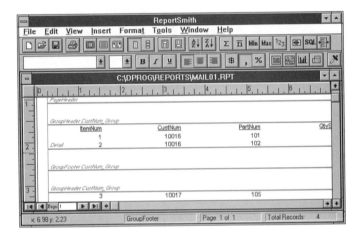

The report now is organized as follows:

```
Header for the entire report

Header of group #1
Group #1
Footer of group #1

Header of group #2
Group #2
Footer of group #2

...
```

As previously stated, you place the name and address of the CustNum client in each group's header, and in each group's footer you place the summation fields and derived fields that are based on calculations of the group's records.

Placing the Clients' Names and Addresses in the Group Headers

Place the name and address of the CustNum in the group header.

☐ Click the Field Editing icon on the ReportSmith toolbar (see Figure 21.27).

Figure 21.27.

The Field Editing icon on the ReportSmith toolbar.

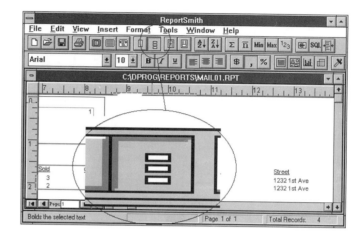

Now that the Field Editing icon is pressed, you can move fields from the column to the header area.

☐ Select the rows of the `LastName` field. (Scroll the report to the left until you see the `LastName` column, and then click on any of the rows under the column heading.)

ReportSmith responds by selecting the `LastName` rows, as shown in Figure 21.28.

Figure 21.28.

Selecting the `LastName` rows.

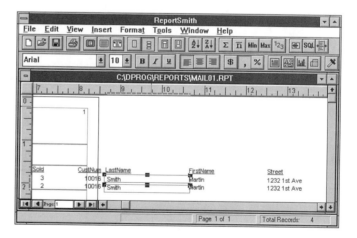

☐ Drag the selected `LastName` rows to the header area of the first group (not to the header area of the report).

☐ Select the rows of the `FirstName` field, and drag them to the header area of the first name.

☐ Arrange the fields in the header area of the first group so that the `FirstName` appears to the left of the `LastName` field.

Now take a look at Figure 21.9; each header group contains the `FirstName` and `LastName`. Of course, in the first group's header group, you see Martin Smith; in the second header, you see Jim Anderson; and so on.

Figure 21.29.

Each header area of a group includes the `LastName` *and* `FirstName` *fields of the group* `CustNum`.

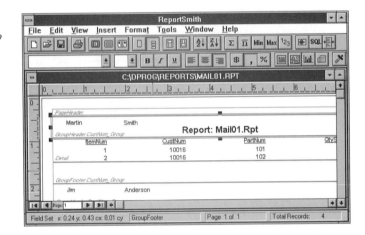

Typically, at this point of the design, you enlarge the header size and add additional fields to the header area (for example, Street, City, State, and ZIP code).

Once you place these fields in the header area of the group, you can delete the column headings of the fields you placed in the group's header area. Note that the `CustNum` column also should be moved to the header area of the group. It doesn't make sense to include a column `CustNum` in the body of the group.

The `ItemNum` column must be deleted because the `ItemNum` is the record number of the Items.DB table and it doesn't provide any information to the client.

☐ Delete the `ItemNum` column and all the other columns except for the `PartNum` and the `QtySold` columns.

☐ Drag the `PartNum` and `QtySold` columns to the left side of the report.

☐ Drag the `CustNum` to the header area of the group.

After inserting the full address in the group header, it should look as shown in Figure 21.30.

☐ Scroll down the report and verify that the second group's header contains the second client's `CustNum` data.

☐ Save the Mail01.Rpt report.

Figure 21.30.

The name and address of the customer appears in the header of each group.

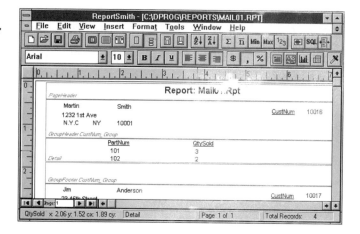

Inserting a Column from Another Table in the Group Body

In this section, you insert a derived column in the body of each group. The derived column is the `SellingPrice` column, which represents the unit price of the item.

However, recall that the `SellingPrice` of an item is stored in the Parts.DB table. As of yet, the Parts.DB table is not part of the Mail01.Rpt report, and so you must add the Parts.DB table to the report.

☐ Select Tables from the Tools menu.

ReportSmith responds by displaying the Tables window.

☐ Click the Add Table button, and add the Parts.DB table.

As shown in Figure 21.31, the report now is made of three tables: Items.DB, Clients.DB, and Parts.DB.

You must now establish a link. You want the Parts.DB fields to appear as columns in the report, where the `SellingPrice` column matches the `PartNum`, and so the common field on which you should link the Items.DB and Parts.DB tables is the `PartNum` field.

☐ Click the Add New Link button.

ReportSmith responds by displaying the Create a New Link window.

☐ Set the link, as shown in Figure 21.32. Select `PartNum` from the list of Items.DB table fields, select the equal-sign (=) option button, and then select the `PartNum` field from the list of Parts.DB table fields.

Figure 21.31.

The report is made of three tables: Items.DB, Clients.DB, and Parts.DB.

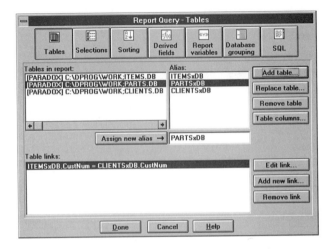

Figure 21.32.

Establishing a link between the Items.DB and Parts.DB tables.

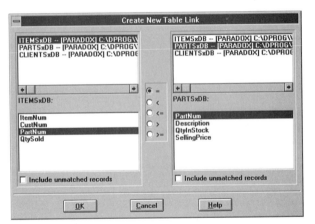

☐ Click the OK button of the Create New Table Link window.

ReportSmith responds by displaying the Tables window with the new link in it. The Tables window (see Figure 21.33) now contains two links: the Items.DB/Clients.DB link, and the Items.DB/Parts.DB link.

☐ Click the Done button of the Tables window.

ReportSmith responds by adding the columns corresponding to the Parts.DB table fields to the Mail01.Rpt report.

☐ Remove all the columns that came from the Parts.DB table except the SellingPrice column.

Figure 21.33.
*Establishing a link between
the Items.DB and Parts.DB
tables.*

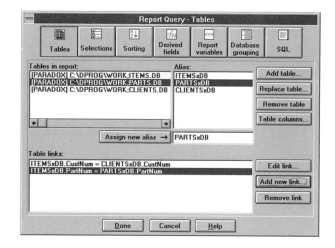

The Mail01.Rpt report now contains the following three columns:

```
PartNum
QtySold
SellingPrice
```

Drag the `SellingPrice` column heading to the left so it appears immediately to the right of the `QtySold` column.

☐ Make sure that the Column Editing icon on the ReportSmith toolbar is pressed, and then drag the rows of the `SellingPrice` column to the left so it is immediately to the right of the `QtySold` column.

The Mail01.Rpt report now looks as shown in Figure 21.34.

Figure 21.34.
*The Mail01.Rpt report after
adding the `SellingPrice`
column.*

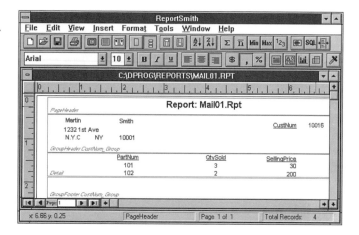

☐ Save the Mail01.Rpt report.

☐ Scroll down the report, and verify that the body of the second group contains the `SellingPrice` column.

☐ Save the Mail01.Rpt report.

Adding a Derived Column

Next, you need to add a derived field to the Mail01.Rpt report—a column indicating the result of multiplying the `QtySold` field by the `SellingPrice` field.

☐ Select Derived Fields from the Tools menu.

ReportSmith responds by displaying the Derived Fields window.

☐ Set the Derived Field Name editbox to **TotalItem**, and select the Defined by SQL option button.

☐ Click the Add button of the Derived Fields window.

ReportSmith responds by displaying the Edit Derived Field window.

☐ Set the formula for calculating the value of the `TotalItem` derived field, as shown in Figure 21.35. Select the `QtySold` field from the list of Items.DB table fields, and click the Insert button. Next, select the `x*y Multiplication` item, and click the Insert button. Finally, select the `SellingPrice` field from the list of Parts.DB table fields, and click the Insert button.

Figure 21.35.

The formula for calculating the `TotalItem` *derived field.*

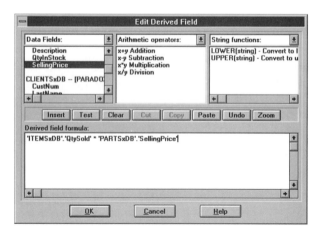

☐ Click the OK button of the Edit Derived Field window.

ReportSmith responds by again displaying the Derived Fields window with the TotalItem *derived field shown as a derived field.*

☐ Click the Done button of the Derived Fields window.

ReportSmith responds by adding the TotalItem Derived column, as shown in Figure 21.36.

Figure 21.36.
The Mail01.Rpt report with the TotalItem *derived column.*

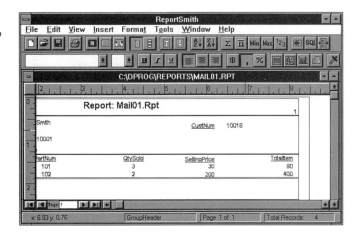

Again, the TotalItem derived column appears in all the groups of the report.

☐ Save the Mail01.Rpt report.

Inserting a Summation Field in the Groups' Footer Areas

You now insert a summation field in each of the footer areas of the groups. The first group's summation field sums all the first group's TotalItem column records. The summation field that is inserted in the footer area of the second group is the sum of all the rows in the second group's TotalItem column, and so on.

☐ Select the TotalItem column heading of the first group, and then click the Summation icon on the ReportSmith toolbar.

ReportSmith responds by inserting in each group's footer area the sum of the TotalItem column records residing in that group.

The summation field of group 1 in the footer area appears as shown in Figure 21.37.

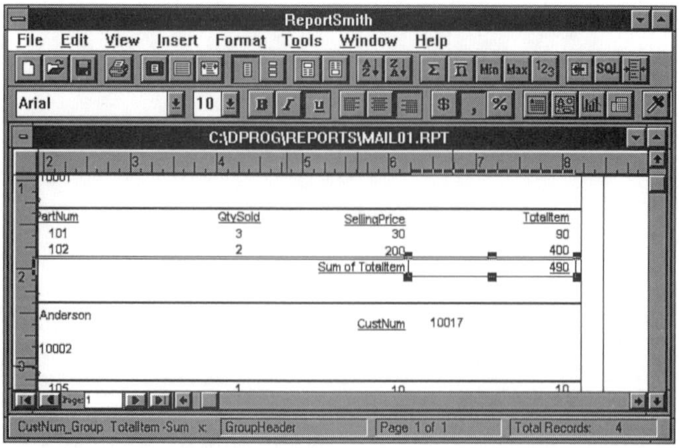

Figure 21.37.
A Summation field is inserted in the footer area of each group.

☐ Scroll down the report and verify that a summation field was inserted in the second group's footer area. Also verify that the value of the summation field is the sum of the records residing in the second group.

☐ Save the Mail01.Rpt report.

Separating the Groups on the Hard Copies

The final step in preparing the Mail01.Rpt report is to print each report so that each group starts on a new page. Printing only one group per page enables you to fold the page and insert it into an envelope. Of course, if a group has many items in it (and therefore multiple pages), you must staple together all the pages belonging to that group, and insert the pages into an envelope.

☐ Select Selection from the Format menu.

   ReportSmith responds by displaying the Format Section dialog box.

☐ Set the Format Section dialog box options, as shown in Figure 21.38. Select the GroupHeader_CustNum_Group item from the Apply to section list, and place a checkmark in the New Page Before. A new page starts before printing each group's header.

☐ Click the OK button of the Format Section dialog box.

   ReportSmith responds by separating the groups. If you print the report, each group is printed on a separate page.

☐ Save the report.

☐ Select Print from the ReportSmith File menu, and print all the pages.

Figure 21.38.

The Format Section dialog box.

ReportSmith prints each group on a separate page. Each page has the same report heading (Report: Mail01.Rpt), the client's name and address, the Detail section with the corresponding column headings, and the footer area with the corresponding summation field.

You also can view each group of the report by using the Navigator control in the lower-left corner of the ReportSmith window.

Printing Labels and Generating Form Reports

In addition to the Crosstab, Columnar, and Columnar-Group report formats, you can use ReportSmith to generate Form reports (each record is printed on a separate page). The Form report format is needed, for example, if you are generating ID cards for employees, or other types of reports where there is a need to separate the report records.

ReportSmith also enables you to generate reports that are printed on labels. You can specify the type of label you're using, and ReportSmith prints each record of the report on a separate label.

Exercises 1 and 2 of this chapter outline the procedures for generating Form reports and Label reports.

Summary

In this chapter, you learned how to prepare Crosstab reports and how to convert a Columnar report to a Crosstab report.

You also learned how to place fields in the groups' header area (for example, for displaying addresses through window envelopes) and how to place summation fields in the footer areas of the groups.

In Exercises 1 and 2 of this chapter, you learn how to generate shipping labels and Form reports, where each record of the report is printed on a separate page.

Q&A

Q Should I use a Columnar report or a Crosstab report?

A It all depends on the particular report you're generating. Typically, a report containing many records is displayed as a Columnar report. For reports that don't contain many records, sometimes the Crosstab report gives the reader a better understanding of the data's meaning.

Q When designing reports, should a checkmark appear to the left of the Boundaries item on the View menu?

A When a checkmark appears to the left of the Boundaries item on the View menu, the report is displayed on the screen with boundaries (each region on the report is enclosed by a rectangle). This helps you to identify the report regions during design and to determine what portion of the report will fit on a page. (You can set the page size and orientation by selecting Page Setup from the ReportSmith File menu). During design time, it is convenient to see the report boundaries.

Quiz

1. To create a Crosstab report, you can do which of the following?

    a. Start a fresh new report and indicate that the format for the crosstab is Crosstab.

    b. First, create a Columnar report, and then convert the Columnar report to a Crosstab report.

    c. All of the above.

2. Prior to inserting a header and footer for each group of records, you must _____.

Exercises

1. Use ReportSmith to generate a Form report. Each Clients.DB table record should print on a separate page.

2. Use ReportSmith to generate shipping labels. Each label should contain the client's name and address from the Clients.DB table.

Answers to Quiz

1. c.

2. Prior to inserting a header and a footer for each group of records, you must create the groups. For example, when you created the Mail01.Rpt report in this chapter, you first created a group (by CustNum), and then you selected the Header/Footer from the Insert menu to display the Header/Footer dialog box, as shown in Figure 21.24. Therefore, the Group Name list contains the CustNum_Group item. You now can select the CustNum_Group item, check the Header or the Footer checkboxes, and click the OK button to insert the header (or footer) in the CustNum_Group groups.

Answers to Exercises

1. Here's what to do.

   ☐ Close all reports on the ReportSmith desktop.

   ☐ Select New from the ReportSmith File menu, select the Form report button, and then select the Clients.DB table.

   ☐ Click the Done button.

   > *ReportSmith responds by generating the report, with each record displayed on a separate page. You can use the* Navigator *control located in the lower-left corner of the report window to move from record to record.*

   ☐ Select Save As from the ReportSmith File menu, and save the report as Form01.Rpt in the C:\DProg\Reports directory.

2. Here's what to do.

   ☐ Close all reports on the ReportSmith desktop.

   ☐ Select New from the ReportSmith File menu, select the Label report, and then select the Clients.DB table.

   ☐ Click the Done button.

   ☐ Use the Insert Field dialog box to insert the fields that you want to appear on the labels. Select a field, click the Insert button, and then click in the label area. Repeat this process for adding other fields in the label.

   ☐ Select Page Setup from the File menu to display a dialog box that enables you to select the Label option and to select a label from a large selection of standard labels.

21

Index

P

Panel control, 68-70
  Align property, 156
  BevelWidth property, 198
parameters
  DeviceName parameter,
    defining, 361-362
  SQL parameters
    defining, 257-259
    modifying at runtime,
      260-263
.Pas extension, 7-8
**PC Speaker radio button,
  attaching code to OnClick
  events, 382-383**
**PC speakers, 328,
  339-340, 382**
**pointers, moving record
  pointers, 318-319**
primary key fields
  creating, 145-148
  sorting records (tables), 44
Print buttons, creating, 286
**Print Report buttons, creating,
  450-452**
printing
  addresses on reports, 536-539
  form reports, 551
  forms, 286
  grouped reports on separate
    pages, 550-551
  labels (reports), 551
  reports, 445-446
procedures, attaching code
  FormCreate( ) (3D virtual
    reality), 409-416
  SetCell( ), 430-431
program code, *see* **code**
programs
  compiling, 174
  executing, 16, 19, 70-71
    runtime errors, 174
  terminating, 17
**project files (.Dpr extension),
  7-8**

**Project Manager command
  (View menu), 73**
projects
  AddView project, 274-293
  Clients project, 194-218
  creating, 5
  FillAnim project, 296-305
  forms, displaying, 72-73
  Hello project, 5-32
  Kennedy project, 328-346
  MM (Multimedia) project,
    348-366, 370-385
  My3DVR project, 390-435
  MyAnim project, 307-324
  MyCust project, 58-107
  MyList project, 220-230
  MyLookup project, 230-246
  One2Many project, 144-165
  OnlyJim project, 248-255
  saving files, 5-8, 154-155,
    162-163
  SearchMe project, 168-189
  SetQuery project, 256-263
  SetRange project, 263-267
  TotPrice project, 114-142
properties
  3D virtual reality controls
    color properties, 414
    setting, 401-403
  buttons
    Caption, 14, 16
    Name, 16
  checkboxes, 93-95
  controls
    creating animations,
      314-316
    setting, 126-131
  data controls, setting
    automatically, 59-63
  DBImage controls
    setting, 299-301
    Stretch, 304
  DBLookupList, 236-237
  DBMemo controls
    AutoDisplay, 302
    setting, 299-301

  edit boxes
    Font, 28-29
    ReadOnly, 29
    Text, 26-28
  fields
    Alignment, 89
    DisplayLabel, 89
    editing via code, 91-92
    Required, 182
    Visible, 90
  forms
    BorderIcons, 202-203
    Caption, 10
    Color, 10-11
    editing, 9-12
    Name, 11-12
    setting controls, 283-285,
      297-298
  Multimedia controls,
    339-340, 375-376
    Error property, 376
  Panel controls
    Align, 156
    BevelWidth, 198
  Query components
    Active, 254-255
    Name, 257
    RequestLive, 254
    setting, 257-259
    SQL, 252-253
  radio buttons, 359-360
  setting for fields (tables),
    87-90
  Table components
    Active, 78, 102
    DataBaseName, 78-79
    Name, 84, 155-156
    ReadOnly, 79
    TableName, 79
  Timer controls, 317-319
Properties tables, 29-30

Add to Your Sams Library Today with the Best Books for Programming, Operating Systems, and New Technologies

The easiest way to order is to pick up the phone and call

1-800-428-5331

between 9:00 a.m. and 5:00 p.m. EST.
For faster service please have your credit card available.

ISBN	Quantity	Description of Item	Unit Cost	Total Cost
0-672-30499-6		Delphi Unleashed (Book/CD)	$45.00	
0-672-30704-9		Delphi Developer's Guide (Book/CD)	$49.99	
0-672-30531-3		Teach Yourself Windows 95 Programming in 21 Days, 2E	$35.00	
0-672-30474-0		Windows 95 Unleashed (Book/CD)	$35.00	
0-672-30611-5		Your Windows 95 Consultant, Pre-Release Edition	$19.99	
0-672-30765-0		Navigating the Internet with Windows 95	$25.00	
0-672-30568-2		Teach Yourself OLE Programming in 21 Days (Book/CD)	$39.99	
0-672-30736-7		Teach Yourself C in 21 Days, Premier Edition	$35.00	
0-672-30667-0		Teach Yourself Web Publishing with HTML in a Week	$25.00	
0-672-30737-5		World Wide Web Unleashed, 2E	$39.99	
0-672-30714-6		Internet Unleashed, 2E	$35.00	
0-672-30520-8		Your Internet Consultant: The FAQs of Online Life	$25.00	
0-672-30459-7		Curious About the Internet?	$14.99	
0-672-30718-9		Navigating the Internet, 3E	$22.50	
❏ 3 ½" Disk		Shipping and Handling: See information below.		
❏ 5 ¼" Disk		TOTAL		

Shipping and Handling: $4.00 for the first book, and $1.75 for each additional book. Floppy disk: add $1.75 for shipping and handling. If you need to have it NOW, we can ship product to you in 24 hours for an additional charge of approximately $18.00, and you will receive your item overnight or in two days. Overseas shipping and handling adds $2.00 per book and $8.00 for up to three disks. Prices subject to change. Call for availability and pricing information on latest editions.

201 W. 103rd Street, Indianapolis, Indiana 46290

1-800-428-5331 — Orders   1-800-835-3202 — FAX   1-800-858-7674 — Customer Service

Book ISBN 0-672-30851-7